Dostoevsky's Unfinished Journey

ROBIN FEUER MILLER

Dostoevsky's Unfinished Journey

Yale University Press
New Haven &
London

Published with assistance from the foundation established in memory of
William McKean Brown.

Set in Sabon Roman type by Keystone Typesetting, Inc.
Printed in the United States of America.

Library of Congress Cataloging-in-Publication Data

Miller, Robin Feuer, 1947–
Dostoevsky's unfinished journey / Robin Feuer Miller.
p. cm.
Includes bibliographical references and index.
ISBN 978-0-300-12015-8 (cloth : alk. paper)
1. Dostoevsky, Fyodor, 1821–1881 — Criticism and interpretation.
2. Dostoevsky, Fyodor, 1821–1881 — Themes, motives. I. Title.
PG3328.Z6M4815 2007
891.73'3 — dc22

2007015553

A catalogue record for this book is available from the British Library.

The paper in this book meets the guidelines for permanence and durability of the
Committee on Production Guidelines for Book Longevity of the Council on
Library Resources.

10 9 8 7 6 5 4 3 2 1

Dostoevsky once described the work of a family
as "an untiring labor of love."
This book is dedicated to Lulu, Alexa Rose, Abigail, and Chris.
We have long been engaged in that happy labor together.

Who is it that can tell me who I am?
— William Shakespeare, *King Lear,* I.4.221

Contents

Preface

This book grew out of an interest in how change occurs or fails to occur. At the same time that I was thinking about this rather nebulous though important issue, I was immersed in reading Dostoevsky. I was struck by the different voices that emerge in his letters, in his notebooks, in his journalism, and of course, in his fiction. Some of these voices engaged me deeply; others enraged me; still others bored me. I found myself wondering, frivolously, what Dostoevsky's e-mail persona would be like. I think he would have flourished in that enveloping, informal medium with its instant feedback.

Because this project has been long in the making, I have been fortunate to have occasion to benefit from the conversations, advice, and wisdom of friends and colleagues. During the past years I have found myself in a prolonged internal dialogue with three critics of Dostoevsky's work who have largely devoted their scholarly careers to writing about him and whose insight, clarity of prose, and sheer brilliance have never seemed to abate: Robert L. Belknap, Joseph Frank, and Robert Louis Jackson. I thank them for their work over the years and for their generosity and encouragement to so many of us in the field. I recently learned that Joseph Frank was a reader of this book for Yale University Press. His engagement with it, when his own writings have been so important for me for the past several decades, makes years of solitary writing suddenly seem genuinely dialogic. Caryl Emerson, Donald Fanger, Malcolm V. Jones, and Deborah Martinsen offered suggestions and critiques of various parts of this manuscript and consistently inspired me by their own work and their passion for it. Donald Fanger is also the writer whose prose I most admire. While I was working on this book in Switzerland, Deborah Martinsen took the trouble to send me photocopies of several works I had forgotten to bring. Upon my return, the precious crate of my books was irretrievably lost in the mail. I am grateful to the several colleagues who lent me those books that I could not easily obtain in a library. My friend and colleague Katherine Tiernan O'Connor encouraged me to forge ahead with the third chapter of this book, and I thank her for that and for many years of friendship. Elizabeth Cheresh Allen, Susanne Fusso, Gary Saul Morson, Donna Tussing Orwin, Irina Paperno, and William Mills Todd III have inspired me with the range of their scholarly interests and their awesome depth of knowledge in so many different areas. Gary Saul Morson was another reader of this book for Yale University Press, and he offered greatly valued advice and encouragement. I have been lucky to work at the press with Jonathan Brent, Sarah Miller, Joyce Ippolito, and Margaret Otzel. I have gained further insight into Dostoevsky through the outstanding work of Liza Knapp, Olga Meerson, Harriet Murav, Richard Peace, Irina Reyfman, Gary Rosenshield, Diane Oenning Thompson, and Andrew Wachtel. Our small field brims with stars.

I also wish to thank several colleagues from Brandeis from whose sharp minds and wisdom I have benefited: John Burt, Mary Baine Campbell, Irving Epstein, Dian Fox, Jacqueline Jones, Susan Lanser, James Mandrell, David Powelstock, and Laura Quinney. I owe deep and special thanks to William Flesch and Robert Szulkin—one could not wish for finer, wiser, wittier colleagues. Linda Boothroyd has helped me in innumerable ways. During my years as Dean of Arts and Sciences, Brandeis initiated what we called a Consilience Seminar. My four years of participation in this group (acting as its leader in the first year) indelibly shaped my intellectual development. Every academic should have the opportunity to work intensively in a small committed group and read widely with colleagues from every corner of the university.

My friend Barbara Campbell encourages me in everything.

My daughter Lulu has given me editorial suggestions, and all three girls— Lulu, Alexa, and Abigail—have urged me on at times of distraction and discouragement. My husband, Chris, has read drafts, offered incisive, spirited, often daunting comments, helped me with manuscript preparation at every stage, and been my constant friend, critic, and partner in long conversation.

He has kept these ideas alive in my brain. This book is dedicated to the four of them.

Earlier versions of parts of this book have appeared as articles or chapters in edited volumes. In all cases, however, these essays have been substantially revised and rewritten for this book. Occasionally page references appear in parentheses in the text. In those cases the first and complete reference occurs in the endnotes for the chapter.

Introduction

What can I but enumerate old themes?
— W. B. Yeats, "The Circus Animal's Desertion"

Dostoevsky's Unfinished Journey explores questions of literary influence and intertextuality in Dostoevsky's work while at the same time investigating his representations in fiction of the dynamic of conversion and healing or, frequently, the failure of this process. Five of the eight chapters offer close readings, and the other three approach problems with a more thematic bent; all the chapters reverberate around questions of intertextuality — literary transformations — and possible paradigms of conversion, both textual and spiritual. Each chapter poses and attempts to answer a different set of interrelated questions.

The first chapter, "Conversion, Message, Medium, Transformation: Dostoevsky and the Peasants," speculates about the timing, the place, and the nature of Dostoevsky's own conversion experience and the degree to which we can even discuss this conversion as a discrete event. I focus here on the thorny problem of Dostoevsky's representation of the peasant. What role did the peasants, either in actuality or in Dostoevsky's ideas about them, play in helping to shape and define this conversion? Whether one is considering Dostoevsky the man, the journalist, the would-be art critic, the religious thinker, or the creative writer, the peasant looms large.

Dostoevsky's representations of the peasant reflect a variety of challenging contradictions: on one hand he tends to portray this figure as embodying quintessential Russian virtues and as constituting a roadmap for Russia's future; on the other hand the peasant often functions as an agent or an emblem of evil. These competing views of the peasant are present in both Dostoevsky's fiction and his nonfictional writings. Even more striking is a hybrid of the peasant that emerges in Dostoevsky's artistic work: the peasant who becomes a difficult text that nonpeasant characters must, in order to grow, decipher. I explore several of the many vexing examples of the peasant that emerge in Dostoevsky's letters, journalism, novels, and his *Diary of a Writer* and find in some of them possible clues for understanding the nature of Dostoevsky's own conversion experience.

The second chapter, "Guilt, Repentance, and the Pursuit of Art in *The House of the Dead*," continues to focus on Dostoevsky's representation of the peasant and offers a reading of Dostoevsky's semi-autobiographical novel and prison memoir, *Notes from the House of the Dead*. This work hovers at the boundaries of several genres. Moreover, within *The House of the Dead* the typical Dostoevskian themes of guilt and responsibility receive a radically different emphasis than they do in his other works, with the possible exception of *Crime and Punishment*. The narrator, a convict himself, reports, "There was no sign of shame or repentance! Yet there was an external, as it were, official resignation, a sort of philosophic calm." I am particularly interested in the variety of ways in which these convicts are transformed at those rare moments when they are engaged in the pursuit of art. It is also, perhaps, at these moments that they undergo some transcendent, albeit fleeting, experience of guilt and even repentance. Surprisingly, many of the convicts are, in one way or another, devoted as the narrator puts it, "for art's sake," to a particular pursuit. It is these various pursuits and their transformative, even healing effect, which occupy my attention in this chapter.

The third chapter, "*Crime and Punishment* in the Classroom: The Elephant in the Garden," is pivotal to the argument of this book, for here I reflect on how Dostoevsky's novel may frequently be transformed in the classroom. It seemed fitting to use this particular novel—which is itself, as Dostoevsky maintained from the outset, about "ideas in the air"—to consider the ways in which any novel takes on new identities as it becomes the subject of classroom discussion. *Crime and Punishment* stands at the center of Dostoevsky's creative oeuvre. It is here that he most fully incorporates his artistic, intellectual, and autobiographical experience to date—although not that of his near execution or his epilepsy, which he reserves for his next novel, *The Idiot*—and heralds, simultaneously, his future trajectory as an artist. It is also in *Crime and Punishment* that he forges the earliest version — though not yet a fully embodied rendition — of that third-person narrator who eventually becomes the narrator-chronicler who is to narrate *The Idiot, The Possessed,* and *The Brothers Karamazov* to such extraordinary effect. An awesome array of fine critical work has already been done on this novel. I do not attempt a survey of it but try instead to understand the importance of this novel to our present time, when the very act of reading, despite high levels of literacy, is in decline and, hence, at risk.

The fourth chapter, "The Gospel According to Dostoevsky: Paradox, Plot, and Parable," takes a close look at some of the instances when Dostoevsky's characters recite short anecdotes that exhibit features that we tend to ascribe to biblical parable. I focus here on four particular instances in which Dostoevsky's characters — and by implication Dostoevsky behind them — create parables, the "gospel," if you will, according to Dostoevsky. I draw my examples from *The Idiot,* "The Peasant Marey," and *The Brothers Karamazov.* Each of the parabolic moments under discussion displays a powerful and uncanny binding together of the deliberate strategies of the artist, well aware of the tastes of his audience, and the didactic, passionate Russian Orthodox believer struggling, as Zosima puts it in *The Brothers Karamazov,* to "scatter the seeds of God's word." As such these parables are moments when Dostoevsky, through the transforming rhetoric of specific characters, could revitalize and reinvent (and even subvert) the traditional Orthodox heritage and render it immediate, modern, and startling.

The fifth chapter, "Transformations, Exposures, and Intimations of Rousseau in *The Possessed,*" continues what has been a longstanding interest of mine in understanding the nature of Dostoevsky's polemic with the ideas of Rousseau, particularly the Rousseau of *The Confessions.* He repeatedly transforms and parodies Rousseau's ideas in his fiction. *The Insulted and Injured, Notes from Underground, Crime and Punishment, The Idiot,* and "The Dream of a Ridiculous Man" all engage in sometimes open, sometimes veiled, but always ferocious argument with Rousseau and his strategies as a narrator, as does, perhaps most famously, Stavrogin's confession in *The Possessed.* In my reading of *that novel,* however, I focus not on this sustained and eloquent attack on nonreligious confession as being no better than indecent exposure and in itself obscene but rather on a quieter instance when the polemic with Rousseau continues, but its strategy changes. Comedy and ridicule predominate.

The sixth chapter, "Unsealing the Generic Envelope and Deciphering 'The Dream of a Ridiculous Man,'" offers a close reading of Dostoevsky's conversion (or anti-conversion) tale. In particular in this chapter, the two strands of the present book — the twin endeavors to unravel possible literary transformations and spiritual conversions — interweave and intersect. I argue that Dostoevsky is responding to the work of Swift, Rousseau, Poe, and especially Dickens but that he ends by offering up his own extremely idiosyncratic and perplexing literary rendering of a spiritual conversion.

In the seventh chapter, "Evocations and Revocations of Anxiety in the Metaphysical Novel: Reading *The Brothers Karamazov* through the Lens of *Melmoth the Wanderer*," I offer an interpretation of *The Brothers Karamazov* that hypothesizes that Dostoevsky learned a great deal about the depiction of anxiety from his avid early reading of the gothic novel, particularly Charles Maturin's *Melmoth the Wanderer*. This chapter centers on the pivotal moment in the chapter "Cana of Galilee," when the central character, Alyosha, undergoes a kind of conversion experience, and also on Ivan's "Legend of the Grand Inquisitor." As in chapter six, I again discover in both these central episodes what seem to be striking instances of simultaneous literary transformation (in this case a borrowing from Maturin) and a depiction of the process of spiritual conversion. Dostoevsky's novel at these two key moments — moments that we tend to think of as "pure Dostoevsky" — vibrates with a strong resonance of Maturin's.

The eighth chapter continues (from chapters one, four, six, and seven) to mount an increasingly focused scrutiny of the phenomenon and the mechanics of conversion in Dostoevsky's fiction. "Perilous Journeys to Conversion: Adventures in Time and Space" returns to four episodes in Dostoevsky's fiction, each of which has been touched upon in a different context in an earlier chapter. In this final chapter, however, I focus on the nature of the conversion experience itself. *The Varieties of Religious Experience* by William James offers a rich and suggestive backdrop against which to contemplate actual moments of conversion as they occur, or do not occur, in "The Peasant Marey," "The Dream of a Ridiculous Man," and for Ivan and Alyosha in *The Brothers Karamazov*. Although James wrote eloquently about Tolstoy, he never mentioned Dostoevsky. Yet James's work offers a means of understanding the Dostoevskian journey toward conversion even more profoundly than it does the Tolstoyan one. James's book has given me a compelling framework for this particular chapter. Throughout Dostoevsky's fiction the experience of conversion is a frighteningly fragile one, for in it the movement toward God threatens, at virtually every moment, to change direction — to collapse into its opposite. Conversion hovers at the edge of perversion, and transformation or healing may, by a shift of the kaleidoscope, become distortion or illness.

I also attempt here a new interpretation of the celebrated interchange in *The Brothers Karamazov* between Ivan and his devil. I have drawn upon Dostoevsky's own ambivalent interest in the medical practices of homeopathy. What is most interesting is that the devil claims to practice metaphysical homeopathy. The two most controversial aspects of medical homeopathy are its fundamental belief that the most minute doses are the most powerful and that like is best cured by like. The symptoms of illness, according to homeopathic wisdom, should be stimulated for they are not necessarily part of the disease itself but rather evidence of the body's attempt to cure itself. What then is the significance of the devil's practice of homeopathy? This is the question I address toward the end of the chapter.

The final chapter, "Concluding Fragments: Some Last Words," speculates impressionistically and freely on ways in which Dostoevsky's fiction grapples with some questions that are important to us today—questions about the possibility of consilience, about the nature of evidence, about order and chaos. Some of today's eloquent and learned writers of popular science—a genre abhorred by Dostoevsky and one dangerously close, in his view, to socialism in its godlessness and attempts at systematization of human experience within the universe—seem to be asking the big questions that contemporary philosophers and novelists currently avoid, questions that do not differ so much, particularly with regard to the passionate way in which they are addressed, from those asked by Dostoevsky. What might Dostoevsky have thought of this?

To some extent each chapter of the present book is not unlike the sequential revolution of a kaleidoscope; the same fragments and colors appear repeatedly within a slightly different configuration. Perhaps this structure simply reflects the kaleidoscopic nature of Dostoevsky's writing in its entirety, for each separate work—be it letter, article, story, or novel—reconfigures anew an array of fragments that is somehow familiar and connected to the other designs along the circle. The pattern of each representation changes, but each is created from the same palette.[1]

Conversion, Message, Medium, Transformation: Dostoevsky and the Peasants

The truth must dazzle gradually.
— Emily Dickinson

He averted his eyes that he might see.
— Charles Robert Maturin, *Melmoth the Wanderer*

This first chapter, unlike the rest of this book, does not examine Dostoevsky's fiction. Readers, I hope, will cast an occasional backward glance at the aspects of Dostoevsky's biography and journalism brought up here. This chapter forms a kind of background or underpinning. Dostoevsky's response to the conditions and the very existence of the vast number of Russian peasants (the *narod*) pervades his biography, his journalism, his writings about literature and art, and his creative work. How much can we know about Dostoevsky's personal experience of a conversion? What was the nature of that conversion, and what role did his interactions with the peasants and his ideas about them play in shaping it? How did Dostoevsky's pragmatic ideas about the need to educate the peasantry combine with his lofty and fervently held ideas about art? How do his views on painting inform his ideas about art in a larger context? If one uses the figure of the peasant as a general example, how can we speculate about the nature of the gap between Dostoevsky's voice as a journalist and his voice as the implied author in his fiction?

Whether we consider Dostoevsky the man, Dostoevsky the political journal-ist, Dostoevsky the religious thinker, or Dostoevsky the creative artist, the peasant — or as Russians of the nineteenth century so often liked to put it, "the problem of the peasant" — constitutes a vital thread that weaves itself into virtually every aspect of his oeuvre. Indeed, every Russian writer of the nine-teenth century, with the possible exception of Anton Chekhov, found it neces-sary to come to terms, both as an artist and as a human being, with the peasant, whose dire situation — whether as enslaved serf or, after 1861, as supposedly "free man" — demanded both recognition and consideration. Moreover, al-though frequently mistreated and abused in the flesh, the peasant in his sym-bolic or collective form was, as one critic has put it, "the repository of some mysterious virtue, defying analysis," who was, in addition, "designated by the potent emotional word *narod,* which can also mean 'people' or 'nation.' "[1]

It is, of course, precisely such divisions and conflicts between the educated Russian's views of the peasant in fact and in theory that contributed to the ongoing nature of "the peasant problem." On one hand, the peasant was despised (a frequent adjective used to describe him was "drunken"); on the other hand, he was held up as the embodiment of Russian virtues and as some ineluctable synthesis of the best of Russia's past and the course of her future. Dostoevsky's views on the peasant reflected all these messy contradictions.

What an irony it is, then, that the great age of the novel in Russia of the nineteenth century does not include a "single significant novel of peasant life."[2] Yet a personal coming to terms with the peasant is crucial to many of the most important heroes of Russian fiction, among them Ivan Turgenev's Arkady Kirsanov and Bazarov, Leo Tolstoy's Pierre Bezukhov and Konstantin Levin, Dostoevsky's Raskolnikov, and Alyosha, Mitya, and Ivan Karamazov, to name only a few. That is, the peasant frequently becomes a term or a way station in the ongoing process of self-discovery of the nonpeasant hero (al-though Dostoevsky's peasants never give his heroes the kind of specific, con-cise, almost formulaic insight that Platon Karataev or the peasant Plato give to Pierre Bezukhov or Konstantin Levin).[3]

What is even more interesting is the way in which the figure of the peasant in Dostoevsky's nonfictional writings differs from its representations in his artis-tic work. My interest lies not in what Dostoevsky believed would happen to the peasants, practically, or should be done about them (his attitude toward reforms) but rather in this fissure between representations of the peasant in his nonfiction versus in his fiction. Dostoevsky's deliberate, programmatic, inten-tional use of the peasant in his art — the peasant transformed by art — becomes a difficult text that the nonpeasant hero must, in order to grow, decipher. For the figure of the peasant is, throughout Dostoevsky's artistic canon, intimately bound up with his most cherished ideas about visionary experience, memory, salvation, and grace — that is, his ideas about transformation and conversion.

Dostoevsky's Conversion: What Was It? When Did It Occur? How Were the Peasants Important to It?

Certain key elements of Dostoevsky's life were directly shaped by his views on the peasants. His controversial early involvement in the politically radical Petrashevsky Circle, for which he was imprisoned in the Peter and Paul Fortress in St. Petersburg, in 1849, and then sent to a prison camp in Siberia, was linked to his concern over the situation of the peasants. Joseph Frank has stated categorically that "Dostoevsky had become a revolutionary only to abolish serfdom and only after the seeming dissolution of all hope that it would be ended, to quote Pushkin, 'by the hand of the Tsar.' "[4]

There is another biographical fact to consider as well: Dostoevsky probably believed that his father had been brutally murdered by his serfs. He certainly heard the prevalent rumors about this crime. Yet we, even armed as we are with the critic's arsenal of hindsight, have no reliable way to measure the overwhelming import of this possible occurrence. Dostoevsky himself never directly referred to this event or to its effect on him, Freud's theoretical writings about Dostoevsky notwithstanding.[5] What does this silence mean, especially when juxtaposed to his preoccupations with murder and parricide in his fiction? At the center of Dostoevsky's life, we encounter a highly dramatic event about which he remained silent. He may well even have felt implicated in his father's death, for his frequent requests for money had likely contributed to the cruel demands his father had made on his serfs, serfs of whom the child Dostoevsky had been very fond. Yet the rumors that his father had been murdered also remained a topic that Dostoevsky would never directly approach, despite his artistic preoccupation with murder, with the representation of peasant murderers, and with parricide.

The rumors about his father's murder may well have been the driving force — the psychological reason — behind Dostoevsky's subsequent lifelong and passionate focus on the plight of the narod. Frank has suggested that the sudden death and possible murder of his father became a catalyst for focusing Dostoevsky's intellectual and creative energy on the peasant. He argues convincingly for this possibility: "The existence of serfdom had now become literally unbearable for him, because he could never free himself from the sickening feeling, that in helping to foment its worst excesses, he had brought on his father's death. Only through the abolition of serfdom . . . could the trauma of his guilt be assuaged."[6] Whether or not his father was murdered, the existence of the rumors would have effectively served to underline his father's severity with his serfs. Such severity toward peasants of whom Dostoevsky had been fond, even without a subsequent murder, could have worked powerfully to awaken his sense of social and political injustice and to inspire his profound compassion and concern for the peasants.

Just as the peasant problem gave Dostoevsky the initial impetus for his fateful foray into radical politics, so too did Dostoevsky's core beliefs about the peasants inform his famous conversion. What was the nature of this conversion? Was it spiritual or ideological? Dostoevsky's own conversion, like his fictional representations of the conversion experience, is fraught with mystery and paradox. It is difficult to determine just *when* this conversion actually occurred, although it is possible, in a general sense, to describe the actual change in Dostoevsky's outlook upon his return from prison and exile. The young man sentenced to death for his radical activities who then served ten years as a convict in Siberia and as an exiled soldier in the ranks returned to St. Petersburg a religious, conservative supporter of the tsar and of Russian Orthodoxy. Frank attributes to Dostoevsky (and I agree with him) a genuine conversion experience, true to the American philosopher and psychologist William James's analysis of such a momentous human event, in which, though no outer circumstances changed, the meaning of them did.[7]

Dostoevsky's conversion may not initially have been a particularly religious one with a classic sudden turning toward God but rather may have involved his turning to the peasant convicts, who represented to him all the negative aspects of the narod in stark relief. His turning toward the people was the necessary step in his eventual fully realized embrace of Russian Orthodoxy. In prison Dostoevsky experienced a range of largely negative responses to the peasants he encountered, but he nevertheless discovered within these same peasants the bedrock of hope for himself and for Russia. Frank puts it in the following way: "Such a metamorphosis indubitably took place for Dostoevsky, who, while refusing to gloss over for an instant the manifest harshness, brutality, and backwardness of Russian peasant life, nonetheless became convinced that at its center were preserved the sublime Christian virtues of love and self-sacrifice."[8] But can we really know *where* or *when* this transformation or conversion took place? I suggest that it occurred *before* Dostoevsky ever reached Siberia.

It is usual to emphasize that it was *during* his years as a convict that Dostoevsky underwent the conversion in which he discovered the greatness and beauty of the Russian people and after which he passionately embraced Russian Orthodox belief. Upon his departure from Siberia in 1854 and before he headed into exile in Semipalatinsk, he wrote, in a memorable and deeply felt letter, to the Decembrist wife Madame Fonvizina. She had offered him comfort, wise counsel, and money on his journey as a convict in chains to Siberia some four years earlier. She had also given him a New Testament. He wrote to her of his spiritual condition, a condition that is most often understood as having arisen from his years amid the peasant convicts.

> And not because you are religious, but because I myself have experienced and felt it I shall tell you that at such a time one thirsts for faith as "the withered grass" thirsts for water, and one actually finds it, because in misfortune the truth shines through. I can tell you about myself that I am a child of this century, a child of doubt and disbelief, I have always been and shall ever be (that I know), until they close the lid of my coffin. What terrible torment this thirst to believe has cost me and is still costing me, and the stronger it becomes in my soul, the stronger are the arguments against it. And, despite all this, God sends me moments of great tranquility, moments during which I love and find I am loved by others; and it was during such a moment that I formed within myself a symbol of faith in which all is clear and sacred for me. This symbol is very simple, and here is what it is: to believe that there is nothing more beautiful, more profound, more sympathetic, more reasonable, more courageous, and more perfect than Christ, and there not only isn't, but I tell myself with a jealous love, there cannot be. More than that — if someone succeeded in proving to me that Christ was outside the truth, and if, *indeed,* the truth was outside Christ, I would sooner remain with Christ than with the truth.
>
> But it is better to stop talking about this. Why is it, though, that certain topics of conversation are completely banned in society and, if they are broached, someone or other gives the impression of being shocked?
>
> But let us leave that.[9]

Locating Dostoevsky's conversion experience as having occurred while he was in Siberia, however, becomes problematic and paradoxical when one takes into account that it lay at the end of a long road already paved with intention and conviction. He alludes in this letter to "particular moments of great tranquillity" and says, "it was during such a moment that I formed within myself a symbol of faith in which all is clear and sacred for me." *When* did that fundamental mental paradigm shift occur? He had determined to undergo such a conversion and may very likely have experienced this "particular moment" of cataclysmic tranquility before his penal servitude in Siberia had even begun. In fact, he had set off for prison in Siberia with the expressed intention of discovering humanity, in the form of the Russian people there. By the time he departed on his journey, he had already experienced an acute surge of love for life; he wished to immerse himself in it. At this juncture, however, God did not seem to be on his mind; the Russian people were, and his turning toward them was what led him toward his fervently held Christian belief.

On 22 December 1849, only hours after having endured the horror of a mock execution, Dostoevsky had written to Mikhail, his beloved brother, about the prison sentence that had just, miraculously, replaced his sentence of death:

> Brother, I have not lost courage and I do not feel dispirited. Life is life everywhere; life is within ourselves and not in externals. There will be people around me, and to be a *man* among men, to remain so forever and not to lose hope and give up, however hard things may be — that is what life is, that is its purpose. I have come to realize this. This idea has now become part of my flesh and blood. Yes, this is the truth! The head that created, that lived by the superior life of art, that recognized and became used to the highest spiritual values, that head has already been lopped off my shoulders. What is left are the memories and the images that I had already created but had not yet given form to. They will lacerate and torment me now, it is true! But I have, inside me, the same heart, the same flesh and blood that can still love and suffer and pity and remember — and this, after all is life. On voit le soleil! . . .
>
> Never before have such rich and healthy reserves of spiritual life been seething in me as now. . . . There is no bile or malice in my soul, and I should like so much, at this instant, to love and to press to my heart any of these former acquaintances [with whom he had quarreled]. It is a joy; I experienced it today as I was taking leave of those who were dear to me before I was to die. . . . Life is a gift, life is happiness, each minute could be an eternity of bliss. . . . Now, at this turning point in my life, I am being reborn in another form.[10]

Dostoevsky was to mine these insights for the rest of his life in both his journalism and his fiction. "To be a man among men," among the people; to give form to memories and ideas, to transform one into the other, to realize that each minute could be "an eternity of bliss" if only the gift of life were valued — these elements formed the bedrock of his conversion and his writing and were all present before he ever set out for Siberia.

Two days later, just before his departure to prison, in bidding farewell to his brother and his friend, the school teacher and critic Alexander Miliukov, Dostoevsky again reiterated his intention of discovering humanity in prison. "I'm not going to my funeral; you're not seeing me off to the grave — and in penal servitude there aren't any wild beasts, but men, perhaps even better than I, perhaps more worthy than I."[11]

Both these passionate statements from December 1849 reflected Dostoevsky's predetermined plan of action, his intentional program for his prison years: the discovery of the Russian people. He had determined upon a conversion, an inner transformation, a rebirth, and perhaps — whether in the execution square, within the Peter and Paul Fortress, or somewhere on the St. Petersburg streets linking them — it had *already* occurred.

Five years later, however, just after the completion of his prison term, and after the period during his imprisonment in which his conversion is generally believed to have taken place, his letters show the other side of the coin: the discovery of his isolation from life, his horror, his aversion to the people. Curiously, too, he directly contradicts his earlier assurance that he was not going to a funeral or being sent off to a den of wild beasts: "They were," he wrote to Mikhail on 22 February 1854 (a month after his exile had begun), "coarse, irritable and embittered people. Their hatred for the nobility passes all limits, and for this reason they displayed hostility at the sight of us, along with a malicious joy at seeing us in such a sad plight. *They would have devoured us* if given the chance."[12] Several months later he expressed to his brother Andrei a similar horror at his experience: "I consider those four years as a time in which *I was buried alive and closed in a coffin.* How horrible that time was I have not the strength to tell you, my friend."[13] He *had* seen wild beasts; he *had* been sent to his grave.

Nevertheless, his 1849 vision of discovering the people (the narod), described from the Peter and Paul Fortress on the eve of his journey, had managed to endure, had at last become a reality. The long letter to Mikhail continues; several pages later his mood seems to mellow, and Dostoevsky writes:

> However, people everywhere are people. Even in penal servitude I learned, in those four years, to discern the human beings among the bandits. Believe me, there are profound, strong, beautiful natures among them, and what pleasure it was to find gold under the rough cover. [In his later journalism, Dostoevsky would use a similar image of finding diamonds in filth.] And I didn't find just one or two instances, but several of them. . . . Apropos: how many types of the common people and characters did I carry away with me from the prison camp! . . . There's enough for volumes and volumes. What a wonderful people! On the whole, my time hasn't been wasted. I may not have seen Russia, but I got to know the Russian people well, as well, perhaps, as few know them. Well, that is my little vanity. I hope it is forgivable.[14]

Dostoevsky the author, who throughout his entire creative life tended to boast about the moments when he had discovered something that other writers did not yet know, had reemerged on the literary scene to some degree unchanged. Whatever conversion he may have experienced in his turning toward the narod as offering the key to the spiritual salvation of Russia, his literary vanity about his ability to express "the new" had remained intact. He was still ready to boast about his discovery of new types and his originality as a writer.[15]

The Education of the Peasant and Art for Art's Sake

When Dostoevsky returned to St. Petersburg after his years in the prison camp and as an exiled soldier in the ranks, he founded, with Mikhail, in quick succession, two short-lived journals, *Time* (*Vremia*) and *Epoch* (*Epokha*). In general, the late 1850s and early 1860s — years when the liberation of the serfs was imminent but had not yet come to pass — were a "honeymoon period" during which an air of euphoria prevailed among educated Russians, who unanimously, for a brief time, felt optimistic about the effectiveness of the reforms expected from above.[16] Dostoevsky was thus echoing the general sentiment when he wrote, in 1860, "Indisputably the most important issue [today] is the question of the amelioration of the condition of the peasants."[17] Yet this statement obscures a crucial change that had occurred in Dostoevsky's beliefs. Before he had been sent to prison, Dostoevsky had advocated reform from below. Now, in 1860, he put his trust in Tsar Alexander II's famous statement of 1856, "It is better to begin the abolition of serfdom from above than wait until it begins to abolish itself from below."

After the reforms of 1861, many intellectuals who had welcomed the liberation of the serfs nevertheless remained wary about the issue of peasant education. Some were in favor of educating the peasants through the development of carefully orchestrated peasant readers. Others feared educating them at all, because of the disturbing fact that a disproportionately large number of peasant criminals were literate. Education could be dangerous.[18]

Dostoevsky, in his journalism of the early 1860s, argued powerfully against both these viewpoints (the call for carefully crafted peasant readers and the fear of educating the peasants at all), each of which advocated the continued social engineering of the wretched peasant. He asserted that "the universally human response [to art] is even stronger in the Russian people than in all other nations and is its highest and best characteristic."[19] He had witnessed first-hand this universal response to art while a prisoner in Siberia. As to the question, asked particularly by the radical critics, of how to measure and define what literature is good for the peasants, Dostoevsky's answer was succinctly to the point: "The measuring rod is simple: the more sympathy a poet arouses in the masses, the more he justifies his appearance as a poet."[20]

Dostoevsky instead stressed the need for entertaining literature for the peasants and defended, for the most part, the idea of art for art's sake. It is crucial, argued Dostoevsky, that the peasant's literature be entertaining so that the peasant chooses to read. Although Dostoevsky, since his return from prison and exile, was now willing to accept the tsar's political reforms from above, his ideas about art remained far more radical (though not in harmony with the social utilitarianism of the radical critics). "Everything [having to do with art] that has been imposed from above, everything that has been obtained by force . . . has never succeeded and, instead of being beneficial, has only been harmful. The defenders of 'art for art's sake' are against the utilitarians because by prescribing certain aims for art, they destroy it, for they encroach on its freedom." Dostoevsky boldly elevates art to the realm of a universal human need. "Art is as much a necessity for man as eating and drinking. The need for beauty and creation . . . is inseparable from man and without it man would perhaps have refused to live in the world."[21] It is interesting that this early statement of Dostoevsky's about art and beauty, which sounds so much like the passionate affirmations of his character Stepan Trofimovich Verkhovensky in *The Possessed* (1872), first comes to the fore in a journalistic discussion about the Russian peasants and their reading habits.

Dostoevsky as Would-Be Art Critic

Dostoevsky's attitude toward painting was largely shaped by his views on literature; he thus also advocated, more or less, art for art's sake in painting and was wary of any painting that seemed to value "tendency" — the utilitarian portrayal of a particular social or political message — over the artist's creative freedom. His favorite painter was Raphael, his favorite painting the *Sistine Madonna*. Dostoevsky's second wife, Anna Grigorievna Dostoevskaya, has written about her first visit with Dostoevsky to the Royal Picture Gallery in Dresden. "My husband went past all the rooms and took me straight to the *Sistine Madonna* — the painting he considered the finest manifestation of human genius. . . . Fyodor Mikhailovich prized the works of Raphael more highly than anything else in painting and considered the *Sistine Madonna* his greatest work."[22] Dostoevsky's idiosyncratic ideas about visual art are fundamental to the aesthetic conception of several of his works, among them *The Idiot* (1868), *A Raw Youth* (1875), "The Dream of a Ridiculous Man" (1877), and *The Brothers Karamazov* (1880).[23]

An awareness of Dostoevsky's views on the contemporary generation of artists in Russia is important for arriving at a deeper understanding of him as a writer of fiction, but these observations of his about these artists are, however, equally important for the light they shed on his opinions about "the peasant problem" and on the question of tendentiousness in art in general. Another of Dostoevsky's early journal articles, "The Exhibition in the Academy of Arts:

1860–1861," offers a fascinating case in point. Here he had attacked what he saw as the "utilitarian character" of the academy's teaching, which seemed to him to place too narrow an emphasis on anatomy, costumes, and theory.[24] Yet, while critical of the academy, Dostoevsky's views led him in a different direction from that of the *peredvizhniki,* the Russian realist painters, many of whom had hoped to embody in their work some of the ideas about the relationship of art to reality found in the writings of such radical critics as Nikolai Chernyshevsky.[25]

By 1873, in his article from *The Diary of a Writer* "Apropos of the Exhibition," Dostoevsky had formulated his critical views about painting in a manner that was strikingly reminiscent of the ideas he had expressed a decade earlier in his articles about literature and peasant literacy. Upon seeing the work of Vasily Perov, Arkhip Kuindzhi, Vladimir Makovsky, Ilya Repin, and Nikolai Ge, he worried, "I have a great fear when 'tendency' takes hold of a young artist, especially at the beginning of his career; and what do you think causes me the most concern? Precisely that the purpose of this tendency will not be achieved."[26]

It is not that Dostoevsky was against art that sought to convey a definite message. Even as we acknowledge the profoundly dialogic and polyphonic qualities of Dostoevsky's fiction, one can also argue that Dostoevsky himself was, particularly in his journalism but also in his fiction, a didactic, tendentious, and manipulative writer. Yet in his stories and novels he never believed that such "messages" could be expressed at the expense of art. In his own fiction writing, he had been known to destroy whole portions of his manuscripts, as he did, for example, with *The Possessed,* if he felt his work was becoming too transparently tendentious. His journalistic voice, however, frequently brimmed with the very tendentiousness he warned artists in every medium to avoid and which he instinctively abhorred in his fiction. "Apropos of the Exhibition" continues, in a tone of frequently tedious, though polemical, ironic sincerity. But Dostoevsky does interlace his polemic with sober observations. He is serious when he observes that "any work of art without a preconceived tendency, a work created exclusively out of the demands of art . . . contributes far more."[27] Dostoevsky asserts that only art which emanates from a genuine and free creative impulse can ever prove really useful.

Dostoevsky then brings these observations about the chilling effects upon unfettered artistic impulse of deliberate tendentiousness or social utilitarianism to bear on Repin's famous painting *The Boatmen of the Volga.* He discovers that he likes the painting immensely in spite of his negative expectations. "No sooner had I read in the newspapers of Mr. Repin's barge-haulers than I got frightened. Even the subject itself is terrible: we have accepted somehow that barge-haulers are the best means of representing the well-known social notion of the unpaid debt of the upper classes to the People. I came expecting to see these barge-haulers all lined up in uniforms with the usual labels stuck to their foreheads." But upon actually gazing at the painting, he decides that the figures are not tendentious. "But what happened? To my delight, all my fears turned out to be in vain. . . . Not a single one of them shouts from the painting to the viewer, 'Look how unfortunate I am and how indebted you are to the People!' And in that alone we can credit the artist with a great service." Dostoevsky argues that only when he, or any spectator, has initially liked the painting and not felt he was being preached at was it impossible "not to think that you are indebted, truly indebted to the People. . . You will be dreaming of this whole group of barge-haulers afterward; you will still recall them fifteen years later!"[28] The artist, in Dostoevsky's view, has thus conveyed a message about the peasant through appealing to the spectator's aesthetic sensibility rather than directly to his or her social conscience.

Moreover, the invocation of the power of memory ("You will be dreaming of this whole group of barge-haulers afterward; you will still recall them fifteen years later!") is a crucial element of Dostoevsky's general ideas about art and its transformative powers. In his novels and stories, memory and artistic invention frequently combine to produce a visionary experience in which a character may be ripe for conversion. In "The Peasant Marey" (1876), for example, the same fusing of time past and future ("fifteen years") comes into play.[29]

Nevertheless, Dostoevsky ends his preaching — nearly ranting — critique with a warning to Repin and by implication to the other artists: "Yes, Mr. Repin, it's a long, long trip to reach Gogol; don't let your well-earned success go to your head. Our genre painting has made a good start and we have talented people, but it lacks something to enable it to broaden and expand." He laments that, "as far as I could gather from conversation with some of our major artists, they fear the ideal like some kind of unclean spirit. No doubt this is a noble fear, but it is a prejudicial and unjust one. Our artists need a bit more boldness, more independence of thought, and, perhaps, a bit more education." Dostoevsky considered the ultimate failing of this group of painters to be that they claimed to value reality more than the ideal or a reality transformed by art. Dostoevsky sought to expose their point of view as false: he maintained, for example, that any portraitist who sat down to paint, in studying and gazing at his subject's face, inevitably sought to "arrest that moment in which the subject resembles himself most." That moment, in his view, constituted an ideal, a reality transformed by art. Thus, concluded Dostoevsky, any artist, whether he admitted to it or not, necessarily sought some version of the "ideal" amid the real.[30]

Dostoevsky had particular praise for Vladimir Makovsky's painting *Listening to the Song of the Nightingale* and suggested that it expressed the quintessential aspects of Russian genre painting. Dostoevsky discovered in "little pictures such as these" a "love for humanity, not only for the Russians in particular but even for humans in general."[31]

In his journalistic writing, however, Dostoevsky frequently forced his compelling insights and ideas to an indefensible (and, to this reader at least, ridiculous) extreme. This is precisely what occurs throughout this article. Disturbingly, his discussion of Makovsky's painting and of Perov's *The Hunters at Rest* modulates into an unpleasant occasion for asserting that the meaning of these works cannot be understood by foreigners (a "German or a Viennese Yid"). Dostoevsky even maintained, rather nastily and illogically, that "we [Russians] would understand a similar picture from German life just as well as they themselves and would even take as much delight in it as they and experience almost the same German feelings as they; but they would understand absolutely nothing of one of our Russian paintings."[32] As a general rule, Dostoevsky's journalistic voice occasionally deteriorates to the point of buffoonery and grandiose exaggeration, as it does here, so that he undercuts his own cherished ideas, much as Lebedev (or even Myshkin) does in *The Idiot.*

Nevertheless, despite this peckish nationalistic outburst, throughout his article Dostoevsky continues, in a more sober vein, to be bothered by, as he sees it, the habit that "our contemporary artists" have of equating idealization with lying. The resulting attempt to adhere strictly to realities (both past and present) results, in his view, in a far worse kind of untruth. In discussing historical painting in general and in particular Ge's *The Last Supper,* he argues that when these contemporary Russian artists portray a historical event, such an "event will *necessarily* be imagined in its completed aspect," that is, not exactly as it occurred in reality, "but with the addition of all its subsequent developments that had not yet occurred at the historical moment in which the artist is trying to depict a person or event." Thus, argued Dostoevsky, an artist who wants "to avoid this imaginary error" will tend to try "to fuse . . . both realities — the historical and the current." As a result of this "unnatural combination," Dostoevsky suggested, arises "the worst kind of untruth."[33] Dostoevsky uses Ge's *Last Supper* as his example of an unnatural blending that results in this kind of lie: he criticizes Ge for creating a Jesus who, though he may be "a very good young man," is "not the Christ we know." He goes on, "Nothing at all is explained here; there is no historical truth here; there is not even any truth of genre here; everything here is false. No matter from which point of view you judge, this event could not have happened this way: everything here is disproportionate and out of scale with the future. . . . In Mr. Ge's picture some good people have simply gotten into a quarrel; the result is something false, a preconceived idea. And falsity is always a lie and not realism at all. Mr. Ge was trying for realism."[34]

Dostoevsky was no art critic. Yet his alternately shrill, tendentious, thoughtful, and affectionate diatribe rings consistent with his abiding ideas: the overriding fear of an art that is overly tendentious, the belief that the most successful art captures and transforms both memory and the real by presenting an idealized (synthesized) version of reality, and the conviction that anyone — whether it be a peasant coping with a book or an aristocrat gazing at a painting of a peasant — must first *like* what he or she sees, be entertained by it, for only then can the viewer begin to be convinced by its "message."

The Disjuncture between Dostoevsky's Representations of the Peasant in Journalism and in Fiction

The disconcerting disparity between Dostoevsky's journalistic voice and the way he depicted similar ideas in his fiction had come to the fore quite dramatically by 1861. In his first of two articles entitled "Pedantry and Literacy," Dostoevsky had highlighted his awareness — so painfully depicted as well in *Notes from the House of the Dead* (1861) — of "the gulf that separates us [the educated or noble class] from the common people." His eloquent advocacy for educating the peasants, for respecting them, and for believing in their innate ability to respond to complex works of art had been powerfully expressed throughout this and other essays of 1861. But into this particular essay Dostoevsky also injects a tonal register that is absent from the semifictional, semi-autobiographical *House of the Dead.* In "Pedantry and Literacy" the reader encounters what is to become a persistent messianic note in Dostoevsky's journalism. He states categorically, "We must now try to earn the trust of the common people; we must get to love them, *we must transform ourselves completely so as to become indistinguishable from them.* Can we do it? Do we know how to do it? Are we equal to it?"[35]

This identical theme is expressed in a less extreme, more nuanced, and far more effective way through fiction in *The House of the Dead.* Here the narrator, Goryanchikov, and Dostoevsky, as the author giving his narrator voice, think, with rich symbolism, about the Russian narod as an instrument of grace. "One has but to take off the outer superimposed husk and to look at the kernel more closely, more attentively, and without prejudice, and some of us will see things in the people that we should never have suspected. There is not much our wise men could teach them. On the contrary, I think it is the wise men who ought to learn from the people."[36] This passage is also interesting because it shows that, as early as 1861, Dostoevsky was already thinking about how potent seed imagery could be as an expression for his own ideas about how grace operates in the real world.

Dostoevsky's final novel, *The Brothers Karamazov* (1881), is above all about the ways in which both good and evil travel through the world. It draws its epigraph from John 12:24, "Verily, verily I say unto you, except a corn of wheat fall into the ground and die, it abideth alone; but if it die, it bringeth forth much fruit." Dostoevsky himself had come near enough to death in 1849 to have known that sensation of falling into the ground and dying. During those very moments he had undergone an intense feeling of connection with his fellow human beings. He had thus already experienced a feeling of rebirth as he set out from the Peter and Paul Fortress in 1849. Shortly afterward he had begun to read the New Testament given to him by Madame Fonvizina; he had read it intensively and exclusively for four years and kept the book tucked under his pillow. In *The House of the Dead*, the narrator's suggestion that one remove the husk to look at the kernel more closely reflects what might have been Dostoevsky's own experience and, at the same time, offers up a compelling link between this early work and Dostoevsky's last novel.

A decade later, in the 1870s, when his position as a great writer was already secure, Dostoevsky frequently wrote about the Russian peasant in his ongoing and widely read *Diary of a Writer* (1873–1881), a work unique to Dostoevsky's oeuvre and to literature in general in its complex combination of journalism and fiction.[37] Dostoevsky's journalistic pronouncements about the peasants—the narod—in *The Diary* are frequently expressed in a strident, messianic, tendentious mode that is at odds with the more complex image of the peasant that consistently emerges in his creative art. This juxtaposition comes into the sharpest relief when one compares the fictional with the nonfictional parts of *The Diary* itself.

But this fissure between his journalistic and his fictional discourse seems always to have been present in Dostoevsky's writing. Take, for example, the important question of whether the peasant criminal experienced a sense of remorse or guilt. In *The House of the Dead*, the narrator, Goryanchikov, repeatedly emphasizes the lack of guilt or repentance on the part of the peasant convicts. He reports, "There was no sign of shame or repentance! Yet there was an external, as it were, official resignation, a sort of philosophic calm. . . . I doubt whether one of the convicts ever inwardly admitted his lawlessness!"[38] Later Goryanchikov reiterates this observation and continues to highlight it and mull it over: "I have said already that in the course of several years I never saw one sign of repentance among these people, not a trace of despondent brooding over their crime, and that the majority of them inwardly considered themselves absolutely in the right . . . surely it would have been possible during all those years to have noticed, to have detected something, to have caught some glimpse which would have borne witness to some inner anguish and suffering in those hearts. But it was not there, it certainly was not there."[39] This is a startling and unexpected insight and one of the most chilling observations that the narrator makes.

Yet, some twelve years later, in *The Diary of a Writer*, Dostoevsky, from within his discourse — his bully pulpit — as a journalist, makes precisely the opposite assertion. He contradicts what had been a foundational point of view in his earlier fictional work. He now maintains that these same peasant convicts he had encountered in Siberia did indeed consider themselves guilty:

> The People [narod] do not deny crime, and they know that the criminal is guilty. The People know that they also share the guilt in every crime. But by accusing themselves, they prove that they do not believe in "environment" [that is, that one can point to one's environment as justification for the commission of a crime]; they believe, on the contrary, that the environment depends completely on them, on their unceasing repentance and quest for self-perfection . . . "Let us become better, and the environment will be better." This is what the Russian People sense so strongly but do not express in their concealed idea of the criminal as an unfortunate . . . I was in prison and saw criminals. I repeat: it was a hard school. Not one of them ceased to regard himself as a criminal. . . . No one discussed his own crimes . . . Yet I believe that perhaps not one of them escaped the long inner suffering that cleansed and strengthened him. I saw them lonely and pensive; I saw them in church praying before confession; I listened to their single, unexpected words and exclamations; I remember their faces. Oh believe me, in his heart not one of them considered himself justified![40]

How different the tone of a passage like this is from the same thought expressed in fiction.

In *The House of the Dead*, Goryanchikov similarly describes seeing the peasant convicts in church:

> It was long since I had been to church. The Lenten service so familiar to me from far-away days of childhood in my father's house, the solemn prayers, the prostrations — all this stirred in my heart the far, far away past, bringing back the days of my childhood, and I remember how pleasant it was walking over the frozen ground in the early morning to the house of God, escorted by guards with loaded guns. . . . We stood all together in a group close to the church door, so far back that we could only hear the loud-voiced deacon . . . I remembered how sometimes standing in church as a child I looked at the peasants crowding near the entrance. . . . I used to fancy then that at the

church door they did not pray as we did, that they prayed humbly, zealously, abasing themselves and fully conscious of their humble state.

Now I, too, had to stand in the background, and not only in the background; we were fettered and branded as felons . . . and I remember that this was positively pleasing to me in a way; there was a special subtlety in this strange pleasure. "So be it," I thought.[41]

Dostoevsky, as an artist, was keenly aware of the power of parable, of the value of *not* expressing his own most cherished ideas in too straightforward or didactic a way. (This idea had even surfaced in his heartfelt letter to Madame Fonvizina about his spiritual condition.) In his journalism, however, he irresistibly ventured more closely toward this dangerous precipice of direct statement, even though he himself, as we have already seen in his article on the 1873 painting exhibition, realized the riskiness of such a tendentious approach. (One cannot but recall Myshkin in *The Idiot* and his poignant descriptions of how, when he tried to express his ideas directly, he debased them. He had ruefully lamented his lack of a sense of measure: "There are certain ideas; there are lofty ideas, about which I must not begin to talk, because I should certainly make everyone laugh. . . . My gestures are not appropriate; I have no sense of measure; my words do not correspond with my thoughts, but only degrade them.")[42] Dostoevsky's acute awareness of the pitfalls inherent in the writing of journalism with a messianic tendency — his often professed wariness about stating his most cherished ideas directly — was insufficient to deter him from the repeated practice of doing just that. Journalism remained an irresistibly attractive form of expression for him.

Yet as early as 1861 Dostoevsky had written: "Indeed, the moment you wish to tell the truth [*istina*] according to your convictions, you are at once accused of uttering copybook maxims. . . . Why is it that if in our age we feel the need to tell the truth we have more and more to resort to humor or satire or irony in order to sweeten truth as if it were a bitter pill?"[43] And fifteen years later, in 1876, Dostoevsky returned yet again to what was for him an irresolvable authorial conundrum: the conflict between the desire he experienced to state his convictions directly and the impossibility of doing so effectively. He had already written about this as a young man to his brother Mikhail, shortly after the appearance of his first work, *Poor People* (1846).[44] Now, as the already famed author of *The Diary*, he wrote about this discursive conflict in a remarkable letter to Vsevolod Solovyov. He was writing to Solovyov about his article "The Eastern Question," which had just appeared in the June 1876 issue and which was, in effect, a rant about Russia's historical role as unifier, first, of all the Slavs and, eventually, of all humanity:

And so, you liked the June issue of *The Diary*. I'm very glad for that. I have a great reason for that. I had never yet allowed myself in my writings to take *certain* of my convictions to their conclusion, to say *the very last word*. One bright correspondent from the provinces even reproached me for starting up conversations about lots of things in *The Diary*, touching on lots of things, but never yet having taken them to their conclusion, and encouraged me not to be timid. And so I up and stated the last word of my conviction — my dreams regarding Russia's role and mission amid humanity, and I expressed the idea that this would not only happen in the near future but was already beginning to come true. And what do you think — exactly what I had foreseen happened; even the newspapers and publications friendly to me right away started yelling that I had paradox on paradox, and other journals didn't even pay any attention, while, it seems to me, I have touched on a most important question. That's what taking an idea to its conclusion means! Pose any paradox you please, but don't take it to its conclusion, and it will turn out wittily, and subtly, and comme il faut, but take any risky utterance to its conclusion, say, for instance, suddenly, "Such and such is in fact the *Messiah*," right out and not in a hint, and no one will believe you, precisely because of your naïveté, precisely because you carried it through to the conclusion, said your very last word. But, on the other hand, if many of the most famous wits, Voltaire, for instance, instead of gibes, hints, bare suggestions and insinuations, had suddenly ventured to state everything they believed, had shown their whole underpinning all at once, their essence, then, believe me, they wouldn't have obtained even a tenth of the earlier effect. Moreover, people would just have laughed at them. [Dostoevsky then goes on to quote a famous line from Tiutchev's poem "Silentium" (1836).] And man somehow doesn't at all like the last word in anything, a "spoken" thought, saying that "A thought spoken is a lie" (*Mysl' izrechennaia est' lozh'*).[45]

Dostoevsky had already expressed a remarkably similar notion in his 1871 article "Apropos of the Exhibition": "He need only keep in mind the golden rule that a word spoken may be silver, but an unspoken one is gold."[46] But in his journalism, as I hope is becoming evident, he did not seem to be able to follow his own advice — even on the same page — or take heed of his own pithy precepts.

Thus Dostoevsky's pronouncements about the peasants offer us a telling case in point, a concrete illustration of the veracity of this annoying "paradox" against which he railed so eloquently but in which he also believed so fervently. For in his journalism Dostoevsky does, at times, attempt to say things directly. He states repeatedly that he regards the peasants — with all their flaws, their opacity, their tendencies to debauchery — as the front line in Russia's quest for salvation. Moreover, in his *Diary* article "Vlas" (1873), Dostoevsky attributed to the narod the capability of making precisely the kind of direct statement of a "final conviction" that he himself, for artistically strategic reasons, knew, despite his own journalistic outbursts, it would be better to avoid. "I still hold that these very same and sundry 'Vlases,' repentant and unrepentant, will say the last word; they will say it and will show us a new path and a new way out of all these apparently insoluble tangles we find ourselves in." No matter what terrible crimes this hypothetical yet quintessential peasant Vlas commits, "He will save himself and us as well, for I repeat once more, the light and the salvation will come radiating from below (in a form that our liberals may find entirely surprising; and there will be a good deal of amusement in this)."[47]

Dostoevsky's journalism virtually abounds with these kinds of statements; such pronouncements may have contributed to the view expressed by writers from Virginia Woolf to Milan Kundera that, for better or worse, the Russian soul is the chief character in Russian literature. It may in fact be sweeping, categorical journalistic pronouncements like those made in "Vlas" that have contributed more to some of the overarching and inaccurate generalizations about Dostoevsky's fiction than his fiction itself, which tends always to present a more dialogic, open-ended representation of any problem or even of "the Russian soul."[48]

In his article "Vlas," Dostoevsky wrote, "I think that the principal and most basic spiritual need of the Russian People is the need for suffering, incessant and unslakable suffering, everywhere and in everything. I think the Russian People have been infused with this need to suffer from time immemorial."[49] Yet how do such statements attributing to the peasant a "need for suffering," the ability to "show us the new path," or to lead the way "to light and salvation" actually affect us as readers? Do we pause? Do we experience that delicious frisson of recognition? Are we swept away by the power and beauty of these ideas, by their irresistible force? Are we convinced, persuaded? I think not.

It is only through Dostoevsky's *artistic* representations of the peasants — that is, the peasant transformed by art — that we begin authentically to care about them, that we begin to consider their enigma, their beauty, their power of spirituality. His journalistic representations of them, in fact, resemble the artistic productions for which he had taken Ge to task. Dostoevsky's journalism discloses itself under a bright light, and its deficiencies and flaws are impossible to hide; his fiction is an art of half shadows, of silences, of parabolic representations and gaps, where "last words" and finalized convictions have no place, but where idea and character alike emerge in a full and compelling embodiment. (Virginia Woolf describes the interplay of light and dark in Dostoevsky's artistic work in a way that powerfully links such lighting with the processes of thought and consciousness that he represents. "Alone among writers, Dostoevsky has the power of reconstructing these most swift and complicated states of mind, of rethinking the whole train of thought in all its speed, now as it flashes into light, now as it lapses into darkness, for he is able to follow not only the vivid streak of achieved thought but to suggest the dim and populous underworld of the mind's consciousness where desires and impulses are moving blindly beneath the sod.")[50]

I will cite two final examples to illustrate this disjuncture between Dostoevsky's voice as a journalist and as an artist. (Each will receive extended treatment in later chapters.) In *The Idiot* Dostoevsky struggled with some of these same themes about the peasant that we have already remarked in his journalism. But in the novel, the representations of the peasants — in all their degradation, who nevertheless suggest a pathway to faith and salvation — do, I think, make the reader pause and decide to engage with the work, to grapple with these large, unwieldy ideas. How does the artist Dostoevsky, as opposed to the journalist, bring about this act of engagement on the part of the reader? Through parable, through enigma, through those lacunae inherent in every human conversation. And years later, in 1876, when Dostoevsky himself may have been endeavoring to describe his own conversion, his own winding path toward belief, he again turned, through the medium of art, to an iconic depiction of the Russian peasant — the peasant Marey — and to the representation of the peasant through a complexly layered anecdote composed of several disparate, seemingly opposing parts.

It is interesting that the two consecutive entries in *The Diary* (February 1876) "On Love of the People. An Essential Contract with the People" and "The Peasant Marey" taken together offer a microcosmic view of the tension between Dostoevsky's journalistic commentaries on the peasant and his rendering of the peasant as transformed by artistic vision. The two discourses share a common theme, but their effects are vastly different.

In the nonfiction article, "On Love of the People," Dostoevsky addresses head-on that seeming contradiction between an acknowledgment that the people are "devoted to darkness and depravity" and the idea that they represent Russia's best hopes. Once again we hear the familiar, impassioned, banal, and unpleasant rhetoric: "He who is a true friend of humanity, whose heart has even once throbbed for the sufferings of the People — he will understand and overlook all the impenetrable deposits of filth that weigh down our People and will be able to find diamonds in this filth. I repeat: judge the Russian People not by the abominations they so frequently commit, but by those great and sacred things for which, even in their abominations, they constantly yearn."[51]

For the reader who can think back to fictional moments in Dostoevsky's canon such as Myshkin's story of the peasant who prayed to God as he slit his friend's throat, this statement about diamonds in the filth may have a genuine resonance. A reader unarmed with such an arsenal of anecdote and parable may fail to be moved by Dostoevsky's passionate but didactic assertions; these assertions may fall short of the mark and read simply as boring harangue. Dostoevsky then claims that "the question of the People and our view of them, our present understanding of them is our most important question, a question on which our whole future rests; one might even say it is the most practical question for the moment." Yet even as he categorically stresses the absolute primacy of this problem, Dostoevsky admits that "however, the People are still a theory for all of us and still stand before us as a riddle. All of us who love the People look at them as if at a theory and, it seems, not one of us loves them as they really are but only as each of us imagines them to be."[52]

Having stated this truth, which seems to bring him and his readers back to a starting point where they all must admit that they do not know the people at all and have only a personal theory to fall back on (and theory, as opposed to an artistically embodied "ideal," in Dostoevsky's view, is always dangerous), Dostoevsky, like Myshkin before him, suddenly decides to give his own *profession de foi* indirectly, through an anecdote: "But reading all these *professions de foi* is a bore, I think, and so I'll tell you an anecdote; actually it's not even an anecdote, but only a reminiscence of something that happened long ago and that, for some reason, I would very much like to recount here and now, as a conclusion to our treatise on the People. At the time I was only nine years old. . . . But no, I'd best begin with the time I was twenty-nine."[53] The wandering attention of the reader abruptly becomes focused; the boredom of both author and reader gives way to extreme interest.

At this point in *The Diary of a Writer* Dostoevsky has abruptly shifted narrative gears and, within a single sentence, moved from the discourse of journalism to that of fiction. The moving, authentic, semi-autobiographical, yet fictional conversion tale that follows offers up an image of the people, as embodied in the peasant Marey, that is, ironically, both a "theory" and an "enigma." It derives its force, however, from the ways in which Dostoevsky has chosen to represent "the problem of the people" to himself and to his readers. Like his created character Myshkin, Dostoevsky strategically forges a reminiscence composed of discrete parts that will combine to suggest to the reader a parable for religious faith. Both *The Idiot* and "The Peasant Marey" contain a peculiar blend of fancy and fact, but in both it is the Russian peasant, represented through the lens of fiction, who embodies the potential for pointing the way to spiritual knowledge.

I have not even touched upon Raskolnikov's final need, in his quest to achieve a meaningful confession, to bow down amid the peasants in the marketplace, or upon the portrait of a peasant holy man so central to *A Raw Youth,* or upon the peasant women of *The Brothers Karamazov,* or upon the hypothetical peasant babe for whom Mitya goes to Siberia, or upon the prophetic, singing, drunken peasant whom Ivan leaves to die and then saves, or upon those peasant jurors who stand so firm amid a sea of psychological and sociological evidence. But these and many others are the peasants of Dostoevsky whom we remember — the peasants transformed by art — the concretely yet artistically realized peasants who in their specificity manage to convey the general ideas about the peasants as bearers of grace that Dostoevsky had hoped but failed to express effectively in his journalism.

Let us now leave the world of Dostoevsky's journalism and turn to *Notes from the House of the Dead.*

2

Guilt, Repentance, and the Pursuit of Art in
The House of the Dead

There's no repentance in the grave.
— Isaac Watts, *Solemn Thoughts of God and Death*

"He is the artist of his own life."
— Spoken by the dreamer of himself, Dostoevsky, *White Nights*

Dostoevsky's *Notes from the House of the Dead* hovers at the boundaries of several genres. To the degree that it constitutes a memoir of his life in a
prison camp, *The House of the Dead* is an autobiographical work. But it may
also be read as a documentary novel — one that conforms to the broad traditions of realism. Seeking to achieve a kind of photographic accuracy, it avoids
being overtly didactic, and the first-person narrator, Alexander Petrovich Goryanchikov, unlike virtually all of Dostoevsky's other first-person narrators,
endeavors to minimize his prejudices and suppress the oddities of his personality in favor of factual, dispassionate reportage. His narrative is framed by the
notes of the general "editor" who discovers Goryanchikov's manuscript after
his death.[1] The relationships among Dostoevsky, the editor, Goryanchikov, and
his text are fascinating and complex. It is interesting to hypothesize about the
narrative texture in this work, to juxtapose the different readings of it that
emerge depending on whether one chooses an emphasis on autobiography or

fiction, or on the role of the author, the editor, or the narrator. Ultimately, however, the narrator's gaze—whether it be autobiographical or fictional, or some hybrid of the two—is focused not inward but outward on his subjects. It is the verbal snapshots, the documentary impulses, that imbue this particular work with its elusive quiddity.

To affix the label of realism to one of Dostoevsky's works without the qualifying oxymoronic adjectives *fantastic* or *romantic* is to separate it from the main body of his fiction. Perhaps because this novel is somewhat anomalous to Dostoevsky's fiction as a whole in that it is *not* a work of fantastic or romantic realism, it should come as no surprise that the great master of Russian realism, Tolstoy, writing in 1868, found *The House of the Dead* to be his favorite among Dostoevsky's works. Tolstoy was also the first to note that *The House of the Dead* does not fit into a particular generic mold. In penning one of his most often quoted observations about *War and Peace* (1868–69) and its connection to the Russian literary tradition, he had observed that no artistic prose works of significance in Russian literature from the time of Pushkin "completely fit the form of novel, narrative poem or novella":

> . . .The history of Russian literature since the time of Pushkin not merely affords many examples of such deviation from European forms, but does not offer a single example of the contrary. From Gogol's *Dead Souls,* to Dostoevsky's *House of the Dead,* in the recent period of Russian literature there is not a single artistic prose work rising at all above mediocrity, which quite fits into the form of novel, epic, or story.[2]

The House of the Dead may even be read as a realist gothic novel, in so far as the action takes place in a remote, isolated locale existing under tyrannical rules that differ from those of the surrounding society but have the potential, nevertheless, of grotesquely mirroring that society. The favorite locales in the gothic novel are the castle, the monastery, and the prison. Like its gothic predecessors, *The House of the Dead* explores the psychology of the victim and the victimizer; it abounds with chiaroscuro landscapes and displays a world where the beautiful and the horrible are oddly and inextricably intertwined. Moreover, as in the gothic novel, the reader of *The House of the Dead* is cast in the difficult role of a frequent spectator of violence.[3]

Robert Jackson has concluded that however we define the genre of *The House of the Dead* (and in addition to the ways I've mentioned one could also affix the labels of sketch, vision, and, following Dante, as Dostoevsky in part means us to do—descent into hell), it also affects us in a way approximating a work of visual art, for it forms "a series of gigantic frescoes of human experience and destiny."[4] Ultimately, however, *The House of the Dead* resists attempts to place it firmly within any one category of prose writing but continues to linger at several boundaries, while coming to rest within none.

Dostoevsky's _House of the Dead_ also resists classification within his own canon on another particularly crucial issue, an ideological one. Dostoevsky's short works and novels aver that for the most part a criminal experiences an innate sense of guilt or responsibility for his or her crime — so that whether or not society condemns the criminal, he or she ultimately arrives at a personal assessment of the transgression. In short, save for a very few exceptions (such as Pyotr Verkhovensky in _The Possessed_), Dostoevsky's characters tend either to possess or to grow into the possession of a conscience. But _The House of the Dead_ presents an altogether different view of the criminal's attitude toward the crime. It is important to reiterate, as I emphasized in the previous chapter, that the convicts Dostoevsky describes are, for the most part, peasants.

It is a commonplace to observe that Dostoevsky's major novels share a concern with questions of guilt, responsibility, and repentance. Yet in _The House of the Dead,_ a text exclusively concerned with convicts (that is, those guilty of crimes who have been forced by society to take on, by their servitude, a ritual responsibility for their deeds), Dostoevsky treats the double-faceted question of guilt and repentance in a manner that bears little resemblance to the way these themes work in the rest of his novels, for, as we have seen, questions of guilt and repentance are for the most part irrelevant to the daily lives of the convicts.

I quote in full two passages cited more briefly in chapter one. In the first, the narrator reports: "There was no sign of shame or repentance! Yet there was an external, as it were, official resignation, a sort of philosophic calm. . . . I doubt whether one of the convicts ever inwardly admitted his lawlessness. If anyone who was not a prisoner were to try reproaching the criminal for his crime, upbraiding him (though it is not the Russian way to reproach a criminal), an endless stream of oaths would follow" (4:13, 38–39). Later he observes, "I have said already that in the course of several years I never saw one sign of repentance among these people, not a trace of despondent brooding over their crime, and that the majority of them inwardly considered themselves absolutely in the right . . . surely it would have been possible during all those years to have noticed, to have detected something, to have caught some glimpse which would have borne witness to some inner anguish and suffering in those hearts. But it was not there, it certainly was not there" (4:15, 41).[5] These peasant convicts "inwardly considered themselves absolutely in the right" and were thus able to step over precisely those barriers that Raskolnikov in _Crime and Punishment_ would find himself unable to cross.

How do we fit these statements into our established ideas about Dostoevsky's belief that the criminal does, at least at moments, feel guilt and assume responsibility for the crime? Just as the convicts never meditate on their crimes and their guilt, neither does the narrator — who murdered his wife — ever meditate upon his relation to his crime (except perhaps indirectly through the chilling inserted narrative, "Akulka's Husband," whose narrator, Shishkov, had murdered his wife). The ethical situation becomes more complicated when, in the passage I have just quoted, the narrator uses as his prime example of the unrepentant convict the case of a parricide who with unconscious grotesque humor describes his "*parent* [as] . . . never [having] complained of any illness right up to the end" (4:16, 42). The narrator's bleakly comic example muddles and befuddles his argument, for it is this very parricide who is later declared to be innocent; so of course, in his case, a lack of guilty or responsible feelings would be most understandable.[6]

In fact, the only time the editor of the notes interrupts Goryanchikov's narrative is near the end of the book (at the beginning of the chapter titled "The Complaint"), in order to tell the reader of the parricide's innocence. He recalls Goryanchikov's previous assertion that this prisoner exemplified "an instance of the callousness with which the convicts will sometimes speak of their crimes." Goryanchikov had also added, as the editor points out, "Of course I did not believe in that crime" (4:195; 299). But Goryanchikov, we learn, even though he had an instinctive suspicion about the convict's innocence, did not possess all the facts and did not know for certain that the parricide was innocent. His primary characterization of the parricide is thus misleading, for to speak callously of a crime you did not commit amounts to a kind of cosmic irony, whereas to speak callously of a crime you did commit suggests genuine immorality or a lack of repentance. After declaring that he had "received information from Siberia that the criminal really was innocent and had suffered ten years in penal servitude for nothing," the editor concludes, "There is nothing more to add. There is no need to enlarge on all the tragic significance of this fact . . . we believe, too, that if such a fact can be possible, this possibility adds a fresh and striking feature to the description of *The House of the Dead,* and puts a finishing touch to the picture" (4:195; 299–300).

Why would the editor choose to undercut his narrator at this point? Do we have here an early example of the later Dostoevsky's fondness for pitting his authorial voice against the narrative voice already present in this work? Certainly *The House of the Dead,* like Dostoevsky's later novels, exhibits a multilayered narration, in which the primary meanings or messages are frequently to be found at the greatest narrative distance from the "author" — witness the searing narrative of "Akulka's Husband." Akulka's voice, to the extent that we hear it, is buried within the fifth layer of narration in this work, if we start from the author and move successively to the voices of the editor, the narrator, Akulka's husband Shishkov, and finally to that of Akulka herself.

At any rate, after the editor has gratuitously interrupted his own presentation of the late Goryanchikov's narrative with this news about the parricide's innocence, he abruptly returns us to it. But what is this "fresh and striking feature," this "finishing touch to the picture" to which the editor alludes? Was it that the unrepentant parricide was later proved innocent? But what about the others — the vast guilty majority who never showed "one sign of repentance"? Is the editor indirectly suggesting that some of them may also have been innocent? The editor also emphasizes that the falsely accused parricide's "young life" had been "crushed." In his subsequent novels Dostoevsky makes sure that readers experience intense compassion for the sufferings of the innocent. Yet is the reader asked to make any leap of compassion here? Has the reader even been taught the terms of the question? No. Do we perhaps here witness Dostoevsky working out the framing of the questions that will infuse his subsequent literary productions? *The House of the Dead* has long been regarded as a sketchbook from which Dostoevsky later drew to work out fuller portraits, fuller characterizations. The work, however, also bursts with images, plot fragments, and narrative strategies that Dostoevsky transforms in his subsequent fiction. One finds an embedded or implicit series of questions that remain largely unexplored by Goryanchikov or even the editor but to which Dostoevsky will repeatedly return.

Moreover, through his narrator, Dostoevsky goes on to suggest a theory of crime and guilt that exhibits, in comparison with his other works, an atypically rigid sense of *class* consciousness. "I have said already," writes the narrator, "that I saw no signs of remorse even when the crime was against one of their class [that is, "against one of their own," in Russian]; as for crimes against officers in control of them, they did not count them at all. . . . The criminal knows and never doubts that he will be acquitted by the verdict of his own class, who will never, he knows, entirely condemn him . . . so long as his offence has not been against his equals, his brothers, his fellow peasants" (4:147; 230).

Yet it was toward these peasant convicts who showed no signs of remorse that Dostoevsky repeatedly turned, often within the pages of this work, to find what he believed to be great and good about the Russian people — their innate sense of justice, their instinctual belief in equality amid the community, their ability to be morally transformed by a work of art, their humility and devotion in the performance of the rituals of Christmas. The narrator portrays all these positive qualities in the convicts as well, and they are not qualities to dismiss easily. But do they allow us to understand the prisoners' lack of remorse, their lack of the sense of having transgressed some moral law? The pieces of this puzzle do not fit compactly together. The moral dualities embodied in the peasant convicts are as difficult to untangle as the generic dissonances between reading this work as fiction or as memoir.

Dostoevsky may have been unsatisfied with his portrayal of the peasant convicts' attitude toward guilt in *The House of the Dead*. As we saw in chapter one, later on, in 1873 in his *Diary of a Writer*, Dostoevsky reversed his position and maintained that the convicts *were* morally aware of their crimes.[7] At any rate, such unresolved, even fragmentary ambiguities in *The House of the Dead* exemplify the intimate but often oblique relationship of this work to the rest of Dostoevsky's fiction. Thus, although *The House of the Dead* is a sourcebook for Dostoevsky's later writing (much as Chekhov's account of his journey to Sakhalin was to be thirty years later), its stance toward guilt, responsibility, and repentance — subjects that form a cornerstone of all Dostoevsky's future creative work — is nevertheless unique and unfinalized, not in the sense of being philosophically, deliberately dialogic but simply in an unfinished way. Andrei Sinyavsky has suggested that Dostoevsky found in prison not only a rich source for new material and an extended occasion for scrutinizing his past but also the experience of having passed through death (*opyt prokhozhdeniia smerti*) — both in those dreadful moments on the scaffold and during the difficult years that followed — the years spent in *The House of the Dead*.[8]

What were these rich sources? In what way is *The House of the Dead* a casebook for Dostoevsky's future work? It is usual to emphasize that during his years as a convict Dostoevsky discovered the greatness and beauty of the Russian people and that therein lay the primary "rich source" for his new material. But as I suggested in the previous chapter, one must not lose sight of the fact that Dostoevsky was determined to make this discovery about the Russian people *before* his penal servitude in Siberia had even begun. He had set off for prison with the expressed intention of discovering the Russian people there.

We have already explored at some length the question of whether or not Dostoevsky had set himself the task of undergoing a transformation or conversion while in Siberia ("I'm not going to my funeral; you're not seeing me off to the grave"). His letters to his brothers following his reprieve from execution had borne poignant testimony to this determination not to find "wild beasts" there but men "perhaps even better than I." Later, upon his release from prison, in 1854, his letters to his brothers had on one hand expressed disillusionment and despair: "They would have devoured us if given the chance" and

"I consider those four years as a time in which I was *buried alive and closed in a coffin*. How horrible that time was I have not the strength to tell you." But he had also managed to find the "gold under a rough exterior" that he had been so determined to find. His words gush with emotion: "Believe me: there are among them those who are deep, strong and beautiful . . . what a marvelous people." Present too, however, was a more neutral and even ironic discourse: the voice of Dostoevsky the practical artist appeared rather coolly to appraise the literary currency his experience had given him: "On the whole, my time hasn't been wasted. I may not have seen Russia, but I got to know the Russian people well . . . as few know them. Well, that is my little vanity."[9]

Was Dostoevsky buried alive in the prison camp, or did he undergo a conversion — or both? Or, as I have suggested, could this conversion have happened earlier, after his reprieve from execution and before his journey to Siberia and back — before his extended immersion amid the Russian people — even began? Whatever Dostoevsky's actual experience in prison might have been, he was ready upon his release, and boastfully so, to transform it into art.

Seven years later, Dostoevsky published *The House of the Dead*. This work is the intricate product of his idealized visions of humanity — which had been made sharper by his experience of the scaffold and its euphoric aftermath — grafted on to his protracted collision in Siberia with reality *in extremis*. The work is a hybrid of intention and experience, of visionary desire in competition with horror amid loneliness and isolation, of events recollected after the fact (though one cannot say "in tranquility") and then artistically reshaped and transformed.

Most important, all these visionary desires, religious and philosophical intentions, and actual experiences are refracted not through the unmediated voice of Dostoevsky himself but through the moderate and for the most part cool tones of Goryanchikov, his narrator. Goryanchikov's is not the polemical, rhetorically passionate, occasionally even shrill, unmediated authorial voice that we have already encountered in some of Dostoevsky's journalistic writing of the same period. Dostoevsky had filtered his voice in *The House of the Dead* through the editor and the narrator, and the closely held beliefs about the peasants encountered in his letters and journalism are transformed and rendered more effective through these layers of fictional discourse.

Dostoevsky continued to be haunted by his created persona Goryanchikov. In 1876, he was still complaining, ruefully to be sure but also with humor, about the tendency of his readers to confuse the narrator with the author. "I wrote my *Letters from a Dead House* fifteen years ago under the name of a fictitious person. . . . Since that time many people have been under the impression . . . that I was exiled for the murder of my wife."[10] Such complaints of course were not new for Dostoevsky. After the publication of his first work, *Poor People* (1846), he had written, "Our public has an instinct, as does any crowd, but it lacks education. They don't understand how one can write in such a style. They've gotten used to seeing the author's mug in everything; I didn't show mine, however. But they can't even imagine that it's Devushkin speaking and not I, and that Devushkin can't speak in any other way."[11]

Dostoevsky's own mixed emotions about the peasants, his various sources of inspiration — the peasants he had imagined he would meet in prison, those he actually did meet, and the hybrid ultimately rendered up in his fiction — and the narrative layers of his own text interfered with as well as enhanced each other. It is no surprise then that *The House of the Dead* contains mutually coexisting messages of hope and despair, of irrevocable death and the possibility of renewal, of unresolved pain and delight achieved amid unspeakable squalor.

At the beginning of his career, in 1846, Dostoevsky had boasted that Vissarion Belinsky and the other critics found that his originality lay in his analytical style. "They (Belinsky and the like) find in me a new, original current consisting of the fact that I write with Analysis, not Synthesis, that is, I go into the depths, but by taking things apart atom by atom I seek out the whole, while Gogol takes the whole directly and for that reason is not as profound as I am."[12] *The House of the Dead* may constitute just such an example of analysis in its minute examination of prisoner after prisoner, event after event, atom after atom. Although this work may reflect an analytic search for "the whole," however, it is anomalous. Dostoevsky's later novels (which contain more of the synthesis to which he alludes) each emanate from some directly apprehended, poetic whole, from an idea expressed and transformed by his artistic execution of it. To the extent that *The House of the Dead* embodies the layers of narration typical of Dostoevsky's later fiction, it already partakes somewhat of the synthetic style that was to become a marker of his mature work. This work nevertheless continues to reflect an analytic process of seeking the whole "atom by atom" and remains to some degree fragmentary and unfinished.

We have already seen that in the late 1850s and early 1860s Dostoevsky was thinking about theories of art. As early as 1856, while still in exile, he had written from Semipalatinsk to A. Y. Vrangel that he had decided to write an article, "Letters about Art," that would be "the fruit of a decade's deliberations": "I'd thought the whole thing through down to the last word already in Omsk. Perhaps many people will disagree with me on many points. But I believe in my ideas and that is enough. I want to ask Ap[ollon] Maikov to read the piece beforehand. In several chapters there will be whole pages from the pamphlet. [He is referring here to another essay he had abandoned because "it was turning out to be a purely political pamphlet."] It is actually about the mission of Christianity in art. Only the problem is where to place it."[13] Two years later he wrote to Mikhail, still from Semipalatinsk, about his ideas for a literary newspaper. He envisions "a literary feuilleton, analyses of the journals, analyses of what's good and what's mistaken, and enmity towards *nepotism,* which is so widespread now; more energy, passion, wit, staunchness — that's what's needed now! I'm saying this so passionately now because I have several literary pieces in this manner jotted down and outlined: e.g., *about contemporary poets, about the statistical movement in literature,* about the futility of *directions* [tendencies] in art — essays that are written provocatively and even sharply, but mainly, with a light touch."[14] Within a few years, after his return to St. Petersburg, in the early 1860s, Dostoevsky had published some of his most famous journalistic writings about art. However, these "Letters on Art" were sadly to join the ranks of his unwritten canon, along with *The Drunkards, Atheism, Fathers and Children,* and *The Life of a Great Sinner* among others.

The House of the Dead offers fundamental and vital clues, albeit indirect ones, to Dostoevsky's ideas about art during the 1850s and early 1860s. These ideas appear necessarily through the lens of fiction and are thus nuanced differently — are transformed by fiction — though they are related to the ideas we have already encountered in his journalism. In both spheres the question of "art for art's sake" emerges as primary. Surprisingly, many of the convicts are, in one way or another, devoted, "for art's sake," to a particular pursuit. The narrator observes, "In obedience to a natural craving and a sort of sense of self-preservation, everyone in the prison had his special craft and pursuit" (4:16; 43). Language — particularly proverbs and eloquent streams of abuse — was frequently chosen by the prisoners as a favorite arena for the exercise of art for art's sake. "And what masters of abuse they were! They swore elaborately, artistically," exclaims the narrator (4:13, 39). Later he marvels, "I could not imagine at first how they could swear at each other for pleasure, find in it amusement, pleasant exercise, enjoyment. . . . A dialectician in abuse [*dialektik-rugatel'*] was respected. He was almost applauded like an actor" (4:25; 54).

While still a newcomer to the prison, the narrator, in seeking to understand the behavior of his fellow convicts, often finds the key to their otherwise irrational behavior in their love of doing something for art's sake (*iskusstvo dlia iskusstva*). Nor is this perception displaced by the narrator's subsequent experience during his years in prison. Thus, early on he describes a smuggler as one who "works from inclination, from passion. He is on one side a poet." Goryanchikov tells of a vodka smuggler who had a dreadful fear of being beaten and who was paid only "the merest trifle" for the vodka he smuggled into the prison, yet despite all this, he continued his smuggling activity. He "sometimes act[ed] with a sort of inspiration. . . . The queer fellow loved art for art's sake" (4:18; 46). Another artist described much later, the convict barber, sharpened his worn-out razor day and night. "He evidently enjoyed his art," writes the narrator, "and was proud of it. And he carelessly took the kopeck he had earned as though he did the work for art's sake and not for profit" (4:78; 130). Among the convicts who selected the new prison horse there were "genuine connoisseurs [*znatoki*] in horse-flesh," two of whom engaged in a "chivalrous duel" over which horse should be bought—a matter of high seriousness, although neither was himself putting up the money (4:186; 286–87). These peasant convicts, like Dostoevsky's famous dreamers in *White Nights* (1846), *Notes from Underground* (1864), *A Gentle Creature* (1876), and "The Dream of a Ridiculous Man" (1877) are all, for good or for ill, artists of their own lives.[15] From the 1860s on, the alienated, isolated, educated urban dreamers for whom Dostoevsky is so well known may have been partly engendered by these peasant convicts. The dreamer in the earlier work, *White Nights,* is a more romantic character who exudes a sentimentality that is absent from the convicts and the subsequent dreamers. The other defining features of Dostoevsky's post–Siberian underground urban dreamers differ strongly from the peasant convicts who all lived an intensely communal life in a rural setting and who were largely uneducated.[16] But these peasant convicts and the urban dreamers share, however, an instinctive hunger for an artistic pursuit of some kind.

What do these unlikely peasant-convict artists have in common with each other? The smuggler, the barber, and the convict horse dealers find fulfillment and enjoyment in a process, in an activity that, during the moments when they are engaged in their "creative" endeavors, eclipses the final result: the smuggled object, the earned kopek, even the horse are of secondary importance. In his later fiction Dostoevsky expanded this idea of process taking precedence over product or theory until it became an identifying marker for his work. To give only two brief examples amid many: in *The Idiot,* Ippolit muses that Christopher Columbus "was happy not when he had discovered America" but rather in the time just before he had discovered the New World. "Life is what matters," writes Ippolit, "life alone—the continuous, eternal process of discovering life and not the discovery itself at all!" In *The Brothers Karamazov,* Alyosha urges Ivan to love life more than the meaning of it.[17]

This idea was to become a commonplace of Dostoevsky's oeuvre, a transferable standard bearer from one work to another. But the peasant convicts who pursued an activity for art's sake were its trailblazers, and their role as such has been overlooked. They are expressing their freedom, their unfettered motion in the stream of life, as much as will any of Dostoevsky's later charismatic, compelling, and larger-than-life characters. Indeed, given the extreme regimentation of nearly every aspect of their prison existence, such "artistic" activities constituted virtually the sole way in which the convicts could exercise their freedom. The love of process and life that the convicts, despite their actual fetters, are able to express through their artistic pursuits further separates them from Dostoevsky's urban dreamers.[18]

But there is a negative side to the pursuit of art for art's sake as well. In Dostoevsky's works the knife always cuts both ways, and the artist who is overcome with vanity can combine his artistic energies with evil intentions. Art for art's sake can express freedom, but it can also serve those who deny themselves nothing, for whom "everything is permitted," and who thereby allow themselves unlimited freedom. Such a one, for example, is the brutal and sadistic Lieutenant Zherebyatnikov. The narrator compares him with the Marquis de Sade, describing him as an "epicure in administering punishment" who "was passionately fond of the art of punishing, and he loved it precisely for the sake of art [*edinstvenno dlia iskusstva*]. He enjoyed it and, like the worn-out aristocratic debauchees of the Roman Empire, he invented all sorts of subtleties, all sorts of unnatural tricks to excite and agreeably thrill his crass soul" (4:148–49, 231).

The narrator perceives Zherebyatnikov's counterpart, Lieutenant Smekalov, as "lacking in artistic fancy," but Smekalov too nevertheless longs, above all, to be an artist. He would obsessively repeat the same joke to those about to be flogged. The narrator understands this to be the vanity of an author. Smekalov "himself composed [his joke]," and he repeated it "because of literary vanity" (4:151; 235–36). Smekalov's own wit (in this case a blasphemous rhyme combining the prisoner's prayer with the order to commence flogging) would enflame him, and "with an inspired gesture" [*s vdokhnovennym zhestom*], he would order the beating to begin (4:151, 236) and then retire from the scene a happy author, delighted because of his successful rhyme. Karla Oeler has eloquently deconstructed Smekalov's dark creativity. She describes how Smekalov improvises on the well-known prayer "Our Father" and uses rhyme. "His rhyme connotes, mockingly, that the victim's flogging accords with divine will, for were the prisoner to continue reciting the prayer, he would come to the lines, 'thy will be done, on earth as it is in heaven.' By interrupting the prayer and inserting his own rhyme, Smekalov shows that the words that presumably express that will . . . can be rhymed with something quite different. Smekalov's travesty of the 'Our Father' transforms verses central to a patriarchal Christian ethic into empty rhetoric or even blasphemy."[19]

The last in the narrator's gallery of torturer-artists is the executioner, whose dexterity and "knowledge of his science and his desire to show off before his fellow convicts and the public stimulate[d] his vanity. He exert[ed] himself for art's sake" (4:156; 242). The narrator emphasizes that the executioners he has known have all conducted themselves like gentlemen [*po-dzhentl'menski*] and cared deeply for the ceremony and theatricality with which they made their appearance on the important stage of the scaffold (4:156; 243).

These artists of the craft of punishment — the floggers and executioners — sought to express their freedom in the most perverted degree, through what the narrator labels the "unlimited mastery of the body, blood and soul of a fellow man." He writes: "I do not know how it is now, but in the recent past there were gentlemen who derived from the power of flogging their victims something that suggests the Marquis de Sade and the Marquise de Brinvilliers. I imagine there is something in this sensation which sends a thrill at once sweet and painful to the hearts of these gentlemen. There are people who are like tigers thirsting to lick blood. Anyone who has once experienced this power, this unlimited mastery of the body, blood and soul of a fellow man made of the same clay as himself, a brother in the law of Christ — anyone who has experienced the power and full license to inflict the greatest humiliation upon another creature made in the image of God will, against his will, lose the mastery of his own sensations" (4:154, 240). That is, the torturer's boundless freedom over others leads in the end to his or her own complete loss of freedom, for the torturer has lost control over his or her own sensations and desires. Unlimited freedom over others inevitably disintegrates into obsession, into compulsion, into habit. "The man and the citizen," writes Goryanchikov (although we hear Dostoevsky's voice behind the narrator loud and clear), "is lost forever in the tyrant, and the return to human dignity, to repentance and to regeneration becomes almost impossible" (4:154; 241). Lest readers believe themselves comfortably distanced from these human monsters, Goryanchikov concludes: "The characteristics of the torturer exist in embryo in almost every man of today" (4:154; 241).

The pursuit of art in the prison — and by analogy in the world at large — is thus morally neutral; the artist who truly endeavors for art's sake may be exercising his or her freedom or, like the torturer-artists, may lose that freedom in the exercise of obsessive tyranny over others.

Nearly every convict in the prison is an artist of some kind, if only an artist of thought, of dreams.[20] Paper, pencil, and any other traditional tools of the artist were of course strictly forbidden to the prisoners. The pursuit of money, an emblem, as the narrator puts it, of "coined freedom" was also naturally very precious to the convict (4:17; 44). Surprisingly, however, of even more value was his ability to dream. "What is more precious than money for the convict? Freedom or some sort of dream of freedom. The prisoners are great dreamers" (4:66, 112). Even the quiet prisoner who suddenly commits some outrageous deed is a kind of artist, for his outbreak is, in the narrator's words, "simply a poignant hysterical craving for self-expression" (4:67; 113). At best, this peculiar mode of art — the commission of an outrageous deed — this fantastical form of self-expression had the power to bring only isolated moments of relief from bondage.

More than a hundred pages later, Goryanchikov revisits this theme: "Here all were dreamers, and this was apparent at once. What gave poignancy to this feeling was the fact that this dreaminess gave the greater number of the prisoners a gloomy and sullen, almost morbid expression . . . The more fantastical his hopes, the more conscious the dreamer himself was of their fantastical character, the more stubbornly and shyly he concealed them in his heart, but he could not renounce them . . . I fancy that the harshest of his assailants were just those who perhaps outstripped him in their own hopes and dreams" (4:196; 300–301). These convict dreamers resemble Dostoevsky's urban dreamers in sharing secret, fantastical hopes and dreams, which they conceal with a certain shyness.[21] The only nondreamers among the convicts were two who had lost all hope, and both of these — an old believer and an obsessive reader of the Bible — sought release through prayer and martyrdom. Interestingly the narrator does not hold these two devout nondreamers up as a religious ideal (as Dostoevsky's later narrators might have done) but characterizes them in strictly psychological terms: "Without some goal and some effort to reach it no man can live" (4:197; 302).

Pitted against this depiction of convicts and jailers who discover some degree of freedom as dreamers, fantasizers, or artists (practicing in no matter how unlikely a medium, though without the traditional tools of the artist) is the chilling possibility of an utter lack of freedom. The narrator locates the concrete representation of this lack of freedom in prison life in its compulsory work, its compulsory communal living, and in the practices of flogging and fettering. *Compulsory* work and *compulsory* community (both italicized by Goryanchikov) horrify the convicts and the narrator because they are perversions — corrosive transformations — of what they naturally love. It is their freely chosen work and their spontaneous sense of community that sustains and protects the prisoners. When labor and community become compulsory, however, they become a "torture" (4:19–20; 48–49).

The dread of being flogged and the experience of it also deprive a man of freedom and undermine or even annihilate moral sensibility. "The condemned man is overcome by an acute, but purely physical terror, involuntary and irresistible, which suppresses the entire moral essence of a human being"

(4:152, 238). The narrator's analysis of the horrifying moment just before punishment is to be received corresponds to the treatment in *The Idiot* of the moment before a prisoner is to be executed. In these moments human beings are devoid of hope and lose moral awareness. Moreover, the victim and the executioner begin grotesquely to resemble each other, for each is completely mastered by a horrifying passion.

At this juncture, in his double role as spectator and teller, the narrator also treads on dangerous ground. He comes close to being obsessed with the psychology of punishment and experiences the perilous thrill of both victim and victimizer: "I was excited, overwhelmed and terrified . . . I began suddenly and impatiently going into all the details . . . I had a great desire to know . . . about the various grades of . . . punishments . . . I tried to picture to myself the psychological condition of men going to punishment . . . I could not help watching with interest the prisoners who . . . were leaving to run the other half of the gauntlet to which they had been sentenced" (4:152–53, 237–38). "Excited," impatient for "all the details," "a desire to know," "could not help watching with interest" — this is also the language of a reader hungry for the plot who abandons the other aesthetic, moral, and structural considerations that might more often engage him or her. Through Goryanchikov's narration the language of the reader of a thriller and the spectator of the infliction of violent punishment converge. Both such a reader and a spectator are selves decoupled from moral considerations, negatively transformed by the power of art or of actual spectacle. After the completion of *The House of the Dead*, similar questions about the nature of negative aesthetics consistently continued to interest Dostoevsky.[22]

Not only the torturer but also the victim, the narrator, and the spectator are all debased, if only temporarily, by their varieties of participation in such violence; each is enthralled, mesmerized, transfixed by the gruesome spectacle. Even the narrator loses, momentarily, his moral awareness as he is absorbed by ravenous curiosity. Let me digress for a moment. Dostoevsky had read Charles Maturin's novel *Melmoth the Wanderer* (1820). This work contains a scene in which the narrator witnesses from a window the mob murder of his greatest enemy and later describes it to his listeners: "While witnessing this horrible execution, I felt all the effects vulgarly ascribed to fascination . . . I echoed the wild shouts of the multitude with a kind of savage instinct . . . then I echoed the screams of the thing that seemed no longer to live, but still could scream . . . I remained uttering shout for shout, and scream for scream . . . The drama of terror [the narrator concludes] has the irresistible power of converting its audience into its victims."[23] The primary purpose of Dostoevsky's narrator is to expose the evil of such violence to the reader, but at moments both the narrator and the reader (as he or she avidly reads Goryanchikov's vivid, urgent, relentless descriptions) involuntarily lose themselves in these acts of violence.

Overarching these horrors of compulsory work, compulsory community, and flogging is the fact of the prisoners' fetters, both the signifier and the symbol of their lack of freedom. The fetters shackle them until their release, whether in life or death. They are the ever-present, nagging, painful, physical embodiment of every other constraint the prisoner must endure. The young consumptive prisoner Mihailov, who in dying casts off his clothes and finally his precious cross, "as though even that were a weight that worried and oppressed him," must die in fetters. But the narrator's graphic description of this death is one of the moments in the novel of unfettered grace, when evil can give way to good.

Robert Belknap has identified a repeated, haunting tripartite configuration in *The Brothers Karamazov,* the presence of which usually indicates the working of grace: the slanting rays of the sun, a memory of childhood maternal love, and prayer.[24] It is striking that some twenty years before the writing of *The Brothers Karamazov* the narrator's description of Mihailov's death incorporates those identical elements. Mihailov left a "pleasant memory" among the convicts. He died in the afternoon and the narrator "remember[s how] the glowing, slanting rays of the sun pierced through the green frozen panes of our windows" onto the dying man. After the dying convict has cast off his cross, another convict gently replaces it on the newly dead man and crosses himself silently. At this moment the sergeant enters; his eyes meet those of the convict Tchekunov, who says, nodding, "as it were involuntarily, 'He too had a mother'" (4:140–41; 220–22). In *The Brothers Karamazov* the setting sun, prayer, and a precious memory of maternal love coalesce to form a precise constellation and contribute to the depiction and operation of grace in the world. This constellation also enhances the symbolic unity of the novel. In *The House of the Dead* these elements remain more impressionistic, for Mihailov's death is an isolated moment amid other such isolated, usually disconnected moments. Moreover, the narrator is careful to dissociate himself from this event. He frames his account of Mihailov with a carefully casual introduction and conclusion. "I really do not know why he comes back to mind so distinctly," he begins. And he concludes, "But I have digressed from my subject" (4:140–41; 220–22). Such dismissals are of course immediate signals to the reader to pay attention.

More important, the memory of Mihailov came to Goryanchikov unawares, but at the needed time, as it would come a decade later in the 1870s to "Dostoevsky," the narrator of another semi-autobiographical, semifictional narrative of prison life, "The Peasant Marey." Similar instances of memories appearing at the needed moment occur for Dostoevsky's more purely fictional characters as well. Usually these memories come to the fore at a moment when anhedonia may be acute, but when it may also be about to give way to some kind of conversion experience or, as in the case of characters like Svidrigaylov or Stavrogin, to a deconversion, to the final experience of despair and eventual suicide. Here, however, in the scene in which Goryanchikov recalls and depicts Mihailov's death, are present the elements of that positive constellation that Dostoevsky will repeat in later works: the slanting rays of the sun, prayer, and a precious memory. Goryanchikov may or may not think he has "digressed from [his] subject," but the author has squarely announced to his reader that it is no digression but the heart of the matter.

Increasingly throughout his writing life Dostoevsky found inspiration for future work in his previous writings. Such may be the case in this passage describing Mihailov's death and in its future creative transformation in *The Brothers Karamazov*. Dostoevsky seems already to have been aware of this creative habit of recycling, for he wrote to Mikhail from Semipalatinsk in May 1858, "I . . . jot down a scene immediately, just as it first appears to me, and I'm happy with it, but then I revise it for entire months, a year. I'm inspired by it several times, not just once (because I love this scene), and several times will add or take out something, as has already happened with me, and believe me that it's turned out much better. If only it were inspiration. Of course, there would be nothing without inspiration."[25] This letter from Semipalatinsk offers a crucial insight into the way Dostoevsky, throughout his entire literary career, transformed both memory and invention, and would return repeatedly to rework particular ideas, scenes, or memories — "I'm inspired by it several times, not just once."

At another critical moment in Goryanchikov's account, the overheard story of "Akulka's Husband," the narrator also downplays the significance of his narrative, as he had done with his description of Mihailov's death. Goryanchikov introduces this powerful embedded narrative as having initially resembled a nightmarish, delirious dream. He is awakened in the prison hospital by the whispers of Shishkov, who had been telling his story to Tcherevin. Like the episode in *The Confessions* in which Jean Jacques Rousseau tells of having stolen a ribbon and then allowing a servant girl to be blamed for the theft, "Akulka's Husband" is about displaced desire. Rousseau had blamed Marion for the theft, but he had initially stolen the ribbon because he desired her and had wanted to give it to her.[26] Shishkov (and his drunken alter ego, Filka Morozov) desires and even loves Akulka, though he shames, beats, and eventually brutally murders her. Goryanchikov abruptly ends his transcription of this terrible story with no further comment. Such instances of the narrator's seeming dissociation from his narrative at crucial junctures were to become a standard technique of Dostoevsky's later fiction.

Just as the convicts and the narrator are all, to some degree, artists, so are they spectators of art, members of an audience. Just as there are good artists and evil ones, so are the roles of the spectators charged with moral tension, as we have already seen. The prison theatricals, in contrast to the witnessing of corporal punishment, enable the convicts to experience the best delights of an audience. The narrator presents their response to art as an ideal one: "On every face was expressed the most naive expectation . . . A strange light of child-like joy, of pure, sweet pleasure, was shining on these . . . branded brows and cheeks" (4:122, 193). The convicts are united at this moment in positive, free community, joy, and innocence. The narrator is relatively unconcerned with the substance of the actual dramas: "What absorbed me more than all was the audience; they were all completely carried away." The experience of dramatic art offers the convict actors and spectators alike the ultimate escape from servitude. "Imagine prison, fetters, bondage . . . the life of days as monotonous as the drip of water or a dull autumn day, and suddenly all those oppressed are allowed for one short hour to relax, to rejoice, to forget" (4:124; 196). The artistic pursuit of either creating or watching the theatricals, which unites the prisoners and allows them a moment of freedom, also carries with it the power of spiritual regeneration. The narrator writes, "They were morally transformed [*nravstvenno meniaetsia*] if only for a few minutes" (4:129–30; 204). Such is the positive, transformative power of art.

Conversely, as we have also seen, the witnessing of an immoral spectacle — that of corporal punishment — could, albeit temporarily, bestialize the audience. When Lieutenant Smekalov tells his joke and orders the thrashing to begin, he explodes with laughter. "The soldiers standing round grin too, the man who thrashes grins, even the man who is being thrashed almost grins" (4:151, 236). As in Maturin's novel, the victim, torturer, and spectator become, for a single ghastly moment, one.

By now it has become evident how the ideas about art that reverberate throughout *The House of the Dead* mesh easily with Dostoevsky's articles "Pedantry and Literacy" and "Mr. — bov and The Question of Art," which were published at about the same time (1861) in *Time*. In these articles, as we have already seen, Dostoevsky calls for entertaining literature for the peasants and largely champions the idea of art for art's sake. Dostoevsky understood that the literature read by the peasants must be entertaining so that they would choose to read. Dostoevsky as a writer was consistently a strategist and manipulator. Pragmatically, however, he had to reconcile the desire to persuade his readers with his competing belief in individual freedom. Dostoevsky's pronouncement in his journalism that "the defenders of 'art for art's sake' are against the utilitarians because by prescribing certain aims for art, they [the utilitarians] destroy it" exerted only a limited rhetorical force.

But when, as in *The House of the Dead,* art for art's sake becomes equated with freedom and stands in opposition to compulsory work, compulsory community, and fetters, its persuasive force moves far beyond the ephemeral journalistic rhetoric of these articles of the 1860s. The message brands itself on the reader's psyche. Art for art's sake may be a dangerous thing, but without it life could become unbearable. Moreover, in *The House of the Dead* the narrator maintains that art for art's sake — the dreams and artistic pursuits of the prisoners — is necessary to preserve the very lives of the men (4:66, 196–97; 112, 301–2). In "Mr. — bov," Dostoevsky extends this idea beyond the prison gates, makes it apply to all, and thereby directly formalizes his notion about the necessity of art for mankind when he argues that "art is as much a necessity for man as eating and drinking."[27] The same message about the necessity of art for human existence that is dramatized in *The House of the Dead* emerges in that literary work with more force than when Dostoevsky had stated these ideas explicitly and polemically in "Mr. — bov" or the article "Pedantry and Literacy."

I suggested earlier that *The House of the Dead* exhibits Dostoevsky's powers of analysis, of, as he had put it, going into the depths and examining the atoms while still searching for the whole. But this analytic style belonged to Dostoevsky's early pre-prison and exile period. By January 1856, that is, before he even wrote *The House of the Dead,* he had reworked his theory of artistic creativity and instead had emphasized the synthetic rather than the analytic process in literary composition. In a letter to Apollon Maikov, Dostoevsky praised the young writer Pisemsky and then added, "When you're young ideas just pour out, you shouldn't seize every one of them on the run and immediately express it, rush to have your say. It's better to wait awhile for more synthesis; to think more, wait for a lot of minor things expressing the same idea to gather into a large whole, into a single large-scale image, and then express it. Colossal characters created by colossal writers were often the result of a long, intense process of creating and refining. You shouldn't express all the intervening experiments and sketches."[28]

Indeed, one could argue that this desire for synthesis was present in Dostoevsky all along. For example, his predetermined plan to discover humanity in prison was, in fact, a synthetic program for action to which he had tried, with mixed success, to make events adhere. Dostoevsky's philosophy of art may have changed during the turbulent years in Siberia, for in 1856, he seems to emphasize the virtues of synthesis over those of analysis. Nevertheless, we should not try to wedge *The House of the Dead* too tightly into either his old (analysis) or new (synthesis) framework. This semifictional autobiography or semi-autobiographical fiction does, undeniably, contain some fleeting "experiments and sketches" of the kind that he had warned Maikov against, but it is both from these sketches and from the indelible images projected by the bathhouse, the hospital, and the prison itself that Dostoevsky could eventually synthesize the irresistible "images in relief" and "colossal characters" of his later fiction.

It is throughout *Crime and Punishment,* but especially in its epilogue, that Dostoevsky first transmutes and synthesizes the experience of prison itself into high art. Here, for example, the aesthetic force of the long chapter on the arrival of spring and the meditation on tramps ("Summertime") from *The House of the Dead* is condensed into single highly-charged sentences like the following: "How could one ray of sunlight mean so much to them, or the virgin forest, or a cool spring . . . that the tramp dreams of and longs for like a lovers' meeting, with the green grass all round it and a bird singing in the bushes?"[29] This sentence reads as though it were a poetic distillation of the first part of "Summertime," in which Goryanchikov describes at length the allure of the life of a tramp.

"Summertime" is remarkable too for its nature descriptions — some of the longest Dostoevsky ever wrote. One passage in particular captures the marvel of the arrival of spring:

> Apart from the fact that in the warmth, in the brilliant sunshine, when, in all your soul, in all your being, you feel nature with infinite force springing into life again around you, prison doors, guards and bondage are harder to bear than ever — apart from that, with the coming of spring and the return of the lark, tramping begins all over Siberia and Russia; God's people escape from prison and take refuge in the forests. After stifling dungeons, law courts, fetters and beatings, they wander at their own free will wherever they please, wherever it seems fair and free to them; they eat and drink what they find, what God sends them, and at night they fall asleep peacefully under God's eye in the forest, or the fields, troubling little for the future, and free from the sadness of prison, like the birds of the forest, with none to say good night to but the stars (4:174; 268).

This exuberant passage reads like a prison-house version of the famous opening lines of Kenneth Grahame's *Wind in the Willows* (1908). The reader encounters in both, one a work of prison literature, the other a British turn-of-the-century children's classic, the same sentimental homage to the magic of spring, the same depiction of universal restlessness.

Like the narrator in *The House of the Dead,* the convict Raskolnikov is not well liked; unlike Goryanchikov he does not tell the readers much about the lives of his fellow convicts. But through the mediating presence of Sonya, whose letters to Dunya and Razumihin stylistically resemble Goryanchikov's narrative voice, Dostoevsky found the means of describing the convicts' capacity for love. The narrator reports that:

> At first Sonya's letters seemed to Dunya and Razumihin somewhat dry and unsatisfactory, but in the end they both found that they could not have been better written, since from these letters there finally emerged a most complete and accurate picture of their unhappy brother's lot. Sonya's letters were full of the most prosaic actuality, the simplest and clearest description of every circumstance of Raskolnikov's life as a convict. They contained neither statements of her own hopes, nor speculations about the future, nor descriptions of her feelings. Instead of attempts to explain his psychological condition and his inner life generally, there were only facts, his own words, that is, and detailed reports of his health, of what he expressed a wish for at their interviews, the questions he asked her or the commissions he entrusted to her. All this she communicated with extraordinary minuteness. In the end, the picture of their unhappy brother stood out in relief, exactly and clearly drawn in his own words; there could be nothing misleading about it, because it consisted wholly of factual reports.[30]

Sonya's resemblance as a narrator to Goryanchikov is striking. This account of Sonya as a writer could be — with the exception of a few passages, such as the more romantic nature excerpt just cited from "Summertime" — a description of the overall texture of Goryanchikov's narrative: "somewhat dry and unsatisfactory," "a most complete and accurate picture," "dry, prosaic actuality," "the simplest and clearest description" "neither statements of . . . hopes nor speculations about the future," "extraordinary minuteness," "the picture . . . stood out in relief."

Moreover, readers of Dostoevsky interested in the development of his narrative voice can see in this description at the end of *Crime and Punishment* of the narrative style of Sonya's letters a forecast, a prefiguring of Dostoevsky's own narrator-chronicler, the voice he would use to such extraordinary effect in *The Idiot, The Possessed,* and *The Brothers Karamazov.* Dunya and Razumihin are cast in the role of ideal readers: at first they are impatient with the narrator's dryness, but they come to see that it could not have been better written. How different her letters are from the letter from his mother that

Raskolnikov receives at the beginning of the novel. This letter, with its descriptions, insinuations, commissions, omissions, and ulterior motives helps to set in motion so much of the ensuing plot. Sonya's letters, on the other hand, partake of Goryanchikov's style and narrative methodology. They do not generate plot; instead, they signal the most general contours of the voice of the narrator chronicler who is to narrate Dostoevsky's next novel.

In "Summertime" in *The House of the Dead,* the other shore of the nearby river, with its vast expanse of open steppe, had become a romantic visual symbol of freedom:

> I speak of the river-bank so often because it was only from there one had a view of God's world, of the pure clear distance, of the free solitary steppes, the emptiness of which made a strange impression on me . . . On the river-bank one might forget oneself: one would look at that boundless solitary vista as a prisoner looked out to freedom from his window. Everything there was sweet and precious in my eyes, the hot brilliant sun in the fathomless blue sky and the far-away song of the Kirghiz floating from the farther bank. One gazes into the distance and makes out at last the poor smoke-blackened tent of some Kirghiz. One discerns the smoke rising from the tent, the Kirghiz woman busy with her two sheep . . . One descries a bird in the limpid blue air and for a long time one watches its flight: now it darts over the water, now it vanishes in the distance . . . Even the poor sickly flower which I found early in spring in a crevice of the rocky bank drew my attention almost painfully (4:178–79; 274–75).

This image of the opposite bank of the river seen from the prison camp reappears transformed and reincarnated at the end of *Crime and Punishment.* Although it is the same springtime season, gone are the touches of romanticism and sentimentality. The spare and powerful description of the opposite shore merges with a vision of the Old Testament and of Abraham tending his flocks. "From the high bank a broad landscape was revealed . . . There, in the immensity of the steppe, flooded with sunlight, the black tents of the nomads were barely visible dots. Freedom was there, there other people lived, so utterly unlike those on this side of the river that it seemed as though with them time had stood still, and the age of Abraham and his flocks was still the present."[31]

Time past merges with time present to create a timeless image out of time. (Chekhov was to draw on a similar quality in his most Dostoevskian short story, "The Student.")[32] These moments from *The House of the Dead* and *Crime and Punishment* likewise prefigure the moment in *The Brothers Karamazov* of Alyosha's vision of Cana of Galilee, when the biblical past and the present fuse in an equally intimate and personal way.[33] Moreover, the narrators of *The House of the Dead* and the epilogue to *Crime and Punishment* portray the flow of time in prison in the same way: they describe in detail the first year of prison life; the remaining years are telescoped or compressed almost to nothing. But Raskolnikov realizes what Goryanchikov and the other prisoners in *The House of the Dead* could sense only unconsciously and could express, haltingly, only through their various free artistic pursuits. "Life," thinks Raskolnikov, or at least we are given to think he thinks, "had taken the place of logic and something quite different must be worked out in his mind."[34]

Crime and Punishment *in the Classroom:*
The Elephant in the Garden

hum and buzz of implication.
—Lionel Trilling, "Manners, Morals and the Novel"

"Every man needs air, air, air! . . . More than anything!"
—Svidrigaylov, *Crime and Punishment*

"Yesterday somebody said to me that a man needs air, air, air! I must go to him at once and find out what he means by that."
—Raskolnikov, *Crime and Punishment*

"Do what justice demands. I know you do not believe me, but it is the sacred truth that life will sustain you. Afterwards you will regain your self-esteem. Now you need only air, air, air!"
—Porfiry Petrovich, *Crime and Punishment*

Dostoevsky's *Crime and Punishment* (1865) lies at the center of his career and at the heart of this book. In this chapter, I have taken a different approach than the series of close readings, critical appraisals, and speculations that inform the other chapters. While the underlining focus remains that of the transformations and conversions so vital to Dostoevsky and his work, I endeavor here to offer an approach to this novel that is embedded in the present time, and, more particularly, in the actual space and air of the classroom. This chapter is, therefore, both mundane and practical, but it is as important to my argument as a whole as this novel is to Dostoevsky's oeuvre. Novels exist on the private space of the printed page, and they are transformed and reincarnated by the imaginations of each reader. But novels also find existence through conversation and discussion — most often in the classroom. The students and teacher in a classroom or any reading community that gather to discuss a novel inevitably rethink it in some organic way. These conversations and discussions, while not real performances of the novel per se, do contain aspects of the performative in that the novel, for the duration of the time it is under discussion, lives a life in the words and the gestures of its several simultaneous readers. At these moments it is literally "in play"; in "the air," much like the many conversations in which Raskolnikov partakes or the snatches of conversations that he overhears.[1] Works of imaginative literature have a public as well as a private existence.

Although many who write what is conventionally known as literary criticism are also teachers of literature and venture often into the confounding terrain of the classroom, we tend to resist writing about the business of actually teaching a work of literature.[2] This subject is somehow considered unimportant, beneath the threshold of intellectual interest, and unhelpful in contributing to a deeper or more meaningful reading of any particular literary text. As I make my own first foray into this realm, I do so with a conviction that thinking about works of literature in conjunction with the imagined experience of those people who are reading a work for the first time or who are reading it in a group is an important activity in itself. This chapter, which is devoted to the workaday subject of teaching *Crime and Punishment,* also addresses the pragmatic and broader contexts of the teaching of literature in universities and reading generally.

We have already seen that Dostoevsky lived much of his life in the public sphere; he also valued and participated in the debates about his own works within it. He regarded his fiction as literally connected to recent events in the past, the present, and the future. Moreover, *Crime and Punishment* is about the swirl of ideas and words in the air — for the most part, the notoriously stifling and constrictive air of St. Petersburg. It is fitting, then, to look at the novel's current incarnations in the sometimes equally stuffy air of our classrooms. The stale, potentially infectious air that seeped into the novel wafts out of it as well.

The briefest of excursions into contemporary culture reveals that our world is, in its own ways, as rife with disease, extremism, ideology, and despair as the worlds that Dostoevsky commonly depicts. Today's virgin readers of *Crime and Punishment,* like the novel's original readers in 1866 and 1867, still find themselves unnervingly alive to this work, still fevered by it — still shocked, despite our nearly daily and perhaps desensitizing television immersion in police, mob, and crime dramas.[3] Why does this novel continue to exert this force? If ours is a society where the reading of literary work is, in fact, at risk, will fictions like *Crime and Punishment* continue to be read? Will they help to keep reading alive? Dostoevsky would not have hesitated to ask practical questions like this, nor should we.

Is Reading at Risk?

In the United States, I would argue, it is. In June 2004, the National Endowment for the Arts issued a report entitled *Reading at Risk.* This report — an exhaustive one — is based on a large sampling over time and was conducted by the U.S. Bureau of the Census, polling 17,000 adults from most demographic groups. The results are sobering, to say the least. The report reads: "For the first time in modern history, less than half of the adult population now reads literature, and these trends reflect a larger decline in other sorts of reading." It finds that the "rate of decline has accelerated, especially among the young" and gloomily concludes, "More than reading is at stake."[4]

Reading at Risk cites the ways in which print culture "affords irreplaceable forms of focused attention and contemplation that make complex communications and insights possible. To lose such intellectual capability — and the many sorts of human continuity it allows — would constitute a vast cultural impoverishment."[5] This is not to say that literary reading is not still an important component of our leisure activity: the report finds that the proportion of people reading literature is higher than participation in most other cultural, sports, and leisure activities except for television watching, moviegoing, and exercising.[6]

The data unambiguously show that people who read also play a more active role in their communities. This may contradict our traditional notion of the reader as someone solitary who escapes society through the intensely private, intimate, often subversive act of reading. A decline in reading, in fact "parallels a larger retreat from participation in civic and cultural life. The long-term implications of this study not only affect literature but all the arts — as well as social activities such as volunteerism, philanthropy, and even political engagement. . . . As more Americans lose this capability, our nation becomes less informed, active, and independent minded. These are not qualities that a free, innovative, or productive society can afford to lose." Finally, as if this were not bad enough, the report projects that "at the current rate of loss, literary reading as a leisure activity will virtually disappear in half a century."[7]

The writers of this document go on to make a brief comparison with the reading habits of Canadians and Europeans. Canada conducted a similar survey in 1998 and found that 67 percent (as opposed to 47 percent in the United States) of its adult population read a book during the survey year. A European study (of October 2002) cited the average reading rate in fifteen European countries as 45 percent, with Sweden, Finland, and the United Kingdom the highest (72 percent, 66 percent, and 63 percent, respectively) and Portugal and Belgium the lowest (23 percent, 15 percent).[8] All Western nations, to varying degrees, share the same predicament. Those who write about and teach literature are also laborers in the effort to keep the reading of literature alive.

It is against this backdrop that professors in the United States assign large, unwieldy, difficult novels like *Crime and Punishment*. In this first context of reading, then, *Crime and Punishment* is merely a stand-in for any other complex literary text, be it poem, short story, play, or novel. Reading is at risk; our first, most basic job, whether we like it or not, the one we tend not even to talk about — the elephant in our garden — is to persuade our students to love reading and to continue to be readers throughout their lives. They may take only one or two literature courses while at the university. This is our chance.[9]

Finding an Analogy: The Novel as Tragedy

Crime and Punishment is the most tautly structured of Dostoevsky's novels. In that way it is somewhat atypical, so that when students go on to read his other novels they frequently find that the fictional world they have entered, with the possible exception of *The Brothers Karamazov,* does not exhibit the same luminescence of architectural design. Malcolm V. Jones has put it this way, "Although the novel takes the hero through successive scenes of disorder, from which he only occasionally finds release, the plot itself is, by Dostoevskian standards, a relatively orderly one."[10]

One way to engage students quickly with unfamiliar and potentially daunting material is to make an analogy with a text or genre they think they already know. Thus I have found that Konstantin Mochulsky's delightfully old-fashioned volume *Dostoevsky: His Life and Work* (1967) is helpful in an introductory class of English-speaking students who have read some Shakespeare and one or two classical Greek tragedies in translation. Mochulsky, you may remember, argues that *Crime and Punishment* is a "tragedy in five acts with a prologue and an epilogue."[11] Others have also made this link to tragedy — Vyacheslav Ivanov first (and famously) called Dostoevsky's novels "novel-tragedies" and, more recently, Joseph Frank has maintained that this novel elevates the Russian nihilist to "artistic heights equaling the greatest creations of Greek and Elizabethan tragedy."[12]

A testing of Mochulsky's hypothesis about whether the novel is "a tragedy in five acts" offers an occasion for fruitful discussion, even before students have actually finished reading the novel. One can throw it out as a hypothesis early on and return to it in subsequent class meetings for reevaluation. Along the way, students will find themselves looking at the action of each part of the novel.

In a nutshell, Mochulsky suggests that Part I is the prologue that "depicts the preparation and perpetration of the crime." Part II then is Act I; it portrays the immediate effects of the crime upon Raskolnikov. In Part III (Mochulsky's Act II) Raskolnikov realizes that Porfiry Petrovich suspects him, and he also has the dream in which he tries to kill the old woman again but finds that despite the blows of his axe, she remains alive and laughs at him. Mochulsky locates the climax of the "novel tragedy" in Part IV (Act III) in the counterpoint between Raskolnikov's interactions with Svidrigaylov ("the bath-house with its spiders") and Sonya (the resurrection of Lazarus). Mochulsky identifies an "unexpected peripetea" in the painter Nikolay's confession at the moment when Porfiry had intended to expose Raskolnikov as the murderer. Part V (Mochulsky's Act IV) contains the scandalous scene of Marmeladov's funeral dinner, Raskolnikov's realization — "Was it really the old woman that I killed? I killed myself" — and his confession to Sonya. These scenes, important though they are, also serve to create a crucial "slowing of the action before the final catastrophe." That catastrophe occurs in his fifth act (Part VI of the novel). It is here that Dostoevsky depicts what Mochulsky labels as the "parallel ruin of the two 'strong individuals' — Raskolnikov and Svidrigaylov."

Mochulsky does not grant that Raskolnikov is undergoing any kind of spiritual change even at this late point in the novel. On the contrary, he asserts that Raskolnikov "does not have enough strength of will to commit suicide, and so he surrenders himself to the authorities. This is not a sign of penitence but of pusillanimity." Finally, in his scheme, the tragedy ends with an epilogue, an epilogue that Mochulsky passionately maintains betrays the thrust of the novel as a whole. He concludes, "The novel ends with a vague anticipation of the hero's 'renewal.' It is promised, but it is not shown. We know Raskolnikov too well to believe this pious lie."

I have offered up a summary of an argument some readers probably know well, because Mochulsky's take on *Crime and Punishment* can be a valuable approach for beginning a classroom discussion of the novel. Why? First, it casts a kind of order, a semifamiliar structure — that of a tragedy — on to a

large mass of turbulent, difficult, often self-contradictory events and utterances with which the students are struggling as they read the novel. Indeed,
although *Crime and Punishment* is Dostoevsky's most single-mindedly con-
structed novel and though it may be the most carefully stitched fiction he ever
produced, the construction is more like a hem-stitch than a woven tapestry.
Tug on one thread, and you may begin to unravel, or at least reconfigure, the
whole fabric. For example, Raskolnikov drops a pair of earrings after the
crime. The young man who picks them up finds himself swirled into the central vortex of events. If a reader begins to focus on this particular event with
microscopic intensity, the shape of the whole alters profoundly. Choose almost
any action, coincidence, or item at random from the novel and it will offer a
link to something else; the pattern on the kaleidoscope will change as will the
perspective of the whole. Thus Mochulsky's accessible comparison of the
structure of this novel with the structure of a tragedy offers a simple way to
begin to talk about the organization of the novel.

Nevertheless, students find themselves simultaneously drawn irresistibly to
the tangle of events and ideas, to disorder, even as they are seeking pattern and
order. Likewise Mochulsky embeds an idiosyncratic, subversive, even cynical
interpretation in his orderly description of the novel. He finds Raskolnikov's
conversion to be largely bogus, a "pious lie" on the part of an author opportunistically eager to get his novel accepted by his readers and by his editor
Mikhail Katkov's thick journal. Is he suggesting, then, that the novel's omniscient narrator is, at worst, a liar and at best, unreliable? He hypothesizes that
Raskolnikov's primary emotion is not repentance or even regret but shame.
Raskolnikov is, above all, ashamed because he had come to his ruin "blindly
. . . and stupidly . . . through some decree of blind fate." Mochulsky's highlighting of Raskolnikov's persistent sense of shame is crucial to his argument.
Shame functions, in his view, as a roadblock to any real repentance on Raskolnikov's part.[13]

Even as Mochulsky underlines Raskolnikov's sense of shame, he finds no
contradiction in continuing to envision him as a grandly tragic hero. Mochulsky concludes, in italics, "*Raskolnikov has been brought to destruction like a
tragic hero in battle with blind Destiny*. But how could the author present this
bold truth about the new man to readers of Katkov's well-meaning journal in
the 1860's? He had to cover it by throwing an innocent veil over it. He did this,
however, hurriedly, carelessly." This careless cover-up, which Mochulsky even
implies is a kind of shameful cover-up, is, in Mochulsky's view, the epilogue.

Surely some might argue that Mochulsky is wrong: wrong about the structure (a tragedy in five acts, with prologue and epilogue), wrong about the
nature of Raskolnikov's experience, and wrong about the author's reasons for

writing his epilogue. Dostoevsky's letters actually chronicle his own surprise that the planned longer ending to his novel had evolved into a short epilogue. Usually his works turned out to be lengthier than he had planned, but in this case the last part grew shorter.[14] But it is always useful for students to see their teachers in dialogue with the critics; it helps them forge their own reading of a text separate from that of professor or critic, yet hopefully informed by them as well.[15] It is the process of making such distinctions and decisions that will fix the novel in their minds.

The Portability of Readerly Insight

Although we want our students, in some concrete, intellectually informed way, to understand this difficult writer and his difficult novels, we also want them to begin, through the act of reading, to learn how to use literary texts both to formulate meaningful questions and to empathize with others different from themselves. The most cherished teachers, like the most enduring novels, model for us the process of finding and asking questions; they do not claim to offer definitive answers.

The formulation of such questions begins to occur most naturally during class discussions. The American poet Jay Parini recently characterized his task as a professor in a seminar (and many of our smaller classes, even at the undergraduate level, in fact become seminars) in a way that aptly describes what happens in a successful classroom interaction among the students, the teacher, and the text: "It seems useful to recall that one 'conducts' a seminar. The analogy with a musical conductor is appropriate and instructive. The subject of the seminar (and the texts or problems being considered) forms a kind of score; the students will already have, with greater or lesser degrees of success, mastered that score before coming to class. The expectation is, in fact, that they will have prepared for class by reading the material, by thinking up something to say. The work of the conductor is to draw out this intellectual music, to arrange it, set the tempo of play."[16] Thus the teacher, while remaining as faithful as possible to her own understanding of the text, needs also to find a way, within the classroom, to bring it into play. Only then will students begin to possess it. Surely Dostoevsky, the master of polyphony, the seeker after "a new word," the author of *The Diary of a Writer,* the avid correspondent, the writer whose every utterance is dialogic, the poet of "ideas in the air," would encourage a free-flowing classroom discussion of his work, would consider it an organic part of his work — its existence in the air, in the atmosphere beyond the printed page.

Possession of a novel by a reader is essentially a private, individual act. But the reading of literature in the classroom also serves a more public, even civic function. It is worthwhile, even urgent, for us as teachers to be mindful that literature and discussions about it are important for our lives as citizens in the public sphere, in culture. Our responses as readers are partly formative of the entire ecosystem of culture both high and low. Recently the American philosopher Martha Nussbaum has explored the ways in which literature and our readings of it form an essential component of our public discourse, and, by extension, our democratic society. Nussbaum argues that "thinking about narrative literature" has "the potential to make a contribution to the law in particular" and "to public reasoning generally."[17]

Nussbaum's search for a vehicle that allows one to empathize, to understand "the other," is no sentimental endeavor; the capacity that literature engenders in us to understand, not only ourselves, but those different from ourselves can contribute, she argues, to the rational formulation of just law and policy:

> The literary imagination is a part of public rationality, and not the whole. I believe that it would be extremely dangerous to suggest substituting empathetic imagining for rule-governed moral reasoning, and I am not making that suggestion. In fact, I defend the literary imagination precisely because it seems to me an essential ingredient of an ethical stance that asks us to concern ourselves with the good of other people whose lives are distant from our own. Such an ethical stance will have a large place for rules and formal decision procedures, including procedures inspired by economics. . . . On the other hand, an ethics of impartial respect for human dignity will fail to engage real human beings unless they are made capable of entering imaginatively into the lives of distant others and to have emotions related to that participation.[18]

The student of literature, the reader of *Crime and Punishment,* enters emotionally into the lives of "distant others," but realizes and necessarily contemplates also the importance, whatever his sympathies might be, of society's "rules and decision procedures." Indeed, to read *Crime and Punishment* is to make a perpetual series of journeys back and forth between the intensely private sphere of Raskolnikov's individual consciousness and the communal realm of laws, ideas, religion, and the population and air of the city that always surrounds and permeates him. More particularly, Nussbaum goes on to argue that the genre of the novel, "on account of some general features of its structure, generally constructs empathy and compassion in ways highly relevant to citizenship."[19] Certainly one could read many scenes in *Crime and Punishment* with such civic questions in mind, nearly every scene, in fact. Even in the moments of his most private reverie, his dreams, or the narrator's representations of the flowing fragmented particles of his hero's consciousness,

Raskolnikov is always rubbing up against the values and practices of the world in which he lives.

To my mind, Nussbaum argues here as a modern-day Portia with much to tell us about the foundational qualities of mercy and compassion, qualities formed and tested in large part by our activity as readers of literature. But most exciting, in her paradigm, the qualities of the best reader in the private world of fiction and the best judge in the real world of events are nearly interchangeable. Near the end of her book she writes, "Intimate and impartial, loving without bias, thinking of and for the whole rather than as a partisan of some particular group or faction, comprehending in 'fancy' the richness and complexity of each citizen's inner world, the literary judge . . . sees in the blades of grass the equal dignity of all citizens — and more mysterious images, too, of erotic longing and personal liberty . . . But in order to be fully rational, judges must also be capable of fancy and sympathy. They must educate not only their technical capacities but also their capacity for humanity. In the absence of that capacity, their impartiality will be obtuse and their justice blind."[20]

Crime and Punishment offers its readers innumerable fictional opportunities to contemplate the overlap and the friction between individual and social justice and to make weighty judgments about both individuals and the society in which they live. Our capacities of fancy and sympathy are taxed throughout; each of us arrives at our own notion of poetic justice in this novel. If we adhere to Nussbaum's point of view, we can argue that this readerly knowledge is portable and can render us more capable of making rational, ethical judgments in the real world.

Reading and Rereading the Novel

Crime and Punishment, like *Pride and Prejudice* or *Huckleberry Finn,* is a novel that some students from the United States read in high school. In the college classroom, one sometime hears them say, with disappointment, "Oh, I've already read that." Yet many students quickly decide that it is worthwhile to reread. Teaching any novel that some students have already read can offer an opportunity to engage in a more intensely dialogic exercise, for one can coax students to juxtapose the memory of the first reading, and concurrently of a childhood or adolescent self, with subsequent ones. They can thus engage in an authentic conversation with themselves, while at the same time creating a dialogue with their fellow students, the teacher, the critics, and, most important, the novel.[21]

Whether we first read *Crime and Punishment* as adolescents or as adults, most of us are gripped by it. V. S. Pritchett wrote incisively of Dostoevsky that he "is still the master [because] he moves forward with us as the sense of our own danger changes." Octavio Paz, in a different context, has concurred, "Dostoevsky is our great contemporary."[22] These statements could serve as epigraphs for *Crime and Punishment*. Our present sense of danger is particularly alert these days to the ways in which ideas — half-baked or otherwise — spread in the same ways that fearsome viruses travel through the world. The air is their medium. In this novel, Dostoevsky, with his typical novelistic economy, has prophetically conjoined the two. Ideas are viruses; viruses are ideas; they are equally contagious, and they are both airborne.

In the epilogue that Mochulsky dismisses so angrily and with such contempt but of which Dostoevsky seems to have been proud is the description of Raskolnikov's final and unforgettable dream, a dream that Raskolnikov has near Easter: "He had dreamt in his illness that the whole world was condemned to fall victim to a terrible, unknown pestilence which was moving on Europe out of the depths of Asia. All were destined to perish, except a chosen few, a very few. There had appeared a new strain of trichinae, microscopic creatures with intelligence and will. People who were infected immediately became like men possessed and out of their minds. But never, never had any men thought themselves so wise and so unshakable in the truth as those who were attacked."[23]

What is our current age but one in which each of us, whatever our nationality, our race, our profession, has been exposed to and likely infected with precisely such a virus? Moreover, the very language of Raskolnikov's dream, with its references to the chosen few, suggests that he has already been infected. Is the dream itself, like Ivan's encounter with his devil, a marker of the beginning of a homeopathic recovery?[24] The specters of very real infectious microorganisms (such as the AIDS virus) and the virus of ideology merge here for a contemporary reader in a way that Dostoevsky would have undoubtedly relished, since he was, above all, a poet, albeit in prose, of the ideas in the air.

The virus Raskolnikov imagines is a disease in which absolute certainty (conviction) is, paradoxically, laced through with uncertainty (anxiety). It is a commonplace of the present study to suggest that ideas, motivations, psychology, and by the time of *The Brothers Karamazov*, even the devil himself — most ideas or items in Dostoevsky's world — have a positive and a negative charge. Hence, to return to Raskolnikov's dream in the epilogue: each individual stricken with the virus thought himself wise and unshakably possessed of the truth. Nevertheless, "all were full of anxiety, and none could understand any other; each thought he was the sole repository of truth and was tormented when he looked at the others, beat his breast, wrung his hands and wept . . . they could not agree what was evil and what good. They did not know whom to condemn or whom to acquit" (6:420; 461).[25] The collective judgments necessarily made by any society had become impossible. The individuals in Raskolnikov's dream lacked the crucial ability to make the kind of informed judgments that Nussbaum has described as being an essential feature of citizenry: to paraphrase Nussbaum, they are unable to think "of and for the whole rather than as a partisan of some particular group or faction"; despite their anxiety and torment, they cannot see "in the blades of grass the equal dignity of all citizens." Is Raskolnikov's dream a representation of the most absolute ideology being wrapped in a paralyzing mantle of relativity and undirected unproductive sympathy? Or is this a visionary dream of a world simply barren of conviction, of empathy, without justice — poetic or otherwise? Both alternatives are dreadful. Passages like these speak to our own contemporary and confusing sense of danger — physical and ethical — in a powerful way.

Moreover, although this novel has its epilogue, Dostoevsky still manages, as he virtually always does in all his work, to frustrate our expectations of an ending. We hear nothing of the reassuring hammering and banging that accompanies the endings of most nineteenth-century blockbuster novels. (E. M. Forster, in his 1927 *Aspects of the Novel,* remarks: "The writer, poor fellow, must be allowed to finish up somehow, he has his living to get like anyone else, so no wonder nothing is heard but hammering and screwing.")[26] Our novel may indeed have offered up to us something like a prologue, five acts of a tragedy, and an epilogue, but despite that formal exterior pattern, there is no inner closure, no answer to any single important question. Questions like, "Why did Raskolnikov commit murder?" or "At what moment did he begin to repent his crime?" or "What constitutes an authentic confession?" or "Does Raskolnikov undergo a religious conversion?" are fully ripe for discussion, but never for a full solution. Is "ripeness" all? Throughout Dostoevsky's canon, the more closely one looks at any possible event or motivation, the more important its precursors seem. Yet such are precisely the paradoxes we expect from our most deeply engaging literature. Just as Maynard Mack said of *King Lear* that the "bent of the play is mythic: it abandons verisimilitude to find out truth," so could we perhaps say of *Crime and Punishment* that it abandons answers to find understanding.[27]

The Aftereffects of an Unwritten Novel and a Discarded Narrative

I turn now to some other strategies for teaching this novel. Before initiating a discussion of Part I, it is worthwhile to consider the question of Dostoevsky's several "unwritten novels" including *Fathers and Children, The Life of a Great Sinner,* and, most important, *The Drunkards,* which hovers behind *Crime and Punishment.* Perhaps because many people fancy themselves to be the authors of several unwritten novels, students are engaged by being invited to think about the ways in which something that remained unwritten, that doesn't even really exist, may have informed something written.

In 1865 Dostoevsky wrote a few lines in his notebook describing *The Drunkards:* " — We drink because there is nothing to do. — You lie! — It's because there is no morality. — Yes, and there is no morality — because for a long time (150 years) there has been nothing to do."[28] Most critics, including Frank, have concluded that this unwritten novel expends itself in the Marmeladov subplot.[29] Personally, I am not so sure. *The Drunkards* may be less unwritten than we tend to think. In fact the ramifications of drunkenness — and Dostoevsky had used this very phrase, "ramifications of drunkenness," when he had written to Andrei Kraevsky about his intention to write *The Drunkards* — permeate this novel in a variety of ways; they are not neatly confined to the Marmeladov subplot. In June of 1865, Dostoevsky had written to Kraevsky of his current plan, "N.B. My novel is called *The Drunkards* and will be in connection with the current question of drunkenness. Not just the question is analyzed, but also represented are all its ramifications, primarily pictures of families, the raising of children in that environment, and so on and so forth."[30] Sometime during the late fall of 1865, Dostoevsky reincarnated this plan and infused it into *Crime and Punishment.* Although we tend to think of this as a novel about crime and about punishment, it is equally a family novel, and there are vivid "pictures of families," and of "the raising of children in that environment." There are four families at its center: the murdered pawnbroker and her sister, the Raskolnikov family, the Marmeladov family, the Svidrigaylov family. There are several other families at its periphery.[31]

The theme of drunkenness extends well beyond the Marmeladov subplot. The Petersburg streets that Raskolnikov wanders abound with drunkards, male and female, young and old, as does his dream of the beating of the horse, which takes place in a rural setting. In one of the earliest notes, we learn that Zametov got Raskolnikov "to drink like a pig."[32] But what is more interesting, even the novel's most positive male character, Razumihin (whose name connotes reason and balance) drinks. The notebooks for the novels repeatedly emphasize Razumihin's propensity for drink. Most extended passages about him in the notes also contain some mention of alcohol. He drinks two bottles of beer, for example, while trying to spoon-feed Raskolnikov soup.[33] In fact, at one point, Dostoevsky suggests that Razumihin is "extremely worried by the fact that . . . while drunk, he let out to Raskolnikov that he was suspected of the murder."[34] In his most extended notebook characterization plan for Razumihin (dated January 2, 1866 — one of the few parts of the notes that can be dated accurately), Dostoevsky writes, "Razumihin has a very strong nature, and as often happens with such strong natures he submits completely to Dunya. (N.B. This trait, too, is often met among people, who though most noble and generous, are rough carousers and have seen much dirt.)" Dostoevsky is at pains, in this plan, to emphasize Razumihin's tendency to drink, noting that after a quarrel with Dunya about Sonya, "he went on a spree." And finally, "N.B. Razumihin took to drink; she herself came to him, to the drunkard. . . . 'What a fine guy you are. And you're not going to drink.' 'I will.' 'What a little devil you are, you are worth 15,000 to me now, you know.' 'I'm going to bite your little finger.' He bites it very hard."[35] Such were his thoughts about Razumihin at the very time that the novel was actually beginning to appear in *The Russian Messenger*. Dostoevsky was prepared to have one of his most positive characters be a heavy drinker. The reader, then, can make no easy equation between drinking and moral weakness.

Thus you can begin by provoking a speculative classroom discussion about how we can discuss an unwritten novel, but this conversation will likely evolve into an exploration of whether Dostoevsky ended up writing this particular novel after all. Raskolnikov himself seems to carry out the murders in a state of spiritual drunkenness — he is drunk, as it were, on his ideas. Frank calls our attention to the fact that "no one has noted, so far as my knowledge goes, the analogy that exists between Raskolnikov's psychology before and after the crime with Dostoevsky's description of what frequently occurred in the case of real-life peasant murders. Such a peasant, house serf, soldier, or workman often has lived in peace for most of his life; but suddenly, at a certain point, 'something in him seems to snap; his patience gave way and he sticks a knife into his enemy and oppressor. . . . The man is, as it were, *drunk*, in delirium. It is as though once having overstepped the sacred limit, he begins to revel in the fact that nothing is sacred to him.' "[36] Frank's insight here is acute, and he convincingly links the intellectual student Raskolnikov to the gallery of peasant convict murderers Dostoevsky had encountered in Siberia.

But what is most fascinating to me is that Dostoevsky chooses to conceive of this peasant murderer as undergoing a sudden, delirious conversion (or perversion) to a state of dark, spiritual drunkenness; he has become addicted to his own idea. His spiritual drunkenness, his delirium, leads him to transgress, to "overstep" the limit. Raskolnikov is thus linked, as Frank convincingly demonstrates, to these peasant murderers, but he is also, by virtue of sharing their peculiar kind of drunkenness, perhaps the most important drunkard of all in this written or unwritten novel, *The Drunkards*. The themes of alcohol and addiction are potent ones for our students. Dostoevsky's representation of these themes, both in his plan for *The Drunkards* and in *Crime and Punishment,* is subtle, unpredictable, and far from formulaic. For all the ideological eccentricity of Tolstoy's reading of *Crime and Punishment,* it is, in this regard extraordinarily incisive:

> Raskolnikov did not live his true life when he murdered the old woman or her sister. When murdering the old woman herself, and still more when murdering her sister, he did not live his true life, but acted like a machine, doing what he could not help doing — discharging the cartridge with which he had long been loaded . . .
>
> He lived his true life when he was lying on the sofa in his room, deliberating not at all about the old woman, nor even as to whether it is or is not permissible at the will of one man to wipe from the face of the earth another. . . . *That question was decided . . . when he was doing nothing and was only thinking, when only his consciousness was active: and in that consciousness tiny, tiny alterations were taking place.* It is at such times that one needs the greatest clearness to decide correctly the questions that have arisen, and it is just then that one glass of beer, or one cigarette, may prevent the solution of the question, may postpone the decision, stifle the voice of conscience and prompt a decision of the question in favour of the lower, animal nature — as was the case with Raskolnikov.[37]

Although Tolstoy probably never knew of Dostoevsky's intention to write a novel called *The Drunkards,* he would seem to concur that Dostoevsky had managed to write that novel after all — though with a different title.

The second point about the genesis of the novel that offers an effective bridge into the story proper is the fact that Dostoevsky originally conceived this as a first-person narrative that would have possessed, as evidenced by his notes for it, all the ambiguities of point of view and audience that *Notes from Underground,* his short novel of 1864, had exhibited.[38] As students read Part I, they can begin to identify and discuss the vestiges of this first-person narration that lurk there: much of the narration comes to us through actual conversation, crucial snatches of overheard conversation, interior monologue, dreams, and the reading and subsequent deconstruction of a letter (more on that in a moment). Part I is a kind of textbook compendium of first-person narrative strategies, even though the actual narrative is in the third person. Once Dostoevsky "discovered" this third-person narrator he described him in his notebook in the following way: "Rummage through all the questions in this novel. But the plot's structure (*siuzhet*) is such that the story *must be narrated by the author and not by the hero.* If it is to be a confession, then everything must be made clear *to the utter extreme.*" For some reason Dostoevsky here associated the need for clarity with the first-person confessional mode. It is not logically evident why if it is "to be a confession, then everything must be made clear *to the utter extreme.*" Nevertheless, as we see, in Dostoevsky's mind at the time, this was the case.

His train of thought in this passage continues: if it is not to be a confessional narrative, but rather one from the author, the shape of the whole text changes: "But from *the author.* Too much *naiveté* and frankness are needed [the implication is that it is a first-person narrative that needs this frankness]. [Instead] an omniscient and infallible author will have to be assumed; he will have to appear as one of the members of the new generation . . . *Another Plan.* Narration from the point of view of the author, a sort of invisible but omniscient being, who doesn't leave his hero even for a moment."[39] There is speculation about when Dostoevsky actually made this shift from first to third person in the narration, though we do know that it occurred sometime during the late fall and early winter of 1865, most probably in November.

Moreover, in the letters up until November of 1865, Dostoevsky consistently referred to his work in progress as a "story;" after that it becomes a novel. The shift in narrative voice coincided with a fundamental generic shift from story to novel. It is particularly interesting that when Dostoevsky *first* wrote about *Crime and Punishment,* he described the work as, above all, about a young man who succumbs to the unfinished ideas in the air. In September he had written to Katkov that the action of the story is contemporary and that it is about a young man who yields to "certain strange, 'unfinished' ideas floating in the air." Throughout this letter (which also offered an extended outline of the plot) as well as in another letter to his friend Alexander Vrangel, Dostoevsky continued to refer to the work as his "story."[40] In letters written in November 1865, however, this designation changes: the story had become "a novel."[41] From here on, all references in the letters to *Crime and Punishment* are to a novel.

Curiously, he wrote in February 1866 to Vrangel of the work's genesis in the following way: "At the end of November much had been written and was ready; I burned it all; I can confess that now. I didn't like it myself. A new form, a new plan excited me, and I started all over again."[42] Yet as we can see from his other letters, and to some degree from the notebooks—whose entries are difficult to date—the important conceptual change had actually occurred in early November, when he had begun to describe his work as a novel instead of as a story. Moreover, Frank points out that having decided to recast his novel in the third person, Dostoevsky "began to rewrite from scratch; but he did not, as he told Vrangel in February 1866, burn everything he had written earlier. On the contrary, he was easily able to integrate sections of the earlier manuscript into his final text . . . simply by shifting them from the first to the third person."[43]

Why did Dostoevsky make this important narrative shift from a first-person narrator to a third? By abandoning the first-person confessional mode, Dostoevsky could, to some degree, escape the claustrophobic air of Raskolnikov's psyche which he had felt he needed, from within, to somehow make clear to the reader. It had become impossible to accomplish this. Most important, in my view, for some unknown reason, switching to a third-person narrator also released Dostoevsky from the task he had set himself of identifying a primary motivation for Raskolnikov's ghastly crime. With the switch to a third-person narrative he simultaneously put that task aside. In the earlier parts of the notebooks, Dostoevsky had repeatedly asked himself why Raskolnikov had committed murder. The possible motivations — all again important foci for classroom discussion — are many: the *Pere Goriot* riddle (abbreviated by Dostoevsky as "the idea of Rastignac"), the desire of Raskolnikov to test himself to see if he was a great man (a Napoleon) or a louse, the awful pressure of his family situation, his immediate physical impoverishment, the devil — the list of possible motivations goes on.

Dostoevsky's abrupt shift in narrative perspective seems oddly to have paralleled a vital conceptual shift in the creation of both the novel proper and its hero. During the time that the novel was still in its first-person format, Dostoevsky seemed more intent upon finding a particular, definite answer to that question of why Raskolnikov committed murder, an answer that would outweigh other answers. He writes to himself, "*The Chief Anatomy of the Novel: it is absolutely necessary to establish the course of things firmly and clearly and to eliminate what is vague, that is, explain the whole murder in one way or another and make its character and relations clear.*"[44] The early notebooks for the novel document Dostoevsky's frustration with the competing tangle of motivations in which no particular cause emerged as primary or sufficient.

Recasting the novel through the voice of a third-person narrator, one who could be both inside of Raskolnikov's mind and outside it, mysteriously though illogically seems to have allowed Dostoevsky to embrace a completely different strategy for representing the problem of motivation. It liberated him from having "to eliminate what is vague" or from having to "explain the whole murder in one way or another." Instead, for some unknowable reason, the mantle of a third-person narrator enabled Dostoevsky to embrace rather than seek to disentangle this chaos of motivation. The plentitude of motivations becomes, in its entirety, the substance of the novel and of Raskolnikov's character.

Dostoevsky has thus returned to his first description of the work as about a young man who has "yielded to the unfinished ideas in the air." The point is those *many* unfinished ideas that enter his being. No single idea can possibly emerge as *the* motivation for murder. Konstantine Klioutchkine has argued that the "hot and suffocating air" dominating the novel would have been "apparent to the reader of the time." He quotes a telling passage from *Time* (1861). "*Summer Heat and Literary Suffocation—Imaginary Theory—The Need for Fresh Air:* Petersburg summers are always suffocating, but people condemned to the studious reading of books, newspapers, and journals are especially stifled. . . . They are engulfed by an ocean of empty speech, banality, falsehood, and meaningless phrases." He concludes, "The characters of the novel are placed not only in the hot summer of 1865, but also in the stifling milieu of repetitive and non-referential speech proliferating in the press."[45] Could Dostoevsky himself have been the author of this feuilleton, as he was of so many of the pieces in *Time?* If so, it would show the extent to which this theme of the linking of summer heat, literary suffocation, and stifling theory was already on his mind several years before he had even written to Katkov of his hero who had succumbed to "the unfinished ideas in the air."

At any rate, once Dostoevsky had decided upon a third-person narration he rapidly settled down to representing his hero's tragic duality (or duality squared, for lack of a better way to express it), rather than trying to resolve it. Ironically, within the confines of a third-person omniscient narrator, polyphony and dialogism gained firmer grounding in Dostoevsky's novels generally, whereas those same qualities of polyphony and dialogism in his shorter works seem to have thrived best in those stories that have a first-person narrator.

Frank's keen analysis posits a different rationale on Dostoevsky's part at this crucial juncture in the writing than the one I have just suggested. "Why Dostoevsky abandoned his story can only remain a matter for speculation, but one possibility is that his protagonist began to develop beyond the boundaries in which he had first been conceived." He goes on to allude to "the perpetual quarrel in Dostoevsky criticism over whether the motives finally attributed to Raskolnikov are or are not contradictory."[46] For Frank, the series of different motivations Raskolnikov experiences do not represent characterologic contradictions or authorial struggles but, rather, a coherent set of sequential metamorphoses that the hero undergoes — "a metamorphosis that results from his gradually dawning *grasp* of the full implications of what he has done."[47] Frank, then, sees the progressive series of Raskolnikov's motivations as emanating in a complex yet reasonable way from his character, whereas I find most compelling the fact that once Dostoevsky had shifted his narrative to the third person, he no longer needed to "explain the whole murder in one way or another" but could instead give himself over to the portrayal of the simultaneous multiplicity (rather than a metamorphosis) of Raskolnikov's motivations, his yielding to those unfinished ideas, those viruses in the suffocating Petersburg air.

Through the representation of the dialogic movement of Raskolnikov's thoughts, words, and deeds juxtaposed to those same movements within the other characters — Marmeladov, Sonya, Dunya, Porfiry Petrovich, and Svidrigaylov in particular — Dostoevsky is able to convey how all of the potential motivations for the crime are operative while also counterposing them to the motivations of these other characters. My use of the phrase "dialogic movement of Raskolnikov's motivations" is a kind of shorthand and is misleading, however, for it implies an ordered, sequential process within Raskolnikov and within the other characters as well. The actual narrative effect resembles far more an unruly conversation, replete with rude interruptions, silences, moments of not listening, and moments of acute attentiveness. Dostoevsky could not possibly have rendered these characters with the same fullness while operating through the confines of a first-person narrative without resorting to cumbersome devices. Dostoevsky remained, however, consistently drawn to first-person narrative, even when he ultimately rejected it. His two first-person novels — *The Insulted and Injured* (1862) and *A Raw Youth* — bear eloquent testimony to Dostoevsky's Herculean struggles with the complexities of wielding a first-person narration in works that also possessed a broad canvas of characters and a plethora of events and subplots.[48] These two novels display an episodic quality and a tendency to confusion that somewhat undercuts their still substantial force.

To return to *Crime and Punishment* and the question of Raskolnikov's motivation: Dostoevsky seemed to have made two nearly simultaneous decisions. First, he had fundamentally shifted his authorial task, and hence the idea of the novel. No longer did he believe it was crucial to locate and represent a dominant motive for Raskolnikov's committing murder. He chose instead to portray the multivalence of the human personality, one who had yielded to the "unfinished ideas in the air." Second, this profound reconfiguration of the idea behind the novel coincided with the shift in narrative point of view from first person to third.

Adrift in Part I

The seven chapters of Part I are crammed with dramatic action. I will touch briefly on only four: chapters two, three, four, and seven. It is unnerving to take stock of what I am leaving out, most glaringly Raskolnikov's rehearsal of his crime, his dream about the horse, his tears and prayer that he not commit murder, his detour through the Haymarket, not to mention all the rest of this novel and its many characters and plots.[49]

The first chapter begins abruptly and tersely with Raskolnikov's dramatic rehearsal (or testing) of the crime. So in chapter two, when he enters the seedy tavern and encounters Marmeladov, readers — students — whose appetite has already been whetted by what seems to be a riveting psycho-thriller of a novel soon to be complete with an investigator and an array of clues, false leads, shaky evidence, psychological theories, confessions, and even a trial — may be frustrated by what seems to be a sudden and annoying slowing of the action, not to mention a boring digression foisted upon our hero and upon the reader by a loquacious drunk.

At this point in discussing the novel with students, I frequently turn to *Dostoevsky* by John Jones. In his chapter on Dostoevsky's first novel, *Poor People* (an epistolary novel written in 1846 before his decade long sojourn as a convict in Siberia and then as a soldier reduced to the ranks), Jones writes: "And now to another petty clerk, Mr. Marmeladov." He then quotes at length from the passage in the second chapter of the novel, in which Marmeladov relates his story to Raskolnikov. Then he observes, "Many people will remember reading this for the first time, perhaps in adolescence, and wondering what was happening to them. Marmeladov comes from nowhere. He is a sideshow and gets no reflected interest from the main story of murder and detection. He looks like a retired clerk. He is dirty and has been drinking. That is about all. The book has scarcely begun. He will be dead, though we aren't to know, long before half-way. He buttonholes Raskolnikov. He is a tavern bore. Then this voice, and a simultaneous onslaught on intellect and emotions that is more like being cuffed about by a god than reading a book."[50]

Cuffed about by a god — this over-the-top statement in fact captures the effect that Dostoevsky can, at times, achieve when he decides to pull out the stops.[51] The narrative pitch in Marmeladov's long, drunken narration is piercingly on key. Jones mulls the reader's response here: "What is it, for example, that stops the reader in his tracks and sends him reeling? . . . No apparent work has gone into committing us to Marmeladov, and there is no access at all to his wife except through the vodka haze of his story, at once gappy and repetitious and muffled."[52] But it is precisely within that boozy narrative that we encounter the concise and tragic drama enacted by Katerina Ivanovna and Sonya, while Marmeladov — at once the cause of the tragedy and the incoherent chorus or witness to the action (as well as its narrator) — lies blurrily on the floor. Indeed, in Dostoevsky's next novel, *The Idiot*, Nastasya Filippovna's tragic story also first comes to us through the muddled narrative of another questionable character. Dostoevsky was to continue to use this technique to good effect.

A similar dynamic in which the reader's expectations are abruptly foiled is operative in the next two chapters (three and four) in which Raskolnikov reads the letter from his mother. By now, and throughout chapter three, readers are perhaps more alert to the fact that a seeming digression or slowing of the action may in fact end by constituting a new kind of intensity of plot, albeit embedded or interpolated. The careful reader may find herself making what seem to be savvy analogies between the situations of Sonya and Dunya and the relative willingness of Katerina Ivanovna and Pulcheria Aleksandrovna to accept such sacrifices. Not to mention the passive or absent male protagonists who seem to do no more than bear witness, grumble, lie on the floor, or potentially reap the material benefits of such sacrifice. At this point students may be feeling quite confident about their capacities to work with this text. They are attentive readers; they are back in control.

Yet in chapter four Raskolnikov offers up his own deconstruction of his mother's letter. Raskolnikov very likely proves himself to be a far more astute reader than we. He is willing to do more than make rough analogies; he pursues his thoughts to their logical moral conclusion; he asserts that the sacrifice his own beloved sister is willing to make is even more abhorrent than Sonya's turn to prostitution. "Do you understand that a Mrs. Luzhin's cleanness is exactly the same thing as Sonechka's, or perhaps even worse, fouler, more despicable, because you, Dunechka, can after all reckon on comforts into the bargain, and with the other it is a question simply of dying of hunger" (6:38; 37). Our students find themselves confronted by a character — another student — who, whatever terrible acts he might commit, can make more perceptive judgments, can observe, can analyze himself and others better than we can. What then is our role as readers in this text? Are we merely spectators to the action, putty in the hands both of the narrator and his protagonist? I have found that students enjoy discussing this conundrum.

When the murders actually occur (in chapter seven, a mere twenty pages or so later), readers — students — find themselves facing yet another challenge, a moral and psychological rather than an intellectual one. Raskolnikov murders the old woman brutally: "He struck her again and yet again, with all his strength, always with the blunt side of the axe, and always on the crown of the head. Blood poured out as if from an overturned glass and the body toppled over on its back" (6:63; 66).[53] Raskolnikov then begins rifling through the pawnbroker's possessions and pledges. A footstep sounds; Lizaveta enters the room. An even more grisly murder occurs, a murder that is, as Raskolnikov himself instantly realizes, a "second, unpremeditated murder" (6:65; 68). Then, relentlessly, comes the passage in which Raskolnikov, on one side of the hastily closed door, listens to the conversation between two young men, who are almost stand-ins both for Raskolnikov himself and also for the reader —

the student Koch and a young man studying to be an examining magistrate. They rattle the door and speculate on why there is no answer to the bell, since the door has been bolted from the inside.

At this juncture I ask students whether they find themselves hoping that Raskolnikov will escape this situation or hoping he will be caught. One page after reading a minute description of two horrendous murders, most students — and most of us readers — will find themselves rooting for his escape. At this point, it is not an intellectual challenge that confronts readers, but a moral one. Why do we side with Raskolnikov? Why are we on his side of the door? Why do we make, if only momentarily, intellectual and moral judgments in fiction that we might not make in life?

By spending what may seem to be an inordinate amount of time on Part I, students may be better equipped to be readers of the rest of the novel. At least they are more aware of the different kinds of challenges that may come to them in subsequent chapters, and they are alert to the work they must keep doing: they must continue to examine their own intellectual and moral assumptions as well as those of the characters. Reading may be at risk; it is also a risky business.

Trifles and Blind Spots

For much of the novel Raskolnikov experiences a terrible certainty that he will be brought down by trifles, by the small things he forgets or cannot control. The fact that he leaves the door hanging open while he murders the pawnbroker is perhaps the first and most unnerving of those trifles, yet it is one that, by virtue of its terrifyingly familiar, nightmarish quality, may help to bind the reader's sympathy to Raskolnikov. Moreover, throughout much of the novel Raskolnikov simply cannot seem to remember that he committed two murders, not one. Only once his interviews with Sonya have commenced does he begin to take into account that he has also murdered Lizaveta and to absorb what the dreadful meaning of that terrible murder might be.

Even worse, after he has overheard Lizaveta in the marketplace, Raskolnikov recalls the first time he had heard of Lizaveta's existence. He remembers a conversation between two students he had overheard six weeks earlier in a tavern just after his own first visit to the pawnbroker. At the time he was struck by the coincidence that the students were speaking of the pawnbroker with the same loathing for her which he also felt, and that, like him they were infected by the Rastignac idea. But Raskolnikov is blind to what is perhaps the main point: he also hears then that Lizaveta is "constantly pregnant" ("*pominutno byla beremenna*," 6:54; 55). Raskolnikov never returns to this recollection (from before the murder) again. Has Raskolnikov actually murdered a pregnant woman? What is the moral impact of this? Does he ever realize this possibility? Neither the narrator nor Raskolnikov ever returns to this subject, but perhaps it will remain activated in the minds of some students. Such trifles and blind spots are the crux of the matter. After students have some understanding of Raskolnikov's intellectual and moral grounding in the "unfinished" ideas and events of his time, whether in the air, on the streets, or in the media, they can move on to attempting to define those elusive trifles and to enumerate the uncanny blind spots that confound Raskolnikov — the trifles and blind spots that really constitute the palpitating center.

In his notes for the novel, Dostoevsky explores the theme of Lizaveta's pregnancy more fully. He even occasionally suggests that she has a child. There is this curious entry: "It happened this way with Sassia: He caresses Sassia, and she came to him. . . . And it was clear that she herself was glad to have a pretext for coming. She said that she is the daughter of Lizaveta (and that she knew Lizaveta). When he admitted his guilt to her, then suddenly, no Sassia."[54]

This same Sassia (Lizaveta's child) then appears at the Marmeladovs'. A few paragraphs later, appears the following note, "Child. Oh you lovable creature; (this is Lizaveta's). About Lizaveta." And then, " 'Why can't I become a Gaas? Why is everything lost?' The baby. Who will forbid me to love this baby? . . . And suddenly: I am astonished why I don't pity Lizaveta. Poor creature."[55] Frank surmises that this Gaas may be "a saintly Moscow doctor who aided convicts," although he does not speculate about the significance of Lizaveta's possible offspring.[56] Moreover, Sassia calls Sonya "auntie." Equally interesting in the notes is the suggestion that a character Bakavin, who is a prototype for Zosimov in the novel, may have been one of Lizaveta's lovers and had made her pregnant:

> "He lived with Lizaveta," Nastasya blurted out as soon as he left. . . . She did his wash for him. Also he paid little [crossed out] didn't pay her anything for it.
>
> "No, it just isn't true at all!" Razumikhin cried out. "She had someone else. I know."
>
> "Well, maybe there (was) a third and perhaps a fourth," Nastasya said laughing. "She was a girl who tried to please. It's not that she herself had to she did it by her own will, but she sort of bore it out of humility. She didn't know how to say no. Every mischief-maker had fun with her. But the infant they found was his (the doctor's)."
>
> "What baby?"
>
> "But don't you know? They performed a Caesarean on her. She was six months' pregnant. A boy. Born dead." . . .
>
> When they left, . . . I [Raskolnikov] fell on my back and caught hold of my head.[57]

We learn too that (as Nastasya suggests in passing in the novel) Lizaveta had mended Raskolnikov's shirt, and Sonya tells him that he still owes Lizaveta ten kopecks for mending: "You haven't paid it yet . . . (and she was murdered pregnant; they used to beat her for nothing, and whoever wanted could outrage her)." ~~I knew her and she mended my linen. She's an idiot. The old woman beat her when she was pregnant. I saw it myself. Pregnant, pregnant, sixth~~"[58] Dostoevsky starkly brackets in the notes the significance of Raskolnikov's sudden recollection that he had killed Lizaveta as well as the old woman: "[N.B. Lizaveta? (Poor thing) Lizaveta! And why is it that I haven't thought of her a single time since then? It's as if I had not killed her. Killed her? How horrible that really is!]" And then, in the jottings for Raskolnikov's confession to Sonya, Dostoevsky has Raskolnikov tell her that he now thinks only of Lizaveta, and not of the pawnbroker, "And it's curious that I do not think of the old woman but only of Lizaveta. Poor Lizaveta."[59]

Not only does Dostoevsky remove this disturbing material about Lizaveta — about her being a mother, having another stillborn child, and being more closely connected both to Raskolnikov and to the character who becomes Zosimov — from the final version of the novel, he condenses it into a single, powerful, minute particle of charged matter, the phrase "constantly pregnant." At the beginning of the novel before he has committed the murders, once Raskolnikov has overheard that Lizaveta was constantly pregnant, he never returns to this thought again, nor does the narrator. This trifle, this blind spot, once it is noticed by the reader, becomes a kind of trompe l'oeil. Once the reader has observed this unsettling detail, Raskolnikov's consistent failure to remember it becomes emblematic of the disconcerting trifles and blind spots that render this novel a metaphysical thriller as well as a proto-detective novel.

In conclusion, nearly everything is missing. I have brought up no discussion of fantastic realism, of the polyphonic novel, of the dialogic imagination, of sideward or squinting glances, of thresholds, of coffin-like rooms, and of drenching rains. Nothing much about Marmeladov, Sonya, Katerina Ivanovna, Dunya, Svidrigaylov, Razumihin, and the magnificent Porfiry Petrovich. Nothing at all about Luzhin or Lebeziatnikov. Nothing about Dostoevsky's technique of doubling, very little about dreams, about Napoleon, the architecture of St. Petersburg, and its canals and bridges, about articles "concerning crime," about the possibility of authentic confession or solid repentance. Not to mention nothing about five-year-old girls hiding behind cupboards, folded one-hundred-ruble notes tucked in pockets, or watchmen named Achilles.

Nothing at all about Dostoevsky's passionate and ongoing polemic with

Rousseau or about another odd detail — that when we first encounter Razumihin in Part II (chapter two) he suggests to Raskolnikov that they should undertake a joint project of translating Rousseau. "There are some very boring pieces of gossip marked out in the second part of the *Confessions,* and we will translate them; someone or other has told Kheruvimov that Rousseau is in his way a sort of Radishchev. Of course, I don't contradict him; he can go to the devil!" (6:88; 95). This second part of Rousseau's *Confessions* was one of the foci for Dostoevsky's lifelong rage and emblematic to him of the problems inherent in any confessional narrative.[60] The fact that Razumihin proposes this particular translation project is another essential trifle, another blind spot, another unexplored connection to the Rastignac idea which, ultimately, also found its source in Rousseau's *Confessions*. There is nothing to do but return to the text, to its final words, "All that might be the subject of a new tale [*rasskaz*], but our present one is ended." Or, perhaps that tale has already been told by the many critics who have written so forcefully and eloquently about this monumental novel and, most important, by Dostoevsky himself.

In closing, one firm insight that I have about entering a classroom to teach *Crime and Punishment,* or any hefty novel or the shortest of poems, is to have, yourself, recently inhaled as much of it as possible, or at least some part of it, before going into class. This is more important than reviewing notes or reading secondary material. When some portion of the literary work is alive in my brain, my intellect, my imagination — a virus all its own — infecting me, perhaps confounding me, I tend to be better off than when I have distilled a particular reading of the text and bottled it for a measured dose to distribute to my class.

Dostoevsky's life and his literary work abound with transformations and with conversions. Dostoevsky's starting point for this novel was, as we have seen, the theme of "ideas in the air" and how they came to enter into the being of his hero. They transformed themselves; they mutated in his psyche. *Crime and Punishment* literally becomes, in the classroom, an idea in the air. It transforms itself; it mutates as it enters, also in "unfinished" form, the minds of its many readers and infects them.

4

The Gospel According to Dostoevsky:
Paradox, Plot, and Parable

After this, Jesus knowing that all things were now accomplished, that the scripture might be fulfilled, saith, "I thirst."
—*John 19:28*

Experiment to me
Is every one I meet
If it contain a kernel?
The Figure of a Nut

Presents upon a Tree
Equally plausibly,
But Meat within, is requisite
To Squirrels, and to Me.
—Emily Dickinson, c. 1865

Many complain that the words of the wise are always merely parables and of no use in daily life, which is the only life we have. When the sage says: "Go over," he does not mean that we should cross over to some actual place, which we could do anyhow if the labor were worth it; he means some fabulous yonder, something unknown to us, something too that he cannot designate more precisely, and therefore cannot help us here in the very least. All these parables really set out to say merely that the incomprehensible is incomprehensible, and we know that already. But the cares we have to struggle with every day: that is a different matter.

Concerning this a man once said: Why such reluctance? If you only followed the parables, you yourselves would become parables and with that rid yourself of all your daily cares.

Another said: I bet that is also a parable.

The first said: You have won.

The second said: But unfortunately only in parable.

The first said: No, in reality: in parable you have lost.

— Franz Kafka, "On Parables"

At numerous moments throughout Dostoevsky's canon, characters recite short anecdotes that exhibit features we tend to ascribe to biblical parable. In general, when Dostoevsky's characters deliver such utterances, they are attempting to apprehend, comprehend, or otherwise turn toward what they imagine to be their authentic Russian heritage. At the same time these anecdotes are frequently transformative, either for the character telling the story or for those who hear it. This chapter examines four instances in Dostoevsky's fiction that exemplify this parabolic impulse and works to decipher within them the collisions between authentically Russian spiritual affirmation and Dostoevsky's predilection for expressing his ideas through Western European literary strategies and forms.

As we have already seen, Dostoevsky's biography and his writings embodied a lifelong give-and-take between his religious orthodoxy and his fascination with Western literary narratives, plots, and themes. His often-quoted letter of 1854 to the Decembrist wife Madame Fonvizina vividly describes how he "thirsted for faith as the withered grass" thirsts for water.[1] In this remarkable letter Dostoevsky calls himself a child of his century, "a child of doubt and disbelief." But he maintains that, despite his doubt and disbelief, nevertheless, during a moment of "great tranquility" he had been able to form a simple "symbol of faith" within himself through his image of Christ. He then concludes, "More than that — if someone succeeded in proving to me that Christ was outside the truth and if, indeed, the truth was outside Christ, I would sooner remain with Christ than with the truth. But it is better to stop talking about this. Why is it, though, that certain topics of conversation are completely banned in society and, if they are broached, someone or other gives the impression of being shocked? But let us leave that."[2] This frequently quoted passage in Dostoevsky's letter tends to be read as a complex *profession de foi*. It is important to remember, however, that it is a statement made in a single letter in the 1850s to a heroic woman whom he revered and who had been kind to him, but who was not one of his regular epistolary correspondents. Nevertheless, this compelling statement, with its haunting formulations, constitutes a Dostoevskian version — "the thirst to believe" — of what William James would later famously describe as "the will to believe." In this letter Dostoevsky affirms his orthodox faith even as he acknowledges his continuing doubts and the influence of the philosophies and political ideologies of his time.

What is of even more interest to me, however, is his claim "but it is better to stop talking about this. . . . But let us leave that." Such statements and seeming disclaimers occur with paradigmatic regularity in Dostoevsky's letters and journalism, and are often indicative, I think, of the moment when he crosses over from discourse into art, from straight lines to parabolas, from didacticism to parable. In short, Dostoevsky will frequently "stop talking about this" and talk about it instead through parable or some other indirect generic mode of expression.

As a writer of fiction depicting the contemporary issues of his time, Dostoevsky had frequent resort to biblical parables. The story of the raising of Lazarus and its implications for *Crime and Punishment* leap immediately to mind. Jostein Børtnes has already eloquently called our attention to and analyzed Dostoevsky's knowledge of the Bible as well as his "intimate knowledge of old Russian hagiography."[3] In this context Børtnes' analysis of the role in *Crime and Punishment* of the story of the raising of Lazarus is most illuminating, for he shows that in the Orthodox tradition this particular story "has a complex symbolical meaning where it is understood as an expression of the *divine power* of Christ to restore man to his original immortality and at the same time as a prefiguration of the imminent death and resurrection of Christ."[4]

In this chapter, however, rather than following the admirable tradition of understanding the complex role of religious quotation and allusion in Dostoevsky's fiction, I focus on Dostoevsky's importation of his own idiosyncratic parables into his work, the "gospel" according to Dostoevsky.

First, a word about parables generally: definitions of the term "parable" embody their own paradoxicality. On one hand, there are those understandings of parable that stress that parables *teach* a moral through an extended metaphor. Consider, for example, the following three characterizations of the genre of parable: "Teaching a moral by means of an extended metaphor," or, "A short, simple story illustrating a moral lesson. In a parable, the story is developed not for its own sake but only in so far as it reinforces the moral, which is always explicit. The parables of Christ, such as those of the Good Samaritan and the Prodigal Son, are the most famous examples of this genre," or, "A *parable* is a very short narrative about human beings presented so as to stress the tacit analogy, or parallel, with a general thesis or lesson that the narrator is trying to bring home to his audience. The parable was one of Christ's favourite devices as a teacher."[5] These definitions all tend to emphasize shortness of form and clarity of meaning; they each suggest that parables are anecdotes or stories that illustrate and teach a moral attitude or religious principle.

On the other hand, there exists another way of understanding parable that, quite neatly and precisely, contradicts this first view of parable as a metaphoric teaching or fictional illustration of a moral view or lesson. Take, for example, the following: "If a story that otherwise qualifies as a parable reaches moral closure rather than leaving the reader caught in a paradox that requires moral choice, the story is not a parable."[6]

The meaning of parable has possessed this irresolvable duality since biblical times. Hence, there is one view that "parables of the kind found in the New Testament were always essentially simple, and always had the same kind of point, which would have been instantly taken by all listeners, outsiders included."[7] Parables, in this understanding of them, are inclusive. But there also exists the notion of parable as an exclusive genre. Frank Kermode offers a fascinating explanation for the origins of this understanding of parable as an exclusive genre: "When Jesus was asked to explain the purpose of his parables, he described them as stories *told to them without* — to outsiders — with the express purpose of concealing a mystery that was to be understood only by insiders. So Mark tells us: speaking to the Twelve, Jesus said, 'To you has been given the secret of the kingdom of God, but for those outside everything is in parables; so that they may indeed see but not perceive, and may indeed hear but not understand; lest they should turn again and be forgiven' " (*Mark* 4:11–12).[8] Mark thus emphasized the dark side of parable — its express purpose of being a story told to outsiders with the intent to conceal rather than reveal a mystery. Mark recognized and underscored the special power of parable to keep those "outside" from perceiving or understanding. Kermode adds that Mark further "distresses the commentators by using the word 'mystery' as a synonym for 'parable,' and assuming that stories put questions which even the most privileged interpreters cannot answer." Kermode succinctly expresses the duality or basic generic dialogism inherent in the genre when he concludes that "parables, it seems, may proclaim a truth as a herald does, and at the same time conceal truth like an oracle."[9]

Where Does Dostoevsky Fit Here?

The Russian religious thinker G. M. Fedotov has suggested that the gospel parables which speak of the "God of mercy" and that breathe a "spirit of love" are the ones that made a particularly deep impression in the Russian religious tradition.[10] These particular parables, while they would be terrifying to the transgressors of the law of mercy or to the violators of love (in Kermode's terminology, the outsiders) would serve, according to Fedotov, to comfort believers. In Kermode's terminology and following Mark, these parables would not be understood by the outsiders (Fedotov's transgressors and violators), but would be understood by the insiders (Fedotov's believers). Dostoevsky's own idiosyncratic parables exhibit precisely such a dualistic tendency.

Dostoevsky, as an artist, was always keenly aware of all these contradictory powers of parable to conceal as well as to reveal. As a genre the parable neatly reflected the value, as he had put it, of not expressing his own most cherished ideas in too straightforward or didactic a way. In 1861, as we have already seen, he had written, "Indeed, the moment you wish to tell the truth [*istina*] according to your convictions, you are at once accused of uttering copybook maxims. . . . Why is it that if in our age we feel the need to tell the truth, we have more and more to resort to humour or satire or irony in order to sweeten truth as if it were a bitter pill?"[11] Dostoevsky often found that he could best "sweeten" the fundamental Orthodox religious truths he wished to convey by "resorting" to the large repertoire of narrative forms that other writers of fiction of his century, particularly the writers of Western Europe, made use of as well.

Fifteen years later, in 1876, as we have already seen in chapter one, Dostoevsky was still complaining in much the same manner. In the letter to Solovyov thanking him for his praise of the recent article in *The Diary of a Writer* on "The Eastern Question," Dostoevsky had lamented that until now he had not allowed himself to "say the very last word" about certain of his convictions. He had cited the example of Voltaire and had maintained that if Voltaire, instead of resorting to hints, suggestions, and insinuations had simply stated his ideas directly, he would have been laughed at. In this remarkable letter, Dostoevsky had gone on to quote his favorite line from his favorite poem, "Silentium" by Fyodor Tiutchev, "A thought spoken is a lie."[12]

With these general thoughts about parable in mind, let us now turn to four of the many moments in Dostoevsky's fiction when he ushers forth, either through the actual words of his characters or through a rapid-fire connection of events over a short period of time, parables of his own. These moments exhibit all the complexity of biblical parables in their attention to questions of moral and religious truth. But they also serve handily to advance the plot of a wily novelist, and as such, they strain away from the impulse toward directly expressing, as he did in his journalism, the values of the ByzantoSlav tradition and veer toward the literary traditions and narrative strategies of Western Europe. Such doubly charged moments are the hallmark of Dostoevsky's fictional universe.

In the beginning of Part II of *The Idiot*, Prince Myshkin arrives in St. Petersburg and pays a visit to his rival Rogozhin, who will shortly attempt to murder him. In the gap between Parts I and II of the novel, Myshkin had spent some six months rediscovering or reacquainting himself with the authentic Russia (both Moscow and the Russian countryside) from which he had been absent for so many years. The reader learns only the skimpiest of details about these crucial six months, although the narrator-chronicler implies that during this time Myshkin had sought deliberately to reestablish his bonds with Russia and to reinvent himself as a Russian. Nevertheless, the influences of Myshkin's lengthy sojourn in Switzerland before the events of the novel began and his prolonged contact there with Western ideas (especially those of Rousseau) continue to inform his vision and shape his character as well. Myshkin and Rogozhin stand beneath a reproduction of a famous Western work of art, a Holbein representation of the dead Christ just after he has been taken down from the cross. (This painting has a fundamental aesthetic import for the novel.) Rogozhin suddenly asks Myshkin if he believes in God. Myshkin does not answer Rogozhin's question directly, but, in true parabolic fashion, and as if "inspired by a sudden recollection," replies instead with an indirect *profession de foi*, "as for faith, I last week, in two days, had four different encounters" (8:182; 239).

The parable begins. Myshkin first tells Rogozhin about meeting a well-known atheist on a train with whom he had tried to discuss the existence of God. But, during their conversation, Myshkin had sensed that their discourse, based as it was upon reason and logic, could not find a way to approach the fundamental question about faith in God. He had then stopped for the night, he tells Rogozhin, at a provincial hotel, where the night before a peasant, completely sober, had murdered his friend for his silver watch, praying, as he raised his knife, "God, forgive me for Christ's sake" (8:183; 239). The next morning, while walking around the town, Myshkin had met a drunken soldier who had pressed him to buy a "silver" cross they both knew was tin. After the swindle, Myshkin had wandered off, thinking to himself about this drunken peasant precisely what Dostoevsky would later express in his journalism. "No, it's too soon for me to condemn this peddler of Christ. God alone knows what is hidden in those weak and drunken hearts" (8:183; 240). A few years later, in his *Diary* article, "The Environment" (1873), Dostoevsky had reiterated his character's thought and asked, "Who has peered into the innermost places of their hearts? Is there anyone among us who can claim truly to know the Russian People?" (21:15; *Writer's Diary,* 1:134).

Myshkin then tells Rogozhin that an hour later he had met a young peasant woman who was in the act of crossing herself with great devotion because her six-week-old baby had just smiled for the first time. She had explained her emotion to Myshkin with a simile that is both simple and startling. It is startling because, without fanfare or pride, she uses a divine example to explicate a mortal one. "There is joy for a mother in her child's first smile, just as God rejoices when from heaven he sees a sinner praying to him with his whole heart" (8:183; 240). It is more usual to attempt to understand the divine in terms of the earthly or the human—"I thirst for faith as the parched grass thirsts for water." Myshkin discovers in her words a shaft of meaning that suddenly illuminates for him the essence of his Russian Christianity. He tells Rogozhin, "The essence of religious feeling doesn't depend on reasoning and it has nothing to do with wrongdoing or crime or atheism." Myshkin is alluding to the swindling peddler, the murderer, and the atheist, and comprehending all of them as mysteriously within God's ken (8:183; 240). Myshkin further concretizes his sense of the interconnectedness of human beings in God's world by imagining that "the simple peasant mother," who had understood the full nature of God's parental joy in his children as she was savoring her own, might perhaps actually *be* the wife of the drunken soldier who had sold him the tin cross.

In Myshkin's parable the peasant mother's joy in her baby's smile cannot undo the atheist's disbelief, the peasant's murder of his friend, or the peddler's dishonesty. But the surge of joyous emotion that she, Myshkin, and perhaps eventually the reader, feel at this linking of her happiness to God's subtly but irrevocably transforms what has gone before. Myshkin's parable does not teach a moral truth but one that reaches beyond questions of morality and traditional religious dogma into a different realm entirely. There is, somehow, a mysterious connection between good and evil in these events that Myshkin has so deliberately linked together, particularly in the virtually oxymoronic notions of a praying murderer and a cheating, drunken peddler of Christ. Myshkin's fourth encounter with the peasant mother bestows unity to the four events by incorporating the mysterious world of evil into the still more mysterious world of good.

Nevertheless, this parable with all its complexities also has specific and practical novelistic functions within the plot of *The Idiot*. It serves either to prefigure (structurally) or to inspire (characterologically) the religious Rogozhin's imminent attempt to murder Myshkin. And, as he and Myshkin will shortly exchange crosses themselves, Dostoevsky both humorously and with dramatic high irony brings to mind the image of the cheating peddler of Christ. Moreover, the four discrete events of the parable, taken as a whole, accede to the typical demands of successful fictional plotting. They move from darkness to light, from renunciation and denial of God, murder, and dishonesty to a celebration of maternal and divine joy, in order to convey a message about the essential nature of religious faith. These separate and "true events" happened, Myshkin tells Rogozhin, over the course of two days, but what would be their overall effect if their order were different? What if the baby's first smile had preceded the story of the murder? Would we perhaps then even have a parable of despair, a story as potentially dark as the message conveyed by the reproduction of Holbein's *Dead Christ* under which the two men stand?

Nearly a decade later, in 1876, when Dostoevsky had sought indirectly to describe his own conversion, his own faith, he turned, like Myshkin before him, to the Russian peasant and to another parabolic anecdote, "not even an anecdote: just a remote reminiscence," composed, again, of several disparate, seemingly contradictory parts filtered carefully and strategically through the medium of art. Autobiographical details intermingle with fictional ones; one transforms the other: the resulting hybrid describes a conversion.[13] Like his character Myshkin, Dostoevsky, in "The Peasant Marey," takes a reminiscence composed of discrete parts that will combine to suggest a parable about religious faith.

As Dostoevsky begins his "Peasant Marey," he is at pains to dissociate it from the typical *profession de foi*: "But reading all these *professions de foi* is a bore, I think, and so I'll tell you a story; actually, it's not even a story, but only a reminiscence of something that happened long ago and that, for some reason, I would very much like to recount here and now as a conclusion to our treatise on the People. At the time I was only nine years old. . . . But no, I'd best begin with the time I was twenty-nine." (22:46; *Writer's Diary,* 1:351). But where Dostoevsky, the journalist, is at pains in this transitional passage between his journalistic entry, "On Love of the People. An Essential Contract with the People," and "The Peasant Marey" to separate his "reminiscence of something that happened long ago" from being yet another boring *profession de foi,* Dostoevsky the artist has written a parable that is, in part, a classic (albeit not boring) conversion tale and a *profession de foi*.

Dostoevsky (in this particular work, he is "Dostoevsky" — that is, part author, part created narrator — an extension of that autobiographical-fictional hybrid that is the story itself) begins by describing the second day of the last Easter week he had spent, more than two decades earlier, in prison. The peasant convicts were indulging in a drunken celebration, and one of the nonpeasant political prisoners, a Pole, had just muttered to Dostoevsky, "Je häis ces brigands" (I hate these brigands). Dostoevsky then lay down on his bed, closed his eyes and began to reminisce, to dream. Reality and invention begin to merge, to penetrate and transform each other. "All through my four years in prison I continually thought of all my past days, and I think I relived the whole of my former life in my memories. These memories arose in my mind of themselves; rarely did I summon them up consciously. They would begin from a certain point [or, perhaps, "speck"], some little thing that was often barely perceptible, and then bit by bit they would grow into a finished picture, some strong and complete impression. I would analyze these impressions, adding *new touches to things experienced long ago; and the main thing was that I would refine them, continually refine them, and in this consisted my entire entertainment*" (22:46; *Writer's Diary*, 1:352, emphasis added). This image suggests a series of circus mirrors, for the artistic memories, musings, reveries, and inventions of the narrator of 1876 are precisely about the artistic memories, musings, reveries, and inventions of his convict self years earlier. The "Dostoevsky" of 1876 is reinventing that self from the past who himself had invented his own present and past. Such invention and reinvention or creation and recreation of self is an endless, unfinalizable, and unfinished process. This short work constitutes a kind of snapshot, a still or freeze-frame of a process, in which time present is superimposed on times past, and the resulting triple-exposure is subject to a subsequent harmonizing, yet fictional, touch-up of the whole.

Dostoevsky then recalls how, while lying there in the prison, he had suddenly recalled "a moment I thought I had completely forgotten." He had remembered back twenty years to his childhood, to a slightly chilly August day, when he had been rambling among the bushes near a ravine. He had wandered into a birch grove to search for mushrooms, when he suddenly and clearly had heard, "amid the deep silence," the cry of "wolf!" In terror, he had screamed and rushed out of the woods into the nearby field to the peasant Marey, whom he had earlier heard plowing close by. Marey then began to comfort the frightened child in an affectionate but perfunctory way, until he saw the child's genuine fear. Dostoevsky (in 1876) remembers (how as a convict he had remembered) that the peasant had then caressed him gently with his "thick earth-soiled" finger with its black nail and had gazed at him with a "broad, almost maternal smile." At this moment the peasant Marey had entered lovingly and with empathy into the frightened child's fantastical, fairy-tale world. "I'll keep an eye on you as you go. Can't let the wolf get you!" he had added with the same motherly smile. "Well, Christ be with thee. Off you go" (22:48; *Writer's Diary*, 1:353–54).

Dostoevsky, the convict, then muses how subsequently, on the rare occasions when, as a child, he had met Marey, he had not spoken to him. Yet now in prison, twenty years later, the long-buried memory had "settled unnoticed in my heart with no will of mine." It had "suddenly" come to him "at the time when it was needed." "I recalled the tender, maternal smile of [the] poor serf, the way he crossed me and shook his head: 'Well you did take a fright now, didn't you, lad!' And I especially remember his thick finger, soiled with dirt, that he touched quietly and with shy tenderness to my trembling lips . . . and had I been his very own son he could not have looked at me with a glance that radiated more pure love" (22:49, *Writer's Diary*, 1:355). The peasant's motherly smile and "delicate, almost feminine tenderness" had comforted him at his moment of imagined danger in childhood; now twenty years later, at a moment of genuine danger — at a moment of decisive spiritual crisis and loathing for his fellow man — the memory (or, as he had described it at the outset, *the recollection or impression to which he had added new touches*) of the peasant's smile had comforted him perhaps even more profoundly than it had when he was a physically terrified nine-year-old. The memory of Marey's tender smile and his empathetic, comforting words had shown to him the essence of religious feeling.

This two-tiered memory interlocking childhood and young adulthood again becomes, some twenty years later — in middle age — the occasion for both artistic transformation and spiritual conversion. The autobiographical and the artistic impulse combine *("I would analyze these impressions, adding new touches to things experienced long ago")* to express a visionary experience, and the result is the forging of a parable. At each of these three autobiographical moments art, fancy, and invention play a strategic role as well. The child had imagined the cry of wolf and Marey had consented to enter that imaginary world with him; the convict had liked to add "new touches" to things long ago outlived; the successful journalist-writer engages in such pursuits constantly — they are by now his livelihood. Authentically Russian religious belief is made manifest and encased in the artistic vision of the nineteenth-century romantic or fantastic realist.

When the convict Dostoevsky at last opens his eyes and gazes around, he realizes a conversion has occurred. Nothing has changed, but everything is different. "I remember I suddenly felt that I could regard these unfortunates in an entirely different way, and that suddenly, through some sort of miracle, the former hatred and anger in my heart had vanished." Dostoevsky then relates how he had looked over at a particularly drunken, brawling peasant, and had thought to himself, "Why, he might also be that very same Marey; for I cannot peer into his heart" (22:49; *Writer's Diary*, 1:355).[14]

Why have I taken you through the stages of a story with which many readers

of Dostoevsky are already familiar? Because the artistic structure of Dostoevsky's intimate parable about faith uncannily resembles Myshkin's parable
about faith. In fact we almost have in Myshkin's anecdote "as to faith" and
Dostoevsky's "story . . . not even a story, but only a reminiscence of something
that happened long ago," what might even be interpreted as two gospel versions of the same parable, at least with regard to its elemental building blocks.
Each starts out as the narration of a memory. The cold hatred of the Poles with
which Dostoevsky begins his distant reminiscence recalls the atheist on the
train with which Myshkin initiates his account of a recent memory. The Pole
and the atheist — moral equivalents in Dostoevsky's canon anyway — each
preach a forceful, persuasive ethic of despair. The peasant Marey, with his
luminous smile that partakes both of intense mother-love and divine love,
recalls, in a haunting way, the peasant woman who rejoices in her baby's first
smile. Each anecdote has embedded within it the equation of a maternal smile
with God's love for man; in each parable the path to grace and salvation is
somehow connected to the mystery of a loving smile that cannot undo pain
and suffering, but still stands strong in the face of a world full of evil.

Each parable pulls its final punch by positing a simple, magical, preposter-
ous, impossible identity between two unrelated figures. Just as Myshkin finds
intense comfort in imagining that the peasant woman may actually be the wife
of the swindling, drunken soldier, so too Dostoevsky hypothesizes that the
peasant convict brawling at his feet may actually be the peasant Marey. In each
parable good and evil are intimately intertwined, and their very intertwining
serves to strengthen the good rather than the evil. Moreover, neither Myshkin
nor the newly converted convict Dostoevsky (at least as he is created by the
"great writer" Dostoevsky some twenty years later) can say what is in the
peasant's heart. Yet each nevertheless tells his tale — a parable about the recep-
tion of faith, of grace — and by telling it enacts yet another act of faith, a
spreading of that grace.[15] Religious parables keep being told: they are short
and applicable, in a variety of ways, to many contexts.

Although Dostoevsky's parables exhibit these traditional features, they also
depend simultaneously on deliberate artistic, fictional devices of narration,
sequence, plot, and surprising identities in order to achieve their effectiveness.
Myshkin concludes by coming back full circle to the atheist with whom he had
begun (8:184; 241). Likewise Dostoevsky closes his "Peasant Marey" with a
return to the Pole with whom he had begun. He, like the atheist on the train,
could not give himself up to an emotion beyond reason. At this point, however, Dostoevsky cannot resist inserting a telltale streak of his nationalistic
contempt for Poles. This moment resembles the comments considered in chapter one about the inability of "a German or a Viennese Yid" to appreciate

Russian genre painting that had so undercut the rhetorical force of his 1873 article "Apropos of the Exhibition."[16] Here Dostoevsky concludes dismissively that the Pole is an "unfortunate man! He had no recollections of any Mareys and no other view of these people but *'Je häis ces brigands*'" (22:49–50; *Writer's Diary*, 1:355). The fictional Myshkin's parable thus suggests a preliminary expression, in both structure and theme, of Dostoevsky's semi-autobiographical, yet semifictional parable of conversion, "The Peasant Marey." Art influences reality, although both are a hybrid of fact and fancy, of impressions, specks, and inventions. Moreover, each parable finds it necessary to exclude (the atheist, the Pole) as well as to include (the narrator himself, some other characters, and readers). As such each belongs to the type of parable that is both inclusive and exclusive.

A third moment in Dostoevsky's fiction bears a striking resemblance to both these parables: the scene early on in *The Brothers Karamazov* when the elder Zosima leaves his cell to converse with a group of five peasant women. Here Dostoevsky, working behind the backs of his narrator-chronicler and Zosima, constructs an indirect parable of events: he leaves it up to the reader to connect them. There is no initial announcement like Myshkin's "as for faith" or Dostoevsky's offhand remarks about boring *professions de foi*. The reader himself may become, if he chooses to do so, the maker of parables.

Among a crowd of some twenty peasant women, Zosima speaks to five. The first peasant, "a possessed woman," is led up to Zosima. The liberal-minded and sociologically inclined narrator-chronicler inserts his own interpretation here to describe how the woman's primitive Christian belief, "aroused by the expectation of the miracle of healing, actually causes a brief cure" (14:44; 39). The second woman Zosima meets is "one from afar." It is well known that this passage has a wrenching autobiographical significance, for into the language of this uneducated peasant woman Dostoevsky pours his own intimate, desperate grief for his own recently dead child.[17]

As she laments the death of her little boy, this peasant woman brings him poignantly to life for us. Zosima first consoles her with conventional church wisdom. This moment somewhat resembles the kind but perfunctory comfort Marey first offered the child Dostoevsky. Zosima tells her that her babe is rejoicing in the company of God and the angels. The woman is a believer; she has experienced no loss of faith, yet this answer offers her no comfort. Divine justice pales before the enormity of earthly injustice and loss. Zosima quickly abandons his strategy of applying standard church dogma. He reaches instead into the biblical past and, like Marey, into the depths of his own heart to offer her counsel. "It is 'Rachel of old . . . weeping for her children and will not be comforted because they are not.' Such is the lot set on earth for you mothers.

Be not comforted. Consolation is not what you need. Weep and be not consoled, but weep" (14:46; 41–42). He urges her to remember and not to forget.

Zosima's third encounter is with a peasant woman who has not heard from her son for a year. She is tempted to resort to superstition by offering up prayers for her son as though he were dead, in the hope that such a prayer would trouble his soul and cause him to write. In short order Zosima chastises her, forgives her, and then predicts that her son will either write or return home very soon. In his fourth encounter Zosima comforts a woman who confesses to him that she has murdered her husband. He assures her that God will forgive her and that she must think only of continual repentance. "If you are penitent, you love. And if you love, you are of God. All things are atoned for, all things are saved by love. If I, a sinner, even as you are, am tender with you and have pity on you, how much more will God?" (14:48; 44). Finally, Zosima meets a healthy peasant woman with her baby girl.

As in Myshkin's parable about faith, the order of these events is crucial. What would be the effect if Zosima had spoken with this woman early on, and his series of interviews had ended with the woman who was "possessed" or the woman who had murdered her husband? This young mother has come simply to see him, to bless him, and to ask him to give the sixty kopecks she has brought with her to someone even poorer than herself. Like Myshkin when he meets the peasant mother whose baby has just smiled for the first time, and like the child Dostoevsky who basks in the radiance of Marey's maternal smile and gentle touch, we here see Zosima receiving inspiration (or grace) rather than giving it (or passing it on), although Zosima does then bless (in the spirit of thanks) the woman and her child. This final encounter also underscores Zosima's conviction that all of us are part of a chain of being in which we nurture and are nurtured, love and are loved.

Zosima's conversations with these five peasant women strongly and clearly recall Myshkin's parable about faith. Zosima, like Myshkin, encounters a murderer (this time a woman) who maintains faith in God. He even assures her that God will forgive her. His last meeting, like Myshkin's, is also with a mother who has a healthy baby in her arms. Both these peasant mothers with their babes function structurally almost like the concluding couplet of a sonnet: they each send an illuminating shaft of meaning up through "the lines" that have preceded them. And Marey too, with his tender, motherly smile at the child Dostoevsky, infuses Dostoevsky's parable with harmony and radiance.

But this parabolic chapter in *The Brothers Karamazov* simultaneously performs vital, useful, practical functions for the plot of Dostoevsky's novel as well as offering a preliminary grounding to some of its primary themes. Although it presents itself as a digression from the main action, in fact, like

Myshkin's anecdote about faith, Zosima's conversation with each of the peasant women prefigures and duplicates the main action. As such it offers a telling example of how Dostoevsky had structured his novel, how he managed to balance part with whole and to weave an organic tapestry between them. For the peasant woman whose child has died, the infinitely precious memory of that child becomes a strong but delicate thread in an Ariadne's web which, if she clings to it and remembers, despite her sorrow and loss, can offer her a path out of the labyrinth of pain and despair. (The reader and some of the other characters in the novel are here offered a paradigm for what they must do as well, as they confront the loss of other children.) In a similar way, the layers of memory experienced, invented, and represented by Dostoevsky in "The Peasant Marey" offered him a path through a labyrinthian darkness. His memories had spanned nearly sixty years; the events forming Myshkin's parable of faith had taken place over two days; Zosima's encounters with the five peasant women occur within an hour or so. But the parabolic force they exert is the same.

Finally, the fourth and last parabolic moment in Dostoevsky's fiction discussed in this chapter — and for me the most paradoxical and most haunting: Grushenka's story of the onion. Dostoevsky had been particularly pleased at being able to reproduce this story in his novel. He had written to his editor, "I particularly beg you to proof-read the legend of the *little onion* carefully. This is a gem, taken down by me from a peasant woman, and of course published for *the first time*."[18] But this story had already appeared in A. N. Afanasev's 1859 collection of Russian legends, and Dostoevsky had probably forgotten that he had already read it there.[19] Dostoevsky, like his own fictional subjects, is forgetting and then remembering something vital "at the needed time."

In *The Idiot* Myshkin had stood before the graphic reproduction of the Holbein painting of the dead Christ whose dark power was great enough to cause loss of faith, especially Russian Orthodox faith in a redeemed and risen Christ.[20] There is no such painting before the suffering, doubting Alyosha Karamazov; there is, instead, a living icon of which he forms a part, a tableau vivante, whose other figures and elements are the treacherous, Judas-like Rakitin, a bit of sausage meat, a bottle of vodka, and, on Alyosha's lap, a seductive woman, Grushenka.

Grushenka learns that Zosima has just died, quickly slips off Alyosha's lap "in dismay," and a few moments later begins her parable of the onion, a story she had heard in childhood from her nanny Matrena. The legend, according to Sarah Smyth, "is the objective link which binds Grushenka with the 'enlightenment' of the Russian people. The legend was inspired by and nurtured in the people; it represents for her the source of life."[21] This story, coming as it does at the beginning of the second half of the novel, assumes a symbolic weight, comparable to other elements as diverse as words, seeds, and bows that all both contribute to the poetic language of the novel and form a matrix to become its overarching symbols. These elements, moreover, are all connected with memory, grace, and love. As we have seen in the other examples of parable in this chapter, "at the needed moment" Grushenka brings forth a precious memory: she tells the grieving, potentially rebellious Alyosha a story from her childhood about a wicked old peasant woman who had, in the course of her long life, performed only one good deed: she had once given away an onion. Yet this old peasant woman's single good deed, like a seed long dead, nevertheless embodied the potential of bearing strong fruit. It could be enough to save her.

The parable's beginning, with its description of the lake of fire in Hell, unmistakably recalls the opening of Ivan's poem of the Grand Inquisitor. "Even this," he had laughed to Alyosha, "must have a preface — that is, a literary preface." Ivan goes on to cite the apocryphal text about Mary's journey to Hell, "The Wanderings of Our Lady through Hell." Ivan gives a succinct, compelling rendition and interpretation of this twelfth-century apocryphal tale:

> "Our Lady visits Hell, and the Archangel Michael leads her through the torments. She sees the sinners and their punishment. There she sees among others one noteworthy set of sinners in a burning lake; some of them sink to the bottom of the lake so that they can't swim out, and 'these God forgets' — an expression of extraordinary depth and force. And so Our Lady, shocked and weeping, falls before the throne of God and begs for mercy for all in Hell — for all she has seen there, indiscriminately. Her conversation with God is immensely interesting. She beseeches Him, she will not desist, and when God points to the hands and feet of her Son, nailed to the Cross, and asks, 'How can I forgive His tormentors?' she bids all the saints, all the martyrs, all the angels and archangels to fall down with her and pray for mercy on all without distinction. It ends by her winning from God a respite of suffering every year from Good Friday till Trinity day, and the sinners at once raise a cry of thankfulness from Hell, chanting, 'Thou art just, O Lord, in this judgment.' Well, my poem would have been of that kind had it appeared at that time." (14:225; 228)

In these same prefatory remarks Ivan also refers twice to Dante's *Inferno*.[22]

The Hell of Grushenka's folktale sharply resembles that of the apocalyptic text Ivan recounts, for both depict Hell as a place in which loving hearts travel to seek mercy for suffering sinners. But her story also bears the markings of a Dantesque vision of Hell, for it is populated by sinners whose sinfulness continues on in Hell. These sinners do not, like those in Ivan's tale, raise a cry of thanks to God and praise the justice of the brief yearly reprieve from suffering he has given them. Nor, of course, do they receive any such reprieve. Both Mary, in Ivan's account of the apocryphal text, and the old peasant woman's guardian angel in Grushenka's parable manage, amazingly, to prevail upon God to reconsider his dread sentence. (This God, like the God of Job, is dialogic; he seems open to conversations and persuasions from others whether they be satanic adversaries or benevolent allies.) In Ivan's story, the sinners, because of Mary's unremitting intercession on their behalf (even in the face of God's anguished pointing to the body of her son nailed upon the cross), had received respite from suffering once a year from Good Friday to Trinity day.

Grushenka's story is far more daring, bold, and unusual. The guardian angel persuades God literally to give the old peasant woman a second chance: the old woman can hold on to the onion her guardian angel is holding out to her and be pulled out of the lake of fire and thereby saved, unless the onion breaks. Grushenka depicts the scene between God and the guardian angel with a narrative clarity and simplicity of form that resembles Ivan's: "So her guardian angel stood and wondered what good deed of hers he could remember to tell to God: 'she once pulled up an onion in her garden,' said he, 'and gave it to a beggar woman.' And God answered: 'You take that onion then, hold it out to her in the lake, and let her take hold and be pulled out. And if you can pull her out of the lake, let her come to Paradise, but if the onion breaks, then the woman must stay where she is'" (14:319; 330).

By telling her story about the onion, Grushenka has given Alyosha both an onion ("You've raised my soul from the depths") and a meta-onion (the entire parable of the onion). Yet moments later, as he takes his leave of her, he smiles at her tenderly and exclaims, with tears, "I only gave you an onion, nothing but a tiny little onion" (14:323; 335). Who has given whom an onion? Or, does the successful giving of the onion depend, as in the parable, wholly on mutuality, on shared responsibility? The angel holds out the onion to the sinner, and the other sinners hold on to her. No one must let go of it or push anyone else away. Grushenka's story literalizes Zosima's idea about the chain of interconnectedness among all things.

Thus the parable of the onion functions in the novel as an emblem of conversion, salvation, and the joy of mutual gift-giving between two souls each at the brink of crisis. As such, for characters and readers alike, for us insiders who, according to the Gospel of Mark, can "perceive" and "understand," it is one of the most uplifting moments in the novel, a moment when a complex idea can become simultaneously symbolized and concretized in the image and fact of a single onion. But the parable Dostoevsky has created here from this old Russian folktale, which he claimed ironically to have discovered but in fact had only himself remembered at "the needed moment," functions in an *opposite* way to how it would function if it were unadorned, a simple tale standing alone, without its surrounding layers of novelistic husk, that is without the characters, events, other stories, and ideas that constitute the many layers of any novel by Dostoevsky.

What turns this folktale, this fable, into a parable? Taken by itself, the story of the onion is the story of a damned soul. Even when given a second chance for salvation, in the depths of Hell, the suffering sinner again sins. The intercession of the guardian angel may be touching; it may reflect the willingness of the Christian God to show mercy, but both are to no avail. In true Shakespearean fashion, the old woman's character literally is her fate. She is twice damned, because she cries out to the others, "It's my onion, not yours." Her selfish cry thereby breaks the chain of interconnection and mutual responsibility among herself, the other sinners, the onion, the angel, and God.

But for Alyosha, for Grushenka, and for the reader of the novel, this irrefutable and stark fact of the old woman's now utter and irrevocable damnation, her renewed and now certainly eternal sufferings in the lake of fire, are somehow forgotten. This dark and dreadful moment, because of Dostoevsky's exquisitely artistic rendering of it as a function not only of itself alone but in the larger context of what is taking place between Alyosha and Grushenka, is seen as a moment in the novel of almost boundless joy. A tale of damnation operates, mysteriously, even miraculously, as a joyful moment of redemption. Fables are usually cautionary by nature — "look what will happen if." Standing by itself, this old folktale could be a cautionary fable.

But in its novelistic context, and through Dostoevsky's parabolic rendering, there is virtually no cautionary, didactic vestige remaining even in this verbatim rendering of the fable. Instead, the act of *telling,* of giving to one another through the valuable gift of words, of sharing a memory that arose at "the needed time," is so highlighted that the actual semantic thrust of the story is subverted and undermined. The emphasis shifts to memory and to the potentially great redemptive force of even a single good deed. No matter that the old woman's good deed *was not enough* to save her. That crucial fact is forgotten by all as Dostoevsky, with one of his typically crafty novelistic sleights-of-hand, and at the same time inspired by his potent Orthodox Christian belief, makes his characters, his readers, and perhaps himself imagine, perhaps only momentarily, that, even in the face of this contrary example, the redemptive force of the onion in each of our pasts *will be enough* to bring about both the salvation of the individual and the Kingdom of God.

Each of these four parabolic moments in Dostoevsky's work — Myshkin's anecdote about faith, "Dostoevsky's" account of "The Peasant Marey," Zosima's brief encounters with the five peasant women, and Grushenka's folktale about the onion — displays a powerful and uncanny binding together of the deliberate, premeditated strategies of the consummate writer of fiction, well aware of his readers' tastes, responses, and reading habits, and the passionate Orthodox believer struggling, like Zosima and Alyosha, to scatter the seeds of God's world (word) throughout this one. These parables constitute moments when Dostoevsky, through the rhetoric of his characters' words and through his own canny ordering of events and manipulation of larger contexts, could revitalize, reinvent, reshape, and reconstruct the Orthodox heritage and, through the medium of contemporary fiction, render it immediate, modern, and startling.

Transformations, Exposures, and
Intimations of Rousseau in The Possessed

For I the Lord thy God am a jealous God, visiting the iniquity of the fathers upon the children unto the third and fourth generation of them that hate me.
— *Exodus 20:5*

It is [the reader's] business to collect these scattered elements and to determine the being which is composed of them; the result must be his work.
— Rousseau, *The Confessions*

"Plato, Rousseau, Fourier, aluminum columns — all this is fit perhaps for sparrows, but not for human society. But since the future social form is necessary precisely now, when we are all finally going to act, so as to stop any further thinking about it, I am suggesting my own system of world organization . . . Starting with unlimited freedom, I conclude with unlimited despotism."
— Shigalev, in *The Possessed*

SHE: Why do I never see you, my dear friend? I am worried about you . . . a whole week has gone by. If I had not been told that you are in good health I should suppose that you are ill . . . Oh dear, what can be the matter with you? You have no business in hand, and you can have no troubles. For if you had, I flatter myself that you would have come straight away to confide in me. Can it be that you are ill? Adieu, my good friend; and may my adieu bring me a good-morning from you.

HE: I can tell you nothing yet. I am waiting till I am better informed, which shall be sooner or later. In the meantime rest assured that persecuted innocence will find a defender zealous enough to make its slanderers repent, whoever they may be.

SHE: I must say that your letter alarms me. What can it possibly mean? I have read it over more than two dozen times. Really I cannot understand a word of it.

HE: . . . But do you know how I shall atone for my errors in the short time I have still to spend near you? By doing what no one else will do; by frankly telling you what the world thinks of you . . . Notwithstanding all the self-styled friends who surround you, when you see me depart you can say farewell to truth. You will never find anyone else who will tell it to you.

SHE: I did not understand your letter of this morning. I told you so because it was the truth. I do understand this evening's. Have no fear that I shall ever answer it. I am too anxious to forget it.

After the terrible falling out between Stepan Trofimovich and Varvara Petrovna, Stepan prepares to quit his *amie* forever. Do we read here an epistolary exchange between them which Dostoevsky drafted in his notebooks, but never inserted into the novel proper? Certainly the dear friends were, continually — for twenty years — in the habit of writing each other, whether both were living under the same roof, or whether Stepan had moved into his cottage on the grounds of Varvara's estate. Varvara, like the "she" of the letters, prided herself on being full of common sense, and, although lately distracted by the influence of new, self-styled friends, was nonetheless devoted to Stepan. Stepan, though extremely sentimental and often frightened, was equally devoted to Varvara.

There are, unquestionably, certain compelling similarities between this pair and the true authors of these excerpts. A strong-willed, middle-aged woman is writing to a sentimental, timorous, middle-aged man. She is impatient. He is preoccupied with imagined conspiracies and persecutions. She is decidedly plain; he, rather ridiculously, prides himself on his attractiveness to women. Throughout their relationship, his role is more feminine, hers more masculine. She even supports him financially. He lives on the edge of her estate, and their frequent letters travel, at most, across the park. She is Mme D' Épinay; he is Jean-Jacques Rousseau.[1]

Dostoevsky's reaction to Rousseau, as we have already begun to see, spanned the length of his writing career. Most often, Dostoevsky alternated between vitriolic polemic with and frequently outrageous parodies of the "Jean-Jacques" of the *Confessions. The Insulted and Injured, Notes from Underground, Crime and Punishment, The Idiot,* "The Dream of a Ridiculous Man," and *A Raw Youth* all contain both polemic and parody directed at Rousseau.[2] In *The Possessed* Stavrogin's written statement, which is read on printed sheets by the monk Tikhon, embodies one of Dostoevsky's most substantial moral critiques of the Rousseau of the *Confessions* and of the genre of the written confession in general. Leonid Grossman was the first to remark upon the significant presence of Rousseau in Stavrogin's confession in his remarkable essay "Stilistika Stavrogina."[3] Since Grossman wrote his essay, many other scholars have further explored the presence of Rousseau in this novel. Brian Wolfson, for example, in his fascinating article "*C'est la faute à Rousseau:* Possession as Device in *The Demons*" articulates the many aspects of Rousseau present in Stavrogin and argues convincingly that the chapter "At Tikhon's" forms "an integral part of the novel's text."[4] He highlights the connections between Stavrogin's document and Rousseau's *Confessions:* "The nature of Tikhon's principal objection, it seems, is moral: Stavrogin's document is animated not by a need to repent but by a powerful desire to justify himself. . . . The suggestion that Stavrogin's intentions might be as vile as his grammar merely develops a formulation already present in Stavrogin's document — in the passage that links rhetorically the Rousseauist confessional form and the vice of self-abuse" (103).[5]

It is always, fortunately, tricky to write about sources, influences, and literary transformations in Dostoevsky's fiction. A single fictional episode in Dostoevsky's canon, if it has any sources at all, is most likely to have at least two sources, if not more. Thus, for example, the famous scene of Kirillov's suicide bears an uncanny resemblance to a similar scene in Charles Dickens's *Martin Chuzzlewit* (chapter 51). But it bears an equally unsettling resemblance to material from Victor Hugo's *Le dernier jour d'un condamné.*[6] Or, in *The Idiot,* Ferdyshchenko's narrative about stealing a three-ruble note from the table of his hostess and allowing her servant, Darya, to be blamed for the deed finds its sources in the famous Marion episode of Book II of Rousseau's *Confessions* as well as in Dostoevsky's own previous work (the episode in *Crime and Punishment* between Luzhin and Sonya in which Luzhin tried to frame her for stealing money that he has insidiously dropped into her pocket, another scene in which Rousseau's presence lurks). All of these episodes are, among other things, about displaced desire.

Likewise Stavrogin's confession in *The Possessed* contains distinct echoes of Valkovsky's in *The Insulted and Injured* and of the underground man in *Notes from Underground.* Significantly, all three confessions draw upon Rousseau's.[7] Moreover, Stavrogin initially had intended to make his confession public — in a random way — to the multitudes, not just to a small circle of readers who deliberately choose to read it. By the time Tikhon reads Stavrogin's statement, it has already been printed, and as Stavrogin pulls the sheets from his pocket, he tells Tikhon, "Here are the sheets which are intended for distribution. If only one man reads them, then, know that I shall not conceal them any longer and they will be read by everyone."[8] Rousseau had also sought to thrust his *Dialogues* (an extension of his *Confessions*) upon the world in like fashion. After an unsuccessful attempt to place his *Dialogues* on the high altar of Notre Dame, he had given copies of them to Étienne Condillac and to a visiting Englishman, and at last, he tried to hand out a circular to passersby in which he pleaded for his voice to be heard by all Frenchmen.[9]

Dostoevsky had explicitly linked the genre of literary confession with the acts of indecent exposure and masturbation as early as his 1861 novel *The Insulted and Injured*. His subsequent repeated linkage of this genre with these practices may have placed him within a kind of cultural convention of his time, though his position is undoubtedly more extreme: Dostoevsky repeatedly implies that a literary, purely secular confession constitutes simultaneously an act of private masturbatory self-gratification and an obscene act of self-exposure to others. Thomas Laqueur begins his book *Solitary Sex: A Cultural History of Masturbation* by asserting that "modern masturbation can be dated with a precision rare in cultural history." It was, as Stephen Greenblatt has put it, "the creature of the Enlightenment."[10] In earlier periods masturbation, though frowned upon, was not imbued with such a weighty baggage of the dangerous and the immoral. What is most interesting, in both Laqueur's book and Greenblatt's review of it, is the linkage among masturbation, fiction, and reading. Greenblatt eloquently highlights this important connection:

> There is a second modern innovation that similarly focused the anxieties attached to solitary sex: solitary reading. "It was not an accident" (Laqueur again) that *Onania* was published in the same decade as Defoe's first novels. For it was reading — and not just any reading, but reading the flood of books churned out by the literary marketplace — that seemed from the eighteenth century onward at once to reflect and to inspire the secret vice. The enabling mechanism here was the invention of domestic spaces in which people could be alone, coupled with a marked increase in private, solitary, silent reading. The great literary form that was crafted to fit these spaces and the reading practices they enabled was the novel. Certain novels were, of course specifically written as *Rousseau* put it, to be read with one hand. But it was not only through pornography that masturbation and the novel were closely linked. Reading novels — even high-minded, morally uplifting novels — generated a certain kind of absorption, a deep engagement of the imagination, a bodily intensity that could, it was feared, veer with terrifying ease toward the dangerous excesses of self-pleasure."[11]

Underpinning this linkage between solitary reading and solitary sex was the ungovernable power of the freewheeling imagination in both activities. Greenblatt continues:

> It was not only the solitude in which novels could be read that contributed to the difference between the two attacks; the absence of the bodies of the actors and hence the entire reliance on imagination seemed to make novels more suitable for solitary than social sex. Eighteenth-century doctors, tapping into ancient fears of the imagination, were convinced that when sexual excitement was caused by something unreal, something not actually present in the flesh, that excitement was at once unnatural and dangerous. The danger was greatly intensified by its addictive potential: the masturbator, like the novel reader — or rather, precisely as novel reader — could willfully mobilize the imagination, engaging in an endless creation and renewing of fictive desire. And shockingly, with the spread of literacy, this was a democratic, equal opportunity vice. The destructive pleasure was just as available to servants as to masters and, still worse, just as available to women as to men.[12]

D. H. Lawrence had, in like spirit, characterized his dislike of reading Dostoevsky and of the other "morbidly introspective Russians" in similar terms (although he later changed his mind). He found Dostoevsky to be "morbidly wallowing in adoration of Jesus, then getting up and spitting in His beard. . . . It's all masturbation, half-baked, and one gets tired of it."[13] Rousseau's notion that there were certain novels that were written to be read with one hand pithily expresses his contempt for a certain kind of novel and a certain kind of reading. How ironic then that metaphorically speaking, from Dostoevsky's vantage point, Rousseau's *Confessions* constitute precisely such a one-handed text.

According to Laqueur, by the beginning of the twentieth century, in large part due to Freud, masturbation was no longer demonized, though its connections with the literary remained. Greenblatt maps the evidence of this change through his reading of Marcel Proust:

> Conjuring up his childhood in Combray, Proust's narrator recalls that at the top of his house, "in the little room that smelt of orris-root," he looked out through the half-opened window and:
>> with the heroic misgivings of a traveler setting out on a voyage of exploration or of a desperate wretch hesitating on the verge of self-destruction, faint with emotion, I explored, across the bounds of my own experience, an untrodden path which for all I knew was deadly — until the moment when a natural trail like that left by a snail smeared the leaves of the flowering currant that dropped around me.
> For this brief moment in *Swann's Way* (1913), it is as if we had reentered the cultural world that Laqueur chronicles so richly, the world in which solitary

sex was a rash voyage away from the frontiers of the natural order, a headlong plunge, into a realm of danger and self-destruction. Then, with the glimpse of the snail's trail, the landscape resumes its ordinary, everyday form, and the seemingly untrodden path is disclosed — as so often in Proust — to be exceedingly familiar.[14]

Though the linkage between these two practices — reading and masturbation, that each draw so heavily upon imagination and that each frequently occur in solitude — no longer seems dangerous, the analogy remains potent.

Like Proust, Dostoevsky and his characters set out with "heroic misgivings" upon "untrodden paths." But unlike Proust, even as they probe the innermost recesses of self, they cannot overthrow embarrassment and shame. Perhaps this is why, despite Dostoevsky's many modernities of form and philosophical outlook, he remains so firmly a novelist of the nineteenth century.

In the 1871 version of Stavrogin's confession, Dostoevsky actually has Stavrogin mention Rousseau. Stavrogin admits that although he gave himself up to the same vice as did Rousseau, he abruptly stopped this habit (presumably masturbation) at seventeen (11:14). Hence we may deduce that Stavrogin had probably read Rousseau's *Confessions* during his youth, and, if he read them later, it is then significant that he chose to compare this early stage of his biography to Rousseau's.

And who, until he turned sixteen, was Stavrogin's tutor, the director of his reading and of his "moral development" (10:35; 53)? Stepan Trofimovich Verkhovensky. Of their relationship, the narrator-chronicler observes, "We must assume that the teacher (*pedagog*) somewhat upset the nerves of his pupil. When, at the age of sixteen, Nikolai was taken to the *lycée,* he looked debilitated and pale, and was strangely quiet and pensive" (10:35; 54). Are these not the shared cultural signals in the nineteenth century of reading too much and of masturbation?[15]

Numerous sources for the character of Stepan Trofimovich Verkhovensky exist — among them, Alexander Herzen, Boris Chicherin, Korsh, Durov, Nikolai Kukol'nik, Ivan Turgenev, and Vissarion Belinsky.[16] Most important, however, is T. N. Granovsky, whose name stands for Stepan's throughout many of the notes for the novel. Stepan Trofimovich, it is customary to point out, represents a repository of the beliefs of the men of the forties in Russia — the liberal, intellectual, Westernizers. Nevertheless, despite these many sources, Stepan Trofimovich is a surprisingly new creation in Dostoevsky's canon (much as Vronsky is in Tolstoy's).[17] Thus, however many antecedents we may discover in Russian intellectual history for Stepan, he is, above all, a fully realized and highly original fictional character. Deborah Martinsen, following the philosophy of Catherine Wilson, has characterized Stepan Trofimovich as a "self deceiver." According to Wilson, "the self-deceiver does not simply possess inconsistent beliefs. He is said, rather, to have made himself believe what he knows to be not true."[18]

Having asserted Stepan's ultimate independence from all the Russian historical figures Dostoevsky drew upon in order to create him, by now it is clear that in this chapter I have added another historical name to the list, that of the European incarnate, Jean-Jacques Rousseau. Although it would be fascinating to consider the ways in which Dostoevsky transformed aspects from all these many historical people into his fictional character and to contemplate that hybrid as a totality, my focus here centers on Rousseau. Rousseau himself — as the father of French Romanticism, as the author of the *Confessions* (above all a celebration of the individual), as a lifelong exile first from Geneva, then from France, and as a political and social thinker who rebelled against the established order — exerted a powerful influence, both negative and positive, over "the men of the forties" in Russia. He was, in effect, a spiritual godfather, hated by some, revered by others, of this generation.

In 1846 Belinsky, upon reading the *Confessions,* wrote, "I am now reading the *Confessions.* In all my life few books have affected me so powerfully as this one has."[19] Indeed, Rousseau's influence has been crucial for Russian writers on all sides of the political spectrum: Karamzin, Chernyshevsky, Tolstoy, Dostoevsky, to name only a few. Thomas Barran has documented the complex influence of Rousseau on Russian writers in the late eighteenth and early nineteenth centuries. He gives a persuasive reading of Karamzin's 1802 story "My Confession" as a work that points out the folly "of others who try to find or create themselves by imitating Rousseau." The story is, in Barran's reading, "the first significant piece of anti-confessional fiction in classical Russian literature." He finds that "Karamzin was able to split Rousseau's legacy into two categories: works written by the benevolent genius, and works produced by the tormented paranoid."[20] That view of the two Rousseaus or a split Rousseau has endured, both within Russia and outside it. In *The Possessed* Dostoevsky also draws on this notion. The Rousseau-like qualities of Stepan Trofimovich are not, of course, the darker ones evidenced in the character of Stavrogin. Dostoevsky's larger point about the pernicious influence of Rousseau's ideas, however, and possibly one even more ominous than the result of any scrutiny of Stavrogin as a freestanding character, is achieved through the depiction of the father-son, tutor-pupil paradigm. Thus Stepan Trofimovich and Stavrogin are far more closely linked to each other than they may seem to readers at first glance.

Stepan Trofimovich's life bears crucial resemblances to Rousseau's. Dostoevsky's creation of Stepan thus holds yet another clue to his ideas about Rousseau. Thus, it is a sleight of hand of typical Dostoevskian skill, economy, and genius that Rousseau's vexed presence should hover, though in very different ways, on both sides of the complex moral equation worked out in the novel (just as it does in history) — on the liberal "father" and his biography, and on his mysterious, revolutionary, symbolic "son" (or pupil) and his problematic use of the confessional genre.

I have already suggested that Dostoevsky's unwritten novel, *The Drunkards,* may in fact exist under its revised title, *Crime and Punishment.* Likewise, Dostoevsky had brooded about writing a novel entitled *Fathers and Children.* Certainly each of his last three novels could all have had this subtitle, but perhaps, ironically, *The Possessed* merits it most of all. It was not until later in 1874 (after he had written *The Possessed*) that Dostoevsky actually produced a written sketch of his idea for such a novel. Nevertheless, it is *The Possessed,* with its passionate and variegated polemic with both Turgenev the man and with his *Fathers and Sons* (1861), that addresses the theme of fathers and children in a way that may be even more complex than in his next two novels. The irony of this deepens even more when one considers that this is a novel that is extremely short on actual biological fathers. They are simply absent. Even Stepan Trofimovich's paternity of Pyotr Stepanovich is cast in doubt. Yet this work is, at the same time, the most profoundly generational of Dostoevsky's novels and perhaps even the most filled with strange "accidental" families.[21] The reader makes intimate contact with the conflict of generations through the ideas of the characters. Martinsen has described this generational conflict of ideas expressed through words as one that is so intense that the demarcations between ideas as weapons in the conflict and as the actual arena for that conflict become blurred: "In this fight, each generation's rhetoric serves not only as a weapon but as the battlefield."[22]

The characters of this novel, more than any other of Dostoevsky's creations, fulfill the prophecy of the narrator of *Notes from Underground* (1864) that men are so susceptible to ideas that they will contrive to be created by them. The underground man's manuscript breaks off with this very thought: "We are oppressed at being men — men with a real individual body and blood, we are ashamed of it, we think it a disgrace and try to contrive to be some sort of impossible generalized men. We are stillborn, and for generations past have been begotten, not by living fathers, and that suits us better and better. We are developing a taste for it. Soon we shall contrive to be born somehow from an idea. But enough; I don't want to write any more from 'Underground.'" The "editor" then adds the words that conclude the work: "The notes of this paradoxalist do not end here, however. He could not refrain from going on with them, but it seems to us that we may stop here."[23]

By ending *Notes from Underground* in this way, Dostoevsky has doubly underlined the importance of his notion that men and literary characters are being begotten from ideas. The underground man abruptly announces, having expressed this idea about men being created by ideas, that he no longer wishes to write any more from "Underground." The "editor" either does not pay attention to the underground man's deliberate words of closure or he simply chooses to ignore them. Either way this allows the editor to highlight or foreground the same idea. First, the editor directly contradicts the underground man's words — "I don't want to write anymore from 'Underground,'" and tells his readers that the underground man's notes "do not end here." Although the underground man "could not refrain from continuing going on," it has seemed to the editor that precisely at this juncture and with the expression of this final thought about men contriving somehow to be born of ideas that the editor finds it fitting to end. It is in *The Possessed* that the characters have contrived most fully to be born of ideas.

The most striking resemblances between Stepan Trofimovich and the Rousseau of the *Confessions* lie in certain elemental biographical details. The narrator-chronicler twice stresses that Stepan Trofimovich is fifty-three years old. Dostoevsky was notorious for muddling the ages of his characters. Their age gains frequently did not mesh with the passage of time in his novels. Stepan is no exception. The narrator-chronicler, in his introductory chapter, describes him as being fifty-three, and then later, as the action of the novel begins, Varvara Petrovna, in urging Stepan to "propose" to Dasha, exclaims impatiently, "What do your fifty-three years matter?" (10:19, 61; 33, 86). It is unclear, however, whether the first reference to his age describes Stepan during a period several years before the main events of the novel occur. What is clear, however, is that Dostoevsky has mentally assigned the age of fifty-three to Stepan, regardless of the passage of time in the novel. Rousseau's *Confessions*, begun in 1765 — fifty-three years after his birth — describe the first fifty-three years of his life.

Like the exiled Rousseau, Stepan emphasized his own "civic role" and, the narrator-chronicler tells us, enjoyed the "pleasant fancy of being a public figure. For example, he was extremely fond of his position as a 'persecuted' man, or, as it were, an 'exile'" (10:7; 20). Rousseau, despite his genuine political problems, labored under the delusions of an increasingly acute persecution mania. "In the abyss of evil in which I am sunk I feel the weight of blows struck at me; I perceive the immediate instrument; but I can neither see the hand which directs it nor the means by which it works. . . . The authors of my ruin have discovered the unimaginable art of turning the public into the unsuspecting accomplice of their plot" (*Confessions,* 544).

Rousseau regarded himself, always, as an exile. The narrator-chronicler outlines Stepan's similar delusions. "How's that for the power of one's own imagination? He himself believed sincerely for his whole life that he was constantly regarded with suspicion in certain spheres, that his steps were continually known and watched" (10:8; 22). Stepan, like Rousseau in his persona of Jean-Jacques, prided himself on spending his life as a "living monument of reproach" (*"voploshchennoi ukoriznoiu"*) to his country (10:11; 27). Yet Dostoevsky undercut his character by having the narrator-chronicler point out repeatedly that the "whirlwind of concurrent events" that had precipitated Stepan into his life as a watchful and watched exile had not, in fact, ever occurred. The reader of Rousseau's *Confessions* must for himself distinguish between fact and fancy in the writer's autobiography. To the degree that Dostoevsky did indeed draw upon Rousseau as a model for Stepan Trofimovich, however, he consistently made his own creation more ridiculous than its real-life source, just as he made Stavrogin darker and more demonic.

Throughout most of his life Rousseau was dependent upon women for emotional as well as financial support. Fittingly, he called Mme de Warens, the greatest love of his life, "mamma." When we first encounter Stepan Trofimovich, he is already the veteran of two marriages and has, for the last twenty years, lived under the wing—emotionally and financially—of Varvara Petrovna Stavrogina. In Book IX of the *Confessions* Rousseau describes his relationship with Mme d' Épinay. For two years he lived in a cottage (the Hermitage) on her estate of Montmorency, where he found it, at first, "delightful to be the guest of [his] friend" (*Confessions,* 376). Stepan also enjoyed a "refined and delicate" union with his "friend," Varvara Petrovna. Both women —notably plain and middle-aged—have literary pretensions: each is extremely proud, at first, to be the guardian and protector of an important literary and political figure. Both men are also preoccupied with matters of education: Rousseau, the author of *Émile,* was also working out a "system of education" (*Confessions,* 381) for the son of Mme de Chenonceaux; Stepan, of course, was the tutor of Stavrogin as well as of Lise Tushina and Dasha Shatova. Each man carries on a kind of sexless flirtation with his protectoress or patron and has as a rival a more famous "German" — Grimm for Rousseau and Karmazinov for Stepan.

Yet both Rousseau and Stepan, despite a mutual preoccupation with education and despite their extreme sentimentality and self-proclaimed sensitivity, have given their own children away to the care of others. They have betrayed the very bonds whose import they affirm. Rousseau deposited each of his five children, as infants, into a foundling hospital. Upon the death of his first wife the "grief-stricken" Stepan sent his five-year-old son Pyotr, "the fruit of a first, joyous and still unclouded love" from Paris to Russia to be brought up by distant relatives (10:11; 26).

Each man proclaims, with breathtaking hypocrisy, his continuing concern and love for these banished children. Rousseau initially admits that he might have erred. He presents himself as a man with all the qualities of an ideal father: "my warm-heartedness, my acute sensibility . . . my innate goodwill . . . my burning love for the great, the true, the beautiful . . . my horror of evil in every form," and so on (*Confessions*, 333). Although these words have a comic, bombastic ring, Rousseau is writing in all seriousness about himself. He describes the pain he felt on sending them off, but he ultimately defends his decision. "All things considered, I made the best choice for my children" (*Confessions*, 334). Likewise, the supposedly "grief-stricken" Stepan had already been separated from his wife and child three years before his wife's death. And Dostoevsky resorts to pure humor in ridiculing this situation as he has Stepan describe to the narrator-chronicler a conversation with the now grown Pyotr, whose estate Stepan has already squandered, "you wretch . . . hasn't my heart been aching for you all my life, though I did send you away by parcel post?" (10:171; 220–21). For each man theories of education and claims about the love of his children conceal a dreadful fact of abandonment. These fathers, who each presume themselves to be important educators of the young, have betrayed not only their children but the fundamental bonds of parenthood. Yet each self-deceiver believes himself to be a loving father and a worthy teacher.

In addition each man finds it necessary to carry on a frantic correspondence with his protectoress. The day's exchange of letters between Rousseau and Mme d' Épinay that appear at the beginning of this chapter greatly resemble the kind of correspondence passing between Stepan Trofimovich and Varvara Petrovna. "It is true," writes the narrator-chronicler, "that he was passionately fond of writing, that he would write to her even when he was living in the same house, and during his hysterical episodes he would write two letters a day" (10:13; 29). All parties, of course, carefully preserved their correspondence.

Moreover, each woman made a kind of child or creation out of her middle-aged male ward. "But one thing," writes the narrator-chronicler of Stepan, "he failed to notice to the very end, namely that he had at last for her become her son, her creation, one might almost say her invention" (10:16; 29). In fact, "she herself designed even the suit he wore all his life" (10:19; 33). Mme d' Épinay had taken a similar maternal, creative interest in the most intimate aspects of the existence of her Jean-Jacques. Rousseau describes how one freezing morning he opened a parcel from Mme d' Épinay "and found in it a little under-petticoat of English flannel, which she informed me she had worn, and out of which she wanted me to make myself a waistcoat. . . . This mark of more than friendly attention seemed to me so tender — it was as if she had stripped herself to clothe me — that in my emotion I kissed the note and the petticoat twenty times in tears" (*Confessions*, 407).

In 1762, when Rousseau claimed in the *Confessions* to have "given up literature" and to have resorted to a simpler, more pure life, he in part expressed his changed attitudes and independence by a change of dress. "I assumed Armenian costume. It was not a new idea, but had occurred to me several times. . . . It recurred to me often at Montmorency" (*Confessions*, 554). His change of costume, he stresses, also facilitated the treatment of his bladder complaint. Similarly, near the end of the novel, Stepan Trofimovich asserts his new independence with a change of costume. He sets out in an outfit he, too, has been mentally designing for some time — high boots like a hussar, a coat with a wide buckle, a broad-brimmed hat, a walking stick, a bag, and an umbrella. Both getups are ripe for literary and cultural deconstruction.

Each man, at times of intense emotional disturbance, suffers from a humiliating physical complaint that acts as a humbling bodily counterbalance to his lofty mental attitudes and ideas.[24] Rousseau's notorious bladder trouble finds an echo in Stepan's attacks of gastric catarrh. But *emotional* disturbance, unlike these embarrassing physical ailments, can ultimately drive each of them suddenly to cast off his role as dependent male: wounded dignity and the perceived betrayal of a grand friendship precipitates each to undertake a dramatically conceived flight. Years after the fact, Rousseau is still at pains to describe the indignation he had felt at Mme d' Épinay when at last relations between them had completely broken down. Still incensed by her last letter, which began, "After having shown you for many years every possible evidence of friendship and sympathy, I have nothing left for you but pity" (*Confessions*, 451), he writes: "It was necessary to depart immediately, whatever the weather, just as I was, even if I had to sleep in the woods and on the snow that then covered the ground . . . I found myself in the most terrible embarrassment that I have ever known in my life" (*Confessions*, 452). Likewise, Stepan Trofimovich, also in the face of encroaching winter, cannot bear Varvara Petrovna's pity and disdain. He plans a departure every bit as imminent and dramatic as Rousseau's. He tells her that as soon as the fête is over, "I shall take up my bag that very evening, my pauper's bag, and leave all my belongings behind me. . . . I always thought that there was something higher than food between us . . . And so I go on my way to make amends. I'm setting out late in the year, in the late autumn, a mist lies over the fields, my future road is covered with the rigid hoarfrost of old age" (10:266; 345).[25]

Immediately after their respective flights, they each become seriously ill.

Rousseau eventually recovers; Stepan Trofimovich does not. Rousseau's prolonged wanderings were largely inspired by his unshakeable, nightmarish, largely imagined fear of conspiracies against him. He describes how he had received anonymous letters, and he writes that "it is my nature to fear the dark; I dread and loathe its black presence; mystery always disquiets me. . . . If I were to catch sight of a figure in the night wrapped up in a white sheet, I should be afraid" (*Confessions*, 521–23). Similarly, as Stepan begins his flight, he meets Lise and tells her, "I'm running from a nightmare, from a delirious dream" (10:412; 534).

At this point, however, Dostoevsky's integrity as an artist surpasses his ideological fury. Throughout the novel Stepan Trofimovich has repeatedly enacted and embodied aspects of Dostoevsky's image of the loathed Rousseau whose ideas, confessions, and conversions were bogus, false, and productive of harm to others. Rousseau's ideas, in Dostoevsky's mind, had become viruses of the most malignant strain. They had had already formed a part of the disease of harmfully contagious ideas that we saw operative in the air of *Crime and Punishment*. Within the world of *The Possessed*, they constitute an epidemic; they resemble the plague of which Raskolnikov dreamt in the epilogue. When readers compare Stepan Trofimovich to Rousseau, it quickly becomes evident that he is equally self-delusional, equally responsible for spreading attractive ideas that frequently have negative, violent, dire consequences. Nevertheless, this character whom Dostoevsky has portrayed with unrelenting, albeit affectionate, irony undergoes an authentic conversion experience.

Dostoevsky's polemic with Rousseau in this novel is three-pronged. The literary, printed confession Rousseau had made so famous finds its ugly demise in Stavrogin's printed sheets. Rousseau's political ideas express themselves as fully diseased in the political reasoning of Shigalev. Wolfson demonstrates how Shigalev has included Rousseau "in his pantheon of proto-revolutionary thinkers, albeit in a conventional context. . . . As Dostoevsky reveals through Stavrogin, Shigalev's formula is essentially a projection of the Rousseauian notion of the relationship between the self and the others onto a social and political realm. The degeneration of Shigalev's system into a dictatorship parallels the rise of an emotional tyranny out of a crusade in the name of cultivating the elusive 'uniqueness.' "[26] It is Stepan Trofimovich, however, who has, within the world of the novel, been the primary carrier of this virus of Rousseauian ideas. Yet, in the end, Dostoevsky allows him to recover, at least partially. He grants him a kind of ideological immunity to the disease he has spread to so many others.

Thus it is at this moment of the greatest biographical similarity between these two sentimental old men — who both declare, at long last, independence from a protecting female — that Stepan Trofimovich begins, morally and spiritually, to transcend Rousseau. Rousseau's departure from the Hermitage was inspired mainly by his wounded vanity. Although Stepan's vanity has suffered an equally painful blow, his comic yet passionate and courageous farewell to Varvara contains a significant prediction. "You have always despised me, but I shall end up like a knight who has remained faithful to his lady, for your opinion has always been dearer to me than anything in the world. From this moment on I shall accept nothing, but shall honor you disinterestedly" (10: 266; 345). Stepan's words prove true.[27]

It is customary to regard Rousseau's *Confessions,* like those of St. Augustine, as a work that describes a crucial conversion.[28] For me, at least, any moment of conversion or authentic spiritual growth in Rousseau is difficult to locate, and when found, is unconvincing at best. Stepan Trofimovich, on the other hand, despite — and perhaps because of — the depths of ridiculousness to which he is capable of descending, does undergo, just before his death, an authentic conversion experience, one of the most moving Dostoevsky ever represented.

Stepan Trofimovich sets out on the high road with no particular destination. In describing this decision on Stepan's part, the narrator-chronicler, despite his habitual irony, also displays respect and understanding for the old man's flight. He sets himself to imagine what was in Stepan's mind as he set out: "No, better simply the high road, better simply to set off for it, and walk along it and to think of nothing so long as he could put off thinking. The high road is something very very long, of which one cannot see the end — like human life, like human dreams. There is an idea in the open road, but what sort of idea is there in traveling with posting tickets? Posting tickets would mean an end to ideas. *Vive le grand route* and then as God wills" (10:480–81; 664). (This description of the high road that is intimately connected with human life and dreams recalls the wistful, dreamy mood in which the narrator of *The House of the Dead* gazed upon the riverbank and its distant opposite shore [4:178–79; 274–75].)[29]

Dostoevsky's engines for the rendering of a conversion experience begin to get into gear. Stepan Trofimovich meets the "gospel-woman," Sofya Matveevna, who is another "peddler of Christ" reminiscent of both the "cheating peddler of Christ" in Myshkin's parable about faith and the attractive young woman whose baby has just smiled for the first time. As we have seen elsewhere in Dostoevsky's writings, a memory occurs at the needed moment. Stepan suddenly remembers that he has been wanting to read the Gospels "for a long time." "The idea occurred to him at the moment that he had not read the Gospel for thirty years at least, and at most had recalled some passages of it seven years before when reading Renan's *Vie de Jésus*" (10:487; 653). Stavrogin, with deadly vanity, had wanted to hand out his printed confession to the multitudes. Stepan Trofimovich, in contrast, seems ready to put his own story aside and attempt to immerse himself in the living stream of something much larger, that world where all are responsible for all. "You see I . . . *J'aime le peuple.*" He tells the gospel-woman, "I will gladly sell your beautiful little books. Yes, I feel that perhaps there is an idea, *quelque chose de tres nouveu dans ce genre*" (10:490–91; 658). The passage brims with a mixture of Stepan's sincerity and foolishness, the narrator-chronicler's admiration laced with his ridicule of him, and, perhaps, a smattering of authorial awareness of and self-irony at his own artistic passion for portraying "the new" that Dostoevsky parodies here.

Stepan Trofimovich's flight of fancy escalates. He begins to dream of promulgating the living gospel "according to Stepan":

> The peasants are religious, *c'est admis,* but they don't yet know the gospel. I will expound it to them. . . . By verbal explanation one might correct the mistakes in that remarkable book, which I am of course prepared to treat with the utmost respect. I will be of service even on the high road. . . . Oh, we will forgive, we will forgive, first of all we will forgive all and always. . . We will hope that we too shall be forgiven. Yes, for all, every one of us, have wronged one another, all are guilty!"
>
> "That's a very good saying, I think sir."
>
> "Yes, yes . . . I feel that I am speaking well. I shall speak to them very well . . ." (10:490–91; 658)

Even as Dostoevsky portrays the ridiculousness and the vanity of his character, he allows Stepan to display a veritable passion of sincerity that exposes but does not ultimately undercut him.

Stavrogin had "confessed" a heightened, dramatized version of his life to Tikhon. Stepan Trofimovich also "confesses" a heightened, dramatized version of his life to an embarrassed and reluctant Sophia Matveevna. In his exaggerated version of his autobiographical confession, Varvara Petrovna figures as an "enchanting brunette" and Darya Pavlovna as a "blond." But unlike Stavrogin, Stepan ultimately bows down before his confessor, and at last speaks the very kind of truth that neither Rousseau nor Stavrogin could ever utter, "It was all lies that I told you this evening — to glorify myself, to make it splendid, from pure wantonness — all, all, every word, oh, I am a wretch, I am a wretch!" (10:480–81; 664). At last Sofya Matveevna, like Sonya Marmeladova before her, reads the Gospel aloud. She reads him three passages: She chooses the first of these, the Sermon on the Mount; then Stepan Trofimovich asks her to "read something more, just the first thing you come across. . . . Wherever it opens, wherever it happens to open" (10:497; 666). She reads from the Apocalypse. Finally, the dying Stepan Trofimovich requests a particular passage from the Bible: "Now read me another passage. . . . About the pigs . . . About the pigs . . . that's there too . . . *ces cochons.* I remember the devils entered into swine and they all were drowned. You must read me that; I'll tell you why afterwards. I want to remember it word for word. I want it word for word" (10:498–99; 667). The passage is also, of course, the epigraph to the novel, the very passage the narrator-chronicler tells us, at this decisive moment, that *he* (as opposed to the author, Dostoevsky) had chosen as "the epigraph of my chronicle" (10:498; 668).

Thus Stepan Trofimovich, the narrator-chronicler, and Dostoevsky share a preoccupation with this passage from the Bible. Its import for readers could not be underscored more strongly. These swine are the infectious ideas polluting Russia's air, the little devils — the trichinae — that had entered Russia. Stepan continues: "They are all the sores, all the foul contagions, all the impurities, all the devils great and small that have multiplied in that great invalid, our beloved Russia . . . and I perhaps at the head of them, and we shall cast ourselves down, possessed and raving, from the rocks into the sea, and we shall all be drowned — and a good thing too, for that is all we are fit for. But the sick man will be healed and 'will sit at the feet of Jesus'" (10:499; 668).[30] Dostoevsky has imparted to the dying Stepan Trofimovich his own precious and potent metaphors involving ideas, devils, and disease. Moreover, he permits him to be healed.

Throughout his life Rousseau had struggled to determine the nature of truth — to learn how to discover the lie immersed in truth and to decipher the truth concealed in the lie. The preoccupation with uncovering the essential meanings of truth and falsehood may be an essential part of any autobiographical enterprise, or of any character whose main activity is the scrutiny of the self. For those lies that we tell are intimately related to our desires. But so are our proclaimed truths. Just as we often suppress those ideas or desires that seem to us the truest, so may those same ideas or desires be the ones we seek most persistently to express. Lionel Gossman addresses some of these considerations in his essay "The Innocent Art of Confession and Reverie." "Perhaps in autobiography, as in many other forms of imaginative writing, there are two impulses. One is to release a discourse that has been suppressed, to permit what could not be said, was not said, and is indeed unsayable — the thing that is at the heart of the writer's activity as a writer — to be said, or rather to be approximated. The other impulse is to imprison it again, to disguise it, to keep it at arm's length, by means of substitutions and displacements."[31] We have already seen how parables as a genre work both to conceal and to reveal. Gossman has identified a similar duality in the confessional genre: the desire to say what could not be said competes with the impulse to imprison it again. Dostoevsky has graphically illustrated this duality as well as that other primary confessional tension between wishing to utter the truth and lying.

Rousseau's final work, the autobiographical *Reveries of the Solitary Walker* (1782), revisits, now in the guise of meditation rather than revelation, many of the themes of the *Confessions*. In *The Reveries*, completed shortly before his death, Rousseau devotes the entire "Fourth Walk" to a close scrutiny of the nature of truth. He asks himself which truths should be revealed, which concealed. He looks back at his *Confessions* and at "the number of things of my own invention which I remembered presenting as true. . . . What surprised me most was that when I recalled these fabrications, I felt no real repentance. I, whose horror of falsehood outweighs all my other feelings . . . by what strange inconsistency could I lie so cheerfully without the slightest twinge of regret?"[32] This question leads Rousseau to a discussion of ethics, morality, and the nature of lies that function in the service of truth and vice versa.

Stepan Trofimovich shares Rousseau's preoccupation with truth and lies, with memory and invention (and so, of course, always, did Dostoevsky and some of his other important characters, particularly, as we have already seen, Razumihin). On the threshold of death, Stepan seems about to discover certain permanent meanings about truth. He, too, links this understanding of truth to confession, to what one chooses to reveal and to conceal. "My friend [Sofya Matveevna, the 'gospel-woman'], all my life I've been lying. Even when I spoke the truth, I never spoke for the sake of the truth but for my own sake" (10:497; 645). Yet Dostoevsky seems never to be able to resist having his characters take such statements one step farther, so that they ultimately join him in his own realm of unfinished paradox: "*Savez-vous,*" continues Stepan, "perhaps I am lying even now. The trouble is that I believe myself when I am lying" (10:497; 645). Such statements do not reveal an unfinalized world view as much as they do a final conviction that in some unfathomable way the truth and the lie partake together of some greater, inscrutable, yet perfect whole. The truth will out, but the lie will in — always concurrent. Curiously, Tolstoy, who had in his youth revered Rousseau, in later life commented to Gorky that "Rousseau lied and believed his lies."[33]

Aside from these correspondences between Rousseau and Stepan Trofimovich, there remain the vital differences between the interests and ideas of these two men, one real, the other fictional. Except for their mutual pursuit after definitions of truth, their other philosophical and intellectual interests do not really coincide. In these spheres, Stepan draws life from the Russian intellectuals of the 1840s. But Rousseau offers the rudimentary point of departure, the biographical frame. Each man unconsciously presents himself to his readers as an epitome of the sentimental, middle-aged man dependent on a strong-willed woman. Each exhibits a strong dichotomy between his timid self and his lofty words — his doctrines that will brook no compromise with honor. Each partakes of two separate existences — a biographical life filled with weakness, veniality, and compromise and a self created through language whose standards are unyielding.

If we admit Rousseau's presence in the character of Stepan Trofimovich, both Dostoevsky's ongoing polemic with Rousseau and the structure of *The Possessed* (often criticized as imperfect) become finer and more subtle. For if Rousseau stands behind both Stepan, the man of the 1840s, and Stavrogin, the mysterious dark hero figure of the 1860s, then the two generations, so deeply in dispute with each other, are also inextricably linked. The portrayal of this chain of guilt, this sharing of responsibility for the condition, the "madness," possessing Russia, is, as we know, one of Dostoevsky's main endeavors in *The Possessed*. Early in the novel, the narrator-chronicler had observed of Stepan and Stavrogin, "there was not the slightest difference between them" (10:35; 53). Each is, in his own way, a hopeless romantic. Each embraces borrowed European ideas that prove to be at best useless, at worst destructive, and many of these borrowings derived ultimately from Rousseau. Yet despite his comic ridiculousness, Stepan eventually transcends Rousseau, while Stavrogin in his confession cannot, despite his tragic awareness, separate himself from destructive vanity.

However, even if Stepan ultimately manages to escape comedy and achieve a genuine dignity and even greatness by the end of the novel, the traces of his guilt linger. Just as *The Brothers Karamazov* portrays the working of a mechanism by which grace travels through the world, so is *The Possessed* concerned with depicting the chain reactions of evil influence. Thus those ideas that seem gently comic in a character like Stepan can become, quite easily, transmuted and transformed into the deadly philosophies of others. We experience Stepan's desire to be greater than he is in the comic mode — hence his silly claims that he is an "exile," his insistence that he is being watched.

But how far removed are these weaknesses, in the end, from those to which Stavrogin succumbs in his confession? His desire to titillate, to describe his deeds as even worse than they are, his vanity are all dangerously akin to all these qualities as they exist in his tutor Stepan. Once again, the closing words of the underground man's narrative offer a telling gloss. He tells his readers, "As for what concerns me in particular, I have only in my life carried to an extreme what you have not dared to carry halfway, and what's more, you have taken your cowardice for good sense, and have found comfort in deceiving yourselves" (5:178; 140).[34] Stavrogin's confession takes Rousseau's *Confessions* to its darkest extremes, while Stepan's character, for the most part, attacks it through parody and ridicule. But the linkages between the tutor and his pupil remain significant.

It is a compelling irony that Dostoevsky himself so often resembled this Rousseau with whom, through his fiction, he so passionately argued. Both Belinsky and Nikolai Strakhov called attention to the negative resemblances between the two. Belinsky said of Rousseau, "I have a great loathing for this man. He so resembles Dostoevsky." Strakhov, in a letter to Tolstoy that was highly critical of Dostoevsky — calling him spiteful, envious, dissolute — added, "Like Rousseau, however, he considered himself the best and the happiest of men."[35] Certainly each man quarreled frequently with his friends, mistrusted them, was jealous of them, yet sought, too, to forgive and love them.

Dostoevsky, nevertheless, resembled Rousseau in positive ways as well. Each man hoped, and in his writings strove, for society's return to a simpler way of life in which the necessary complexities of the individual psyche could be minimized. Each, in his writings, portrayed with compassion the figure of the dreamer who loved, above all, to let his thoughts ramble as he himself wandered about outdoors. Each explored, unabashedly, the sensuality lurking in guilt and in punishment. Each, ultimately, sought for the reader to be the ultimate judge of all he had written. Above all, both Rousseau and Dostoevsky engaged themselves in an unceasing, intense search for authenticity — through seeking to portray the human soul in all its nakedness and in all its layered veils and adornments.

"My husband went past all the rooms and took me straight to the Sistine Madonna—the painting he considered the finest manifestation of human genius."
—Anna Grigorievna Dostoevsky

Raphael (Raffaello Sanzio) (1483–1520), *Sistine Madonna*. Painted for Pope Julius II as his present to the city of Piacenza, Italy. The church at Piacenza was dedicated to Pope Sixtus II (left), on the right Saint Barbara, 1512–1513. Oil on canvas, 269.5 × 201 cm.

"Not a single one of them shouts from the painting to the viewer, 'Look how unfortunate I am and how indebted you are to the People!' . . . You will be dreaming of this whole group of barge-haulers afterward; you will still recall them fifteen years later!"
— Dostoevsky

Ilya Repin (1844–1930), *The Boatmen of the Volga*, 1873. Oil on canvas, 131.5 × 281 cm.

Dostoevsky believed that "little pictures such as these" expressed a "love for humanity."

Vladimir Makovsky (1846–1920), *Listening to the Song of the Nightingale.*

TRETYAKOV GALLERY, MOSCOW, RUSSIA. PHOTO CREDIT: SCALA / ART RESOURCE, NY.

Unfortunately, Dostoevsky believed that the meaning of such paintings as these could not be understood by foreigners (such as a "German or a Viennese Y.d").

Vasily Perov (1834–1882), *The Hunters at Rest*, 1871. Oil on canvas, 119 x 183 cm.

STATE TRETYAKOV GALLERY, MOSCOW, RUSSIA.

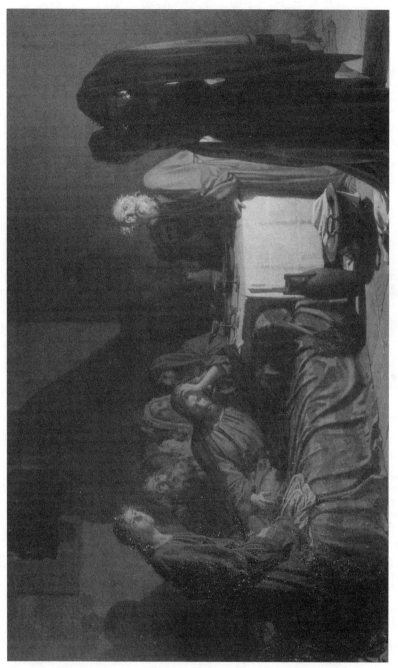

"Nothing at all is explained here; there is no historical truth here; there is not even any truth of genre here; everything here is false."
— Dostoevsky

Nikolai Ge (1831–1894), *Last Supper*, 1863. Oil on canvas, 283 × 283 cm.

"Why, that's a painting that might make some people lose their faith. . . . As for faith, I had four different encounters in two days last week." (Myshkin, *The Idiot*)

Hans the Younger Holbein (1497–1543), *Dead Christ*, 1521.

"The gentle emerald sea softly lapped the shore and kissed it with manifest, visible, almost conscious love. Tall, beautiful trees stood in all the glory of their green luxuriant foliage, and their innumerable leaves . . . welcomed me."
— "Dream of a Ridiculous Man"

Claude (Gellee) Lorrain (1600–1682), *Landscape with Acis and Galatea,* 1657.

Contemplation

"He stands, as it were, lost in thought . . . but if he were asked what he had been thinking about, he would remember nothing. . . . He may suddenly, after hoarding impressions for many years, abandon everything and go off to Jerusalem on a pilgrimage . . . or perhaps he will suddenly set fire to his native village, and perhaps do both." (The narrator-chronicler's description of Ivan Kramskoy's painting, *The Brothers Karamazov*)

Ivan Kramskoy (1836–1887), *The Meditator,* 1876. Oil on canvas.

THE MUSEUM OF RUSSIAN ART, KIEV, UKRAINE.

6

Unsealing the Generic Envelope and Deciphering "The Dream of a Ridiculous Man"

"I am not what I am."
—Iago in *Othello*

It is from the fruitful union of the grotesque with the sublime that the modern spirit is born.
—Victor Hugo

Real life is full of the ridiculous and is only sublime in its inner meaning.
—Dostoevsky in a letter of August 25, 1879

I turn now from Dostoevsky's long and tangled novel, *The Possessed,* to one of his shortest stories, "The Dream of a Ridiculous Man" (1877), which first appeared in *The Diary of a Writer.* This story was the final piece of fiction to appear in *The Diary.* It represents both a philosophical and a narrative culmination in the short form of much of Dostoevsky's thinking about conversion. At the same time, this brief text literally bristles with Dostoevsky's reworkings and transformations of other literary works, including some of his own. Thus this story becomes a repository in miniature of the central ideas with which the present study is grappling.

We know that Dostoevsky was a reader of Shakespeare. Like Shakespeare,

Dostoevsky was preoccupied by what I think of as the "Iago factor" — the problem of seemingly unmotivated evil. How is evil disseminated through the world? How can one write about what motivates it? By what mechanism does it travel? This theme permeates Dostoevsky's work, as does its converse: how does goodness travel through the world? In both cases the answer is frequently the same — through the power of words. Dostoevsky was as preoccupied with understanding the varieties of evil as he was with comprehending the nature of goodness; most of all, perhaps, he recognized that the border between the two could sometimes be difficult to discern.

Dostoevsky's "The Dream of a Ridiculous Man" (1877) is about just that: the power of the word to subvert, to pervert, and, possibly, to convert. Yet it is a typical Dostoevskian irony that a story focusing both structurally and semantically on the power of words should be so difficult to understand. It is a story whose central character (the narrator), upon choosing the vocation of preacher (*propovednik*), pleads above all to be understood, but whose author relentlessly wraps his creation in a verbal mantle of ambiguity.

For the most part, recent critical debates about "The Dream" have centered around the question of the sincerity and ultimate moral goodness of the main character, the dreamer.[1] Yet this fundamental and traditional question about interpretation of character has not been asked in a simple way. The most interesting critical explorations of the ridiculous man's character tend to concentrate on efforts to categorize the generic envelope in which he presents himself to us. If, the reasoning goes, that can be determined, then the character himself can be better understood. If, for example, the form of the story is utopian, the dreamer is a forward-looking idealist. If it is anti-utopian or dystopian, he is a disillusioned solipsist. If the form of the story is a fantastic dream sequence, our hero cries out to be understood psychologically. Or, as I argue in the last section of this chapter, if this is a conversion tale of the Christmas story variety, the main character, emboldened by his vision, cheerfully accepts and embraces his inevitable ridiculousness in the eyes of the world.

I have divided this chapter into four sections, each of which glances at this story from a different vantage point with regard to genre. These various vantage points in turn suggest competing tissues of meaning. The point, however, is that all exist simultaneously and continually reconfigure themselves before the reader's gaze. This tale represents, for both character and reader alike, an unfinished journey par excellence.

Dostoevsky, as we have already seen, was never one to make use of a genre or specific literary form in a straightforward manner. While nearly every key feature, unit of plot, and character in his canon ultimately descend from some traceable source or sources, that starting point functions primarily as a springboard. More often than not, Dostoevsky's borrowings ultimately lead him in such startling new directions that the final result bears few traces of the inspirational nugget. Such, I suggest, is the case with the relationship between "The Dream" and its inspirational texts, particularly "A Christmas Carol" (1843) by Charles Dickens.

Indeed, "The Dream" confirms the palimpsest-like nature of Dostoevsky's fiction generally, a palimpsest that extends to form, narrative tone, and theme alike, a palimpsest, moreover, in which the different layers of structure and meaning both collide and interact. It is in this context of fluid interaction and contradiction, then, that readers can most creatively approach Dostoevsky's work. Henry James, whose dislike of Dostoevsky's novels is well known, explicitly embraced a similar diversity of vision in his own work. The description of the tasks of the author and the reader that he sets forth in the preface to *What Maisie Knew* (1897) can illuminate and validate our response to Dostoevsky at his most baffling moments: "The effort really to see and really to represent is no idle business in the face of the constant force that makes for muddlement. The great thing is indeed that the muddled state too is one of the very sharpest of the realities, that it also has colours and form and character, has often in fact a broad and rich comicality, many of the signs and values of the appreciable."[2]

These overarching generalities about palimpsests and Jamesian muddlement inevitably encase any close analysis of "The Dream." Nevertheless this story — one of Dostoevsky's shortest — teems with sources.

Swift, Rousseau, Poe

"All things in common nature should produce
Without sweat or endeavour: treason, felony,
Sword, pike, knife, gun, or need of any engine,
Would I not have; but nature should bring forth,
Of it own kind, all foison, all abundance,
To feed my innocent people."
— Gonzalo, in *The Tempest*

"What objections can be made against a writer, who relates only plain facts, that happened in distant countries . . . ? I have carefully avoided every fault with which common writers of travels are too often justly charged. Besides, I . . . write without passion, prejudice or ill-will . . . I write for the noblest end, to inform and instruct mankind; over whom I may, without breach of modesty, pretend to some superiority."
— Gulliver, in *Gulliver's Travels*

The ridiculous man's descriptions of the customs of the people living on his visionary island of that "other/not other" Greek archipelago resemble, most of all, the way of life of the Houyhnhnms, those spiritually sensitive yet rational horses whom the rapidly disintegrating Gulliver came to love so much on his fourth voyage. Gulliver's admiration closely prefigures that of the ridiculous man for his island-dwellers: "Neither is reason among them a point problematical as with us . . . it is not mingled with, obscured or discolored by passion and interest." When the Houyhnhnms die, "their friends and relations [express] neither joy nor grief at their departure . . . they take a solemn leave . . . as if they were going to some remote part of the country." Gulliver is deeply impressed that the Houyhnhnms had in their language no words for lie, doubt, opinion, or evil. The verb *to die,* moreover, meant "to retire to one's first mother."[3] Indeed, the ridiculous man's discourse — an enclosed monologic narrative — calls Swift's Gulliver to mind as well. By the end of his account, Gulliver too has become a kind of preaching madman, yet, unlike the ridiculous man's all-encompassing affirmation, his is a doctrine of sweeping aversion to all mankind. Gulliver's encounter with an ideal, unfallen society has rendered him unable to bear the human weaknesses, even the very humanity, of his contemporaries at home — all of which the ridiculous man actively embraces after his "return."

The ridiculous man's vision also offers us yet another chapter in Dostoevsky's lifelong literary reaction to Rousseau. I have already sought to demonstrate how Dostoevsky most often chose to polemicize with the Rousseau of the *Confessions* and to rework and recast certain of its key episodes, most notably Rousseau's account of the stolen ribbon, which had given Dostoevsky a richly laden structure of twisted desire with which to experiment.[4] Certainly the framing narrative context of "The Dream" is also that of a confession in the truest sense: the narrator admits to a secret crime, repents of it, and, in the course of his narrative, chooses a new path.[5]

In order to find the most tangible Rousseauian influence in "The Dream," however, one must turn to the work of the other Rousseau, Rousseau the political thinker and analyst of human society. The inhabitants of the ridiculous man's visionary island may be cousins to Gulliver's Houyhnhnms, but they also are siblings of the natural men Rousseau conjures up in his *Discourse on the Origins of Inequality* (1755). These natural men live by instinct, an instinct untroubled by passion and informed by the emotion of pity. The innate kindness and goodness of those whom the ridiculous man visits in his dream mirror this capacity for pity. Rousseau identifies pity in the natural man as an instinctive human drive that contributes to the "mutual preservation of the whole species. . . . It is pity which in the state of nature takes the place of laws, morals, and virtues, with the added advantage that no one there is tempted to disobey its gentle voice."[6] Superficially, perhaps, this Rousseauian notion of pity may seem to resemble Dostoevsky's ideas about compassion, expressed so eloquently by Myshkin in *The Idiot*. But the difference between these two conceptions is vast, for Rousseau's brand of pity can exist in a world without God, whereas in Dostoevsky's scheme it cannot.

By responding so intensely in one short story to two works—*Gulliver's Travels* and *A Discourse on Inequality*—whose ground bases of purpose are so different, Dostoevsky creates an extraordinarily strange hybrid. For Swift's intentions are deeply satiric. Even as Swift asks us to admire certain aspects of the Houyhnhnms' civilization, he clearly challenges us to reject Gulliver's mad vision of distaste at the end. We may sympathize with Gulliver and understand his sorry predicament, but we assuredly are not expected to undergo with him the same psychic transformations that result from his wanderings. The reader's alternating responses of sympathy, identification, and separation carry over, to some extent, from Swift's work to Dostoevsky's story, although the degree to which Dostoevsky asks his readers to accept or reject the ridiculous man's vision has been a major source of critical debate.

By contrast, Rousseau's entire narrative is in deadly earnest. Moreover, he claims to prefer his natural men to the civilized variety. As much as the ridiculous man's island-dwellers resemble these natural men, it seems that neither the ridiculous man nor his creator prefers them to humans as they exist in reality. Dostoevsky's polemic with Rousseau takes on a new form here: unlike Rousseau, he refuses to idealize a perhaps nonexistent past, although he expresses love for it. He can appreciate its lost beauty, but both he and his character actively love humans even more in their fallen (civilized) state. That paradoxical yet accepting love is nowhere present in Rousseau's *Discourse*.

Much has already been written about the fantastic nature of "The Dream" and its links to the Russian tradition of the fantastic, particularly in such works as Aleksander Pushkin's "The Queen of Spades" (1833), Nikolai Gogol's *Petersburg Tales* (1842), and Vladimir Odoevskii's *Russian Nights* (1844). The editors of the Russian edition of Dostoevsky's work acknowledge these links but suggest that Dostoevsky's subtitle, "A Fantastic Story," reflects the author's interest in Edgar Allan Poe. This subtitle, of course, links "The Dream" to another story Dostoevsky had recently published in *The Diary of a Writer* in 1876, "A Gentle Creature." Both stories share the same subtitle, to neatly contrasting effect. In "A Gentle Creature" the fantastic element clearly relates to its narrative form, a Hugo-like stenography of the mind. The fantastic qualities of "The Dream," in contrast, are thematic and semantic. By introducing the idea of Poe's influence, however, the editors considerably sharpen the focus of this admittedly murky picture. They suggest that we turn back to the preface Dostoevsky wrote for three short stories of Poe that appeared in the journal *Time* in Russian translation: "Mesmeric Revelation," "The Black Cat," and "A Tale of the Ragged Mountains."[7] Both Dostoevsky's preface and these stories deserve a closer look than I shall give them here, but the editors of Dostoevsky's complete works eloquently call attention to the generic and thematic correspondences between these three stories and "The Dream."

In his 1861 preface, Dostoevsky had particularly admired Poe's ability to create a brand of fantasy in which a single fantastic event was convincingly bounded by a series of occurrences that otherwise conformed to the laws of everyday reality. He also called attention to the particular strength of Poe's imagination and his ability to accumulate and convey details. Dostoevsky specifically praised Poe's description "in one of his stories of a journey to the moon" ("The Unparalleled Adventure of One Hans Pfaall"), especially the narrator's detailed, almost hour-by-hour account of the journey (9:88).[8] The ridiculous man, during his dream, also makes a voyage through space that is in some ways similar, primarily in its peculiar blend of fantasy and reality and in its careful account of the journey per se.

Moreover, Dostoevsky's general observations about Poe apply neatly to "The Dream" as well. "The Tale of the Ragged Mountains" shares certain special affinities with "The Dream." Although the ridiculous man's dreamlike state might bear some resemblance to a phenomenon that interested Dostoevsky—mesmerism (as in "Mesmeric Revelation")—"A Tale of the Ragged Mountains" seems to be the story in which correspondences with "The Dream" are the most striking. I enumerate five of them here. In that story Mr. Augustus Bedloe's "dream" occurs, as does the dream of the ridiculous man, in November. He sets off into the hills near Charlottesville, Virginia, and there, under the influence of morphine, makes a visionary journey to another world: "In the quivering of a leaf—in the hue of a blade of grass . . . in the humming of a bee—in the gleaming of a dew drop—in the breathing of the wind—in the faint odors that came from the forest—there came a whole universe of suggestion—a gay and motley train of rhapsodical and immethodical thought." He discourses at length, as does the ridiculous man, on the phenomenon of dreams from the point of view of the dreamer and goes on to assert: "You will say now, of course, that I dreamed; but not so." He also, like the ridiculous man, refers to the uncanny knowledge a dreamer often has that he is dreaming. Moreover, he prefigures the ridiculous man in dreaming that he has already died and describing his feelings after his own death.[9] Each dreamer continues after "death" to retain his individual consciousness and sensations.

The editors have also discerned in "The Dream" the presence of Emanuel

Swedenborg, whose works Dostoevsky read in A. N. Aksakov's translations. Dostoevsky was both attracted and repelled by Swedenborg's ideas, and as Czeslaw Milosz has demonstrated, Dostoevsky opportunistically borrowed from Swedenborg "what suited his purpose." Swedenborg's belief in the existence of other worlds and the possibility that one could journey to them, as well as his notion of a "private hell," have found strong echoes in Dostoevsky's fiction. It is especially striking that Dostoevsky's use of seed imagery, which appears throughout his works and is particularly important to *The Brothers Karamazov* and to Zosima's ideas about how grace travels through the world, may be an echo of Swedenborg. Zosima's ruminations about how God took seeds from different worlds and scattered them perhaps finds its most direct source in Swedenborg. Most important for Dostoevsky — as Milosz points out — is Swedenborg's notion of correspondences (which was also so crucial for Charles-Pierre Baudelaire, whose translations of Poe Dostoevsky knew).[10] Indeed, it seems to me that the most significant movements in the plot of "The Dream" occur through precisely such correspondences: it is the interconnections, the metaphoric equivalences, among the little girl, the gaslight, the star, and the subsequent vision of the Golden Age that give the story its poetic, associative cohesiveness.

The Dream: A Utopian-Dystopian Hybrid

One condition alone is given to the lot of man: the atmosphere of his soul consists of a merging of heaven with earth. . . . It seems to me that the world has taken on a negative sense, and that out of a lofty, refined spirituality has emerged a satire.
— Letter of Dostoevsky, 9 August, 1838

The different critical readings of this story have contributed to its permanently "unfinished" aura. For example, Michael Holquist and Gary Saul Morson have eloquently, though from different perspectives, explored the question of whether "The Dream" is a utopian or an anti-utopian work. The use of the word "dream" in the title would have suggested to a contemporary nineteenth-century reader both romantic fantasy and utopian vision.[11] The message of the story (with its quotation near the end from Christ's Sermon on the Mount: "The main thing is to love your neighbor as yourself") is, in Holquist's view, "utopian at least as much as Christian in that it seeks to eradicate differences between selves [so that] the pronouns 'you,' 'I,' 'mine,' and 'yours,' would collapse into a homogenized one." Yet Holquist goes on to emphasize that the form of this story — a monologue — undercuts this thematic message, for the structure of the story highlights the "aloneness" of the narrator. Eventually Holquist discovers that the ridiculous man's utopianism may be best understood in Freudian terms, "since what is utopian in his scheme is precisely that he fails to distinguish between the phantom wholeness of his dreams, home of desire, and the waking world of the others, home of necessity." The tension that Holquist so well describes in this story between "dream" and "utopia" serves a double purpose. On the one hand, as Holquist demonstrates, we see that the competition in the story between utopian and anti-utopian or dystopian impulses can be blended into a kind of homogeneous extract of dream material. Holquist quotes Freud to powerful effect: "The alternative either/or is never expressed in dreams, both of the alternatives being inserted in the text of the dream [as] though they were equally valid . . . 'either-or' used in recording a dream is to be translated by 'and.' "[12] On the other hand, by his very focus on the dream elements in this story, Holquist has indirectly underlined the ridiculous man's close link to the tradition of the French utopian "dream" (*rêve*). In general, however, Holquist has sought to resolve the ambiguities so present in this story by giving them a Freudian gloss.

Gary Saul Morson's strategy is different, yet equally persuasive and ingenious. He too concerns himself with the dilemma of the reader forced to choose between the utopian and anti-utopian elements in the story. Although Morson initially labels "The Dream" Dostoevsky's "extraordinary utopian story," he is quick to point out that the story is embedded in and reflects *The Diary of a Writer* as a whole: "The voice of the utopian prophet [Dostoevsky] usually predominates, but that predominance is always precarious, and prophecy is never free from the threat of parody." Holquist resolves the ambiguities of "The Dream" by linking them to the principles of alternation and coexistence operative in Freud's analysis of dreams. Morson likewise apprehends these ambiguities and approaches them directly, positing as he does so that this utopian/anti-utopian tension creates, in effect, a new genre, a genre existing at the edge of each of these conflicting generic impulses: " 'The Dream' is a . . . boundary work, that is, one which has come to be interpreted according to contradictory generic conventions." Even more important, according to Morson, it is also a threshold work, that is, "one designed to resonate between opposing genres and interpretations. Or, to put it differently, 'The Dream' is a meta-utopia embedded in a meta-utopia [*The Diary of a Writer*], an epitome of the larger work's genre and of its ambivalence."[13] Thus Holquist and Morson have each found ways to allow us to read this vexed little story as one whose very contradictions contribute, ironically, to its unity. For each of them, the activity of identifying or defining "The Dream" generically as utopian, as anti-utopian, or as a combination of the two is both the primary and the most interesting task for the reader or critic.

Certainly there is much in "The Dream" to support placing it within the tradition of the utopia. Frank and Fritzie Manuel, in their monumental study *Utopian Thought in the Western World*, have pointed out that the principal elements in European utopias are "a shipwreck or chance landing on the shores of what turns out to be the ideal commonwealth, a return to Europe, and a report on what has been remarked." "The Dream of a Ridiculous Man" offers a visionary version or reworking of these components. Moreover, the Manuels note that as early as 1595 Sir Philip Sidney in his *Defense of Poesie* had defined utopia as a both a form of rhetoric and a way to knowledge that, like poetry, is "more persuasive than history or philosophy in leading men to virtue."[14] Could Sidney have read Dostoevsky's "The Dream"? A ridiculous question, of course, yet in his rhetorical outburst, with all its possibly poetic meanderings, the ridiculous man explicitly seeks to lead his audience to knowledge and virtue.

Moreover, the Manuels assert that in the utopian tradition there is, in any given work, a frequent and ongoing tension between the claims of utopia and those of dystopia, so that, in fact, there has never been a crucial need to choose one label or the other: "The histories of utopia and dystopia are a landscape in chiaroscuro. . . . Utopia is a hybrid plant, born of the crossing of a paradisical otherworldly belief of Judeo-Christian religion with the Hellenic myth of an ideal city on earth."[15] Thus "The Dream" could fit comfortably within the utopian tradition even without resort to Freud or "the dialogics of meta." But before we consign this story, more or less comfortably, to the prescriptive realm of utopia, I would like to suggest that the most crucial boundaries of the story lie on a different front altogether.

Gardens and Paradises

Two paradises 'twere in one,
To live in paradise alone.
— Andrew Marvell

The woods of Arcady are gone.
— W. B. Yeats

"My soul was seized by a sense of heavenly iridescence, freedom, and loftiness: I knew that I was in Paradise. Yet, within this earthly soul, a single earthly thought rose like a piercing flame."
— The narrator in Nabokov's "The Word"

The only paradise is paradise lost.
— Marcel Proust

More problematic than the rather standard utopian content of the ridiculous man's initial encounter with the island-dwellers is his evolving attitude toward them. The key tensions in this story are the Christian ones of fall and redemption (or false redemption). The Garden of Eden or the earthly paradise replaces utopia as the arena for action and analysis.[16] As I see it, the important aspect of the ridiculous man's dream is his ever-shifting, unfinalized position vis-à-vis what he sees and experiences. His human, postlapsarian complexity grafts itself on to the unfallen simplicity of the society he encounters in his journey to this other world. Moreover, although he is attracted by their innocent ways, the inhabitants are equally, if not even more, ready to imitate and be converted by him. Thus, as he responds to them, they are simultaneously modeling themselves upon him. He quickly casts off the typical role of observer of a safely remote utopian society to become instead a tortured figure, roaming amid a secluded but overwhelmingly fragile garden. He undergoes in that garden a moral enactment of the equation two times two equals five posited by his literary predecessor, the underground man. In the face of paradisical contentment and the foreknowledge of all the suffering inherent in fallen man's having to choose between good and evil, the ridiculous man still chooses to fall again. So too do the inhabitants in his paradise.

By separating paradise from utopia, we can, perhaps, fruitfully recast our sense of the ridiculous man's situation and the terms of his choice. However beautiful and harmonious a utopia may be, it exists, for us, in the future. It is created by postlapsarian men and women who have chosen to follow what they believe to be the path of virtue. (Its degradations, in Dostoevsky's canon, are the Crystal Palaces, the hen coops, and the anthills. I know of no positively, purely utopian representation in Dostoevsky's work, except perhaps a single moment in "The Golden Age in the Pocket" (*The Diary of a Writer*) or in the implications of some of Zosima's exhortations.) Paradise, the irrevocably lost world whose image has been created by such widely divergent writers as Milton, Ivan Goncharov, and Dostoevsky, can be imagined and loved — but is reentered only through art or dreams.

W. H. Auden has written of the important distinction between utopia and paradise. I quote him at length because his words give us a firm paradigm against which to consider this deeply elusive and illusive story:

> Our dream pictures of the Happy Place where suffering and evil are unknown are of two kinds, the Edens and the New Jerusalems.
>
> Though it is possible for the same individual to imagine both, it is unlikely that his interest in both will be equal and I suspect that between the Arcadian whose favorite daydream is of Eden, and the Utopian whose favorite dream is of New Jerusalem, there is a characterological gulf as unbridgeable as that between Blake's Prolifics and Devourers.

In their relation to the actual fallen world, the difference between Eden and New Jerusalem is a temporal one. Eden is a past world in which the contradictions of the present world have not yet arisen; New Jerusalem is a future world in which they have at last been resolved.[17]

Could we not understand the ridiculous man's dilemma as one of being caught in the role of an Arcadian dreamer who is preaching an impossible return to the past? His Eden is more irretrievably gone than any other, for he has journeyed there and destroyed it. We have, if you will, a second fall.

Eden is a place where its inhabitants may do whatever they like to do; the motto over the gate is, "Do what thou wilt is here the law." New Jerusalem is a place where its inhabitants like to do whatever they ought to do, and its motto is "In His will is our peace." . . . To be an inhabitant of Eden, it is absolutely required that one be happy and likeable; to become an inhabitant of New Jerusalem, it is absolutely required that one be happy and good. Eden cannot be entered; its inhabitants are born there. . . . The psychological difference between the Arcadian dreamer and the Utopian dreamer is that the backward-looking Arcadian knows that his expulsion from Eden is an irrevocable fact and that his dream, therefore, is a wish-dream which cannot become real. . . . The forward-looking Utopian . . . believes that his New Jerusalem is a dream which ought to be realized.[18]

Auden was writing about Dickens's *Pickwick Papers* (1837) in this remarkable essay, but his words can also suggest a deeply sympathetic model by which to view the ridiculous man. The ridiculous man enacts, in condensed form, the fall of man, the role of the serpent in the garden, and the aspiration of Satan to be as God. All this occurs simultaneously with his memory of that fall and his vision of its lethal effect on others. This is the same kind of polyphony of events, long separated from each other in time, that we saw operative in "The Peasant Marey," although there the narrators past and present were separated by decades, not by eons. Present, past, and future emerge, submerge, and converge. The result — a kind of Edenic utopia — is a generic and thematic oxymoron.[19]

The boundaries of "The Dream" that connect it to paradise or Eden (as opposed to utopia or dystopia) and the fall of man are boundaries demarcated by moral, rather than political or ideological, indicators of place. A character who experiences an Edenic vision emerges from the experience with an inevitable sense of loss and, in some way, undergoes an experience of conversion. Edward Wasiolek and Robert Louis Jackson have, from widely different perspectives, assessed the ridiculous man's dream in light of the experience of conversion. Wasiolek has argued that " 'The Dream of a Ridiculous Man' is blasphemy, and yet it has been taken universally by Dostoevsky's interpreters as sacrament." He points to the ridiculous man's solipsism as the reader's clue for separating this blasphemy from genuine sacrament: "He corrupts the truth by making it his, and as is frequent in Dostoevsky's work, this corruption takes the form of a grotesque imitation of Christ. . . . In Dostoevsky's moral dialectic the highest goods can be corrupted to the deepest evils, and it is often hard to see the difference. But the difference is there and it is absolute."[20] Like Holquist and Morson, Wasiolek is acutely aware of the collisions of meanings and modes in this work; unlike them, he does not see that collision as constituting the chief semantic element. In his view, readers must eventually emerge from their indecision, even if the character does not.

Jackson, like Wasiolek, reads "The Dream" as a work about whose narrator readers must make a final moral judgment, but his conclusion about the nature of that judgment is directly opposed to that of Wasiolek: "The ridiculous man evolves not from a state of apathy to moral-spiritual conviction, but from a state of elevated moral-spiritual consciousness to apathy and then back again to a new level of heightened sensitivity to man and society."[21] In other words, according to Jackson's reading, the ridiculous man undergoes a genuine conversion. If so, then one might describe the ridiculous man's conversion as the realization that, although paradise is lost, men can be, in his words, "happy and beautiful without losing their ability to live on earth."[22] Jackson quotes Paul Evdokimoff, "Along with the beauty of paradise, the ridiculous man has discovered that there is something better than innocence: conscious virtue."[23]

Reawakenings

"My eyes [were] opened and I [saw] everything in quite a different light. Everything reversed, everything reversed!"
— Pozdnyshev, in Tolstoy's *Kreutzer Sonata*

Midway on our life's journey, I went astray
from the straight road and woke to find myself
alone in a dark wood.
— Dante, *The Inferno*

Life is a gift; life is happiness; each minute could be an eternity of bliss.
. . . Now, at this turning point in my life, I am being reborn in another form.
— Dostoevsky, letter of December 1849

On a gloomy, urban winter evening, a lonely and isolated man walks home through the dark city. Its few lights serve not to cheer but to highlight the surrounding gloom. Having turned his back on humanity, in part by rejecting the request of a poor child abroad at night, he prepares to sleep. He is preoccupied with himself, and himself alone. What ensues may or may not be a dream. He undergoes both a vision and a visitation. An unearthly being (or series of beings) takes him on a spiritually uncanny journey, for it is a journey to the familiar, to what he already knows. At some point during the course of the vision be believes he has died. As the dream time passes, he watches himself move from relative innocence to corruption. He watches his fall with helpless despair. He betrays those he had loved. Suddenly he awakens and finds it has all been a dream. Delirious with happiness, he helps a child and actively revels in his own ridiculousness (and impenetrable goodwill) in the eyes of the world.

This paragraph summarizes "The Dream." It also summarizes a work by a writer Dostoevsky knew well, "A Christmas Carol" by Charles Dickens. "The Dream" may be read as a kind of meta-Christmas story, in which the main character undergoes his conversion in the course of a single night and becomes a man of goodwill. Both main characters move from indifference to love, to a struggle toward life itself and away from theories of life, to an acceptance, even a joyous one, of futility, of process over product, of the endlessly unfinished over the perfectly realized. "A Christmas Carol" is, if you will, a story in a major key. "The Dream" transposes the same elements into a minor key and provides the reader with a resolving cadence whose resolutions have proved to be ambiguous. Holquist has argued that although "The Dream" seems to relate a typical Dostoevskian conversion, it does not, for it is instead a thrice-told tale of the narrator's "megalomania and solipsism."[24] This reading, while persuasive, does not fully take into account the ending of the story and the ridiculous man's conscious effort to dissociate himself from solipsism. As he observes, " I have beheld it — the Truth [*istina*] — it is not as though I had invented it with my mind, but I have beheld it, beheld it" (25:118; 737). The ridiculous man has experienced both a vision of paradise and a conversion.

It might seem strange to link together two stories whose emotional thrust is so different. However one chooses to read "The Dream," it remains a baffling, provocative, and ultimately unsettling text. "A Christmas Carol," by contrast, leaves readers awash in a pleasant sea of sentiment. Even as they know that the happy ending is in honor of the Christmas season and that it would be far more prudent to expect, in the real world, that Tiny Tim's chair would indeed be vacant by the next Christmas, readers find themselves willing to believe Tiny Tim saved, to accept Scrooge's conversion as authentic, and to rejoice with him in his purchase of a large turkey for the Cratchits. The end of "The Dream," on the other hand, does not ask readers either to draw upon their capacity for sentimentality nor does it call upon them to rejoice. Nevertheless, the striking structural and thematic correspondences between these two stories deserve a closer look.

The tradition of the Christmas story, brought to perfection by Dickens, embodies a curious welding together of despair and optimism. The groundwork of grim reality is covered, for a moment, by a fragile growth of hope and charity. The author of a Christmas story seeks readers' complicity in setting aside their sense of the way things really are; he asks readers to yield to an optimism that both he and they know is foolish. Dickens invites his readers to become happy and ridiculous with Scrooge: "Some people laughed to see the alteration in him, but he let them laugh, and little heeded them; for he was wise enough to know that nothing ever happened on this globe, for good, at which some people did not have their fill of laughter at the outset. . . . His own heart laughed: and that was quite enough for him."[25]

Dostoevsky, on the one hand, asks us to celebrate with the ridiculous man the fact that he has awoken transformed from his dream and has found the little girl, but Dostoevsky also asks us to experience the chilling, unsettling effect of the ridiculous man's exhilaration: "I love all who laugh at me more than all the rest. Why that is so, I don't know and I cannot explain, but let it be so . . . I don't want and I cannot believe that evil is the normal condition among men. And yet they all only laugh at this very faith of mine" (25:118; 737). He acknowledges his own muddlement, embraces it, and admits that his Edenic dream has been just that: "Even if, even if paradise on earth never comes true and never will be (that, at any rate, I can see very well!) . . . I shall go on preaching" (25:118; 738). He asks us to see the whole process of hope and failure and still to hope. In effect, Dickens is asking the same of his readers in a less abrasive way. But the ridiculous man embodies that human willingness to show oneself as vulnerable and illogical in order to express hope in the power of some higher good. (It is no surprise that the others call him a "holy fool" [*yurodivyi*].)

Although by the ends of their stories Scrooge and the ridiculous man actively embrace their ridiculousness in the eyes of the world, initially each is a character who lives according to a plan or doctrine. At the outset, each one believes that his life is a rational reaction to his milieu. By the end, each has abandoned reason and cares only for the dictates of the heart. This progression follows a similar course in each story. Both "A Christmas Carol" and "The Dream" contain five parts. In Stave 1 of "A Christmas Carol," Scrooge several times refuses requests for Christmas charity and turns away a beggar child who has come to sing at his door. He is indifferent to all around him: "No warmth could warm, no wintry weather chill him" (46). At the beginning he asserts, "If I could work my will, every idiot who goes about with 'Merry Christmas' on his lips should be boiled with his own pudding, and buried with a stake of holly through his heart" (48). He lives according to a political and economic doctrine of rational, miserly indifference: the prisons, the Union workhouses, and the Poor Law should take care of those who suffer. Those who would rather not submit to such institutionalized charity had better die "and decrease the surplus population" (51).

Scrooge's comic but impenetrable isolation from his fellow man is echoed much more somberly by the ridiculous man. In Part 1 he describes how he arrived at the conviction that "nothing in the whole world made any difference." His philosophical indifference leads him to solipsism: "I suddenly felt that it would make no difference to me whether the world existed. . . . I began to be acutely conscious and to feel with my whole being that nothing existed in my own lifetime" (25:105; 718). The ridiculous man expresses philosophically and tragically what Scrooge does in practice and comically. Each man, in the course of his nighttime vision, clashes head-on with his cherished doctrines and ideas and comes to a rejection of them based upon the emotions of the heart.

As Scrooge walks home from work through London, the fog and darkness thicken. The murkiness is lit by the "flaring links" the people carry and by a fire some workers have started. The light illuminates "ragged men and boys"; the lamps of the shop windows briefly make "pale faces ruddy" (52). Dickens here uses the effect of light in the typical gothic way: to deepen rather than to alleviate gloom and poverty.[26] Likewise, while walking home, the ridiculous man gazes first upon a gaslight that "oppressed the heart so much just because it shed a light upon it all" (25:105; 719). He glances up from the gaslight and sees a little star amid the fathomless dark patches of the night sky. Once again Dostoevsky has deepened and rendered metaphysical an element that Dickens has used affectively. The light amid the darkness in Dostoevsky's story sets up a complex pattern of correspondences (of the Swedenborgian or Baudelairean variety suggested by Milosz) that ultimately serves to connect the ridiculous man's despair, the rejection and the ultimate rediscovery of the little girl, and his Edenic vision.

The presence of another darkness, the darkness of death, illumines the first part of each story as well. "A Christmas Carol" begins: "Marley was dead: to begin with" (45). Marley is Scrooge's partner and alter ego, initially indistinguishable from him in every respect. But at the end of Stave 1, Marley's ghost has appeared to Scrooge, who, though he wishes to dismiss the ghost rationally as "an undigested bit of beef, a blot of mustard, a crumb of cheese, a fragment of underdone potato," cannot do so. His assertion that "There's more of gravy than of grave about you" (59) falls flat, though, for he believes in the ghostly vision.[27] Marley warns Scrooge that he will be visited by three spirits and urges him to embrace the doctrine of personal charity, of "Christian spirit working kindly in its little sphere" (62).

Death appears in Part 1 of "The Dream" in the form of the ridiculous man's plan to commit suicide that night. After his dream suicide, he questions God with a hostility not unlike Scrooge's to Marley, although it is, of course, purged of all comicality. The ridiculous man has deliberately turned away from the consideration of any personal charity, and yet it is his instinctive, unconscious bond with the little girl that will save him: "And I should of course have shot myself, had it not been for the little girl" (25:107; 721). In the opening section of each story the specter of death has, in fact, foreshadowed the redemption of an indifferent man.

Scrooge and the ridiculous man both slide imperceptibly into sleep and believe throughout that they are awake. Each continues, both during and after his visionary experience, to be uncertain whether or not it was a dream. While Scrooge awaits the first spirit after Marley's ghost departs, he cannot decide whether he is dreaming: "Every time he resolved within himself, after mature inquiry, that it was all a dream, his mind flew back again, like a strong spring released, to its first position, and presented the same problem to be worked all through, 'Was it a dream or not?'" (67). The ridiculous man also falls asleep "without being aware of it at all" (25:108; 724). Although he reports to us after the fact, he does describe his uncanny awareness during his dream that it is indeed a dream. After his "death," the dark and unknown being flies with him to that bright little star, and the ridiculous man describes the dreamlike quality of this flight: "I cannot remember how long we were flying, nor can I give you an idea of the time; it all happened as it always does happen in dreams when you leap over space and time and the laws of nature and reason, and only pause at the points during which your heart is lost in reverie" (25:110; 726).

The first time the ridiculous man speaks at length about dreams, he tells us how he sometimes dreams about his brother, who, though he has been dead for five years, "takes a keen interest in my affairs." Although the ridiculous man knows, even during the dream, that his brother is dead, he nevertheless "is here beside me, doing his best to help me" (25:109; 724). Although the autobiographical references to Dostoevsky's own beloved dead brother are unmistakable, this passage could also call to mind Marley's appearance to the dreaming Scrooge. Marley, although he has been dead for seven years, takes a keen interest in Scrooge's affairs and tries to help him. Moreover, he laments in words that seem to foreshadow the ridiculous man himself, "Why did I walk through crowds of fellow-beings with my eyes turned down, and never raise them to that blessed Star which led the Wise Men to a poor abode?" (62–63). If we allow ourselves to connect the ridiculous man to Scrooge and, in this instance, to Marley, we can see a biblical (and Christmas) resonance to the bright star that leads the ridiculous man (read "wise man") to that poor abode (read "poor child") and to salvation. At any rate, as he tells his tale, the ridiculous man repeatedly asks himself if it was a dream: "What does it matter whether it was a dream or not?" "What if it was only a dream? . . . Perhaps it was no dream at all!" (25:109, 115; 724, 733). By the end, he wholly rejects the need to separate dreams from everyday life: "What is a dream? And what about our life? Is that not a dream too?" (25:118; 738).[28]

Both Scrooge's and the ridiculous man's conversions may be described as a shifting of the locus of their being from the head to the heart: hence Scrooge's tears and the ridiculous man's deliberate shifting of the aim of his gun from his head to his heart. It is fitting, then, that each of them at the end should have lost his former capacity for reasoned discourse. Each awakens from his dream with a face bathed in tears. Scrooge awakens and laughs for joy: "I don't know how long I've been among the Spirits. I don't know anything. I'm quite a baby. Never mind, I don't care. Hallo! Whoop! Hallo here!" (128). The ridiculous man's joy is, predictably, a more sober intoxication, but it, like Scrooge's, renders his language emotive rather than logical: "Rapture, boundless rapture welled through my entire being. Yes, life and preaching [*propoved'*] . . . After my dream I lost the knack of putting things into words" (25:118; 737–38). The paradoxical notion of a preacher who knows he has lost the knack for words renders his life, rather than his words about that life, a living symbol of faith as opposed to reason.[29]

Scrooge and the ridiculous man each make a fantastic journey in the company of a mysterious being. The Spirits Scrooge sees — the Ghosts of Christmas Past, Present, and Future — fill him with ever greater fear and dread, but each shows for Scrooge a solemn, if not affectionate, concern. His visit to his own childhood constitutes a journey to a personal Golden Age. The ridiculous man, too, quickly realizes that his unearthly guide cares for him: "He did not answer me, but I suddenly felt I was not despised, that no one was laughing at me or even pitying me, and that our journey had a purpose, an unknown and mysterious purpose that concerned only me" (25:111; 727). Scrooge's journey is to the stages of his own life, and thus also concerns him alone.

Scrooge learns by the end, however, that the fates of others are connected to him. Although the ridiculous man does not journey to his own past, he too is led to what he already somehow knows — to the past of all humanity — yet does not know. He travels to a planet that is an exact copy of our earth, to one of the islands of the Greek archipelago. His dream, moreover, has been prefigured and shaped by his thoughts just before going to sleep and is a dramatic recasting of them. After rejecting the little girl, he had returned home and unconsciously transformed his shabby deed into an intellectual proposition. He had asked himself to imagine that if he had once lived on the moon or Mars and had committed a disgraceful deed there, would he afterward, on earth, have felt that such a deed made no difference? (25:108; 723).[30]

Scrooge's cranky comments about the surplus population, also uttered just before going to sleep, likewise come back, quite literally, to haunt him. He begs the Ghost of Christmas Present to tell him if Tiny Tim will live: "Say he will be spared." The Ghost replies that, unless the shadows of the future intervene, Tiny Tim will die and adds, "If he be like to die, he had better do it, and decrease the surplus population" (97). Later Scrooge sees the starving children, Want and Ignorance, hiding under the cloak of the Ghost of Christmas Present and cries out in sorrow, "Have they no refuge or resource?" The Spirit responds, "Are there no prisons? Are there no workhouses?" (109). *The seeds that engender each character's conversion lie encased in the husks of those very doctrines that had led him astray.*

The best clue to the uneasy relationship between perversion ("Nothing makes any difference"; "It's a matter of reducing the surplus population") and conversion ("I'll keep on preaching even if they laugh at me"; "Please let the crippled child live") comes from the ridiculous man. "Dreams," he writes, "seem not to be induced by reason but by desire, not by the head but by the heart" (25:108; 724). If so (and Freud would back him up), *when* does the actual moment of the conversion experience occur for Scrooge and for the ridiculous man? When they each lament, during the course of the dream, the plight of the suffering child? When they each find a new mode of being in ridiculousness? When they awaken from their dreams with tears and joy? Or, does conversion occur at the point when the dream begins? For the very fact of the dream expresses, from its first moment, the desire of the dreamer for conversion. Or, does conversion occur with the first birth of that desire, which is merely enacted in the dream? When does potential desire become spiritual reawakening? How does this kind of transformation occur? Scrooge, the miser who cared only for financial gain, and the ridiculous man, the metaphysical miser who cared only for himself, each adopt a similar code by the end; each story argues for the value of personal goodness and charity, even in the face of defeat.

It has frequently been noted that "The Dream" is Dostoevsky's third reworking of a vision of a Golden Age inspired in part by his response to Claude Lorrain's painting *Landscape with Acis and Galatea* (1657). The position of "The Dream" as a third-generation offspring in this literary genealogy could suggest that we see the ridiculous man as a direct descendant of Stavrogin and Versilov and therefore be deeply suspicious of his vision.[31] In *The Possessed,* Stavrogin's dream hallucination of a Golden Age is associated directly with his destruction of the little girl Matryosha. He too awakens from his dream (in which the slanting rays of the setting sun figure powerfully) with his eyes wet from tears and with a feeling of an "unknown unhappiness." It seems that he too might be ripe for a conversion. When he tries to remember and reenter that dreamscape, however, he sees a bright light with a dark spot in it (an exact inversion of the ridiculous man's star amid darkness) that becomes a spider. He dreams, instead, of Matryosha, who appears locked in a heartrending gesture of reproach. Stavrogin then remembers the spider on the geranium leaf, which he had been watching during the moments when he knew Matryosha was committing suicide in the next room.[32] This is a profound moment of deconversion, of perversion, of failed conversion in which a transformational process nearly identical to that of the narrator in "The Peasant Marey" or the narrator of "The Dream of a Ridiculous Man" leads not to affirmation but to despair. Instead it resembles Svidrigaylov's visionary dream near the end of *Crime and Punishment*. Both these visions involve a child, as of course, so too do those of the narrator of "Marey" and "The Dream," but Svidrigaylov's and Stavrogin's potentially transformative visions end in the irresistible desire to commit suicide.

In *A Raw Youth* (1875), Versilov had also imagined the sun setting as it does in Claude Lorrain's picture, but here it is setting on the last day of humanity, during which a new love is blossoming among men. (The ridiculous man's vision, by contrast, is of a prelapsarian, not a final, dawning.) That Stavrogin and Versilov (and, in part, Svidrigaylov in *Crime and Punishment*), such morally voluptuous characters, should have some fleeting visions of a Golden Age does, of course, lend credence to the idea that the ridiculous man's vision is also morally suspect. Moreover, Dostoevsky draws upon the epilogue to *Crime and Punishment* and recalls Raskolnikov's "terrible dream" about the trichina.[33] The ridiculous man, like other real-life explorers and colonists of Africa and South America, brings disease with him to his visionary island: "Yes, yes, it ended in my corrupting them all! How it could have happened, I do not know, but I remember it clearly. The dream encompassed thousands of years and left in me only a vague sensation of the whole. I only know that the cause of the Fall was I. Like a horrible trichina, like the germ of the plague infecting whole kingdoms, so did I infect with myself all that happy earth that knew no sin before me. They learnt to lie, and they grew to appreciate the beauty of a lie" (25:115; 733). But the parasitic trichina he brings is not smallpox or measles, it is a moral disease of pride and the love of deceit. The ridiculous man, too, tells the inhabitants of his visionary garden that on earth he often could "not look at the setting sun without tears" (25:114; 732). We have already seen, repeatedly, that Dostoevsky is notorious for frequently transposing his most deeply held "final convictions" into the thoughts and words of characters who use them to their own ends.

As early as 1867, while working on the notebooks for *The Idiot*, Dostoevsky had wondered how to work Don Quixote's vision of the Golden Age into his novel (although he actually never did). In the entry for September 8, he had parenthetically remarked, "(Don Quixote and the acorn)." In chapter eleven of *Don Quixote*, the knight eats acorns with some goatherds. He then begins to meditate and discourse on the Golden Age: "Happy the age and happy the times on which the ancients bestowed the name of Golden, not because gold . . . was attainable without labour in those fortunate times, but rather because the people of those days did not know those two words thine and mine. . . . Nor had fraud, deceit or malice mingled with truth and sincerity."[34] When the ridiculous man corrupts the unfallen island inhabitants of his dream, he describes their fall with a direct allusion to Don Quixote and his acorns: "A struggle began for separation, for isolation, for personality, for mine and thine" (25:116; 734).[35] Yet even as the ridiculous man describes his negative act (that is, the process by which he corrupts them all), it becomes, by virtue of its telling, by being preached and rendered cautionary, a positive act.[36] The reader can easily tease out the underlying message: the ridiculous man is really longing for a return to the blurring between mine and thine. He resembles a fallen, wistful, conscious Don Quixote in this respect.

There exists yet another genealogical line that bears fruit in "The Dream," a far more positive one than this kinship to Stavrogin and Versilov, and one that directly links it to the genre of the Christmas story. Indeed, in my opinion, we can also view "The Dream" as a direct descendant of an earlier Christmas story by Dostoevsky, one squarely in the Dickensian tradition.

In the January 1876 issue of *Diary of a Writer*, Dostoevsky had described at length a Christmas party at the Artists' Club. Like Dickens at the time he began work on "A Christmas Carol," Dostoevsky criticized the half-baked charity and the ill-conceived philosophies of education to which impoverished children were subject. (In October of 1843 Dickens too was thinking and writing about the needs of poor children for genuine education. He deplored the fate of the "thousands of children condemned to tread the path of jagged flints and stones, laid down by brutal ignorance." He had thought of publishing a pamphlet entitled "An Appeal to the People of England on behalf of the Poor Man's Child."[37]) Then, in the very next *Diary* entry—a famous one, "The Golden Age in the Pocket"—Dostoevsky had continued his meditation about this Christmas party at the Artists' Club. As he had watched the dancing with weariness and disillusionment, he recounted how

> one quite fantastic and utterly improbable thought occurred to me: "What if
> all these dear and respectable guests wanted, even for one brief moment, to

become sincere and honest? How would this stuffy hall be transformed then? What if each of them suddenly learned the whole secret? What if each one of them suddenly learned how candid, honest, and sincere he really was? . . . Yes, ladies and gentlemen, all that exists within every one of you, and no one, not a single one of you knows anything about it! Oh, dear guests, I swear that each lady and gentleman among you is cleverer than Voltaire, more sensitive than Rousseau. . . . Do you know that each of you, if you only wanted, could at once make everyone in this room happy and fascinate them all? And this power exists in every one of you, but it is so deeply hidden that you have long ceased to believe in it. Do you really think that the golden age exists only on porcelain teacups?

Don't frown at the words *golden age,* Your Excellency: I give you my word of honor that you won't be compelled to walk around in the costume of the golden age wearing only a fig leaf.[38]

Dostoevsky here sounds much like his doomed character Myshkin at the party just before he broke the Chinese vase and had an epileptic seizure. He is also, like Myshkin, allowing himself to come perilously close to (and perhaps even crossing over) that dangerous boundary of expressing a cherished idea directly and without resource to indirection or to art.

He ends his entry with sincere words that are nearly identical to the ridiculous man's: "I am glad I made you laugh, and yet my whole outburst just now is not a paradox but the complete truth [*pravda*]. . . . And your whole trouble is that you don't believe it." (22:12–13; 308). Yet these words, without the cocoon of fictional discourse encasing them, seem both thin and extreme. (Later, in August 1876, Dostoevsky wrote in *The Diary* of his vision of a garden — as opposed to a utopian Crystal Palace — in which mankind would be regenerated. In this garden, children would be born connected to the soil rather than to the pavement or the street and they would spend their childhood in play [23:96; 591].)[39]

The January 1876 version of Dostoevsky's Golden Age — conceived sincerely, with a belief in its possibility, and, most important, as a Christmas thought at a Christmas party — occurs after the morally opaque representations of it in *The Possessed* and *A Raw Youth* and is, moreover, most closely linked with both the character and the narrative texture of the ridiculous man. Throughout this chapter, it has seemed more important to gauge the ridiculous man's attitude toward his transformative vision rather than the actual content of it, and this attitude far more resembles that either of Scrooge or of Dostoevsky's own unmediated voice in "The Golden Age in the Pocket" than it does the attitude or diction of Stavrogin or Versilov.

The very next January chapter of the *Diary* is strikingly Dickensian in outlook, and it is here that we find Dostoevsky's story "The Boy at Christ's Christmas Party." In the entry preceding that story, "The Boy with His Hand Out," Dostoevsky describes meeting an urchin on Christmas Eve who, like the little girl the ridiculous man encounters, is clad, despite the terrible cold, "in clothes more fit for summer" (22:12; 309). Dostoevsky's reworking of Dickens's Micawber into his own Marmeladov has been well studied;[40] a key technique of Dostoevsky's borrowings from Dickens involves darkening and deepening the comic or sentimental Dickensian outlines and rendering them more stark. In Dostoevsky's story, a lost seven-year-old, reminiscent of such children in Dickens, is imagined to have come out from his basement to go begging. But it is the description of the basement that leaves Dickens behind and becomes characteristically Dostoevskian, for it is a basement where hungry, beaten women, suckling their hungry children, take part in bouts of drinking. "These are people who, quitting work at the factory on Saturday night, return to work no earlier than Wednesday evening. In the cellars their hungry and beaten wives drink with them; their hungry babies cry here too. Vodka, filth, and depravity, but vodka above all" (22:13, *Writer's Diary*, 1:309).

After this chilling journalistic description, Dostoevsky immediately begins his story "The Boy at Christ's Christmas Party," in which he seeks to awaken in his readers the same responses, but now through making a direct appeal to their personal emotions and aesthetic sensibilities through art rather than to their social conscience through nonfiction. This brief story is perhaps the most Dickensian of all Dostoevsky's works; the sentimentality it awakens in readers is fueled, as it frequently is in Dickens, by a powerful, dark, cathartic force. Jackson has aptly described this work as "a moving Christmas story, as ecstatic in its religious idealism as it is brutal in its social realism."[41]

This Christmas story, moreover, with its focus on a desperate child abroad on a winter night, calls to mind and prefigures "The Dream." It thus links "The Dream" directly to the genre of the Christmas story and to Dickens. The ridiculous man imagines that the little girl who beseeches him as he returns home may have left the side of a dead or dying mother. In "The Boy at Christ's Christmas Party," the story, though it is in the third person, is told from the child's perspective; he leaves his dying (or perhaps already dead) mother and wanders the streets. During the course of the evening, the freezing child gazes through three windows onto three seemingly benign scenes: a children's Christmas party, a room filled with wonderful Christmas food, and, finally, a collection of finely crafted puppets. We confront these scenes through the child's eyes. Jackson has described the effect of this on our own vision: "Dostoevsky defamiliarizes, indeed almost demonizes, the reader's reality: what had always seemed right and good now seems evil because of its exclusiveness and moral indifference. All that seems the very essence of the Christmas spirit now seems the beauty of the lie."[42]

The story ends with the child's inevitable death; but as he dies, he imagines he is taken up, along with other such children, by Christ to share in a heavenly celebration at his Christmas tree. Christ holds out "his hands to them, blessing them and their sinful mothers. . . . And the mothers of the children stand apart, weeping; each one recognizes her son or daughter; and the children fly to their mothers and wipe away their tears with their tiny hands" (22:17; *Writer's Diary*, 1:313–14).[43] This ending, like the ending of "A Christmas Carol," in which Tiny Tim survives, is not really a happy ending but is the kind of "happy" ending typical of a Christmas story. Even as readers experience a sentimental relief and softened joy, they sense the invading force of a starker, more brutal, shadow closure: the child outside any story, although he may inspire one, who remains lost, cold, and poor, and who is not rescued by fiction, whether it be through a transcendent death or through the ebullient charity of a former miser.

Thus it is Dostoevsky's extended *Diary* entry for January 1876, with its focus on the plight of poor children at Christmastime, its Dickensian Christmas story, and its advocacy, imagined during a Christmas party, of the possibility of a Golden Age, that offers the key literary historical link in my attempt to associate "The Dream" with Dickens's "Christmas Carol." Yet Dostoevsky's ridiculous man repeatedly stresses that his dream occurs on the third of November — hardly a date associated with the Christmas season. Nevertheless, if we read this story, as I have suggested we may, as a kind of meta-Christmas story, the November time frame becomes somehow fitting. For, in fact, Christmas stories tend to describe and urge a change of heart that ultimately extends beyond the Christmas season. Christmas is an occasion for a certain kind of discourse, a time when readers are predisposed to be moved. But both Dickens and Dostoevsky intended their Christmas stories to convey a message that in fact has very little to do with the Christmas holiday and more to do with man's relationship to his fellow man. At any rate, whatever the date of its occurrence, "The Dream" contains the crucial elements of a nighttime visitation, a voyage, and the conversion of a spiritually indifferent and highly rational man into a man of ridiculously good will. "The Dream of a Ridiculous Man" thus embodies the quintessential rhythms of "A Christmas Carol," which seeks above all, as do Dickens's other Christmas stories, to stir and transform the hearts of readers, to lead them away from the confines of reason, and to awaken spontaneous goodwill, compassion, and emotion within them.

7

Evocations and Revocations of
Anxiety in the Metaphysical Novel:
Reading The Brothers Karamazov *through*
the Lens of Melmoth the Wanderer

I had a dream, which was not all a dream.
The bright sun was extinguish'd, and the stars
Did wander darkling in the eternal space,
Rayless, and pathless, and the icy earth
Swung blind and blackening in the moonless air;
Morn came and went — and came, and brought no day,
And men forgot their passions in the dread
Of this their desolation . . .
— Lord Byron, "Darkness"

. . . the world, which seems
To lie before us like a land of dreams,
So various, so beautiful, so new,
Hath really neither joy, nor love, nor light,
Nor certitude, nor peace, nor help for pain;
And we are here as on a darkling plain
Swept with confused alarms of struggle and flight,
Where ignorant armies clash by night.
— Matthew Arnold, "Dover Beach"

"Oh, blind force! Oh, nature! Men are alone on earth — that is what is dreadful! 'Is there a man alive on the battlefield?' cries the Russian hero. I cry the same, though I am not a hero, and no one answers my cry . . . Men are alone — around them is silence — that is the earth! . . . The pendulum ticks callously, heartlessly. Two o'clock at night."
— The narrator of Dostoevsky's "A Gentle Creature"

The nature of literary genre, like that of beauty, will always be problematic, for genre, like beauty, exists both in the perception of the beholder and in the inherent properties of the text itself.[1] Or, as Tzvetan Todorov has put it, "when we examine works of literature from the perspective of genre, we engage in a very particular enterprise; we discover a principle operative in a number of texts, rather than what is specific about each of them"[2] By extension, the discovery of yet another operative principle within that same text would serve to realign the generic classification of the work. This operative principle played out at length in the previous chapter in which, depending on choices of emphasis with regard to genre, we could read "The Dream of a Ridiculous Man" as a utopian or a dystopian text, as a fantastic dream journey to a lost Eden, or as a Christmas story.

It would be virtually a commonplace, then, to assert that Dostoevsky's final novel, *The Brothers Karamazov* (1880), taken as a whole simultaneously embodies several different literary genres or modes of discourse. Nevertheless, this is precisely the assertion that underpins this chapter. I am emboldened to undertake this task, however, because, ideally, the act of generically classifying a work of literature should illuminate and deepen our initial response to the work itself and also enlarge our perceptions of the particular genre in question. In this chapter I focus on *The Brothers Karamazov* in the shadow of a novel that Dostoevsky knew well and that his readers in the nineteenth century also generally knew, but one that is not often read today — *Melmoth the Wanderer* (1820) by Charles Robert Maturin.

It is possible, for example, to place both *Melmoth the Wanderer* and *The Brothers Karamazov* within the category, as Freud defined it, of the uncanny, within Todorov's related classifications of the "fantastic-uncanny" (*The Brothers Karamazov*) and the "fantastic-marvelous" (*Melmoth the Wanderer*), or within the perimeters of the melodramatic novel, as defined by Peter Brooks. Moreover, one can argue, and I believe argue persuasively, that *The Brothers Karamazov* bears many traces of the genre of the gothic novel, of which *Melmoth the Wanderer* is often regarded as the best example. Or, one may read both these novels as metaphysical novels, as works which, like *Moby Dick*

(1851) or *Heart of Darkness* (1899), are primarily concerned with the perennial moral and religious questions of good and evil, faith and despair, but which remain, nevertheless, within the boundaries of the novel and which resist simple reduction into allegory, philosophy, or sermon.

What is most interesting, however, is that these five genres — the uncanny, the fantastic, the melodramatic, the gothic, and the metaphysical — share a preoccupation with dread, with a free-floating, intense anxiety that affects both the characters and the reader. Freud asserts that the uncanny "tends to coincide with whatever excites dread," and that it constitutes "that class of the terrifying which leads back to something long known to us, once very familiar."[3] Thus, the experience of the uncanny is often brought about by repetitions, through recurring situations, events, or the appearance of one's double. Freud goes on to specify that an emotional affect that is repressed can bring about morbid anxiety, and if that morbid anxiety recurs, the sensation of the uncanny is experienced (47). Hence the notions of repetition, anxiety, and repression are key ingredients of the uncanny.

In the realm of art, a writer produces the uncanny, according to Freud, by "pretending to move in the world of common reality." "He takes advantage, as it were, of our supposedly surmounted superstitiousness; he deceives us into thinking he is giving us the sober truth, and then after all oversteps the bounds of possibility" (57). The crucial element is that the reader or character experiences a "conflict of judgment" between his belief in a simple everyday reality and a system of superstitious beliefs he thought he had long ago discarded (56). Fairy tales, of course, do not produce the uncanny, for the existence of the marvelous has been straightforwardly assumed from the outset, so that neither a "conflict of judgment" nor its ensuing anxiety occurs.

The production of the uncanny occurs nearly constantly throughout *Melmoth the Wanderer*, whereas in *The Brothers Karamazov*, only during certain key moments (such as when Ivan's devil appears) does the narrator arouse, within both Ivan and the reader, a complex array of emotions that culminates in bringing about the experience of the uncanny. Ivan's devil embodies his old "superstitious" thoughts as well as other ideas that Ivan imagined he had discarded long ago. His devil is, moreover, a being both familiar and unfamiliar — an extension of Ivan himself, a double once removed, a product of delirium.[4] The reader cannot, without some "conflict of judgment," immediately relegate this little devil to the status of hallucinatory apparition. This conflict becomes the marker of the uncanny as well as of the fantastic.

Todorov draws heavily upon Freud's ideas of the uncanny to create his compelling theory of the fantastic. "The fantastic . . . lasts only as long as a certain hesitation: a hesitation common to reader and character, who must decide whether or not what they perceive derives from 'reality' as it exists in the common opinion. At the story's end, the reader makes a decision even if the character does not: he opts for one solution or the other, and thereby emerges from the fantastic. If he decides that the laws of reality remain intact and permit an explanation of the phenomena described, we say that the work belongs to another genre: the uncanny. If, on the contrary, he decides that new laws of nature must be entertained to account for the phenomena, we enter the genre of the marvelous" (*The Fantastic*, 41). Although Todorov's usage of "the uncanny" in part derives from Freud's, it also differs from it considerably in its particular emphasis of the uncanny as one of two possible outcomes of the necessary hesitation produced by the experience of the fantastic, which, precisely because it is born of hesitation, is always in flux and transition.

The characters and the readers in *Melmoth the Wanderer* and *The Brothers Karamazov* each experience, at times, that "certain hesitation" described by Todorov (what Freud called more generally a "conflict of judgment" and what Todorov later specifies as being, in fact, two "transitory sub-genre[s]" — the fantastic-uncanny and the fantastic-marvelous (*The Fantastic*, 44)), but the conflict is resolved, in the case of *Melmoth the Wanderer,* by a final entry into the genre of the marvelous, whereas because the laws of everyday reality remain intact in *The Brothers Karamazov,* the genre of the uncanny prevails. What is crucial to each work, however, is the "conflict," the hesitation, the anxiety that permeates each novel. It is a moral, ontological anxiety brought about by the overriding problem of the existence of suffering and evil in a universe governed by a supposedly benevolent deity.

At the outset of *The Melodramatic Imagination,* a study focusing on Balzac and Henry James, Peter Brooks writes of these two novelists, "within an apparent context of 'realism' and the ordinary, they seemed in fact to be staging a heightened and hyperbolic drama, making reference to pure and polar concepts of darkness and light, salvation and damnation. They seemed to place their characters at the point of intersection of primal ethical forces and to confer on the characters' enactments a charge of meaning referred to the clash of these forces. Reading these novelists . . . appeared to me to pose problems and to demand understanding of the melodramatic mode: a certain theatrical substratum used and reworked in the novelistic representations."[5] With Balzac and James one discovers, in the course of reading, that behind the facade of common reality an elemental, melodramatic drama expressive of the fundamental roles of human existence is in fact being played out. But in Maturin's and Dostoevsky's novels the reader has entered a heightened world where these "primal ethical forces" are in collision from the very beginning, even though the framing context of realism is maintained as well.

Brooks goes on to characterize the melodramatic mode as one that is "subsumed by an underlying manichaeism," and which preoccupies itself with the "moral occult" and with taboo.[6] The overall movement in both the early French melodramas and the melodramatic novel is not reducible to comedic-romantic solutions or to tragedy. Instead, in Brooks's scheme, the primary theme is usually that of virtue beleaguered and the structure one of fall, exoneration, redemption. Moreover, the melodrama displays a fondness for a "sublime" rhetoric, "whose typical figures are hyperbole, antithesis, and oxymoron" (*The Melodramatic Imagination*, 40).

These statements can easily describe *Melmoth the Wanderer* and *The Brothers Karamazov* as well. Certainly each novel displays a frequently manichaean world view in which God and the devil, as Mitya Karamazov himself puts it, are doing battle within "the hearts of men"; each novel is more concerned with moral taboo, with the fall and redemption or damnation of its major characters, rather than with any permanent resolution of their romantic destinies. The final representations of good and evil are, in the pure melodrama, always unambiguous, whereas for novelists like Maturin and Dostoevsky, the relationships between good and evil are intricately tangled. The demonic Melmoth is, ultimately, a catalyst for the salvation of his victims, and in *The Brothers Karamazov,* each character (except perhaps Smerdyakov) is a composite of good and evil.

Both novels are, above all, rhetorical tours de force in which, frequently, torrents of heightened, powerful language virtually possess and engulf the reader. One can choose passages nearly at random from Melmoth to illustrate its rhetorical texture, woven from strands of hyperbole, antithesis, and oxymoron, for Maturin's is a novel literally composed out of paradox. For example, Maturin describes his heroine Immalee, who was "once so refined amid nature, and now so natural amid refinement," "the improbable had become familiar to her — and the familiar, only improbable." As another heroine, Elinor, gazes at her beloved, "she attempted to converse, but paused to listen — she tried to look up, but felt like the worshippers of the sun, sickening under the blaze she gazed on — and averted her eyes that she might see."[7] Dostoevsky, on the other hand, although he often has his characters and his narrator-chronicler employ similar rhetorical devices, tends to raise paradox, antithesis, and oxymoron to a metaphysical level in his fiction. Thus, for example, the burial of Ilyusha constitutes his resurrection, the life of complete obedience to an elder can be the path for seeking freedom, Ivan's legend of religious despair can inadvertently manifest his undemolished love of Christ, and so on.[8]

The early French melodramas were originally dramas accompanied by music, and Brooks maintains the subsequent importance of music for the melodramatic novel: "Even though the novel has no literal music, this connotation of the term melodrama remains relevant. The emotional drama needs the desemanticized language of music, its evocation of the 'ineffable,' its tones and registers. Style, thematic structuring, modulations of tone and rhythm and voice — musical patterning in a metaphorical sense-are called upon to invest plot with some of the inexorability and necessity that in pre-modern literature derived from the substratum of myth" (*The Melodramatic Imagination*, 14). Bakhtin's observations about the musical, polyphonic nature of Dostoevsky's writing have already become axiomatic for most of Dostoevsky's present-day readers. Recently the critics Michael Holquist, Alexander Makhov, and Caryl Emerson have undertaken a fresh look at the significance of Bakhtin's ideas about polyphony and musicality in the novel. In a forthcoming essay Emerson highlights a significant insight of Makhov's from his essay "The Music of the Word." Emerson offers the following paraphrase of Makhov's argument: "The term polyphony (like the concept of sonata form) originated in Rhetoric and was borrowed by medieval musical theorists from verbal-art criticism: Bakhtin could be seen as taking back the term for literature. . . . In its historical context, sacred polyphony was a musical equivalent to *allegory* — that is, to the musical simultaneity of Old-Testament events and their New Testament analogues."[9]

Likewise, Bakhtin's theories about Dostoevsky's appropriation of certain key techniques of menippean satire are both axiomatic but always subject to revision.[10] In the later manifestations of this genre, Northrop Frye has chosen to substitute the word "anatomy" for the "rather misleading name 'Menippean satire'" and has concluded that a key ingredient in novels of anatomy and its hybrids (such as the *roman à thèse*) is the reader's perception of the work's shapelessness. "There is hardly any fiction writer deeply influenced by it [anatomy] who has not been accused of disorderly conduct" (*Anatomy of Criticism*, 312). Maturin and Dostoevsky have each, from the beginning of their careers, been criticized for their "shapeless" productions, and in each case, analogies to music — to variations upon themes, expositions, recapitulations, and, above all, to polyphony — can provide order and structure when the standard linear developments typical of "pure" realism and traditional narrative structure seem to fail as analytical tools.

What is particularly useful about Brooks's emphasis on the intervening tradition of the melodrama is that it provides a more immediate source for those techniques and values of the menippean satire that both Maturin and Dostoevsky found so attractive. Maturin actually did write numerous melodramas and was initially better known for them than for his novels into which he deliberately imported many of the techniques of the melodrama. Indeed, as one critic has pointed out, "Gothic techniques are essentially visual in their emphasis on dramatic gesture and action and in their pictorial effects, giving the reader an experience comparable to that of a spectator at the theatre." Another has maintained that the gothic novelists were "the first to perceive and emphasize the dramatic method which has since become a platitude of narrative theory."[11] Moreover, Dostoevsky had longed to write dramas of his own. All his works are filled with "stage directions" and dramatic dialogue.[12] His novels, despite their relative lack of prolonged setting descriptions or stage directions, are essentially dramatic creations. His scandal scenes, in particular, make use of the gestures, pantomimes, and heroics of melodrama.

The melodramatic mode, in its preoccupation with taboos, the moral occult, the depiction of characters in their primary psychic and ethical roles, and in its heightened rhetoric that strains for sublime effects, is very close to the gothic, although the gothic tinges all these themes with deeper ambiguities, so that a more unfinalized atmosphere of chiaroscuro prevails. *Melmoth the Wanderer* is, perhaps, first and foremost a gothic novel, and like other gothic novels is concerned with the interplay between the supernatural and the fantastic. The gothic novels of the late eighteenth and early nineteenth centuries were novels of increasing narrative complexity and attempted, in a manner reminiscent of the menippean satire and the melodrama, to incorporate within themselves, as David Punter has observed, "elements drawn from diverse literary and subliterary traditions: the cosmic scope and powerful emotions of tragedy, a poetic reliance on intensity of imagery, the violence, supernaturalism and vivid coloring of legend and folklore."[13] *Melmoth the Wanderer,* more than any other gothic novel, expresses this staggering literary diversity. So too do Dostoevsky's novels, particularly *The Idiot, The Possessed,* and *The Brothers Karamazov*: each displays a similar all-encompassing range of literary and narrative diversity.[14]

At the heart of the gothic tradition in literature lies a metaphysical, semi-mythic, frequently religious quest in which, as G. R. Thompson has put it, an individual, often a self-divided hero, seeks to discover his relationship to the universe.[15] The presence of a mysterious, supernatural world creates, in virtually every gothic novel, a sense of deep anxiety, often a hopeless anxiety that offers no possibility of escape.[16] Although the gothic novel has often been called the novel of terror or horror, what is crucial about these epithets is the response that terror and horror themselves produce, and that response, in its broadest terms, is one of anxiety or dread. (Thus Thompson writes, "The chief element of the Gothic romance is not so much terror as, more broadly, dread — whether physical, psychological, or metaphysical, whether of body, mind, or spirit" ["A Dark Romanticism," 34].)

In the gothic novels this atmosphere of anxiety is created by an overarching structure in which each approach toward danger is succeeded by yet another approach (much like the flight of stairs in a Piranesi [1720–1778] etching) and where the resolution of conflict or the dispelling of mystery is, at best, only temporary and partial. *Melmoth the Wanderer,* for example (which Punter has labeled a "metaphysical Gothic novel" and William Axton has called a "profoundly religious parable")[17] consists of a series of tales of extreme suffering that intersect with each other so that the reader is literally engulfed unremittingly by the spectacles of suffering that the demonic Melmoth visits. In *The Brothers Karamazov* Dostoevsky provokes anxiety in his readers as they watch each of the brothers grapple with the fact of his father's murder and the degree of responsibility each must assume. Dostoevsky further promotes anxiety by the encyclopedic treatment in his novel of the theme of the suffering of children in the world. Ultimately, the reader may find herself asking to what extent she herself is responsible for the evil and suffering she sees around her. Yet Dostoevsky, unlike Maturin, seeks ultimately to balance the extreme tensions he creates in his readers with an equally powerful sense of genuine resolution, at least momentarily achieved. This momentary resolution in turn suggests the eventual possibility of a lasting one.

Starting with Ann Radcliffe, the gothic novelists frequently invoked the names of Salvatore Rosa (1615–1673), Bartolomé Murillo (1617–1682), and Claude Lorrain (1600–1682) to lend to their landscape or figural descriptions a painterly aura. These painters were all noted for their depictions of light intersecting with darkness. As we have already seen, Dostoevsky, from *The House of the Dead* — in his depiction of the dying convict Mihailov whose emaciated body is illuminated by a shaft of light — onward, through such works as *The Idiot, The Possessed, A Raw Youth,* and in particular, "The Dream of a Ridiculous Man" — shared this preoccupation with creating painterly effects of light amid shadow that is also endemic to the gothic novel. In *The Brothers Karamazov,* for example, Alyosha remembers "an open window, the slanting rays of the setting sun (he recalled the slanting rays most vividly of all); in the corner of the room a holy image, before it a lighted lamp, and on her knees before the image his mother, sobbing hysterically with cries and shrieks, snatching him up in both arms, squeezing him close till it hurt, and praying for him. . . . That was the picture!"[18]

Ann Radcliffe's *The Mysteries of Udolpho* (1794) literally abounds with descriptions of the slanting rays of the setting sun. These chiaroscuro landscapes were used by the gothic novelists to invoke the sublime — a combination of the beautiful with the terrifying or painful. Dostoevsky employs his chiaroscuro settings to like effect. (In the passage quoted above, Alyosha also remembers how his nurse ran up to him and snatched him from his mother's arms in "terror" and how his mother's face was "frenzied but beautiful." The moonlit scene at the end of *The Idiot* in which the dead Nastasya Filippovna lies draped amidst her discarded finery similarly invokes the mixture of the terrifying and the beautiful that produced, according to Burke, the sensation of the sublime.) Like Maturin, Dostoevsky most often depicted painterly tableaus either inhabited by or descriptive of human beings rather than uninhabited landscapes.[19]

Maturin usually sought analogies with the paintings of Salvatore Rosa (as did Radcliffe) or Murillo, but the primary effect he sought in his prose remains one of light intersecting with darkness. Consider, for example, the following description of the great fire within the walls of the Spanish Inquisition: "It was a subject worthy of the pencil of Salvatore Rosa or of Murillo. . . . Our dismal garbs and squalid looks, contrasted with the equally dark, but imposing and authoritative looks of the guards and officials, all displayed by the light of torches, which burned . . . fainter and fainter, as the flames roared in triumph above the towers of the Inquisition. The heavens were all on fire. . . . It seemed to me like a wildly painted picture of the last day. God appeared descending in the light that enveloped the skies — and we stood pale and shuddering in the light below" (*Melmoth*, 185). Or later, in the description of the ravaged Everhard, who had sold his blood to get money for his starving family, light once again intersects darkness and horror mingles with beauty: "The moon-light fell strongly through the unshuttered windows. . . . So he lay . . . in a kind of corpse-like beauty, to which the light of the moon gave an effect that would have rendered the figure worthy the pencil of a Murillo, or a Rosa, or any of those painters, who, inspired by the genius of suffering, delight in representing the most exquisite of human forms in the extremity of human agony" (*Melmoth*, 322).

Dostoevsky, like Maturin himself and the artists Maturin names, was "inspired by the genius of suffering"; like Maturin he portrayed, repeatedly, images in which could be discovered horror and beauty united, good and evil intertwined. Each had frequent recourse to painterly descriptions, where the play of light and shadow could suggest an ultimately religious significance, where the shafts of light exposed both man's fallen state and his desire for redemption.[20]

At the beginning of this chapter I suggested that the determination of genre will always be in part problematic, in part a satisfying enterprise that can yield up the discovery of shared "operative principles" among works of art. To illustrate that point, I have chosen to consider as examples two novels that tend not to be compared with each other. But whether we categorize *Melmoth the*

Wanderer and *The Brothers Karamazov* as representatives of the uncanny, the fantastic (whether of the marvelous or uncanny variety), the melodramatic novel, or as some manifestation of or direct descendant of the gothic, all these genres depend upon an expressed concern with metaphysical problems and with, at least for the duration of the act of reading, the evocation of a heightened experience of anxiety on the part of the reader. That anxiety may be expressed as "conflict of judgment" (Freud's uncanny), as "hesitation" (Todorov's fantastic), as a heightened awareness of the struggle between "primal ethical forces" (Brooks's melodramatic mode), or as "horror, terror, and dread" (the gothic). Thus *Melmoth the Wanderer* and *The Brothers Karamazov*, despite their obvious differences, enmesh their characters and readers in a world where each event is in fact an event of metaphysical significance and where the reader frequently finds herself isolated, hesitating, and deeply ambivalent about how to judge what she is witnessing; she is, in fact, until the end, above all an anxious reader. Keeping in mind these strong affinities between these two novels, one can now ask, did Dostoevsky actively transform some elements of *Melmoth the Wanderer* to suit his own purposes in *The Brothers Karamazov?* How might one speculate on such a possible transformation?

Melmoth the Wanderer enjoyed great popular success in Russia, where it was read first in its 1821 French translation and then in a Russian one. In fact, Maturin's popularity was so great that the translation of De Quincey's *Confessions of an English Opium Eater* (1821, revised 1856) also appeared under Maturin's name. Indeed, Dostoevsky first read Maturin's novel as a child and later, as a young man, he read aloud from *Melmoth the Wanderer* to his acquaintances in the Petrashevsky Circle. Although it is impossible to verify specific examples of Maturin's direct textual influence upon Dostoevsky, critics have generally agreed that Maturin's novel did play a significant role in Dostoevsky's development as an artist.[21]

Charles Robert Maturin (b. 1780) was an Anglican Irish clergyman who, in 1805, became the curate of St. Peter's, the most fashionable parish in Dublin. However, this position did not supply enough money to support Maturin and his family. Like Dostoevsky, Maturin wrote novels (and plays) partly in order to attain desperately needed income. His fictional and dramatic works, which were full of Irish nationalism and potentially subversive theological positions, did not help his career in the Anglican Church. In 1824 Maturin died in strange circumstances from an accidental dose of poison.

Melmoth the Wanderer consists of a series of interlocking tales. Its structure has frequently been compared to a series of nesting boxes.[22] Melmoth, a figure who partakes both of the Faust tradition and the legend of the Wandering Jew, has made a fatal bargain with the devil. He has received, in exchange for his soul, a reprieve of life for one hundred and fifty years, and, if during that time, he can find anyone who is willing to exchange places with him, he can be freed from his dreadful contract. Hence Melmoth wanders widely through time and space and visits people at their hour of deepest despair to propose his ghastly trade. The novel consists of the five stories of those whom Melmoth eventually visits — a sane man confined in a madhouse; a Spaniard, Monçada, unwillingly confined in a monastery and tortured by the Inquisition; a wretched but de-voted family who fall from prosperity to the brink of starvation (they some-what resemble the Marmeladov family in *Crime and Punishment*); a young, beautiful girl Immalee, who has grown up completely alone on a remote is-land; and a pair of star-crossed lovers.

Throughout the novel Maturin involves the reader intensely with his char-acters. His novel was quickly recognized as the greatest of the gothic novels and one that, according to Douglas Grant, "anticipates the psychological metaphysical novel of the future. Dostoevsky and Kafka are low on the hori-zon."[23] Punter, who had also attached the label "methaphysical" to *Melmoth the Wanderer,* calls it a "vastly influential book" whose subsequent eclipse in popularity has been caused by "the decline in those reading habits which sustain works of such length and complexity."[24] Aside from his effect on Dostoevsky, Maturin's influence has been greatest on Walter Scott, Honoré de Balzac, Poe, Baudelaire, and Robert Louis Stevenson, but it can also be seen in the works of Pushkin (*Eugene Onegin* [1833]) and in Gogol (especially in *The Portrait* [1835]).[25] Balzac actually wrote a novella that is a sequel to *Melmoth the Wanderer,* entitled *Melmoth Reconciled,* and Baudelaire, who was dissat-isfied with the 1821 French version of *Melmoth,* had planned to retranslate it.

In addition to the generic correspondences between *Melmoth the Wanderer* and *The Brothers Karamazov,* there are certain other compelling similarities between these two novels and their authors. Such correspondences could ar-gue further for the case of some kind of transformation or reconfiguring of Maturin's work by Dostoevsky. Above all, both men, though fervently anti-Catholic, cherished a deeply felt Christian faith, and they were both obsessed with the undeniable presence of terrible suffering on earth. Each sought, through his writing, to come to terms with the problem of suffering and to reconcile its prevalence with a continued faith in God, by maintaining that suffering offered a more direct path than any other to spiritual growth. Both Dostoevsky and Maturin struggled to believe that salvation occurred more readily after one had passed through the "dark abyss" or the "abyss of suffer-ing." Maturin had written in one of his sermons, a year before the publication of *Melmoth the Wanderer:* "The Bible reconciles us to suffering by showing not only that it is the path all must tread, but the path the best have trod — a path consecrated by the steps, by the tears, by the blood of those to whom humanity looks up for solace and for elevation. Patriarchs and prophets, saints and martyrs, and Him whose name must not be named in a page so light, they were all destitute, afflicted, and tormented, and shall we repine?"[26]

Maturin and Dostoevsky lead their characters to the limits of human experience; as thinkers and moralists they each, from worthy motives, describe human suffering and evil. Yet as artists both frequently became fascinated by what they loathed, so that their depictions of suffering and evil are of mesmerizing, sometimes titillating interest for the reader. This tension, this delicate balance, throughout the writings of both men, between their pursuits as thinkers and as artists, creates a further correspondence between them.

As corollaries to this concern with suffering, it comes as no surprise that Maturin and Dostoevsky have each described, at length, the terrible humiliation of poverty, the mind of the criminal (including the parricide), and the way in which time passes in prison. Most interesting, Maturin's extreme fascination with executions and public scenes of punishment and his descriptions of such events from the point of view of victim, victimizer, and spectator may have contributed to Dostoevsky's own creative insight on such subjects. Indeed, both Maturin (in *Melmoth the Wanderer*) and Dostoevsky, as we have already seen in *Notes from the House of the Dead* (but also in *The Possessed*), have shown how, at the most heightened moments in these terrible episodes of punishment, the boundaries dividing the victim, the victimizer, and the spectator crumble, and all are united, albeit momentarily, in a horrible frenzy of fascination. Their artistic and religious preoccupation with the depiction of suffering may also have contributed to the interest Maturin and later Dostoevsky shared in creating the verbal paintings mentioned earlier.

Like *Melmoth the Wanderer*, *The Brothers Karamazov* is, to some extent, a religious, metaphorical *roman à thèse* in which the vast movements of a complex plot can be read as a series of intricate variations or exempla of a single text given directly by the author (as opposed to the narrator) to his readers at the outset. Maturin takes a passage from one of his own sermons: "At this moment is there one of us present, however we may have departed from the Lord, disobeyed his will, and disregarded his word — is there one of us who would, at this moment accept all that man could bestow or earth afford, to resign the hope of his salvation? No — there is not one — not such a fool on earth, were the enemy of mankind to traverse it with the offer!" Dostoevsky takes as his text John 12:24, "Verily, verily, I say unto you, except a corn of wheat fall into the ground and die, it abideth alone: but if it die, it bringeth forth great fruit."

Each novel, in the lengthy course of demonstrating its thesis, depicts as the bedrock of man's life on earth the struggle of good with evil and the necessity for man, at his deepest moments of despair, to exercise his free will, to retain it at all costs, and to choose, in the face of terrible, seemingly unjustified suffering, to remain faithful to God. Paradoxically, each novel portrays scenes of deep suffering and even brutality in the cause of making a generally optimistic religious statement. No one but Melmoth has accepted the devil's bargain; he can find no one willing to exchange places with him. In *The Brothers Karamazov* the deaths of Markel, Zosima, Ilyusha, and even Fyodor do bring forth, eventually, "great fruit."

The five interlocking stories that constitute the narrative of *Melmoth the Wanderer* seem to find a strong resonance in Dostoevsky's plans for his unwritten novel *The Life of a Great Sinner*. Melmoth makes five separate attempts to persuade someone to exchange destinies with him. Each story is vastly different, yet each is fueled by the same proposition. Compare this to Dostoevsky's description of his projected novel: "It will be my last novel. It will be about the size of *War and Peace* and you would approve of the idea for it. . . . This novel will consist of five large novellas. . . . The novellas are completely independent of one another, to such an extent that it will even be possible to read them separately. . . . The overall title is *The Life of a Great Sinner,* but each novella will have its own title. The main question which will run through all the parts of the novel is the question that has tormented me either consciously or unconsciously all my life — the existence of God."[27]

Although it is impossible to establish unequivocal instances of the direct influence of Maturin upon Dostoevsky, in addition to these larger correspondences between them of questions about anxiety and religious faith and similarities of narrative structure that I have described throughout this chapter, there are also several particular images and even passages from *Melmoth the Wanderer* that recur in Dostoevsky's work in a particularly striking, one could almost say eerie, way. Can we discern here actual moments of Dostoevsky's capacities for literary transformation at work? For example, *Melmoth the Wanderer* contains several instances of spider imagery (for example, *Melmoth,* 88) — a favorite Dostoevskian image as well. At another point a man who imagines he has been responsible for his brother's murder finds that someone has mysteriously arranged pillows beneath his head (*Melmoth,* 95). This gesture brings to mind a similar occasion when some kind person places pillows beneath the accused Mitya's head. *Melmoth the Wanderer* also employs an image of the "two-edged sword" (*Melmoth,* 87) to describe the ambivalent nature of monasticism. This resembles Fetyukovich's description of psychology in the equivalent Russian expression as a "stick with two ends" (15:152, 154; 688, 690). Monasticism in *Melmoth the Wanderer* and the techniques of psychology in the course of *The Brothers Karamazov* each come in for serious scrutiny by the author. What is most important, however, is that this cluster of images (the spider, the pillow, the "two-edged sword") occurs in *Melmoth the Wanderer* within an eight-page span and seems to suggest an extended period of heightened attention on the part of Dostoevsky, the reader, which may have later filtered, probably unconsciously, into the creative stores of Dostoevsky, the writer. It is, of course, risky to make such suppositions, but it is at the same time a mistake to ignore them completely.

Moreover, within this same eight-page section of *Melmoth the Wanderer* occurs a passage that, when read out of context, could almost read as a recasting of one of the most important passages in *The Brothers Karamazov*: "I rushed from the infirmary. . . . The garden, with its calm moonlight beauty, its innocence of heaven, its theology of the stars, was at once a reproach and a consolation to me. I tried to reflect, to feel—both efforts failed; and perhaps it is in this silence of the soul, this suspension of all the clamorous voices of the passions, that we are most ready to hear the voice of God. My imagination suddenly represented the august and ample vault above me as a church—the images of the saints grew dim in my eyes as I gazed on the stars. . . . I fell on my knees. I knew not to whom I was about to pray, but I never felt so disposed to pray" (*Melmoth*, 90). The plot surrounding this passage differs from yet also strangely resembles the moment when Alyosha leaves Zosima's body after his vision of Cana of Galilee. Here the young Monçada has also just left the body of a dead monk, an evil one, with whose final exhortations he, like Alyosha, had been entrusted. Alyosha too walks from the dead monk's cell and into the evening garden: "The vault of heaven, full of soft, shining stars, stretched vast and fathomless above him. The Milky Way ran in two pale streams from the zenith to the horizon. The fresh, motionless still night enfolded the earth. The white towers and golden domes of the cathedral gleamed out against the sapphire sky. . . . The silence of earth seemed to melt into the silence of the heavens. The mystery of earth was one with the mystery of the stars. . . . Alyosha stood, gazed, and suddenly threw himself down on the earth. . . . He longed to forgive everyone and for everything, and to beg forgiveness. Oh, not for himself, but for all men, for all and for everything. 'And others are praying for me too,' echoed again in his soul" (14:328; 340).

Beyond these disconnected, haphazard, yet powerful moments of textual similarity and creative transformation that suggest Dostoevsky's possible patterns of unconscious association to Maturin, lies the fact of the structural resemblance between these two profoundly metaphysical novels. Each of these *romans à thèse* displays a structure of complexly layered narration, of narrations within narrations. The "nesting" or "Chinese box" framework so elaborately developed by Maturin is also present in *The Brothers Karamazov,* where in fact Dostoevsky, with a stroke of his own unparalleled genius, makes theme and form unite.[28] For even as what is most valued and close to the author's primary intent is often to be discovered at the core of a narration several times removed from the main narration, so does this very message itself reflect the idea so central to *The Brothers Karamazov:* that the precious kernel of the seed of grace is encased in its own protective husks. For example, the author has the narrator-chronicler report Alyosha's written rendering of Zosima's last exhortations, which contain Zosima's words and those of his brother, Markel. Dostoevsky wrote of this section containing Zosima's narrative, "But above all, the theme is one that would never even occur to any other contemporary writer or poet, and so, it is completely original. It is for this theme that the entire novel has been written."[29] The point, however, is that Zosima's account is removed from the reader by four and perhaps even five — depending upon whether one chooses to differentiate Dostoevsky from the author — degrees of narrative separation.

Melmoth the Wanderer and *The Brothers Karamazov* each contain, as a kind of centerpiece or focal point to the entire novel and one that is buried under successive layers of narrative, a metaphysical dialogue between a dexterous spokesman for the devil and an innocent, less experienced defendant of faith in goodness and in God, whose primary role is that of listener rather than of speaker. In highlighting the similarities between these two interpolated narratives, "The Tale of the Indians" and "The Legend (or Poem) of the Grand Inquisitor," I do not intend to minimize the important differences between them. "The Tale of the Indians" functions in part as a romance, an Edenic romance between Melmoth and a young woman, Immalee, who has grown up alone on a remote island in a state of blissful ignorance and harmony with nature. She falls passionately in love with the satanic stranger, Melmoth, who appears in her garden and who imparts to her intellectual knowledge, as well as the knowledge of suffering and of evil. (It is also important to note that this dynamic also resembles the interaction between Dostoevsky's ridiculous man and the inhabitants of his visionary Eden. They too, as we have seen, come to love the satanic stranger who appears in their garden and teaches them to love the beauty of a lie.) The narrative of "The Tale of the Indians," as does "The Legend of the Grand Inquisitor," quickly takes on the overtones of myth, but whereas "The Tale of the Indians" may be said to evoke, in its broadest contours, John Milton's *Paradise Lost* (1667, 1674), "The Legend of the Grand Inquisitor" shares the more doctrinal interests of *Paradise Regained* (1671) where the main subject has no romantic coloring at all, but focuses rather on the three temptations offered by the devil to Christ.

Despite these fundamental differences in focus, however, "The Tale of the Indians" and "The Legend of the Grand Inquisitor" serve similar purposes as metaphysical centers to their parent novels. In each tale, a bitter old man offers both a passionate and an intellectual explanation for why he has rejected God's world, and in so doing, expresses his contempt for the majority of mankind. Melmoth accuses men of deliberately and unnecessarily choosing to inflict suffering on themselves and each other, whereas the Grand Inquisitor emphasizes instead the common man's weakness and inability to take on the full ramifications of free will and responsibility. But each presents a cynical, pessimistic view of the majority of men and puts forth himself as one who has chosen differently. Yet each addresses his monologue to a "good heart," to a representative of God's world par excellence. In the framing narrative of the Grand Inquisitor's story, Ivan explains his beliefs and narrates his poem to Alyosha, who is throughout the novel regarded by the others as a kind of angel. The Grand Inquisitor addresses his monologue to Christ himself. Both the demonic Melmoth and the Grand Inquisitor seem at moments to experience a haunting love for the God whose creations they have rejected. (Ivan, of course, explicitly proclaims his love for Alyosha.) Moreover, each tale makes use of the Inquisition and its dark atmosphere of death and *auto da fé* for a general backdrop. Immalee (who becomes "Isidora") and her child eventually die inside the walls of the Inquisition, where Melmoth has mysteriously appeared to her within her cell to make his final terrible proposal. The Grand Inquisitor imprisons Christ, upon his brief second coming, for a night within the walls of the Inquisition.

Monçada the Spaniard narrates, from memory, "The Tale of the Indians" to Melmoth's descendant John Melmoth. Monçada, whose adventures have constituted the main plot of the novel thus far, had encountered the tale written on parchment in a subterranean vault, where he had been ordered by the old Jew Adonijah to transcribe the manuscript into Spanish. It had originally been coded in Greek characters representing the Spanish language. Monçada, who had since escaped to Ireland, and who now finds himself in Melmoth's ancestral home, has been telling his own history to John Melmoth. He interrupts it to relate "The Tale of the Indians" (which itself contains within it a narrative of Melmoth's own, "The Lovers' Tale"). Monçada's narrative takes him, literally "many days" (*Melmoth*, 406), and shortly after he completes it, the final denouement of the novel occurs.

Ivan's "Grand Inquisitor," on the contrary, although it lasts a bit longer than the "ten minutes" Ivan suggests it will take to narrate, is as compressed as "The Tale of the Indians" is discursive. Like "The Tale of the Indians," however, it is an extended prose narrative recited from memory. John Melmoth,

Alyosha, and the readers of the two novels are the first to "hear" these narratives (just as Christ is the first to hear the Grand Inquisitor's statement). In each case the primary third-person narrator of the novel as a whole is reporting the narrative of a secondary narrator (Monçada, Ivan), who is narrating the words of a group of tertiary narrators (Melmoth, Immalee, the Grand Inquisitor, and the few words, but mainly the actions, of Christ) to another secondary narrator (John Melmoth, Alyosha). Each of the secondary narrators is also a main character in the novel.

Moreover, the narrative of each tale is interrupted periodically by the ongoing conversation of the two secondary narrators. These interruptions and the dialogues that frame the interpolated narratives serve to make the two layers of narration intersect thematically. Thus, when John Melmoth first interrupts Monçada's "Tale," Monçada replies, "have patience, and you will find we are all beads strung on the same string. Why should we jar each other? Our union is indissoluble" (*Melmoth*, 229). His words, of course, prove true in this novel where all events seem ultimately connected with each other as part of a vast metaphysical jigsaw puzzle. Likewise, the connections between Ivan's poem and the events of *The Brothers Karamazov* function as further confirmation of the interconnectedness of all things in the great ocean of being, an affirmation of which lies at the center of Dostoevsky's novel.

Maturin and Dostoevsky each worried that the compelling denunciations of God's world found in their novels would be interpreted by their readers as genuine authorial blasphemy rather than as arguments voiced by characters whose views are counterbalanced and refuted by the subsequent events and narratives in the novel. Thus Maturin interjects a note into "The Tale of the Indians" explicitly dissociating his views form Melmoth's: "As, by a mode of criticism equally false and unjust, the worst sentiments of my worst characters . . . have been represented as my own, I must here trespass so far on the patience of the reader as to assure him, that the sentiments ascribed to the stranger are diametrically opposed to mine, and that I have purposely put them into the mouth of an agent of the enemy of mankind" (*Melmoth*, 233).

While working on the chapters describing Ivan's rebellion and his poem of the Grand Inquisitor, Dostoevsky expressed similar worries. He had written to N. A. Liubimov, on May 10, 1879, that "this Book Five is, in my opinion, the culminating point of the novel, and it must be finished with special care. As you will see from the text I have sent you, it deals with the theme of the ultimate blasphemy and with the central core of the destructive idea of our times, in Russia. . . . In the text I have sent you today, I draw only the character of one of the principal persons in the novel, as seen in the formulation of his fundamental belief. . . . It is the denial, not of God, but of the significance of

His creation. . . . My hero chooses an argument that, *in my* opinion, is irrefutable — the senselessness of children's suffering — and from it reaches the conclusion that all historical reality is an absurdity."[30] Still worried, three and a half months later, on August 24, 1879, Dostoevsky wrote to Konstantin Pobedonostsev: "You raise the most *absolutely essential* question: that thus far I don't seem to have the answer to all these atheistic arguments, and an answer is indispensable. Yes, you have something there, and this is my major worry and concern. For I attempt, as a matter of fact, to give the answer to this whole *negative side*, in Book Six, 'A Russian Monk.' . . . And that's why I'm trembling over it, wondering whether it will be an *adequate* answer."[31]

The history of the initial response to both these novels bears witness to the fact that whether or not Melmoth's arguments and those of Ivan and his Inquisitor are ultimately refuted, the metaphysical hesitation they have inspired or recreated in their readers has been powerful — perhaps for many readers more powerful than any answers embodied in the novels. As Dostoevsky himself put it, by virtue of the themes of suffering they have each dwelt upon, the arguments of these characters have remained, to some degree, "irrefutable."

Melmoth teaches the innocent Immalee about the world and its suffering people by having her train a magical telescope onto different scenes around the world. She witnesses the various evils perpetrated in the name of organized religions: she views a vast sandy plain covered with skeletons and dying bodies; she sees mothers leaving their infants to perish near temples, and children conveying their aged parents to the riverbank where, "after assisting them to perform their ablutions . . . they left them half-immersed in the water, to be devoured by alligators" (*Melmoth,* 226). Melmoth continues to present his ghastly catalogue of human sufferings until at last Immalee flings herself to the ground crying, "There is no God, if there be none but theirs." The demonic Melmoth has fostered rebellion and denial in Immalee's heart, but her moment of doubt brings her ultimately closer to God than she had been before. When she raises herself to take a last view, she discovers a tiny Christian church, questions Melmoth about it, and he, unwillingly, becomes her teacher of Christian doctrine. Once again she falls to the earth, then raises her glowing face and exclaims, "Christ shall be my God, and I will be a Christian" (*Melmoth,* 228).

A similar sequence occurs between Ivan and Alyosha. A few moments before telling his tale of the Grand Inquisitor, Ivan relates a devastating litany of the unjust sufferings children have had to endure. (Like Melmoth's, many of his examples have to do with Turks.) He presents Alyosha with a verbal panorama of suffering on earth; he does not spare his own Russia: "Our historical pastime is the direct satisfaction of inflicting pain. There are lines in

Nekrasov describing how a peasant lashes a horse on the eyes, 'on its meek eyes,' everyone must have seen it. It's peculiarly Russian. He describes how a feeble little nag had foundered under too heavy a load and cannot move. The peasant beats it, beats it savagely, beats it at last not knowing what he is doing in the intoxication of cruelty" (14:218; 221). He concludes his catalogue of suffering by describing a general who sets his hounds to kill a child as the child's helpless mother watches. Ivan then asks Alyosha, " 'Well, what did he deserve? To be shot?' . . . 'To be shot,' murmured Alyosha, lifting his eyes to Ivan with a pale, twisted smile" (14:221; 224). Like Melmoth with Immalee, Ivan has sparked a moment of rebellion within Alyosha. Ivan eloquently denounces any system, religious or otherwise, that can be built upon the unexpiated tears of a tortured child to "dear, kind God" (14:222; 225). But even as Alyosha agrees with Ivan, his eyes suddenly flash, and he, like Immalee, has a sudden vision of Christ as the only being who does have the right "to forgive everything, all and for all" (14:224; 226).

Ivan's eloquence has worked in much the same way as Melmoth's: each has fostered in his angelic listener a moment of genuine rebellion and doubt that rapidly gives way to a turning toward Christ. Melmoth had, against his will and intent, praised Christianity. Ivan too, by narrating his poem of the Grand Inquisitor and by describing how Christ's kiss glowed in the old man's heart has unwillingly, perhaps even unwittingly, praised the God whom he has set out to mock. Alyosha is surely partly right when he tells Ivan, "Your poem is in praise of Jesus — not in blame of him — as you meant it to be" (14:237; 241).

Melmoth, the Grand Inquisitor, and Ivan never actively turn back to God. Melmoth at last, despite his love for Immalee, proposes his awful bargain to her on her deathbed. Similarly, the Grand Inquisitor, even after receiving Christ's kiss, continues to work against him in his efforts to deprive men of their free will. Ivan's future choices remain in doubt. Yet the virtuous Immalee's final words function simultaneously as a declaration of love for Melmoth and as an act of possible intercession for him. "Paradise," uttered Isidora, with her last breath, "Will he be there?" (*Melmoth*, 405). Likewise Christ's kiss continues to glow in the Grand Inquisitor's heart, and Ivan's love of Alyosha, for the "sticky little leaves" and his acceptance of responsibility for his father's death all indicate the possibility of his redemption, despite his plunge into madness.

The seeds of regeneration have at least been sown, and the reader's hesitation at the end of these novels — whether it is tinged with overtones of the uncanny, the sense of the fantastic, with gothic dread, or with an unresolved metaphysical anxiety — is not untinged with optimism as well. As an artist, Maturin had sought to depict the sufferings that most obsessed and pained him, as a thinking, yet believing man, throughout his life. Yet he wrought, finally, a novel of haunting metaphysical optimism. Melmoth in the end fails to persuade anyone to give up his free will and his salvation in exchange for relief from earthly suffering. Dostoevsky may well have absorbed these impulses, as well as Maturin's fondness for complexly layered narrative, into his own work in a striking way, transforming and grafting them into his own creative vision. He too, as an artist, sought to depict those sufferings that most obsessed him, yet his novel, like Maturin's, still managed to exhibit a haunting metaphysical optimism. Neither the Grand Inquisitor's eloquence nor Ivan's can unravel the beliefs of Jesus or of Alyosha — their fundamental goodness remains intact. And in *The Brothers Karamazov* "the seed that has died" brings forth, in countless ways, "great fruit."

8

Perilous Journeys to Conversion:
Adventures in Time and Space

"I have of late, but wherefore I know not, lost all my mirth."
—William Shakespeare, *Hamlet* 2(2):308–19

What is the meaning of life? That was all—a simple question; one that tended to close in on one with years. The great revelation had never come. The great revelation perhaps never did come. Instead there were little daily miracles, illuminations, matches struck unexpectedly in the dark. . . . In the midst of chaos there was shape; this eternal passing and flowing (she looked at the clouds going and the leaves shaking) was struck into stability. Life stand still here . . .

All was silence.
—Lily Briscoe in Virginia Woolf's *To the Lighthouse*

Time, as it were, fuses together with space and flows in it [forming the road].
—Mikhail Bakhtin, "Forms of Time and Chronotope in the Novel"

One thirsts for faith as "the withered grass" thirsts for water . . . I can tell you about myself that I am a child of this century, a child of doubt and disbelief; I have always been and shall ever be (that I know) until they close the lid of my coffin.
—Dostoevsky, Letter to Madame Fonvizina, 1854

Throughout Dostoevsky's fiction the experience of conversion is a frighteningly perilous one in which the movement toward God threatens, at virtually every moment, to collapse into its opposite, to change direction. Conversion hovers at the edge of perversion; perversion may, by an infinitesimal shift of the kaleidoscope, by a minute rearrangement of identical elements, become conversion. It is a commonplace to discern in Dostoevsky's work frequent moments of the fantastic — the fantastic as defined Todorov — that the reader (and the character) experiences temporally as a period of hesitation before exiting into an interpretation of the text as realistic or marvelous. As we saw in the last chapter, for example, it is possible to read *The Brothers Karamazov* as existing within Todorov's related categories of the "fantastic-uncanny" or the "fantastic-marvelous."[1] For Dostoevsky the experience of conversion is always unfinished, always perilous; it embodies a metaphysical apprehension of the fantastic, a fleeting but unforgettable sensation of "contact with other worlds." By the time Dostoevsky wrote *The Brothers Karamazov* this theme of "contact with other worlds" no longer resonated covertly but was instead a full-bodied presence that announced itself repeatedly and with many variations. But reader and character alike can become fruitlessly enmeshed in the attempt to decide whether "what happened" was real or hallucinatory, and if they do — if they focus solely on trying to name, to classify their experience — its essence, its authenticity, will begin to elude them. The brush with the essential that occurs during a conversion eludes classification. It is from this perspective, as we have seen, that the ridiculous man speaks, when he proclaims in his closing words, " 'The consciousness of life is higher than life, the knowledge of happiness is higher than happiness' — that is what we have to fight against."

Conversions, partial conversions, counter-conversions, deconversions abound in Dostoevsky's fictions. Virtually all of them partake, in some way, of the motif of the journey, a journey that is, for the most part, always unfinished. The road, the crossroads, the shortcut, the bridge, the back alley, the detour, the threshold, the public square — these are the common locales of the Dostoevskian conversion. The road maps for these thoroughfares and byways have been charted by at least six generations of critics; Dostoevsky criticism now constitutes a combination atlas and guidebook, in which the travels and the stopping points of Dostoevsky's travelers have been logged, from St. Petersburg's Izmaylovsky Bridge to the Siberian steppe, from the glossy Crystal Palace to the damp, stuffy bathhouse full of spiders.

In "The Sick Soul," the sixth and seventh of the Gifford lectures (1901–2), William James writes eloquently and at length of Tolstoy's account in *A Confession* (1882) of the loss and recovery of personal faith that assailed him in the last decades of his life. In his works James never mentions Dostoevsky, yet

The Varieties of Religious Experience (1902) offers a means of understanding the Dostoevskian journey to conversion even more profoundly than it does the Tolstoyan one, for "Dostoevsky" (that self, semi-autobiographical, semifictional, who appears in "The Peasant Marey") and some of his other characters undergo experiences that resemble those of many of the mystics in James's case studies. Some of Dostoevsky's characters (most notably Zosima and Alyosha) at their journey's end eventually take on the qualities of saints, as described by James.

In this final chapter I focus on Dostoevsky's ongoing fascination with those inward conversion journeys in which the paradigmatic and necessary shift of the locus of being from the head to the heart is effected by a process of transformation that, in one form or another, partakes of an uncanny journey through time and space. This journey may be simultaneously a journey from the known to the unknown and from the unknown to the known.

A character's journey toward conversion may or may not result in a genuine spiritual awakening. I use here William James's definition of conversion as "the process, gradual or sudden, by which a self hitherto divided, and consciously wrong, inferior and unhappy, becomes unified and consciously right, superior and happy, in consequence of its firmer hold upon religious realities."[2] But the journey to conversion may result in a perversion of such experience. Rather than the polarity between conversion and perversion that one might expect to find, there exists a troubling mutuality or symbiosis between them—a homeopathic rather than an allopathic relationship, if you will—that is, a relationship of like to like rather than one based on difference. X can resemble nothing so much as X_1, but X_1 is toxic, while X is life-giving. (For example, Dostoevsky's ongoing exploration of the dreadful tension between God-man and Man-god—the Shatov/Kirillov dichotomy—embodies a homeopathic rather than an allopathic relationship.)

The four important journeys to conversion in Dostoevsky's work that I consider here are accounts ranging along the narrative spectrum from autobiography transmitted through the lens of fiction to fiction passed on through the lens of autobiography. My texts, "The Peasant Marey," "The Dream of a Ridiculous Man," and *The Brothers Karamazov,* have all been central to other chapters in the present book, but I now return to them within the context of the conversion journey. As early as 1868, in *The Idiot,* Dostoevsky had demonstrated a sustained interest in representing the experience of conversion as a fantastic journey, but such conversion journeys became particularly prevalent in his work from 1876 on.

"The Peasant Marey" offers a paradigm for the experience of conversion in Dostoevsky.[3] Whether we follow Joseph Frank and see in this work a profound visionary expression of Dostoevsky's turning to the people, or whether we follow Robert Louis Jackson and see a three-tiered recollection of a recollection expressing a religious *profession de foi*, we encounter in this work a quintessential example of conversion literature. Frank explicates Dostoevsky's conversion experience and finds present in it the three key ingredients of the archetypal conversion, as defined by William James in his "still unsurpassed" (according to Frank) *Varieties of Religious Experience:* "The sense that all is well with one . . . even though the outer conditions should remain the same . . . , the sense of perceiving truths not known before . . . [and] an appearance of newness [that] beautifies every object."[4] These identical conditions prevail just as neatly in "The Dream of a Ridiculous Man" and in Alyosha's vision of Cana of Galilee, whereas their presence is, at best, experienced only fleetingly and partially by Ivan in his nightmare encounter with the devil.

In James's first lecture in *Varieties of Religious Experience*, "Religion and Neurology" — which has a title worthy of Rakitin or of Ivan Karamazov — he enumerates the qualities of a typical "religious leader" before he has undergone a conversion. James's description reads like many of Dostoevsky's notebook sketches for his heroes and anti-heroes alike: "[They] have been subject to abnormal psychical visitations. Invariably they have been creatures of an exalted emotional sensibility. Often they have led a discordant inner life, and [have] had melancholy during a part of their career. They have known no measure, been liable to obsessions and fixed ideas, and frequently they have fallen into trances, heard voices, seen visions, and presented all sorts of peculiarities which are ordinarily classed as pathological" (*Varieties*, 25). Indeed, in James's view the "two main phenomena of religion are melancholy and conversion," and the successful conversion in Dostoevsky's scheme also involves a journey from one state to the other.

Subsequently, in discussing Tolstoy's *Confession*, James breaks down the notion of melancholy into two key components that characterize the preconversion state in general. The attack of melancholy that can lead to religious conversion, states James, consists, first of all, of *anhedonia* — a passive loss of appetite for life's values. Second, this melancholy casts the world in "an altered and estranged aspect" that eventually, in the desire for "philosophic relief," stimulates a "gnawing, carking questioning" (*Varieties*, 130). (It is interesting to note here James's use of the word "estranged" as applied to Tolstoy in 1902, long before the Russian formalists.) Dostoevsky's characters often exhibit a profound Jamesian anhedonia. The frequent tag phrase, that marker of existential despair, "nothing makes any difference," uttered by Raskolnikov, Ippolit, Stavrogin, the ridiculous man, and Ivan, reflects nothing so much as an acute "loss of appetite for life's values." The sense of estrangement and the "gnawing questioning" of the Dostoevskian hero find expression (and relief) in the otherworldly journey to conversion, a journey brought about by melancholy and the desire to cast it off. This journey defamiliarizes the known.

In all of Dostoevsky's conversion scenes, memory — both that which is consciously remembered and that which is subliminal, literally just beneath the threshold of memory — plays a fundamental role. Thus, that moment of *crisis*, in which the process of conversion may seem so rapid as to be instantaneous, is really the result in James's view, of *lysis*. That lysis is composed of subliminal material. "The older medicine used to speak of two ways," writes James, "*lysis* and *crisis*, one gradual, the other abrupt, from which one might recover from a bodily disease. In the spiritual realm there are also two ways, one gradual, the other sudden, in which inner unification may occur" (*Varieties,* 156). James then classes Tolstoy and Bunyan as examples of "the gradual way." Although he does not cite Dostoevsky, his characters tend to believe that they experience conversion through *crisis*. This has also been the perception of Dostoevsky's readers. In this chapter I argue not that what seems like *crisis* is actually *lysis*, but that perhaps that event of *crisis* takes place at a moment whose import may be less evident than the event generally recognized as "the critical moment."

James observes, echoing a Dostoevskian truism, that "the memory of an insult may make us angrier than the insult did when we received it — that is, the power of 'remoter' facts, often exerts greater force on our actions and beliefs than do actual, present material sensations" (*Varieties,* 59). Some years earlier, Thomas De Quincey, another student of religious and mystical experience (and a writer, moreover, whose work Dostoevsky knew), had asserted: "Of this, at least, I feel assured, that there is no such thing as *forgetting* possible to the mind; a thousand accidents may, and will, interpose a veil between our present consciousness and the secret inscriptions on the mind; accidents of the same sort will also rend away this veil; but alike, whether veiled or unveiled, the inscription remains forever."[5] This idea closely prefigures Dostoevsky's cherished belief that long-forgotten memories will return to the conscious mind at the needed time.[6]

James points out that these subliminal memories are far closer to the conscious mind than the material present in the unconscious. Here he seems to prefigure Bakhtinian ideas and even language when he observes, "Recent psychology has found great use for the word 'threshold' as a symbolic designation for the point at which one state of mind passes into another" (*Varieties,* 119). Moreover, these memories, writes James in a language that seems to be identical to Dosotevsky's, reveal "whole systems of underground life . . . of a painful sort which lead a parasitic existence." They "irrupt into consciousness" with "hallucinations, pains, convulsions" (*Varieties,* 193). Dostoevsky, to designate that threshold point identified by James of spiritual conversion where sublimi-

nal memory intersects with present despair, puts his characters into supernatural, fantastic, and mystical relations with time and space; that is, he uses
the motif of the journey.

The crucial element in James's understanding of religious conversion is the
fact that evil is not destroyed, undone, or rendered impotent, but it is incorpo-
rated, miraculously, into a sense of divine harmony. Indeed, at its very heart,
the experience of conversion, in James's view, exists as a paradoxical response
to the problem of evil: "When disillusionment has gone as far as this, there is
seldom a *restitio ad integrum.* One has tasted of the fruit of the tree, and the
happiness of Eden never comes again. The happiness that comes, when any
does come . . . is not the simple ignorance of ill, but something vastly more
complex, including natural evil as one of its elements, but finding natural evil
no such stumbling block and terror because it now sees it swallowed up in supernatural good. The process is one of redemption, not of mere reversion to
natural health, and the sufferer, when saved, is saved by what seems to him a
second birth, a deeper kind of conscious being than he could enjoy before"
(*Varieties,* 135). James carefully underscores the perils of this process—
that "happiness," however limited, may *not* come; the sufferer is *not* always
"saved."

In fact, the conversionary process can work the other way: "The normal
process of life contains moments as bad as any of those which insane melancholy is filled with. The lunatic's visions of horror are all drawn from the material of daily fact," he writes. This mental state accords with an example
of counter-conversion or perversion that James claims to have translated
from the French but which is, in fact, a moving account of a devastating
personal experience that took him unawares in April 1870. One evening
"without any warning" he experienced "a horrible fear of [his] own existence." Suddenly, "simultaneously" he *remembers* a terrifying, motionless epileptic he had seen in an asylum. "This image and my fear entered into a species
of *combination* with each other. *That shape am I,* I felt, . . . I became a mass of
quivering fear. After this the universe was changed for me altogether. . . . It was
like a revelation" (*Varieties,* 138). James's own work, given this veiled autobiographical account, itself expresses a profoundly moving longing for the
kind of positive religious experience he describes in others. Like Ivan Karamazov, James experiences a demonic negative revelation, the minus instead
of the plus.[7]

"The Peasant Marey"

Alone, alone, all, all alone.
 — Coleridge, *The Ancient Mariner*

How shall I say
What wood that was! I never saw so drear,
   so rank, so arduous a wilderness!
   Its very memory gives a shape to fear.
Death could scarce be more bitter than that place!
   But since it came to good, I will recount
   all that I found revealed there by God's grace.
— Dante, *The Inferno*

In my search for answers to the question of life I felt just like a man who
is lost in a wood.
   I came to a clearing, climbed a tree and saw clearly into the never-
ending distance. But there was no house there, nor could there be. I
walked into the thicket, into the gloom, and saw the darkness, but there
was no house there either.
— Tolstoy, *Confession*

The head that created, that lived by the superior life of art . . . , that head
has already been lopped off my shoulders. What is left are the memories
and the images that I had already created but had not yet given form to.
— Dostoevsky, Letter of 1849

   With this Jamesian model for conversion in mind, let us return for the fourth
time to "The Peasant Marey." In his compelling analysis of this work, Jackson
makes three observations that can offer rich veins for the exploration of other
moments of conversion in Dostoevsky's fiction. By finding in "The Peasant
Marey" a three-tiered structure of experience, vision, and recollection of a
recollection, Jackson calls attention to three crucial matters: one about memory, one about conversion itself, one about the stunning economy of the power
of dream language. Dostoevsky's visionary work is chiseled out of memory in
all its form — conscious, liminal, subliminal, and above all, as we have already
seen at length, memory that has been artistically transformed. We have already
seen how he would constantly relive and reinvent the whole of his former life
through memory. Dostoevsky had described how, when he was a convict:
"These memories arose in my mind of themselves; rarely did I summon them
up consciously. . . . Bit by bit they would grow into a finished picture, some
strong and complete impression. I would analyze these impressions *adding
new touches* to things experienced long ago; and *the main thing* was that *I
would refine them, continually refine them,* and in this consisted my *entire
entertainment.*"[8]
   "The convict Dostoevsky" enters a trance-like state (like that described by

James) where present misery is unexpectedly overtaken by memory. He journeys to a newly remembered, long-forgotten past in which "the child Dostoevsky" journeys out of the ravine and into the bushes and hears a cry of "wolf!"
"The convict Dostoevsky" is in the midst of his painful Siberian sojourn. "The
great writer Dostoevsky" (the voice actually narrating the 1876 account) mentally journeys back to both times, 1830 and 1850, at once. Time becomes
double time: a bright day at the end of August 1830 coalesces with the second
day of Easter week in 1850. The glaring concrete present time of 1850 imperceptibly assumes the fleeting shimmer of the fantastic by containing within it
a day from childhood in 1830: "This disgraced peasant, with shaven head
and brands on his cheek, drunk and roaring out his hoarse, drunken song —
why he might also be the very same Marey" (*PSS*, 22:49; *Writer's Diary*,
1.355).[9]

Jackson goes on to ask a crucial question, "When did the miracle take
place?" Did it happen in the summer of 1830, at the time of the childhood
hallucination? Did it come about during that Easter week of 1850, when
"without any effort of my will . . . [the memory of the wolf and the peasant
Marey] came to my mind at the needed time"? Or could it even have occurred
much later, in 1876, when Dostoevsky "recollected the recollection"?[10]

Indeed, in my view, in considering the nature of conversion in Dostoevsky's
work, it is this question of *precisely when* that becomes primary for the ridiculous man, for Ivan, and for Alyosha as well as for his other characters who
undergo seemingly transformative experiences. This question about Dostoevsky's fictional characters mirrors that same question about his own biography,
for as we saw in chapter one, it is virtually impossible to locate the time and
place in which Dostoevsky's own conversion may have occurred. The important moments in his Siberian and post-Siberian experience seem governed by
his nearly rhapsodic and visionary musings just after he had experienced his
reprieve from execution.[11] Thus this question of "when" is a question that
touches upon a constant paradox of conversion, one that James illustrates
through a quotation of the words of the American philosopher Xenos Clark,
who observed, "The truth is that we travel on a journey that was accomplished
before we set out" (*Varieties*, 307n). Although a conversion experience tends to
be regarded as a discrete event after which one's life is changed, the closer one
tries to look at it, the hazier the borders of this event become. We cannot locate
with certainty the actual moment — *the* critical moment — of conversion for
Dostoevsky in his biography, for the "Dostoevsky" of "The Peasant Marey,"
for the ridiculous man, for Ivan, or for Alyosha or for any of his other characters; we can only witness their journeys and watch their subsequent efforts to
transmit their experience to others.

In "The Peasant Marey" the convict Dostoevsky's memory welled up in response to his horror of his fellow convicts. The child Dostoevsky ran in terror from the imaginary wolf to the motherly arms of the peasant Marey. Jackson discovers a compelling link between the two, one that is fully consonant with Freudian dream interpretation, in the fact that the Russian word for wolf, *volk*, is the German word, *Volk*, for "the people."[12] Dostoevsky's profession of faith, his intimate account of his turning to the people, thus hinges upon a radical semantic conversion: the terrifying "volk" somehow is reincarnated into the redeemed "Volk." Nothing at all in his everyday reality changes, but Dostoevsky "suddenly felt I could regard these unfortunates in an entirely different way and that suddenly, through some sort of miracle, the former hatred and anger in my heart had vanished"(*PSS*, 22:49; *Writer's Diary,* 1:355). Curiously, as early as 1918, the Freudian psychoanalyst Alfred Adler had stumbled upon the psychological importance of this elusive wolf and had lectured on his findings. "This reminiscence is generally interpreted as if it characterized Dostoevsky's bond with the peasantry. *However, the important thing here is the wolf, the wolf that drives him back to man.*"[13]

   But that wolf that drives Dostoevsky back to man exists within all men, even within Marey himself, the figure of safety toward whom the terrified child runs. This is the typical terror of the nightmare into which any ecstatic dream can instantaneously collapse. James Rice, following the lead of the Soviet scholar L. M. Rozenblium, discovers that immediately below the surface of the tender, motherly Marey himself lurks "peasant brutality and the potential for abrupt violence." Rozenblium cites a manuscript passage for "Peasant Marey" that clearly derives from Raskolnikov's dream of the horse in *Crime and Punishment.* "He has moments of inward impatience, and the Tatar within him bursts forth, and he starts beating his little mare, his 'nurse and provider,' across her eyes with his knout when she is stuck in the mud with the cart."[14] In these manuscript pages, that terrifying volk lurks within the iconic one — within Marey himself. The child Dostoevsky does not rush from the imaginary wolf to the welcoming embrace of the motherly peasant. He rushes instead into the arms of a figure who himself embodies both polarities. Marey becomes a disturbingly liminal figure. The proximity, the mutuality, of good and evil is endlessly problematic. Did Dostoevsky remove this passage because he believed his readers would reject his *profession de foi* if it were included? Does this excised excerpt offer us the very crux of the matter?

   Before leaving "The Peasant Marey" I would like to suggest certain nodules in the text that seem to possess a tangle of meaning that Dostoevsky would continue to rework, transpose, and ponder. First, in Dostoevsky's presentation of it, this journey to conversion, at whatever locale in time or space one decides to say it occurred, is located within a frame, a rhyme of sorts. The despairing convict Dostoevsky rushes out of his cell, his heart filled with anger and loathing of the peasant brutality around him. He then hears the words of the Polish convict, "Je häis ces brigands." The story ends with Dostoevsky's second encounter with the Pole and a repetition of the French phrase, but now, of course in a way typical of a conversion experience, and as we have already seen, everything remains the same, yet all is changed. This kind of framing recurs, with variations, for the ridiculous man, Ivan, and Alyosha at their critical moments as well. Second, at the core of "The Peasant Marey" one finds a frightened child, the nine-year-old Dostoevsky. The suffering of a child also posed fundamental questions for the ridiculous man, Ivan, and Alyosha. Third, as we have already seen, the convict Dostoevsky's visions used to begin with some speck or "from a certain point, some little thing that was often barely perceptible." We have here a suggestion of the trance-like state, most prominent in Stavrogin, but evident too in other characters like Raskolnikov, Prince Myshkin, and, most important, for the ridiculous man, Ivan, and even Alyosha.[15] Fourth, Dostoevsky carefully gives the precise time of year when these important events occurred: the time of the auditory childhood hallucination is August, the end of summer; "the day was clear and dry, but a bit chilly and windy; summer was on the wane" (*PSS*, 22:47; *A Writer's Dairy*, 1:352). Marey, as we saw in chapter four, had for an instant almost believed the frightened child, but he had then comforted him with rational, typically adult assurances that it had been a dream; finally, however, seeing the child's continuing distress and that he was not comforted, Marey had gently reentered the child's world of delusion and had assured him that "I shall not surrender thee to the wolf!" The memory had remained hidden, forgotten, in Dostoevsky's mind, and then, without any intellectual effort, had come to the fore "at the needed time" during that terrible Easter week in prison. ("It was the second day of Easter Week. The air was warm, the sky was blue, the sun was high, warm, and bright, but there was only gloom in my heart" [*PSS*, 22:46; *Writer's Dairy*, 1:351]).

The frame, the needy child, the trance-like state, the precise description of the day on which the conversion occurs, the subliminal memories that resurface "at the needed time" — all these five elements function as mysterious talismans that, in one form or another, reappear in subsequent conversion scenes, almost as if Dostoevsky's individual stories and novels were themselves separate worlds, making mysterious contact with one another.

"The Dream of a Ridiculous Man"

One of the Soviet astronauts said in an interview that he had flown very high but had not seen God anywhere.
— Czeslaw Milosz, "Religion and Space"

I now return to the story that occupied our attention in chapter six, "The Dream of a Ridiculous Man." This short story impressed Mikhail Bakhtin by virtue of its "maximal universality," "maximal terseness," and its remarkable "artistic and philosophical laconism." As we have already seen, it is a stunning and vexing tale — stunning, in that despite its laconism, it teems with sources, yet remains hauntingly original; and vexing, in that it has provoked strong disagreement among its readers over the question of whether the ridiculous man's experience was one of conversion or of perversion.[16] Bakhtin links this story to "the dream satire" and to "fantastic journeys" containing a utopian element.[17] Dostoevsky had known full well that his title would immediately carry these utopian associations to any of his educated contemporary readers. Yet, as we have seen, Dostoevsky's title and its utopian or dystopian connotations can easily deflect the reader from the story's most authentic genealogical tie, for "The Dream's" most intimate kinship lies with the conversion tale or the tale of visionary experience. Its structure and thematics particularly mirror *A Christmas Carol* by Charles Dickens, although there are also some important echoes from some of Poe's visionary stories as well.

In "The Peasant Marey" the words of the Polish convict, "Je häis ces brigands," had framed the tale, and, by the different meaning they took on at the end, had highlighted the Jamesian concept that after a conversion, although outward circumstances may remain the same, its features are invested with new and radiant meaning. In "The Dream of a Ridiculous Man," the narrator's knowledge of his own ridiculousness functions as a partial frame to the story. He knows that others find him ridiculous both before and after his conversion journey. Before his dream journey, the realization that he has "always cut a ridiculous figure," along with his solipsistic belief that nothing makes any difference, brings him to the brink of suicide. His anhedonia (to use James's term for "the sick soul") is acute. After his conversion journey, however, this ridiculousness becomes precious to him: "They still regard me as being as ridiculous as ever. But that does not make me angry any more. They are all dear to me now."[18]

Central to Dostoevsky's conversion accounts is the fear, suffering, death, or violation of a child. Whereas in "The Peasant Marey" Dostoevsky, through the agency of memory, had journeyed back and forth through space and time so that he could exist in the story simultaneously as the child, vulnerable to injury, and the adult, capable of both hatred and reconciliation, in "The Dream of a Ridiculous Man," the child acts as the second key part of the frame for the ridiculous man's journey through space and time. The ridiculous man rejects her plea for help at the beginning; he assures us that he has found her at the end. At the beginning, his unwilled pity for her — his discovery that he still, despite his acute melancholy, anhedonia, and solipsism, has the capacity to feel — inspires his dream journey. His encounter with the little girl and his subsequent musings before falling asleep also underscore the difficulty of determining the precise moment when his conversion occurs. But the little girl, as the ridiculous man himself knows well, figures at the heart of the matter and at the center of his subsequent journey.[19]

This frame of the little girl, lost and then found, that punctuates the ridiculous man's journey through time and space calls to mind another visionary work that Dostoevsky knew well, De Quincey's *Confessions of an English Opium Eater.* At the outset of his account, the ridiculous man tells how he did not help the child, but "the little girl, in fact had saved me" (*PSS,* 25:108; 723). De Quincey's experience with the child prostitute, Ann, is not dissimilar. "Then it was, at this crisis of my fate, that my poor orphan companion . . . stretched out a saving hand to me" (*Confessions,* 51). He then loses her in the dreary expanse of London, and during the succeeding years, searches repeatedly for her, wishing desperately to send her "an authentic message of peace and forgiveness. . . . Often, when I walk at this time in Oxford Street by dreary lamp-light . . . I shed tears . . . But to this hour, I have never heard a syllable about her. This, amongst such troubles as most men meet in this life, has been my heaviest affliction" (ibid., 52–53, 64). Likewise, the gaslight afflicts the heart of the ridiculous man, but he finds the child ("And I did find that little girl," [*PSS,* 25:119; 738]) who has, for De Quincey, disappeared forever.

In between these encounters with a female child, each man's flight through time and space occurs. For both men this passage of time, this journey, is impossible to describe clearly. Expanse exists, but time cannot be the indicator of its measure. De Quincey describes the effects of opium: "I sometimes seemed to have lived for seventy or one hundred years in one night; nay, sometimes had feelings representative of a millennium passed in that time" (*Confessions,* 103). His experiences are "wholly incommunicable by words. . . . The sense of space and, in the end, the sense of time were both powerfully affected" (ibid., 103). The ridiculous man describes how certain details in dreams appear with "uncanny vividness . . . while others you leap across as though entirely unaware of, for instance, space and time. Dreams seem to be induced not by reason but by desire, not by the head but by the heart" (*PSS,* 25:108; 724).

To reiterate briefly some of the important elements of the story: The ridiculous man dreams that he dies and is buried. He then flies with an unknown being on a flight whose stopping points are charted by desire. "I cannot remember how long we were flying, nor can I give you reason of the time; it all happened as it always does in dreams, when you leap over space and time and the laws of nature and reason and only pause at the points which are especially dear to your heart" (*PSS*, 25:110; 726). He travels to that other earth, that prelapsarian repetition of our own, where he admires, loves, and eventually corrupts the innocent inhabitants of that other Greek archipelago. He longs for martyrdom and is expelled. They plant in him the seed of love and redemption, even as he is the cause of their Fall. "Like a horrible trichina, like the germ of the plague infecting whole kingdoms, so did I infect with myself all that happy earth" (*PSS*, 25:115; 733).[20] But all these elements are redolent of the visions De Quincey describes.

His *Confessions of an English Opium Eater* prefigure this burial, this journey through space and time, and, most important, De Quincey, too, becomes both the would-be deity and the victim on his visionary travels. "I was the idol; I was the priest; I was worshipped; I was sacrificed. I fled from the wrath of Brama through all the forests of Asia. . . . I came suddenly upon Isis and Osiris: I had done a deed, they said, which the ibis and the crocodile trembled at. I was kissed with cancerous kisses, by crocodiles. . . . Over every form . . . brooded a sense of eternity and infinity that drove me into an oppression of madness" (*Confessions*, 109). He then dreams of the lost Ann; her lost image—for a moment recovered in the dream—hovers at the end of his confession. Like the little girl whom the ridiculous man meets, Ann becomes an icon of redemption illuminated, not by a religious candle, but by a dreary urban lamplight: He remembers a time "seventeen years ago, when the lamplight fell upon her face," and in his dream he is once more "by lamp-light in Oxford Street, walking again with Ann" (ibid., 112).

In the nineteenth and early twentieth centuries, the mystical experiences produced by opium and anesthetics seemed to some to offer a legitimate and productive avenue for investigation of transrational experience. In his chapter on "Mysticism" in *Varieties of Religious Experience* James cites numerous reports that reached him of such experiences. One of these, from a pamphlet by Benjamin Paul Blood, entitled "Tennyson's Trances and the Anaesthetic Revelation," bears a particularly striking resemblance to the ridiculous man's dream: "A great Being or Power was traveling through the sky, his foot was on a kind of lightning, as a wheel is on a rail, it was his pathway. The lightning was made entirely of the spirits of innumerable people . . . and I was one of them. He moved in a straight line. . . . Then I saw that what he had been trying to do with all his might was to *change his course*, to *bend* the line of lightning . . . He bended me, hurting me more than I had ever been hurt . . . and at the acutest point of this . . . *I saw*. I understood for a moment things I have now forgotten. . . . The angle was an obtuse angle. . . . In that moment the whole of my life passed before me, including each little meaningless piece of distress, and I *understood* them. . . . On waking, my first feeling was, and it came with tears, '*Domine non sum digna*'" (307–9). The ridiculous man's journey through time and space is drug free, yet its closest analogues lie in the visionary experiences of those, like De Quincey and others, who have made their spatial and temporal boundary crossings with the help of opium and ether. In fact, the preoccupation with the angles and pathways in space in that James cites from Blood's pamphlet also resembles Ivan's interest in such details.

Even as the ridiculous man conveys to us the miraculous leaping through time and space that is his dream, he is, at the same time, extremely careful, as "Dostoevsky" had been in "The Peasant Marey," to locate his dream at a particular point in time: "I learnt the truth last November, on the third of November, to be precise" (*PSS*, 25:105; 718).[21]

Indeed, Dostoevsky, throughout the entire span of his literary career, was always careful to locate that experience of a journey that occurs outside of everyday time and beyond the boundaries of known space within precise temporal and spatial markers. The result—an uncanny intersection between time and timelessness, between a specific place and a known but unreachable place—generates Dostoevsky's idiosyncratic mode of the fantastic, or of fantastic realism, and is present in as early a work as *The Double* (1846). Golyadkin, like the ridiculous man, wanders in Petersburg near the Fontanka on another foul November night. Both nights are wet, dismal, and cold; the ridiculous man remembers "a rain with a distinct animosity towards people" (*PSS*, 25:105; 719); Golyadkin likewise is abroad and feels that he has "no more life in him." The narrator writes, "It was a dreadful night, a real November night, dank, misty, rainy and snowy, a night pregnant with colds, agues, quinsies, gumboils, and fevers of every conceivable shape and size—put in a nutshell, a night bestowing all the bounties of a St. Petersburg November. The wind howled through the streets, lashing the black waters of the Fontanka. . . . It was raining and snowing all in one . . . And so, alone with his despair, Mr. Golyadkin jogged along." "Snow, rain and all the nameless afflictions of a wet and windy St. Petersburg November night were suddenly and with one accord assailing Mr. Golyadkin." The dreadful weather "[cuts] into him from all sides . . . and [draws] him off his path and out of his mind."[22] He enters a trancelike state and begins to stare fixedly into the canal's black and troubled waters. No conversion occurs. Instead, it is in this atmosphere that he encounters his double.

Ivan Karamazov

"I fear I am not in my perfect mind."
—*King Lear*, IV.7.63

Homo duplex, homo duplex! The first time that I perceived that I was
two was at the death of my brother Henri, when my father cried out so
dramatically, "He is dead, he is dead!" While my first self wept, my
second self thought, "How truly given was that cry, how fine it would be
at the theatre." I was then fourteen years old.

This horrible duality has often given me matter for reflection. Oh, this
terrible second me, always seated whilst the other is on foot, acting,
living, suffering, bestirring itself. This second me that I have never been
able to intoxicate, to make shed tears, or put to sleep. And how it sees
into things, and how it mocks!
— Alphonse Daudet, *Notes sur une Vie*

The fantastic intersection of time with timelessness fittingly envelops the
uncanny aspects of the journey to conversion for "Dostoevsky" in "The Peasant
Marey" and for the ridiculous man on his excursion. In *The Brothers Karamazov,* similar intersections figure importantly for Ivan in his encounter with the
devil, and for Alyosha in his vision. Each man encounters something that is simultaneously familiar and unknown. Dostoevsky "remembers" a long-forgotten occurrence at the "needed time." The ridiculous man visits a replica of our
own unfallen earth. Ivan encounters long-forgotten fragments of his own past
thoughts; the gloomy night dredges up a doubling of his own ideas in a physical
form that is alien and other: a devil.[23] Alyosha's vision combines recent events
and memories with a personal experience of the biblical past.

Ivan's uncompleted journey to conversion — the night on which he makes
his third and final visit to Smerdyakov and on which we witness his encounter
with the devil — occurs, the narrator-chronicler tells us precisely, at "the beginning of November. There had been a hard frost," and "a dry and sharp wind
was lifting and blowing the bits of snow about" (*PSS,* 14:462; 486).[24] This day
has extended through Books X and XI, and in chapter eight, as Ivan approaches Smerdyakov's house, the narrator refers to the morning weather that
he had described a hundred pages previously, "the keen dry wind that had
been blowing early that morning rose again, and a fine, thick dry snow began
falling heavily. It did not lie on the ground, but was whirled about by the
wind" (*PSS,* 14:462; 486). The date and the weather thus strongly recall the
night on which the ridiculous man had had his dream. (Golyadkin also comes
to mind.)

In "The Dream of a Ridiculous Man" it is impossible to say whether or not
the ridiculous man's actual conversion occurred after his journey through
space and time, during it, or before it, when he felt the first stab of pity for the
little girl. In Ivan's case, we cannot speak of a full-blown conversion or of a

sharply defined journey, but he does, like the ridiculous man, sometime in the course of that windy, wet night at the beginning of November, undergo a profound, irrevocable change. He, too, has an encounter with a being outside of everyday space and time. Moreover, Dostoevsky once again demarcates a character's spiritual change through the use of a frame, as he had done earlier in both "The Peasant Marey" and "The Dream of a Ridiculous Man." But now this frame is more curiously displaced, although it bears a strong resemblance both to the Polish convict who utters "Je häis ces brigands" and to the little girl, who each appear twice in their respective stories.

Ivan had earlier told Alyosha that he wished to send back his "entrance ticket" because he had rejected any universal system founded upon the unjustified tears of a child. Like the ridiculous man, he possesses a theory that allows him to reject God. But to underscore the change that is about to occur — his partial new acceptance of his membership in precisely such a universe where good and evil are mysteriously entwined — Dostoevsky does not have him meet a child on that cold November night. Instead, Dostoevsky offers up a kind of worst-case scenario: Ivan encounters a disgusting, drunken little peasant, a figure much closer to Dostoevsky's fellow convicts in his repulsiveness.

Like the Dostoevsky of "The Peasant Marey," Ivan feels a dreadful loathing and hatred for the peasant whom he meets on the way to his third and final interview with Smerdyakov. When the peasant lurches against Ivan, after having just sung his uncanny ditty, Ivan pushes him down on the frozen ground and thinks to himself, "He will freeze" (*PSS*, 15:57; 588). When he leaves Smerdyakov, after the latter's confession of murder, a spiritual regeneration has, at some indefinable point, already occurred for Ivan. "Something like joy was springing up in his heart" (*PSS*, 15:68; 600). He then stumbles again against the freezing peasant. Although exterior circumstances remain the same, in a pattern typical of the conversion experience, their essence has changed for Ivan. He saves the peasant. The frame is familiar, a repeated meeting or encounter — whether with a Pole, a child, or a drunken peasant — encapsulates a religious transformation. The use to which Dostoevsky will put it, however, is in this instance vastly different.

Ivan himself thinks he recognizes in his altruistic "frame act" a symbol of his regeneration, yet he simultaneously puts off going to the prosecutor to give him the money and to confess his role and Smerdyakov's. He goes home instead, and "strange to say, almost all his gladness and self-satisfaction passed in one instant" (*PSS*, 15:68–69; 601). Thus, instead of demarcating the boundaries in which, somewhere, sometime, a full conversion has occurred, this little frame tale of the drunken peasant underscores a failed conversion, a counter-conversion, a perversion of sorts.

Ivan returns home; his eyes fasten "on one point;" he enters a kind of trance-like state (much like Golyadkin's had been). The narrator-chronicler is at pains to describe Ivan's condition clinically and minutely: "As he entered his own room he felt something like a touch of ice on his heart, like a recollection or, more exactly, a reminder, of something agonizing and revolting that was in that room now, at that moment, and had been there before. . . . At moments he fancied he was delirious, but it was not illness that he thought of most. Sitting down again, he began looking round, as though searching for something. This happened several times. At last his eyes were fastened intently on one point. . . . There was evidently something, some object that irritated him there, worried him and tormented him" (*PSS*, 15:68–69; 601–2). After a discussion of the doctors Ivan had already consulted, the narrator-chronicler continues, "And so he was sitting almost conscious himself of his delirium and, as I have said already, looking persistently at some object on the sofa against the opposite wall." The devil appears.

During his interview with the devil, Ivan's mysterious relations with time and space manifest themselves most strikingly. Liza Knapp, who has explored the scientific aspects of this relationship, hypothesizes that "Ivan was unable to accept the harmony of God's universe because he understands the mystery of time—time being the 'fourth dimension' from which his three-dimensional Euclidean mind barred him."[25] Knapp shows convincingly that we may "crack the riddle" of Ivan through taking into account Dostoevsky's excellent knowledge of mathematics, astronomy, and physics and his understanding of current theories about the potential relativity of time. My interest in Ivan's relation to time and space is less scientific and more linked to the many possible "varieties of religious experience" as explored by William James.

Certainly, Dostoevsky's use of time through his literary career has been consistently problematic and has baffled readers as they realize how carefully Dostoevsky orchestrates the passage of time in his work even as that passage is consistently difficult to chart. Dostoevsky, even as he has almost obsessively portrayed particular moments in time, has, as Jacques Catteau aptly observed, evinced an "allergy toward epic time." Instead, he "sees and thinks about the world primarily in space rather than in time."[26] Nevertheless, his characters tend to experience their key moments of spiritual epiphany in terms of journeys—journeys to Siberia, to Europe and back, and, most markedly in the later stages of Dostoevsky's literary career, in journeys through space and time, especially to the past. And these journeys do come to possess a kind of epic quality, for upon their completion, the traveler becomes an epic hero of sorts, ready to transmit an emblematic message to his people, even though he may not be believed.

Bakhtin has remarked upon Dostoevsky's avoidance of the more usual forms of chronotope. "In his works Dostoevsky makes almost no use of relatively uninterrupted historical or biographical time, that is, of strictly epic time . . . [but] concentrates action on points of crisis . . . when the inner significance of a moment is equal to a 'billion years,' that is, when the moment loses its temporal restrictiveness. In essence he leaps over space as well."[27] Yet, as we have seen, Dostoevsky tends to demarcate these spatial and temporal leaps into the beyond by the use of frames that are strictly, rigidly rooted in the very time and space that are then briefly transcended. The point of departure and the point of return to more limited apprehensions of time and space are as crucial to Dostoevsky's overall vision as are the uncanny journeys away.

The devil's appearance before Ivan necessarily forces the reader, along with Ivan, to try to classify the nature of this experience. The devil may be simply a hallucination, the product of Ivan's deepening symptoms of brain fever. If so, he reiterates an old concern of Dostoevsky's. In *The Idiot* Myshkin had wondered whether visionary experience that was the result of illness could still "count," whether its lessons, its momentary glimpses of some higher harmony could be accepted, if they were merely the results of illness. Even earlier, in *Crime and Punishment*, Svidrigaylov had mused similarly about ghosts. James also had considered this question about the relationship between illness and visionary experience, but he dismissed it with the pragmatic conclusion that all that matters is the unshakeable sense one has of having undergone an authentic experience. James, in fact, is close to Svidrigaylov in suggesting that perhaps illness brings with it a broader awareness of other realms.[28]

Ivan himself makes no journey through space and time, but his devil does; he even catches cold along the way. Most important, the devil tells to Ivan Ivan's own "Legend about Paradise"—the story of the philosopher, who rejected everything, and after his death was sentenced to walk a quadrillion kilometers "in the dark." Once this trek was completed, so the story goes, the Gates of Heaven were to open to him. This journey fable offers a prophetic key to the fact and the ultimate results of Ivan's own visionary experience. The devil's telling of Ivan's own story also brings Ivan into intimate contact with the numinous.[29] The numinous is most readily expressed in literature by images of darkness, silence, and empty distance. The philosopher's quadrillion-kilometer walk in the dark thus becomes a nearly perfect expression of the numinous. "Empty distance," writes Rudolf Otto, "remote vacancy is, as it were, the sublime of the horizontal."[30]

The point of the devil's narrative and of Ivan's long-forgotten anecdote is that, after lying there *almost* a thousand years, the philosopher gets up and starts to walk. In reply to the devil, Ivan, desperately embracing the framework of Euclidean time, observes that the philosopher's decision to embark upon this journey is irrelevant, for it would take a billion years to travel such a distance. The devil pleasantly replies, "Much more than that, I haven't got a pencil and paper, or I could work it out. But he got there long ago and that's where the story begins" (*PSS*, 15:79; 611). The story somehow has leapt over an infinity of time and space, and its real beginning occurs only after this cosmic leap. The devil, in the hour he spends with Ivan, slyly urges Ivan toward an irrational acceptance of this other kind of time.

Ivan suddenly recalls that he himself had made up this anecdote at the age of seventeen. By discovering the devil's plagiarism, he thus tries to reduce him to the status of a hallucination. But the devil is a mysterious practitioner of homeopathy. Ivan insists to the devil that he has not the "hundredth part of a grain of faith in [him]." "But," replies the devil, "you have a thousandth of a grain. Homeopathic doses perhaps are the strongest. Confess that you have faith even to the ten-thousandth of a grain" (*PSS*, 15:79; 612).[31] It is here that we come up against a question more fundamental, more difficult, and more important to answer than whether or not the devil is a hallucination. Instead, Dostoevsky invites us to consider whether or not the devil is working to bring about Ivan's salvation or his damnation.

Throughout Dostoevsky's fictional writings, there is, as we have already seen, a curious mutuality between the ways in which good and evil work in the world. Dostoevsky describes the power, the modus operandi, of each in disturbingly similar terms. This mutuality had been expressed earlier on in *The Idiot* by Ippolit. He had described how one can plant the "seed of a good deed," and "all the seeds planted by you, which you perhaps have forgotten, will take root and grow."[32] This idea is congruent with the central motif governing *The Brothers Karamazov*. From its epigraph from John, to Zosima's exhortations, to Alyosha's actions throughout, to Ilyusha's death, to Dr. Herzenstube's pound of nuts, this novel is about the way in which goodness and grace journey through the world.

But, unfortunately, as we have repeatedly seen, evil travels in the same way. In *The Idiot*, for example, "the seed" of Ippolit's last conviction—the desire to commit suicide—also takes hardy root. Even Zosima, in *The Brothers Karamazov*, who can optimistically echo the novel's epigraph and himself cite John 12:24, has a dark vision, equally powerful, of how evil seeds can also bear fruit. He warns of the effect of a passing, spiteful word on a child. "You may have sown an evil seed in him and it may grow" (*PSS*, 14:288–89; 298). Thus, when Zosima goes on to say that "God took seeds from different worlds and sowed them on this earth . . .but what grows lives and is alive only through the feelings of its contact with other mysterious worlds" (*PSS*, 14:290; 299), he may be referring, albeit indirectly, to evil seeds as well as to good.[33] As James has observed, the mystical, saintly view includes evil in its overview; it cannot reduce or banish it.

When the devil, therefore, makes use of seed imagery for his own purpose, whether to convert or to subvert, he intensifies this disturbing symbiosis between good and evil. He wants to sow in Ivan a "tiny grain of faith" that "will grow into an oak tree" (*PSS*, 15:80; 612). For what purpose, we ask. The devil, true to our view of him as wily and full of sophistry, lays out both possibilities. On one hand, he would gain, by a believing Ivan's eventual fall, a greater trophy than a mere atheist ("we have our arithmetic" [*PSS*, 15:80; 613]). On the other hand, the devil—who is boastfully well read—suggests that he might be a variation of Faust's Mephistopheles, one who, by sowing a grain of faith in Ivan, claims to work in the service of God's greater good: "Mephistopheles declared to Faust that he desired evil, but did only good. Well, he can say what he likes, it's quite the opposite with me. I am perhaps the one man in all creation who loves the truth and genuinely desires good. . . . I know that at the end of all things I shall be recovered. I, too, shall walk my quadrillion" (*PSS*, 15:81; 614–15). Both possibilities exist.

What is perhaps most interesting is that the devil claims to practice metaphysical homeopathy. Homeopathy is directly opposed to mainstream medicine, which is "allopathic." Allopathic medicine makes use of remedies that produce effects different from those of the disease being treated. The science of homeopathy, both popular and discredited in the nineteenth century, maintained that illness was best cured by giving medicines that mimicked rather than masked the symptoms of disease. Its motto was *Similia similibus curentur.* ("Let likes be cured with likes").[34] The symptoms of illness should be simulated, according to homeopathic wisdom, for they are not part of the disease itself, but rather evidence of the body's attempt to cure itself. Thus the devil's practice of homeopathy upon Ivan may be understood as an attempt to "cure" his disease of atheism. Can we consider the devil's approach a variety of religious experience? "Knowing that you are inclined to believe in me, I administered some disbelief by telling you that anecdote. I lead you to belief and disbelief by turns, and I have my motive in it. It's the new method, sir" (*PSS*, 15:80; 612). The devil, whether he is a hallucinatory or a truly demonic double, homeopathically duplicates the symptoms of Ivan's disease; he mimics and mocks Ivan's own words, ideas, doubts. Thus Ivan, by recoiling from this toxic doubling of himself, might, according to the principles of homeopathy, begin to heal himself.

The most controversial aspect of homeopathy is its fundamental belief that the most minute doses, called the higher potencies—which are, in fact, *the most diluted* — are the most powerful, the most capable of curing. "Most scientists believe that no medicine diluted to more than a 12c potency would have any biochemical effect, since it is improbable that any molecules of the original substance remain."[35] Yet it is precisely these miniscule doses that homeopathy claims are most effective. It is, moreover, just such a miniscule dose of faith that the devil seeks to administer to Ivan by imitating Ivan's own "symptoms" of disbelief.

The question is, does it work? According to the predictions of the science of homeopathy, we would probably have to argue yes, although by the end of the novel Ivan's "cure" as yet is not finished, but is, rather, still in progress. A homeopathic cure takes time; all the initial physical symptoms greatly worsen before they improve. In fact, their very worsening is supposed to be a sign of improvement, for the homeopathic cure works from the inside out. The internal parts improve first, while the exterior parts are supposed to worsen temporarily. This may be the case with Ivan; certainly by the end of the novel, he lies unconscious, the symptoms of that "brain fever" that had been encroaching for so long, since his homeopathic encounter with the devil are now worse than ever. Yet he had briefly, after his third meeting with Smerdyakov, felt a transient surge of healing joy. Has the devil's small dose of highly toxic words stimulated the beginning of a more permanent healing process? Does Ivan's confession in the courtroom indicate that he has already, like his philosopher, gotten up "from the road" and begun, in the dark, the journey toward belief? Certainly Ivan's statement to the court possessed the most telling earmarks of an authentic Dostoevskian confession: Ivan utters his words publicly, and no one takes them at their face value.

Dostoevsky himself had, as a patient, a firsthand experience with homeopathy. In 1837, just before he set off to engineering school, and a few months after his mother's death, he contracted a throat ailment that reduced his voice to a whisper. Dostoevsky's father tried conventional remedies upon him; when they failed, he practiced, "against his own strictly allopathic professional convictions" a popular homeopathic technique on him.[36] In fact, Rice points out that this was "the only known therapeutic exchange" between Dr. Dostoevsky and his son. Although the homeopathic remedy he used was a popular one, it was also controversial, for it involved administering a slight dose of a toxic substance, "probably belladonna." The treatment failed and "Dostoevsky never recovered the normal use of his voice."[37] Shortly after this episode, in October 1838, a report presented to the Society of Russian Physicians concluded that homeopathy was unsound. Nevertheless, it continued to remain a popular form of treatment. Dostoevsky's early personal experience with homeopathy may well have informed this critical scene from the end of his literary career. If so, it could be an indication to us that the devil's treatment won't work.

In fact, the notebook pages outlining the early plans for Ivan's encounter with the devil are more peculiarly crammed with references to the devil's medical problems than is the final text. Dostoevsky makes repeated reference to the devil's wart, to his cough, to his catarrh of the respiratory canal. He also mentions sulfuric hydrogen gas, Hoffmann's malt liquor, and honey with salt. In Dostoevsky's jottings, the devil repeats several times that he has been vaccinated twice.[38] Vaccinations could certainly be considered to be equivalent to homeopathic provings, for they inoculate against a particular disease by dosing the patient with a small amount of it. A miniscule toxic dose is thus used for curative purposes. Moreover, these notes suggest that Dostoevsky may have planned for the devil either to inoculate Ivan through his words against atheism, or, what to my mind is less likely, to inoculate Ivan against belief. "You believe a small drop. Homeopathic. A little seed-oak. An oak grows up . . . Ivan. That's to convert me" (*PSS*, 15:335; 222). The knife cuts both ways, and it is left for the reader to decide whether the devil's rendition of Ivan's "Legend about Paradise" operates to bring Ivan to belief or to drag him away from it. Could the devil be giving Ivan an onion?[39] At any rate, in the notes Ivan emphasizes the devil's resemblance to him. "He's terribly stupid. He is stupid like me. Exactly like me . . . I am looking at my portrait." Thus, like is treated with like, according to homeopathic wisdom. There is also the curiously homeopathic statement: "Alyosha believed a little drop" (*PSS*, 15:337; 225).

In the text of the novel, Dostoevsky reduces the number of medical references, although they continue to play a role consonant with homeopathy. Ivan accuses the devil of being "myself, myself only with a different mug." The devil agrees that he, like Ivan, "suffers from the fantastic, and so I love the realism of earth" (*PSS*, 15:73; 605). For him, this realism is epitomized in the pleasures of superstition and of "being doctored": He tells Ivan how he has been vaccinated for smallpox, and how he suffers from rheumatism. He then offers up a striking misquotation from Terence. Ivan realizes that he himself has never thought of this misquotation before, and for a moment, Ivan believes in the devil. Seeing this, the devil immediately bursts out with a cynical dismissal of visionary experience: "Listen, in dreams and especially in nightmares, from indigestion or anything, a man sometimes sees such artistic visions, such complex and real actuality, such events, even a whole world of events, woven into such a plot, with such unexpected details from the most exalted matters to the last button on a cuff, as I swear Leo Tolstoy could not create. . . . I am only your nightmare, nothing more" (*PSS*, 15:79; 606). Ivan quickly realizes that the devil is dragging him back and forth between belief and disbelief, between conversion and perversion. In reply, the devil promises to explain later the "special method" he has adopted "for today." That special method, as we have seen, is homeopathy.

The devil thus ridicules the kind of visionary journey that the ridiculous man took in "The Dream of a Ridiculous Man." He chalks these "artistic visions" up to indigestion. But the devil shares the ridiculous man's belief that our earth can be, in some unfathomable way, repeated elsewhere in time and space. "Our present earth may have been repeated a billion times. Why, it's become extinct, been frozen; cracked, broken to bits, disintegrated into its elements, again 'the water above the firmament'; then again a comet, again a sun, again from the sun it becomes earth — and the same sequence may have been repeated endlessly" (*PSS*, 15:79; 611). Victor Terras suspects that this idea of "eternal palingenesis" may have been one of Dostoevsky's preoccupations.[40] Certainly, it offers us a further link between the visionary experience of Ivan and the ridiculous man.

Indeed, in his efforts to cure the cold he caught flying through space in an evening suit, the devil practically tells us that he himself has resorted to homeopathic medicine, which had long been in disrepute in Russia, but had nevertheless remained so popular. He lambastes the establishment Russian doctors. "I've tried all the medical faculty: they can diagnose beautifully . . . but they've no idea how to cure you." He makes fun of fancy European specialists: the one in Paris "who can only cure your right nostril," the one in Vienna who "will cure your left nostril. What are you to do? I fell back on popular remedies" (*PSS*, 15:76; 607–8). On the advice of a German doctor he rubs himself with honey and salt, and when that fails to cure him, he resorts to what seems to be homeopathy. He writes to Count Mattei in Milan. "He sent me a book and some drops, bless him, and only fancy, Hoff's malt extract cured me! I bought it by accident, drank a bottle and a half of it, and I was ready to dance; it took it away completely. I made up my mind to write to the papers to thank him" (*PSS*, 15:76; 608). The devil's gleeful foray outside accepted medical practice into the realm of popular remedies and drops from a count in Milan suggest an anti-establishment resort to homeopathic practices.[41]

Alyosha Karamazov

> with an eye made quiet by the power
> Of harmony, and the deep power of joy,
> We see into the life of things.
> — Wordsworth, "Lines composed a few miles above Tintern Abbey"

Levin listened to the rhythmical dripping of raindrops from the lime trees in the garden, and looked at a familiar triangular constellation and at the Milky Way which with its branches intersected it . . .
"This new feeling has not changed me, has not rendered me happy, nor suddenly illuminated me as I dreamt it would, but is just like my feeling for my son."
— *Anna Karenina*, 8.19

I shall close with a brief look at Alyosha Karamazov's moment of crisis and the fantastic journey that embodies his conversion: his vision of Cana of Galilee. Some of the conversion rhythms of "The Peasant Marey" recapitulate here in a major key. The frame of the Polish convict and his "Je haïs ces brigands" finds an echo in Alyosha's conversations with Rakitin. In despair, Alyosha leaves the body of the decaying elder Zosima. Like the convict Dostoevsky, he rushes outside for relief. In his grief and doubt he lies "face downwards on the ground under a tree" (*PSS*, 14:308; 319). Rakitin, the moral equivalent of the Polish convict, appears. Alyosha then goes with Rakitin to Grushenka, where he and Grushenka enact their mutual "onion-giving."[42] The meeting between Alyosha and Grushenka possesses the same suggestion of preconversion conversion that occurs in "The Dream of a Ridiculous Man," where the main protagonist is somehow saved by the little girl even *before* he undertakes his fantastic conversion journey. Alyosha returns to Zosima's cell, where he will find himself on a visionary journey to the biblical past, but the actual moment of his conversion is impossible to locate. Later in the novel, as we have seen, Ivan's lowest point — his third visit to Smerdyakov — had ended with his having felt "something like joy." In all three cases, but particularly in Alyosha's, it is possible that the fundamental shift to conversion has taken place even before the "conversion journey" through time and space begins.

Rakitin taunts Alyosha as they return to the monastery. "So you see the miracles you were looking out for just now have come to pass!" (*PSS*, 14:324; 336), but Alyosha, like the convict Dostoevsky with the Pole at the end of "The Peasant Marey," finds himself no longer vulnerable to Rakitin's cynicism and hatred. Something has already taken place. He reenters Zosima's cell and is overwhelmed by joy. As he listens to Father Paissy read the passage in the Bible about Jesus's first miracle, he finds himself actually present with Christ at Cana of Galilee. "But what's this? Why is the room growing wider? . . . Ah, yes . . . It's the marriage, the wedding . . . yes, of course" (*PSS*, 14:327; 339). Zosima is there, too. Zosima, who calls him "dear one," "my kind boy," "gentle one," treats him with a motherly affection reminiscent of Marey (*PSS*,

14:327; 339). He raises Alyosha by the hand. Alyosha, like the child Dostoevsky in "The Peasant Marey," expresses his fear. "I am afraid . . . I dare not look." Zosima comforts him. Alyosha awakens and rushes outside to water the earth with his tears. "Something firm and unshakable" had entered his soul; he never forgets that moment. "And never, never, all his life long, could Alyosha forget that minute. 'Someone visited my soul in that hour,' he used to say afterwards with implicit faith in his words" (*PSS*, 14:328; 341).

This event, like the nine-year-old Dostoevsky's encounter with Marey, occurs toward the end of August, at the close of a bright day. "The vault of heaven, full of soft, shining stars, stretched vast and fathomless above him. The Milky Way ran in two pale streams from the zenith to the horizon. The fresh, motionless, still night enfolded the earth." Alyosha lies on the earth amidst "the gorgeous autumn flowers." "The silence of earth seemed to melt into the silence of the heavens" (*PSS*, 14:349; 340). Yet again, Dostoevsky has carefully located a conversion—which involved a journey out of everyday time and space to a precious, living past—within a definite frame of setting and time: a monk's cell and a garden at nine o'clock on an evening in late August. As in "The Peasant Marey," "The Dream of a Ridiculous Man," and Ivan's encounter with the devil, recent events and memories converge with time long past; the subliminal becomes immanent; conversion occurs.

The Dostoevsky of 1876 who wrote "The Peasant Marey," the ridiculous man who loses the knack for words but becomes a preacher anyway, and Alyosha who rises up from the earth "a resolute champion" have each completed a journey of conversion, from which they emerge with tears of joy to embrace an unchanged but newly beautiful world. Their journeys now change direction. Instead of journeying inwardly through time and space to an infinitely precious, fully living past, they must each now travel on the road of everyday reality. They now transmit their message to others, knowing full well they will probably not be believed. To some degree, each has taken on the qualities of a saint. This is not to say they have become emblems or stock characters, or that they lose their individuality. Indeed, argues James, the saint is, above all, the champion of the individual. "With their extravagance of human tenderness, [they] are the great torch bearers of [the belief in the essential sacredness of every person], the tip of the wedge, the cleavers of the darkness" (*Varieties*, 283).[43] At the end of *The Brothers Karamazov*, Ivan is still writhing under the effects—potentially lethal, potentially redemptive—of the devil's homeopathic experiment. When we last see him he remains in that uncleared darkness that Dostoevsky and James both knew so well. Whether Ivan journeys to conversion or to perversion remains a mystery. Or can we assume that perhaps, like his philosopher, "he got there long ago"?

Concluding Fragments: Some Last Words

"Reading as if for life"
— Charles Dickens, *David Copperfield*

I must lie down where all the ladders start,
In the foul rag-and-bone shop of the heart.
— W. B. Yeats, "The Circus Animals' Desertion"

Tiny, tiny alterations — but on them depend the most immense and terrible consequences. . . . And boundless results of unimaginable importance may follow from the most minute alterations.
— Tolstoy, "Why Do Men Stupefy Themselves?"

"It's a strange thing: it's painful, yet the memories are, as it were, pleasant. Even what was nasty, what I was vexed with at the time, is, as it were, purified from nastiness in my memory and presents itself in an attractive shape to my imagination."
— Devushkin, in *Poor People*

Dostoevsky hesitated in his fiction to say his last word or to state, directly, any final conviction. Most often when he did try to do so, he failed. For that his readers can be glad. His journeys remain unfinished. There are fully realized moments, complete unto themselves, but these moments always give way to something else. That is why, with the possible exception of *The Brothers Karamazov,* there is no closure at the end of any of his literary works. They all remain open, unfinished, ready to be reread and reimagined anew, even when some larger message within them has been finalized. Yet even *The Brothers Karamazov* — which closes with Alyosha's electrifying speech at the stone, with its many invocations of memory, joy, and faith, and with the children's heady, responsive cries of "Hurrah for Karamazov," a closure that seems initially resoundingly firm — remains open.[1] Those funeral pancakes will be eaten; everyday life will resume its course. The brothers and the children will scatter and age; some will die, others will find themselves immersed in new plots. All they or we can do is trust, or at least retain the hope, of remembering moments like this at the "needed time." Then, like the convict Dostoevsky lying in his bunk in despair, the memory of such a moment — whether it be generated by life or by literature or by imagination — can be reinvented, reincarnated, added to, transformed. In the case of *The Brothers Karamazov* and the moment that Alyosha exhorts the boys to remember, it is the moment when they have gathered to remember their dead friend, Ilyusha, at whom these same boys had thrown stones. His disturbing and tragic death becomes transformed into an occasion for a kind of surprising joy, just as Grushenka's pessimistic parable about the old woman in the burning lake of Hell was transformed into a narrative emblematic of surprising joy for both Grushenka and Alyosha.

The student who lamented that reading *The Brothers Karamazov* was like trying to carry nine bags of groceries has captured Dostoevsky in our time. So has the young man sitting at the back of the room who started wiping his eyes during a discussion of the scene in *Poor People* about how the bumbling old Pokrovsky, with books sticking out of his pockets, lost his hat as he ran after his dead son's coffin. Varvara describes to Devushkin how the passersby who witnessed the strange scene "took off their caps and crossed themselves. Some stopped and stood gazing in wonder."[2] Dostoevsky reaches into our hearts, enrages us, challenges our theories, subverts cherished beliefs, and even when he does not answer the big questions his works pose, offers up a comfort that is not cold, not lukewarm, but hot. The words of W. H. Auden come to mind,

> O look, look in the mirror,
> O look in your distress;
> Life remains a blessing
> Although you cannot bless.

O stand, stand at the window
As the tears scald and start;
You shall love your crooked neighbor
With your crooked heart.[3]

In 1849 when Dostoevsky traveled through the streets of St. Petersburg on his way to what he thought was his execution, his musings about his life — his memories — merged with thoughts about his reading, most specifically with Victor Hugo. We can be almost certain of this.[4] As we have seen, Dostoevsky's characters also draw equally from memory, from literature, the Bible, or folk-lore at critical moments; these elements combine with each other in unexpected ways. Both he and his characters repeatedly find meaning and comfort in the hybrid created by this mixing of fact and fancy. For Dostoevsky this blending was productive of a higher truth. He might have called it a spiritual truth; today we might prefer to call it an aesthetic one. Nevertheless, we also experience, whatever we choose to call it, that same fusion of life and art at similarly critical moments. What fragment of a particular work of Dostoevsky's, what seed, will lodge in each of us to take root and be remembered at some later time and thus, to some degree, transform us?

Works like *Notes from the House of the Dead, Crime and Punishment, The Idiot, The Possessed,* "The Peasant Marey," "The Dream of a Ridiculous Man," and *The Brothers Karamazov* have engaged each successive generation since their writing. Moreover, each suggests a series of answers to the question "why do we read?" In many of these works the characters themselves are avid readers and are repeatedly influenced by what they read. Their reasons for reading are the same as ours. We read to lose ourselves in plots, to find ourselves in characters, to overhear possible answers to the big questions, to laugh or to cry, to reenact — as complex reading beings — individual, social, and moral dilemmas. Such reasons for reading are axiomatic, automatic, and not terribly compelling, though reading itself is. As I have already observed, in the pedagogically flavored chapter devoted to *Crime and Punishment,* great novels, like great teachers, do not teach us to answer questions but to find a way to pose them.

An attempt to locate or define the impulse toward reading is as uncertain as it is to describe both the position and the speed of a single electron. As readers we seek to have an emotionally intimate encounter with the text as well as to generate a cool appraisal of its trajectory within theoretical, formal, critical, cultural, and historical contexts. But in any given moment a reader experiences one kind of reading at the expense of the other.

Early on in *David Copperfield* (1849–50), a novel Dostoevsky knew and loved, the mistreated and neglected David discovers — to borrow Tsvetaeva's haunting phrase — his childhood bookshelf, which is in fact really the collection of his dead father's books, in a little room adjoining his own. He begins feverishly to read, and soon he is reading, as the adult David narrator (and through him, Dickens himself) tells us "as if for life."[5] We read "as if for life." Such reading is both a complete immersion in the act itself and a contemplation of it. Paradoxically, however, the more we are immersed, the less accurately can we analyze what we are reading, and the more we analyze, the less actively can we be immersed. This uncertainty principle is, in its totality, the act of reading itself, and why we read "as if for life." Dostoevsky and his characters "read as if for life" and are transformed by their reading, as are we.

There are moments in Dostoevsky's fiction that seem to belie the extreme interconnectedness of characters, plot fragments, and those narrative layers that weld his novels and stories into such a tough alloy. Such moments (and for each reader they differ) reach out of the work and into a fictionally unconceived, more everyday space that usually serves as a buffer between reader and text. I shall cite four short examples from a single novel, *The Brothers Karamazov.* One such moment pops up at the end of the first chapter in the novel. The narrator-chronicler is describing how Fyodor Karamazov ran into the street and began shouting with joy at the news of his first wife's death in St. Petersburg. "The story is that he ran out in the street and began shouting with joy." But "others say that he wept without restraint like a little child, so much so that people were sorry for him, in spite of the repulsion he inspired. It is quite possible that both versions were true, that he rejoiced at his release and at the same time wept for her who released him." As the reader — new to the novel and its many characters — works to process this duality in a character who has so far seemed both safely removed to a comic distance and slightly repulsive, the narrator-chronicler abruptly closes his chapter with a generalization that reaches out, somewhat uncomfortably, into that undefined zone beyond the novel proper: "As a general rule, people, even the wicked, are much more naïve and simple-hearted than we suppose. *And we ourselves are too.*"[6]

Another moment in the same work when the narrative, without warning, encroaches upon a boundary beyond its typical borders occurs when Zosima tells the grieving peasant woman from afar whose little child has died, "do not be comforted, you should not be comforted, do not be comforted" (*PSS,* 14:46; 41–42). In chapter four I suggested that we could read Zosima's five encounters with five peasant women (taken as a whole) as constituting a kind of parable about faith. In reading the dialogue between the second of these women, the "one from afar," and Zosima, the reader is drawn into the narrative in an unexpected way to find unexpected comfort in the assertion to "not be comforted." One might say that at this moment the narrative of the novel has again overstepped its usual boundaries and crossed into that other indefinable space closer to the actual reader. What does it mean to be urged to be not comforted? Is this not a message for the present? Is it comforting?

Other such moments break through the fabric of the text at unpredictable intervals. There is, for example, the narrator-chronicler's excursion into art criticism (reminiscent of some of Dostoevsky's own remarks that we have already encountered in his occasional role as art critic) when he describes, in an extended character sketch of Smerdyakov, the "remarkable painting" *Contemplation* by Ivan Kramskoy. The painting depicts:

> a forest in winter, and on a roadway through the forest, in absolute solitude, stands a wandering peasant in a torn caftan and bark shoes. He stands, as it were, lost in thought. Yet he is not thinking; he is "contemplating." If any one touched him he would start and look at one as though awakening and bewildered. It's true he would come to himself immediately, but if he were asked what he had been thinking about, he would remember nothing. Yet probably he has hidden within himself the impression which had dominated him during the period of contemplation. Those impressions are dear to him and no doubt he hoards them imperceptibly, and even unconsciously. How and why, of course, he does not know either. He may suddenly, after hoarding impressions for many years, abandon everything and go off to Jerusalem on a pilgrimage for his soul's salvation, or perhaps he will suddenly set fire to his native village, and perhaps do both (*PSS*, 14:116–17; 115).

Throughout his career as both journalist and writer of fiction, Dostoevsky consistently focused on seeking to understand and portray the experience, the ramifications, and above all, the transformative force of memory — laced with invention — and the role within memory of dreams, of waking dreams, of forgetfulness and sudden recollection. Each chapter of the present work has engaged with the varieties of ways that this transformative process operates in Dostoevsky's work, whether through suggesting how his own literary transformations may have been engendered by his readings of other writers, or by endeavoring to understand how Dostoevsky represented the process of transformation or conversion within his characters and himself. In the passage describing Kramskoy's painting, a brief narrative digression about a peasant lost in thought (almost in a trance) who gazes absently at the surrounding landscape encapsulates all of these themes.

It also urges us, indirectly, to understand Smerdyakov's motivations and his potential for good as well as evil in a way that most readers have chosen not to do. Smerdyakov too, like this strange peasant and like any character Dostoevsky ever created, could have been ripe for conversion, but that transformation never occurs. Do we ever really know whether that third presence in the room to whom Smerdyakov alludes when he confesses to Ivan is God or the devil? Why can there not be four presences, or five — for are we not there as well?

How many readers may even have encountered this unsettling digression about Kramskoy's painting after they too have just gazed at something, perhaps looked up from their reading lost in thought, yet not thinking, having just come to their senses, bewildered? We too — like Dostoevsky, Goryanchikov, Raskolnikov, Myshkin, Stavrogin, the ridiculous man, Zosima, Grushenka, Ivan, Alyosha, and Kramskoy's nameless peasant — hoard our impressions, with their full potential for evil and good. Every reader assembles, voluntarily and involuntarily, consciously and without full consciousness, a rich collection of such impressions. These impressions combine to support a coherent reading of any work of fiction or poetry, but much like the pillow that some unknown person places under the sleeping Dmitry's head after his interrogation and deposition, it is impossible for any reader to know for certain how exactly that supporting understanding — that cherished reading — came into being. We are all "reading as if for life." Thus reading a novel suggests a microcosm for the way we live our lives, for the way in which we assemble our memories and our impressions. Like "the convict Dostoevsky" we live by analyzing our impressions and adding new touches to things experienced long ago.

Dostoevsky brings his readers into his world at unexpected moments and in unexpected ways; the reader never knows from moment to moment — whether the narrative be humorous, heartrending, or journalistic in tone — when a boundary will suddenly be encroached, and either the story will spring uncomfortably, into the reader's world, or the reader, willy-nilly, will find himself inside the novel, almost like the narrator in Woody Allen's comic story "The Kugelmas Episode," who finds himself inside *Madame Bovary,* and worse, exposed and visible to all its other readers at that moment in time.

For each reader, then, fragments, shards or loose threads of the novel jut out of the text into an a-literary zone occupied by the reader. Are these moments loose ends in the novel that do not quite cohere to the internal organization of the text? In the collection, for example, of the four such moments that I have just offered up here, one sees two throwaway digressions by the narrator-chronicler, a message to be not comforted and the unexplained appearance of a pillow. Tug on any one of them, and instead of being a dangling fragment, shard, or loose thread, the whole novel will tumble into your lap, thus illustrating Zosima's frequently cited aphorism that "all things are connected." In the world of this novel and of Dostoevsky's fictional works generally, at least, they are. That world comes tumbling down on today's reader, that uncomforted, yet comforted reader lost in a contemplation fraught with every kind of potential.

A Leaf, a Door, a Stone

Although Dostoevsky was not a poet in the conventional sense, he used symbols as vigorously as any poet, and as an author he was consistently aware of the poet within himself.[7] Moreover, his characters have been recognized by readers as various as Belinsky, Viacheslav Ivanov, Woolf, Coetzee, and Leonid Tsypkin (perhaps by virtually all his readers) as being the fictional embodiments of a profoundly poetic mind. In his evocative but largely forgotten essay "Dingley Dell and the Fleet," upon whose insights I have already drawn in chapter seven, Auden gives a handy definition of such characters, that is, characters who are, somehow, poetic embodiments of an idea. He is not writing about Dostoevsky (he is in fact, amusingly, comparing Sherlock Holmes to Anna Karenina), but his observation is keen and wholly applicable to Dostoevsky:

> All characters who are products of the mythopoeic imagination are instantaneously recognizable by the fact that their existence is not defined by their social and historical context; transfer them to another society or another age and their characters and behaviour will remain unchanged. In consequence, once they have been created, they cease to be their author's characters and become the reader's; he can continue their story for himself.
>
> Anna Karenina is not such a character for the reader cannot imagine her apart from the particular milieu in which Tolstoi places her or the particular history of her life which he records; Sherlock Holmes, on the other hand, is: every reader, according to his fancy, can imagine adventures for him which Conan Doyle forgot, as it were, to tell us.[8]

Auden goes on to hypothesize that it is usually minor writers who possess this mythopoeic gift, although he offers up Shakespeare, Cervantes, and Dickens as exceptions. Surely Dostoevsky belongs on that list as well.

The sticky green leaves of early spring have become a tag phrase for identifying Ivan Karamazov, for they function as a Bakhtinian loophole, an indication early on in the novel that whatever rebellion may lie ahead for this character, the potential for love and affirmation is there too. (Later, Zosima asserts, "every leaf is striving to the Word" [*PSS*, 14:268; 274]). Dostoevsky did not hesitate to use sentimental images in this particular way — think, for example, of the baby, described by Myshkin in his parable about faith, who had smiled at its mother for the first time, or the little girl in "The Dream of a Ridiculous Man," or that grieving peasant woman from afar who comes to Zosima's cell. Dostoevsky was ready to pull all the stops if it would achieve the desired effect of bonding his readers to a character and thereby implicating them in that character's fate. The many other images of lost and injured children throughout his work function similarly. The emotion they call forth ultimately helps dissipate the propensity for theories about life and propels characters into life itself, a consistent aim of Dostoevsky's fiction. There are, of course, notable exceptions to this process. Svidrigaylov and Stavrogin, for example, each violate a female child and end by being unable to embrace that sticky, emotion-laden affirmation of life. They commit suicide. For Ivan, the sticky green leaf stands in juxtaposition to his theories, much in the same way as for Dostoevsky himself his love of Jesus could, at times, stand in juxtaposition to his passion for the truth.

More than a quarter of a century earlier, Dostoevsky had written to Madame Fonvizina, "More than that—if someone succeeded in proving to me that Christ was outside the truth, and if, *indeed,* the truth was outside Christ, I would sooner remain with Christ than with the truth." We have already, in chapter one, considered the importance of this often-quoted letter for understanding Dostoevsky's own conversion. The green leaf becomes an accessible symbol for Ivan's potential for conversion, for his acknowledgment of something living and precious that exists outside of and despite his theories. If we knew, however, that Smerdyakov had also loved the sticky green leaves would we have had hope for him too? Can we find it in our hearts to be moved by Smerdyakov's inability to experience a transformation, a spiritual reawakening, or a conversion? Is there any evidence, despite our knowledge that Dostoevsky believed in evil and in the devil, that he would have wanted us to be so moved? In Ivan's preface to "The Grand Inquisitor," he alludes to the ancient narrative of "The Wanderings of Our Lady Through Hell." "Our Lady visits Hell. . . . She sees the sinners and their punishment. There she sees among others one noteworthy set of sinners in a burning lake; some of them sink to the bottom of the lake so that they can't swim out, and 'these God forgets'—an expression of extraordinary depth and force" (*PSS,* 14:225; 228).[9] Does Dostoevsky "forget" Smerdyakov in similar fashion?

Although Dmitry Karamazov, like Ivan, undergoes a conversion in the course of the novel, Dostoevsky primarily focuses on him as a character for whom many plots are possible. Innumerable scenarios hover around him—scenarios that may or may not have taken place before the events of the novel begin, scenarios that occur during it, and future scenarios. It is fitting then, that Dmitry's trial becomes the arena for an extraordinary debate about the meaning and the ultimate usefulness of evidence in general.

This focus on the nature of evidence is yet another way in which novels like *Crime and Punishment,* in which both Raskolnikov and Porfiry Petrovich know, at virtually every moment, that any piece of evidence, any fact, has multiple interpretations, or *The Idiot,* in which the many characters who seek to create a biography for Myshkin each distort and capture his character in different ways, or *The Brothers Karamazov,* with its complex trial scene in which the same evidence, depending upon who wields it, can argue in contrary ways, touches upon themes that are of compelling interest to readers today. Evidence, Dostoevsky's fiction repeatedly tells us, like psychological theory, is (literally "a stick with two ends") a knife that can cut either way.

This insight becomes a commonplace. In *The Brothers Karamazov* this paradox about the nature of evidence, for example, comes to the fore most dramatically in the scenes devoted to Dmitry's trial. It is frequently epitomized by speculations by the narrator-chronicler and others about whether, on the night of the murder, the door to the garden was open or closed. Upon the determination of that fact seems to hinge the judgment about Dmitry's innocence or guilt in the murder of his father. Grigory's evidence, based on his faulty recollection, becomes crucial. The door becomes the vital piece of evidence, the one small truth on which larger truths hinge.

Yet how many readers of the novel can actually remember, several months after they have finished the novel, whether that door was open or closed? Even as we acknowledge that this is a crucial piece of evidence, do we remember it? What does this forgetfulness signal? Does it perhaps suggest that the individual facts upon which we build a theory may not even be the important ones after all? Should the door, and whether or not it was open or shut, have ever become the locus for determining Dmitry's innocence or guilt? Could not he have been innocent or guilty whether or not the door were open or shut, or even if there were no door at all? The door, then, becomes symbolic of the need for the fact to fit the theory, even when both fact and theory are in doubt. The door and the confusion about it also concretize how difficult it is to recollect clearly, to recognize guilt or innocence, to string together a series of events in a truthful way, to identify evidence as such. For Dostoevsky the more essential truth of any matter does not lie in the recovery of a photographic and completely accurate memory, but rather in that recollection which has been transformed but not contaminated by an act of the imagination. He recognized that evidence itself is unstable and always contextual.

Dostoevsky (and after him, Bakhtin) asks us to recognize him as a writer whose vision (whether narratively, thematically, or with regard to character) hovers precariously and uncomfortably at boundaries and thresholds. In such a realm a door, whether opened or closed, is ultimately irrelevant.

For Dostoevsky the kind of knowledge that factual evidence like this can impart is less meaningful than the more symbolic, epiphanic transformations that can occur at unexpected moments. Dostoevsky's representations of such moments in his fiction tend to coincide with the occasions on which he is in fact trying to impart some kind of portable, durable insight. Moments such as when the narrator of *The House of the Dead* sees the dying convict Mihailov in chains, or Raskolnikov recollects his terrible dream in prison, or Dostoevsky recreates his nine-year-old self and the peasant Marey, or Alyosha speaks to the boys at the stone at the end of *The Brothers Karamazov*—these moments, whether negative or positive, constitute the portable insights about the features of transformation and conversion and the kind of primary experience Dostoevsky deemed most important.

For example, the very fact that Alyosha's speech to the boys at the end of the novel is at a stone reminds us not only of the apostle Peter, but of the commandments that were inscribed on a stone.[10] Although those biblical tablets are lost, or are probably nonexistent, their words have inscribed themselves upon the memories of hundreds of generations, just as Alyosha's pronouncements at the stone inscribed themselves upon the memories of the boys in the novel and upon us as readers. His words have become bread; they offer pleasant nourishment and a basic means to sustain life. Thus Dostoevsky makes use of stones in the novel as a kind of symbol that is itself firm yet always in flux—a stone can be a stone, a weapon, a word, and it can, miraculously, turn into bread; it is the thing itself and something other. It is firm, a bedrock, yet not fixed.[11]

Thus the leaf, the door, and the stone each function differently. The leaf speaks to the reader about the primacy of life over theory. The sticky green leaf signals the reader that Ivan himself is sticky, green, and young—still susceptible to experience. His natural impulses toward life and love exist despite his theory. The door calls our attention to the difficulty of taking any one fact as evidence for the whole. The door does not illuminate Dmitry's character but rather points to a debate in the novel about the nature of evidence. The stone suggests the inherent potential for good and for evil, for conversion or its lack, inherent in all human beings. The stone remains unfixed, a metaphor always in flux, transforming or not transforming into a weapon, into bread, into words —becoming by the close of the novel the foundation of a spiritual edifice built on the unjustified suffering and tears of a child. The poet Dostoevsky used symbols to widely varying effect.

Intellectual Property and Spiritual Plagiarism

I have already considered at some length Dostoevsky's use of seed imagery, beginning in *Notes from the House of the Dead* and finding its culmination in *The Brothers Karamazov*. Grushenka's story of the onion has also played a significant role in these pages. The seed and the onion are emblematic of that same potential in each human being for both negative and positive metamorphosis and transformation. The seed and the onion are likewise suggestive of Dostoevsky's longstanding habits of narration, with his primary strategies as a writer. They have each offered metaphors for describing the narrative texture of his fiction generally. The layers of narration in his work, particularly in *The Brothers Karamazov*, resemble those that compose a seed, moving in from the husk to the kernel. Alternately, narration in Dostoevsky's fiction exhibits features reminiscent of the concentrically spiraling layers of an onion: sliced in half an onion appears to have discrete layers, and each layer in some way replicates the others. But in fact the layers are connected and compose a single entity. The onion can unwind into an unbroken spiral so that each layer is not only a microcosm of the whole, it is the whole.[12] These metaphors for the kind of narrative texture Dostoevsky created are especially powerful in *The Brothers Karamazov* because in that particular novel form and content, with regard both to seeds and to onions — coincide.

Both John 12:24 and the story of the onion told by Grushenka to Alyosha are dominant ideas of the novel that have the open-ended potential of having either a positive or a negative effect. Bad seeds can, as we have frequently seen, as easily take root as well as healthy ones. Although Grushenka's story was about an old woman whose one good deed had *not* been sufficient to save her from the burning lake in Hell, it had been told as an optimistic parable in order to give a redemptive onion to both Grushenka (the narrator) and to Alyosha (her audience) and to readers in general.

Moreover, Alyosha, in giving back the onion to Grushenka, repeats a precious routine that he has already enacted in the novel, that of spiritual plagiarism. He had already given back to Ivan the kiss that Ivan's Jesus had given to the Grand Inquisitor (" 'That's plagiarism,' cried Ivan, highly delighted. 'You stole that from my poem. Thank you though' " [*PSS*, 14:240; 244]. Earlier Ivan had told Alyosha, " 'It's wonderful how you can turn words as Polonius says in *Hamlet*. . . . You turn my words against me. Well, I am glad' " [*PSS*, 14:216; 220][13]). Alyosha, in these three acts of literary and spiritual plagiarism, has returned to Grushenka and to Ivan kernels of grace that each had *already* unknowingly possessed. We have already seen how the devil had plagiarized Ivan as well when he told him Ivan's own, but forgotten, story of the philosopher who had to walk a quadrillion kilometers in the dark. The devil, through his plagiarism, had similarly returned to Ivan something precious that he already, unknowingly, had. Or, put in the terms of "The Peasant Marey," the memory of the story he had composed in his youth had returned to Ivan at the "needed time."

Ironically, when Dostoevsky proudly inserted this tale of the onion into his novel, he thought he was the first to set down this remarkable peasant parable.[14] But he had committed an unwitting act of plagiarism himself. This obsession with being original, with saying something new, an obsession depicted for us by him in nearly all his characters, stayed with Dostoevsky for his entire career. He passionately valued his intellectual property — his originality, even as he unconsciously borrowed and even plundered the work and the ideas of others. But even as he valued originality, he equally cherished the kind of plagiarism that he represents through Ivan, Grushenka, Alyosha, and the devil. Such plagiarisms form an organic connection among texts, characters, and human beings.

More ironic still is that the kind of intellectual ownership that he craved as a writer — that is, his many claims for the originality of his work — is consistently depicted by Dostoevsky in his fiction as a pursuit that is stillborn, isolationist, and representative of the seed that dies and does not bear fruit. What does bear fruit in Dostoevsky's created world is mutuality, the kind of spiritual plagiarism in which Alyosha indulges so freely and to such powerful effect. Only when Ivan recognizes and accepts with "strange eagerness," "nervous" laughter, and an "almost childish delight" (*PSS*, 15:78–79; 611) the fact that his devil had plagiarized his story about the rebellious philosopher in space can Ivan himself get up from the road and begin his own positive journey. The devil's plagiarism mimics Alyosha's to similar spiritual effect, for the devil, in his recitation of the story of the philosopher, had given back to Ivan something valuable that in fact he already had. Without the devil's plagiarism of the parable Ivan himself had long forgotten, Ivan would still be standing on the road in a kind of trance, more like the peasant in Kramskoy's painting than like any philosopher, lost in unconscious, unproductive contemplation.

In our reading of Dostoevsky's fiction today — when issues of intellectual property intersect with the many breathtaking, interactive means at our command to disseminate and receive ideas rapidly — these seemingly simple ideas, drawn from the common produce of the earth, about seeds and onions, exert a special force. Neither a seed nor an onion can be fixed permanently in time, because each is organic, alive, and in itself representative of the capacities for regeneration, change, transformation, and conversion that Dostoevsky had sought to express in so many different ways. His fiction comprises a collection of seeds and onions from different gardens, to paraphrase Zosima. Some of these seeds die and then take root in us. In an ideal sense, Dostoevsky's stories and novels are also onions to be given, consumed, remembered.

Dostoevsky resorts to more kinds of narrative than do most authors in order to achieve his effects. As Bakhtin and others have noted, his novels abound with anecdotes, newspaper articles, legends, several simultaneous narrators — an enormous bag of tricks. Despite the weight of this bag of tricks, during a first heady immersion in the text, it is as easy for a reader to initially overlook it as it was for Alyosha to overlook that little bag around Dmitry's neck. These diverse modes of narration underline the fact that any ongoing written communication replicates a process. As David Lodge wrote in 1990 in his important essay "The Novel as Communication":

> The novel is a form of narrative. We can hardly begin to discuss a novel without summarizing or assuming a knowledge of its story or plot; which is not to say that the story or plot is the only or even the main reason for our interest in a novel, but that this is the fundamental principle of its structure. . . . The novel therefore has a family resemblance to other narrative forms, both the purely verbal, such as the classical epic, the books of the Bible, history and biography, folktales and ballads; and those forms which have non-verbal components, such as drama and film. Narrative is concerned with *process,* that is to say, with change in a given state of affairs; or it converts problems and contradictions in human experience into process in order to understand or cope with them. Narrative obtains and holds the interest of its audience by raising questions in their minds about the process it describes and delaying the answers to these questions. When a question is answered in a way that is both unexpected and plausible, we have the effect known since Aristotle as *peripeteia* or reversal.[15]

A few pages later in this remarkable essay Lodge wryly observes, "every decoding is another encoding." He goes on to quote from his own comic novel, *Small World.* There Morris Zapp gives a lecture that he entitles, "Textuality as Striptease." Zapp's words, like Zosima's, have a particular relevance for us today. Zapp says,

> "If you say something to me I check that I have understood your message by saying it back to you in my own words, for if I repeat your own words exactly you will doubt whether I have really understood you. But if I use *my* words it follows that I have changed *your* meaning, however slightly. . . . Conversation is like playing tennis with a ball made of Krazy Putty, that keeps coming back over the net in a different shape. Reading of course is different from conversation. . . . [But] the same axiom, every decoding is another encoding, applies to literary criticism even more stringently than it does to ordinary spoken discourse. In ordinary spoken discourse the endless cycle of encoding — decoding — encoding may be terminated by an action, as when for instance I say, 'The door is open' and you say, "Do you mean you would like me to shut it?' and I say, 'If you don't mind,' and you shut the door, we may be satisfied that at a certain level my meaning has been understood. But if the literary text says, 'The door was open' I cannot ask the text what it means by saying that the door was open, I can only speculate about the significance of that door — opened by what agency, leading to what discovery, mystery, goal."[16]

Zapp's half-mocking parody of literary theory actually touches upon the same nexus of ideas inherent in the generous acts of plagiarism I have been trying to describe (and even, by lucky coincidence, uses the example of an open door to signify the complexity of reaching agreement on questions about significance, memory, and meaning). We have here in comic form the same concerns with evidence, with mutuality and communication, with the effects of narrative that preoccupied Dostoevsky.

Chaos and Consilience

For readers of Russian literature it is a commonplace to observe that both Tolstoy in novels like *War and Peace* (1869) and Dostoevsky in works like *The Brothers Karamazov* represent through the lens of fiction the large human questions of how to live and how to believe. Each tackles the representation of these immense and general questions against a backdrop of an everyday reality imported from outside the novel. For Tolstoy the primary shapes in that backdrop are historical persons and events; for Dostoevsky they are the political questions, and the moral and religious dilemmas of his own time. In each case the canvas is huge.

Most important, each work exemplifies the attempt to apprehend the nature of causality simultaneously on a local, individual, and a cosmic scale. Pierre Bezukhov and Alyosha Karamazov experience at pivotal moments in their lives an unshakeable intuition about their place in the great chain of being. Pierre tells Andrei, "Don't I feel in my soul that I am part of this vast harmonious whole? Don't I feel that I form one link, one step, between the lower and higher beings in this vast harmonious multitude of beings in whom the Deity — the Supreme Power if you prefer the term — is manifest? If I see, clearly see, that ladder leading from plant to man, why should I suppose it breaks off at me and does not go farther and farther?"[17] Zosima periodically imparts similar beliefs to Alyosha, "Every blade of grass, every insect, ant, golden bee, all so amazingly know their path." "For all is like an ocean, all is flowing and blending; a touch in one place sets up movement at the other end of the earth" (*PSS*, 14:267, 290; 272, 299). Alyosha had fully assimilated Zosima's understanding of the universe when, lying in the earth of the monastery garden, he had sensed, "from the abyss of space . . . threads from all those innumerable worlds of God, linking his soul to them, and it was trembling all over, 'in contact with other worlds' " (*PSS*, 14:328; 340).

These well-known passages have their important philosophical underpinnings, roots, and sources. But equally vital for our present-day reading is the way in which both Tolstoy and Dostoevsky, even as they scrutinize and try to represent the impossibility of demarcating the complex immensity of the collisions and interactions among minute and vast chains of causality, share an overriding, instinctive awareness of what today is called chaos theory. It is precisely the dichotomy between these two kinds of causality that chaos theory also addresses:

> Only a new kind of science could begin to cross the great gulf between knowledge of what one thing does — one water molecule, one cell of heart tissue, one neuron — and what millions of them do.
>
> Watch two bits of foam flowing side by side at the bottom of a waterfall. What can you guess about how close they were at the top? Nothing. As far as standard physics was concerned, God might just as well have taken all those water molecules under the table and shuffled them personally. Traditionally, when physicists saw complex results, they looked for complex causes. When they saw a random relationship between what goes into a system and what comes out, they assumed that they would have to build randomness into any realistic theory, by artificially adding noise or error. The modern study of chaos began with the creeping realization in the 1960s that quite simple mathematical equations could model systems every bit as violent as a waterfall. Tiny differences in input could quickly become overwhelming differences in output—a phenomenon given the name "sensitive dependence on initial conditions." In weather, for example, this translates into what is only half-jokingly known as the Butterfly Effect — the notion that a butterfly stirring the air today in Peking can transform storm systems next month in New York.
>
> When the explorers of chaos began to think back on the genealogy of their new science, they found many intellectual trails from the past. But one stood out clearly. For the young physicists and mathematicians leading the revolution, a starting point was the Butterfly Effect.[18]

Pierre, Alyosha, Zosima, Tolstoy, Dostoevsky — would not they all have affirmed the Butterfly Effect? Might they even not say, reaching across their fictional worlds or from the grave, "We told you so?"

It is a fine thing today to remember and affirm that disciplines as disparate as nineteenth-century Russian literature and chaos studies can nourish and perhaps even inform and transform each other. Certainly a fragment of literary evidence cannot contribute directly to a physical derivation. Nor can the opposite apply. But disciplines nevertheless can be and are linked, or to paraphrase Dostoevsky — are separate worlds in contact with each other — in meaningful ways.

Recent literary works like Tom Stoppard's *Arcadia* (1993) and Michael Frayn's *Copenhagen* (1998) are creations that find their existence within the realm of the consilient. In his pathbreaking and controversial book *Consili-*

ence, the renowned biologist E. O. Wilson tells us (in a diction that frequently sounds like Tolstoy's but with a rhetorical structure of argumentation that echoes Dostoevsky) that "the greatest enterprise of the mind has always been and always will be the attempted linkage of the sciences and humanities. . . . Consilience is the key to unification." He draws his term *consilience* from the philosopher William Whewell, who in 1840 "was the first to speak of consilience, literally a 'jumping together' of knowledge by the linking of facts and fact-based theory across disciplines to create a common groundwork of explanation." Wilson warns his readers that the belief in the possibility of consilience is a metaphysical world view "which cannot be proved with logic from first principles or grounded in any definitive set of empirical tests,"[19] but he nevertheless sets out to demonstrate its truth. The Butterfly Effect and the possibility of consilience are vital, even basic, ideas for us today; our understanding of these contemporary ideas deepens as we read Dostoevsky.

Notes

Introduction

1. G. K. Chesterton's observation some hundred years ago about the Dickensian palette — much disagreed with by later critics, but still somehow apt — possesses some degree of applicability to Dostoevsky's creative oeuvre taken as a whole: "There is no such novel as *Nicholas Nickleby*. There is no such novel as *Our Mutual Friend*. They are simply lengths cut from the flowing and mixed substance called Dickens." See G. K. Chesterton, *Charles Dickens* (1906), excerpted in *Charles Dickens*, ed. Stephen Wall (Middlesex, U.K.: Penguin Books, 1970), 244. Dostoevsky's literary works each constitute a separate world, but these worlds remain, for the reader, in intimate contact with one another.

Chapter 1: Conversion, Message, Medium, Transformation

1. Ronald Hingley, *Russian Writers and Society in the Nineteenth Century,* 2nd ed. (London: Wiedenfeld and Nicolson, 1977), 78.

2. Donald Fanger, "The Peasant in Literature," in *The Peasant in Nineteenth-Century Russia,* ed. W. Vucinich (Stanford, Calif.: Stanford University Press, 1968), 231.

3. Fanger puts it thus: "The peasant, then, cannot speak for himself in nineteenth-century literature, nor can his way of life inspire a long, coherent work." Instead, the peasant's significance "is the writer's own invention or discovery; it answers his needs and is a part of his moral life." The story of the peasant in Russian literature "is the story of the changing moods and attitudes of the most influential segment of educated society, and

it tells us much more about that society than about the peasant himself. In other words, as far as imaginative literature is concerned, the peasant is — in the best and most serious sense of the word — a myth" (ibid., 232). This statement applies neatly to Dostoevsky and Tolstoy but not to Chekhov.

4. Joseph Frank, *Dostoevsky: The Years of Ordeal, 1850–1859* (Princeton, N.J.: Princeton University Press, 1983), 208.

5. One of the rare allusions to his father after 1839 comes in an emotional letter written to Anna Grigorievna from Wiesbaden in April 1871. Here Dostoevsky laments his unintended gambling bout and his ensuing losses, made more dreadful in his own mind for "two reasons" — first, that he had not wanted to distress her, and second, "I dreamed last night of my *father,* and he appeared to me in a terrifying guise, such as he has only appeared to me twice before in my life, both times prophesying a dreadful disaster, and on both occasions the dream came true." See G. M. Fridlender, ed., et al., *Polnoe sobranie sochinenii v tridtsati tomakh* (hereafter *PSS*), vol. 29(1) (Moscow: Nauka, 1972–1990), 197; *Selected Letters of Dostoyevsky,* ed. Joseph Frank and David I. Goldstein, trans. Andrew R. MacAndrew (New Brunswick, N.J.: Rutgers University Press, 1987), 353–54. The previous summer Dostoevsky had recorded another dream about his father. James Rice cites this notebook entry to show how deeply worried Dostoevsky was, not only about his epilepsy, but also about his respiratory problems: "I see my father (for a long time I've not dreamt of him). He directed my attention toward my chest, below the right nipple, and said: 'All's well with you, *but here it is very bad.*' I looked and it actually seemed that there was some kind of growth below the nipple. Father said, '*Your nerves are in disorder.*' Then at father's place there is some kind of family holiday. From his words I concluded that I was in a very bad way. . . . N.B. Awakening in the morning, at noon, I noticed almost at the same spot on my chest that Father had indicated, a place about the same size of a walnut with an extremely acute pain; if you touch it with a finger it's just like touching a painfully bruised spot. Nothing of the kind was there before." See James L. Rice, *Dostoevsky and the Healing Art: An Essay in Literary and Medical History* (Ann Arbor, Mich.: Ardis, 1985), 102.

Eight years later Dostoevsky visited the Darovoe estate his father had owned, which was now inhabited by his sister's family. He wrote about this visit in the 1877 July–August *Diary of a Writer.* Frank contends that despite what must have been Dostoevsky's painful memories of his father (who had been, at best, "stern, harsh, [. . . and] quite unforgiving"), Dostoevsky may ultimately have "judged (and pardoned) his own progenitor." Frank quotes at length a passage from *The Diary* about children who are able to wholeheartedly forgive their fathers on the strength of a single beautiful memory or good deed. Frank's reading rings true. See Frank, *Dostoevsky: The Mantle of the Prophet, 1871–1881* (Princeton, N.J.: Princeton University Press, 2002), 247. See also *PSS,* 25: 180–81. For another astute rendering of the murder of Dostoevsky's father, see Malcolm Jones's account of it. Jones finds an interesting parallel between Dostoevsky's situation and that of Tsar Alexander, who may have known of the intention to murder his father, the emperor Paul I. Jones also discusses the influence of Schiller's *Die Rauber* and its treatment of the theme of parricide. See Malcolm V. Jones, *Dostoevsky: The Novel of Discord* (New York: Harper & Row, 1976), 171.

6. Joseph Frank, *Dostoevsky: The Seeds of Revolt, 1821–1849* (Princeton, N.J.:

Princeton University Press, 1976), 88. Frank gives an excellent account of the murder of Dostoevsky's father, its possible motivations, and a clear summary of the complicated evidence disputing its occurrence. See also Frank's more recent discussion of this subject in *Dostoevsky: The Mantle of the Prophet*, 4–5.

7. Frank, *Years of Ordeal*, 117, 124; Frank, *Dostoevsky: The Stir of Liberation, 1860–1865* (Princeton, N.J.: Princeton University Press, 1986), 55. As this book is going to press, four significant works—two books and two articles—have appeared that each speculate about the nature of Dostoevsky's conversion and about his religious belief more generally. Readers interested in pursuing these topics more fully should turn to Steven Cassedy's elegant *Dostoevsky's Religion* (Stanford, Calif.: Stanford University Press, 2005) and Malcolm V. Jones's groundbreaking *Dostoevsky and the Dynamics of Religious Experience* (London: Anthem Press, 2005), as well as to Nancy Ruttenburg's "Dostoevsky's Estrangement," *Poetics Today* 26, no. 4 (2005); and James L. Rice's "Dostoevsky's Endgame: The Projected Sequel to *The Brothers Karamazov*," *Russian History Histoire Russe* 33, no. 1 (Spring 2006): 45–62. Each author writes from a startlingly different perspective and, taken together, the four works signal an exciting renewal of interest in the nature of Dostoevsky's religious belief.

8. Frank, *Stir of Liberation*, 5.

9. Frank and Goldstein, *Selected Letters*, 68–69. Natalya Fonvizina was the wife of the Decembrist Mikhail Fonvizin; she had followed him into exile. She had been kind to Dostoevsky during his journey to Siberia, at the transit station in Tobolsk. Dostoevsky kept the copy of the New Testament she gave him, the only book allowed in the prison, under his pillow for the next four years. See Frank, *Years of Ordeal*, 73–75. For a discussion of how Dostoevsky may have transformed this moment into art and let it in part form the structure of Ivan Karamazov's spiritual crisis, see Robin Feuer Miller, *The Brothers Karamazov: Worlds of the Novel* (New Haven: Yale University Press, 2008), 54–71. In particular, I argue there that "Ivan's language of negation sounds strikingly like Dostoevsky's language of affirmation so many years earlier when, as a convict, he wrote to Madame Fonvizina. Dostoevsky had then affirmed that his love for Jesus was even greater than his love for truth. Ivan divides his universe into two camps as well: like Dostoevsky, he maintains that something is more valuable to him than truth; but it is not Jesus, it is his own right not to accept that truth" (60). See also Robert Louis Jackson's analysis of a similar moment that occurs toward the end of Dostoevsky's life. Mikhail Bakhtin cites a notebook entry Dostoevsky made in 1881 in a response to remarks by K. D. Kavelin, "A scorching feeling tells me: better that I remain with a mistake, with Christ, than with you." Robert Louis Jackson, *Dialogues with Dostoevsky* (Stanford, Calif.: Stanford University Press, 1993), 284–86.

10. PSS, 28(1):162–63; Frank and Goldstein, *Selected Letters*, 51–53.

11. Konstantin Mochulsky, *Dostoevsky: His Life and Work*, trans. Michael A. Minihan (Princeton, N.J.: Princeton University Press, 1965), 145 (recounted from Miliukov's memoirs).

12. PSS, 28(1):169; Frank and Goldstein, *Selected Letters*, 59. Here and elsewhere I have occasionally slightly altered translations into English.

13. PSS, 28(1):181; *Dostoevsky Letters, 1832–1859*, ed. and trans. David Lowe (Ann Arbor, Mich.: Ardis, 1988), 1:201; emphasis added.

14. *PSS,* 28:172–73; Frank and Goldstein, *Selected Letters,* 62–63.

15. For a fuller discussion of this preoccupation of his, see Robin Feuer Miller, *Dosto-evsky and* The Idiot: *Author, Narrator and Reader* (Cambridge, Mass.: Harvard University Press, 1981), 22–24.

16. Frank, *Stir of Liberation,* 6. Frank describes the political and cultural scene of this period at some length in both volumes two and three. He emphasizes that Dostoevsky's turning to the people mirrors the attitude of much of the Russian intelligentsia during this time, which had "in an overall sense" begun to shift from a Westernizing to a Slavophile point of view. Frank quotes Belinsky's statement of 1847: "I am rather inclined to side with the Slavophiles rather than to remain on the side of the 'humanistic cosmopolitans' " (Frank, *Years of Ordeal,* 229). It was the *pochvenniki* (men of the soil) of the 1860s, among whom Dostoevsky counted himself, who deliberately sought to synthesize the ideas of the Slavophiles and the Westernizers. They believed, as Ellen Chances has put it, that solutions to Russia's overriding problems were to be found by "exploring the virtues enshrined within the breast of the Russian people. The chief virtue was the simple Christian love of one human being for another." See Ellen Chances, *Conformity's Children: An Approach to the Superfluous Man in Russian Literature* (Columbus, Ohio: Slavica, 1978), 95. Indeed, the announcement for Dostoevsky's journal *Time* was also the manifesto for the *pochva* movement of which he was a primary architect. After 1812, "we saw at last that we, too, are a separate, highly unique nationality, and that it is our task to create a new form for ourselves, a native form of our own, drawn from our soil, from our national spirit and national resources." See Leonid Grossman, *Dostoevsky: His Life and Work,* trans. Mary Mackler (Indianapolis: Bobbs-Merrill, 1975), 223. For an interesting discussion of the relation of Dostoevsky's ideas about pochva to his ideas about the narod, see V. P. Popov, "Problema naroda u Dostoevskogo," *Dostoevskii: materiali i issledovaniia,* ed. G. M. Fridlender (Leningrad, 1980), 4:42.

17. Frank, *Stir of Liberation,* 35.

18. The same worries about education prevailed in the United States at this time. The autobiography of Frederick Douglass bears witness to this with extraordinary eloquence. Douglass writes of his various owners: Mr. Auld, for example, maintained that "learning would *spoil* the best nigger in the world. Now . . . if you teach that nigger . . how to read, there would be no keeping him." He wrote of his mistress, who believed, in Douglass's words, "that education and slavery were incompatible with each other . . . All this, however, was too late. The first step had been taken. Mistress, in teaching me the alphabet, had given me the *inch,* and no precaution could prevent me from taking the *ell.*" See *Narrative of the Life of Frederick Douglass, An American Slave: Written by Himself* (1845), ed. Houston A. Baker (New York: Viking Penguin, 1982), 78–82. See also *PSS,* 4:122.

19. *PSS,* 18:99; and "Mr.-bov and the Question of Art," in *Dostoevsky's Occasional Writings,* trans. and ed. David Magarshack (Evanston, Ill.: Northwestern University Press, 1997; first printed 1963), 131. William Mills Todd III gives a fine overview of Dostoevsky's career as a professional writer. He paints a vivid picture of the cultural environment in which Dostoevsky and his brother founded their journals of the early 1860s. "However grimly familiar the literary world must have looked from afar (the same editors and journals, the same police surveillance), Dostoevskii found that much

had changed when he finally returned to St. Petersburg in December, 1859. The age of censorship terror had passed; the Great Reforms were about to change the institutions and social structure of the Russian Empire. Relaxed censorship practices and a new tolerance of political reporting in the press facilitated the growth of journalism: 150 new periodicals (newspapers and journals) appeared between 1855 and 1860, although the lack of a concomitant growth in literacy doomed many new enterprises to rapid failure." This, then, was the context in which Dostoevsky brothers founded their journals. See Todd, "Dostoevsky as a Professional Writer," in *The Cambridge Companion to Dostoevsky,* ed. W. J. Leatherbarrow (Cambridge, U.K.: Cambridge University Press, 2002), 76. For another incisive overview that places Dostoevsky's journalism of the 1860s in a larger journalistic context, see Robert L. Belknap, "Survey of Russian Journals, 1840–1880," in *Literary Journals in Imperial Russia,* ed. Deborah A. Martinsen (Cambridge, U.K.: Cambridge University Press, 1997), 91–117.

In his final novel, *The Brothers Karamazov,* Zosima — the wise elder of the work, echoes these ideas of Dostoevsky, expressed decades earlier: "And there's no need of much teaching or explanation [for the peasant], he will understand it all simply. Do you suppose that the peasants don't understand? Try reading them the touching story of the fair Esther and the haughty Vashti. . . .Don't forget either the parables of Our Lord, choose especially from the Gospel of St. Luke (that is what I did) . . . you will penetrate their hearts" (*PSS,* 14:267; and *The Brothers Karamazov,* trans. Constance Garnett, ed. and rev. translation, Ralph E. Matlaw [New York: Norton, 1976], 273).

20. *PSS,* 18:100; Magarshack, ed., "Mr.-Bov," 134.

21. *PSS,* 18:77, 94; Magarshack, ed., "Mr.-Bov," 96, 124.

22. Anna Grigorievna Dostoevsky, *Dostoevsky: Reminiscences,* trans. Beatrice Stillman (New York: Liveright Publishing, 1975), 117–19.

23. Chapters four, six, and seven of this book as well as its concluding pages offer further discussion of some of Dostoevsky's ideas about art. See also my *Dostoevsky and The Idiot,* 212–13 and passim, and especially the work of Robert Louis Jackson in *Dostoevsky's Quest for Form: A Study of his Philosophy of Art* (Bloomington, Ind.: Physsardt, 1978); and *The Art of Dostoevsky: Deliriums and Nocturnes* (Princeton, N.J.: Princeton University Press, 1981), passim. Anna Grigorievna has described Dostoevsky's admiration for the old masters — Raphael, Titian, Murillo, Correggio, Carracci, Batoni, Ruisdael, Lorraine, Rembrandt, and Van Dyke in particular (*Reminiscences,* 117–19). See also Jefferson J. A. Gatrall, "The Icon in the Picture: Reframing the Question of Dostoevsky's Modernist Iconography," *Slavic and East European Journal* (hereafter *SEEJ*), 48, no. 1 (2004): 1–25. Gatrall's remarks on what constitutes "the real" for Dostoevsky are of particular interest. "In Dostoevsky's modernist iconography the real is never simply an object to be represented, not an effect, nor even an affect, but a problem . . ." (5). See also Konstantin Barsht, "Defining the Face: Observations on Dostoevskii's Creative Processes," in *Russian Literature, Modernism, and the Visual Arts,* ed. Catriona Kelly and Stephen Lovell (Cambridge, Mass.: Cambridge University Press, 2000), 23–58; and Sarah Hudspeth, "Dostoevskii and the Slavophile Aesthetic," in *Dostoevsky Studies* (New Series) 4 (2000): 177–97. Barsht links Dostoevsky's preoccupation with faces to his overall aesthetic in an interesting way. Like Andrew Wachtel, he also discusses the fascinating question of Dostoevsky's views on photography. Hudspeth's

essay shows precisely how, for example, Dostoevsky's views on Raphael's Sistine Madonna mesh with his larger aesthetic concerns. See too Andrew Wachtel, "Dostoevsky's *The Idiot:* The Novel as Photograph," *History of Photography* 26, no. 3 (Autumn 2002): 205–15. For an extended and fascinating discussion of the painterly qualities of Dostoevsky's creative work and, in particular, his sensitivity to color, see Jacques Catteau, *Dostoevsky and the Process of Literary Creation,* trans. Audrey Littlewood (Cambridge, U.K.: Cambridge University Press, 1989), 21–27, 397, 399–408, and passim.

24. Jackson, *Dostoevsky's Quest for Form,* 217. For an interesting discussion of Dostoevsky's article from a different perspective, see ibid., 71–91.

25. See Elizabeth Valkenier, *Russian Realist Art: The State and Society: The Peredvizhniki and the Their Tradition* (Ann Arbor: University of Michigan Press, 1977). In her analysis Valkenier looks carefully at the precise reasons why the first generation *peredvizhniki* were so influenced by Chernyshevsky, although she takes her analysis far beyond simple ideology into the realm of social and psychological motivation. Yet this ideological influence does offer a starting point: it is customary in describing the preoccupation of Russian realist painters with moral and social, not pictorial, problems to trace this predisposition to the influence of Nikolai Chernyshevsky's belief that the arts should eschew striving for the ideal and that they should not merely reflect reality but comment and pass judgment on it as well (ibid., 16–17). Irina Paperno puts it thus: "Chernyshevsky's rejection of idealism in favor or reality is expressed through the rejection of the search for the ideal. . . .Striving for absolute perfection, a combination of all possible virtues devoid of any faults, is the sign of a cold or empty heart, Chernyshevsky claims, and can only be regarded as pathological." See Paperno, *Chernyshevsky and the Age of Realism: A Study in the Semiotics of Behavior* (Stanford, Calif.: Stanford University Press, 1988), 160.

26. *PSS,* 21:72; and Fyodor Dostoevsky, *A Writer's Diary,* vol. 1 (2 vols.), trans. Kenneth Lantz, introductory study by Gary Saul Morson (Evanston, Ind.: Northwestern University Press, 1994), 210–11. For a shrewd analysis of Dostoevsky's views about time in genre painting that can be gleaned from reading "Apropos of the Exhibition," see Morson, *Narrative and Freedom: The Shadows of Time* (New Haven, Conn.: Yale University Press, 1994), 180–82.

27. *PSS,* 21:72; Dostoevsky, *Writer's Diary,* 1.211.

28. *PSS,* 21:74; Dostoevsky, *Writer's Diary,* 1.213.

29. See chapters four, six, and eight for further discussion of this point. The visionary strength of such memory, transformed by artistic invention, forms a bedrock of Dostoevsky's work. Diane Oenning Thompson has called these recollections "iconic memories," and has shown how they shape *The Brothers Karamazov.* See Thompson, *The Brothers Karamazov and the Poetics of Memory* (Cambridge, U.K.: Cambridge University Press, 1991). For another perceptive analysis of "Apropos of the Exhibition" and its place within a Hegelian context, see Jackson, *Dostoevsky's Quest for Form,* 206–12.

30. *PSS,* 21:75; Dostoevsky, *Writer's Diary,* 1:214–15.

31. *PSS,* 21:71; Dostoevsky, *Writers Diary,* 1:208–9.

32. Ibid.

33. *PSS,* 21:76; Dostoevsky, *Writer's Diary,* 1:215.

34. *PSS,* 21:76–77; Dostoevsky, *Writer's Diary,* 1:215–16.

35. *PSS,* 19:7; Magarshack, "Pedantry and Literacy. First Article," 141. Emphasis added.

36. *PSS*, 4:122; Fyodor Dostoevsky, *The House of the Dead*, trans. Constance Garnett (New York: Macmillan, 1959), 192. On occasion in this as in other translations from the Russian I make minor changes.

37. Coming to an understanding of this hybrid form and its significance is the task Gary Saul Morson sets for himself in his incisive *The Boundaries of Genre: Dostoevsky's Diary of a Writer and the Traditions of Literary Utopia* (Austin: University of Texas Press, 1981), passim.

38. *PSS*, 4:14; Dostoevsky, *House of the Dead*, 38.

39. *PSS*, 4:14; Dostoevsky, *House of the Dead*, 41. I address questions about guilt and repentance among the peasant convicts in more detail in the next chapter and attempt to show that Dostoevsky treats these issues differently in this work than throughout the rest of his oeuvre.

40. *PSS*, 21:18–19; Dostoevsky, *Writer's Diary*, 1:138–39. Compare too what Dostoevsky wrote in his 1876 *Diary* article, "On Love of the People. An Essential Contract with the People": "I have a kind of blind conviction that there is no such scoundrel and villain among the Russian People who would not recognize that he is low and vile." *PSS*, 21:42; Dostoevsky, *Writer's Diary*, 1:348.

41. *PSS*, 4:176–77; Dostoevsky, *House of the Dead*, 272. This moving passage has links to Raskolnikov's childhood recollections in Part I of *Crime and Punishment*. The question of Dostoevsky and religion is endlessly complicated. The best single essay on the subject is by Malcolm V. Jones, "Dostoevsky and Religion," in *The Cambridge Companion to Dostoevksii*, ed. W. J. Leatherbarrow, 148–75. Jones's scholarly and sensitive reading ultimately permits us to take haunting passages like this — of Goryanchikov's childhood memory of church — and tease out of them a knowledge about Dostoevsky's own personal views about religion. "And what of Dostoevskii's biography? Whatever other sources may be available, his fiction is itself the best testimony to what was actually going on in Dostoevskii's mind. While we may indeed hope that he ended his troubled life in a haven of spiritual serenity, Dostoevskii himself always insisted that the important thing was not the achievement of the goal but the process of striving to reach it" (172). Readers should also turn to Cassedy, *Dostoevsky's Religion*, and Jones, *Dostoevsky and the Dynamics of Religious Experience*, cited in note 7.

42. *PSS*, 8:283; Fyodor Dostoyevsky, *The Idiot*, trans. Henry and Olga Carlisle (New York: New American Library, 1969), 362. For a longer discussion about both Dostoevsky's and Myshkin's fears about expressing their ideas directly, see Miller, *Dostoevsky and The Idiot*, 10–16, 150–52, 201–5, 224, and passim.

43. *PSS*, 18:53; Magarshack, translation of "Five Articles from *Time*. Introduction," 58–59.

44. *PSS*, 28(1):117–18; Lowe, *Dostoevsky Letters*, 1:121–23.

45. *PSS*, 29(2):101–2; Lowe, *Dostoevsky Letters*, 4:304–5. See also Miller, *Dostoevsky and The Idiot*, 14–15.

46. *PSS*, 21:73 (and again, 75); Dostoevsky, *Writer's Diary*, 1:211 (and again, 213).

47. *PSS*, 21:34, 41; Dostoevsky, *Writer's Diary*, 1:160, 168. Note too that he is again positing that change will occur from below, whereas upon his return from Siberia, Dostoevsky had, in the 1860s, seemed to convey a somewhat opposite point of view (except, perhaps, within the realm of art, where he always tended to center upon the reactions of the reader as opposed to the ideological intentions and tendencies of the author). See, for

example, the discussion earlier in this chapter about the importance for both author and reader of pursuing art for art's sake.

48. The response to Dostoevsky's work has consistently been polarized and colorful. At one extreme is Berdyaev's assertion that "So great is the worth of Dostoevsky that to have produced him is by itself sufficient justification for the existence of the Russian people in the world" (Nicholas Berdyaev, *Dostoevsky,* trans. Donald Attwater [New York: New American Library, 1974], 227). At the other extreme are comments like that of D. H. Lawrence, "It's all masturbation, half-baked, and one gets tired of it" (D. H. Lawrence, "On Dostoevsky and Rozanov" [1936] reprinted in *Russian Literature and Modern English Fiction,* ed. Donald Davie [Chicago: University of Chicago Press, 1965], 99–100) or Nabokov—"I am very eager to debunk Dostoevsky" (V. N. Nabokov, *Lectures on Russian Literature,* ed. Fredson Bowers [New York: Harcourt Brace Jovanovich, 1981], 6). See also Robin Feuer Miller, Introduction to *Critical Essays on Dostoevsky* (Boston: G. K. Hall, 1986), 1–4; and Peter Kaye, *Dostoevsky and English Modernism, 1900–1930* (Cambridge, U.K.: Cambridge University Press, 1999), 1–29 and passim. The exchange between Milan Kundera and Joseph Brodsky in the *New York Times* (January 6 and February 19, 1985) offers another fascinating round in the debate over Dostoevsky's writing. For a fine reading of this exchange and its larger significance, see Caryl Emerson, "Milan Kundera on Not Liking Dostoevsky" (unpublished paper, presented at AATSEEL, New York City, December 2002).

49. *PSS,* 21:36; Dostoevsky, *Writer's Diary,* 1:161.

50. Virginia Woolf, *Books and Portraits: Some Further Selections from the Literary and Biographical Writings of Virginia Woolf,* ed. Mary Lyon (New York: Harcourt Brace Jovanovich, 1977), 118–19.

51. *PSS,* 22:43; Dostoevsky, *Writer's Diary,* 1:347.

52. Ibid., 44, 349.

53. Ibid., 46, 351. For two excellent analyses of this story, see Jackson, *Art of Dostoevsky,* 20–33, and Frank, *Years of Ordeal,* 116–27.

Chapter 2: Guilt, Repentance, and the Pursuit of Art in The House of the Dead

1. At the beginning, the editor offers an introduction in which he explains that he came into possession of Goryanchikov's papers after his death. Among the papers is a manuscript, "unfinished, perhaps thrown aside and forgotten by the writer. It was a disconnected description of the ten years spent by Alexander Petrovich in penal servitude. In parts this account broke off and was interspersed by passages from another story, some strange and terrible reminiscences, jotted down irregularly, spasmodically, as though by some overpowering impulse. I read these fragments over several times, and was almost convinced that they were written in a state of insanity. But his reminiscences of penal servitude ... seemed not devoid of interest" (*PSS,* 4: 8; Fyodor Dostoevsky, *The House of the Dead,* trans. Constance Garnett (New York: Macmillan Dell, 1959), 31–32. When possible, references to *House of the Dead* appear in parentheses in the main body of the text with the Russian page reference from PSS preceding the English one. I have roughly followed the Garnett translation, occasionally changing words or phrases. Dostoevsky

has deliberately framed his novel (an editor coming upon some notes) in the tradition already made famous by Alexander Pushkin, Mikhail Lermontov, and Nikolai Gogol.

Victor Shklovsky was the first to call this work a "documentary novel" (*Povesti o proze* [Moscow, 1966], 64–84). How to categorize *The House of the Dead* with regard to genre has provoked much interesting critical debate. See, for example, Robert Louis Jackson, *The Art of Dostoevsky: Deliriums and Nocturnes* (Princeton, N.J.: Princeton University Press, 1981), 6–7. For an excellent recent discussion and summary of this question of genre, see Karla Oeler's fine essay, "The Dead Wives in the *Dead House*: Narrative Inconsistency and Genre Confusion in Dostoevskii's Autobiographical Prison Novel," *Slavic Review* 63, no. 3 (Fall 2002): 519–34. Oeler maintains that critics have generally placed themselves "somewhere between the extreme poles of defining the text as, strictly speaking, a memoir or a novel (519). John Jones argued that "the novel counterfeits the jumbled actuality of a dead man's memoir, life as he lived and recorded it. And the result is the art of the remiss, of provisional assessment, gossip, idle conjecture, contradiction, uncertainty above all" (Jones, *Dostoevsky* (Oxford: Oxford University Press, 1983), 158. Gary Saul Morson has found the generic hallmarks of the work precisely in its double narrative identity — a compound of the voice of the fictional wife-murderer and a representation of Dostoevsky's autobiographical experience in prison. "In fact," writes Morson, "the novel reads quite differently, depending on which narrator we assume. Did Dostoevskii make a mistake? Perhaps, but I think not. Rather, the work seems, like a Gestalt duck-rabbit drawing, to play on its double status" ("Paradoxical Dostoevsky," *SEEJ* 43, no. 3 (1999): 49–492.

2. Lev Tolstoy, *Polnoe sobranie sochinenii* (iubileinoe izdanie), ed. V. G. Chertkov et al., 90 vols. (Moscow, 1929–59), 16 (1955): 7; and "Some Words About *War and Peace*," in *War and Peace: A Norton Critical Edition*, ed. George Gibian (New York: Norton, 1966), 1366.

3. For more on Dostoevsky's fascination with the gothic novel and his transformations of its conventions in his own work, see chapter seven, as well as my "Dostoevsky and the Tale of Terror," in *The Russian Novel from Pushkin to Pasternak*, ed. John G. Garrard (New Haven, Conn.: Yale University Press, 1983), 103–25; and *Dostoevsky and The Idiot: Author, Narrator, and Reader* (Cambridge, Mass.: Harvard University Press, 1981), 108–25.

4. Jackson, *Art of Dostoevsky*, 6. See also Dale Peterson, *Up from Bondage: The Literatures of Russian and African American Soul* (Durham, N.C.: Duke University Press, 2000). Peterson emphasizes Dostoevsky's "aesthetics of disorder" in *House of the Dead*. Jacques Catteau suggests that in the work Dostoevsky has created a new genre, "the literature of imprisonment," in "De la Structure de la Maison des Mortes de F.M. Dostoevskij," *Revue des Etudes slaves* 54, nos. 1–2 (1982): 63–172 (cited by Oeler, "Dead Wives in the *Dead House*," 521).

5. James Scanlan speculates about this lack of repentance on the part of the convicts and observes that Dostoevsky does not say that "any human being was denied the 'gift' of conscience at birth, or that the gift has been *irretrievably* lost." James P. Scanlan, *Dostoevsky the Thinker* (Ithaca, N.Y.: Cornell University Press, 2002), 93.

6. That the "parricide" Ilyinsky later offered Dostoevsky one source for the character of Dmitri Karamazov has been shown by Robert L. Belknap, among others. See his *The*

Structure of The Brothers Karamazov (The Hague: Mouton, 1967), 15. See also B. G. Reizov, "K istorii zamysla *Brat'ev Karamazovykh*," *Zver'ia* (1936), 549. For a fuller description of Ilyinsky, who, it turns out, was never actually convicted of murder, see Belknap, *The Genesis of* The Brothers Karamazov: *The Aesthetics, Ideology, and Psychology of Making a Text* (Evanston, Ill.: Northwestern University Press, 1990), 61–62. See *PSS*, 4:284.

7. For further discussion of Dostoevsky's shift in assessing the extent to which the peasant convicts considered themselves guilty, see Jackson, *Art of Dostoevsky*, 10.

8. Andrei Sinyavsky, "Dostoevskii i katorga," *Sintaksis*, 9 (Paris, 1981): 108.

9. See chapter one for a fuller discussion of these important letters.

10. *PSS*, 22:46; Fyodor Dostoevsky, *A Writer's Diary*, trans. Kenneth Lantz (Evanston, Ill.: Northwestern University Press, 1994), 1:352. For discussion of this passage in the larger context of Dostoevsky's narrative voice, see my *Dostoevsky and* The Idiot, 14–16.

11. *PSS*, 28(1):117–18; *Dostoevsky Letters*, ed. and trans. David Lowe (Ann Arbor, Mich.: Ardis, 1988), 1:122.

12. Ibid. David Lowe points out in his editorial notes that Belinsky's critique, published in *Notes of the Fatherland* (no. 3, 1846), was not entirely enthusiastic, for it criticized the work for its "longueurs." Even more interestingly he discovers that the "notion of analysis as the basis of Dostoevsky's art belongs to the critic V. N. Maikov, not to Belinsky" (122).

13. *PSS*, 28(1):229; *Dostoevsky Letters*, 1:256.

14. *PSS*, 28(1):316; *Dostoevsky Letters*, 1:351.

15. For an illuminating essay on these works, see Deborah A. Martinsen's introduction to Fyodor Dostoevsky, *Notes from Underground, The Double, and Other Stories* (New York: Barnes and Noble Books, 2003), xiii–liv.

16. The narrator is at pains to point out, however, the surprising fact that most of these convicts, though not formally educated, could read. " 'We are men who can read,' they would often say with strange satisfaction. . . . I may mention in parentheses that they were 'men who could read,' and not in the slang, but in the literal sense. Probably more than half of them could read and write. In what other place in which Russian peasants are gathered together in numbers could you find two hundred and fifty men, half of whom can read and write? I have heard since that someone deduces from such facts that education is detrimental to the people. That is a mistake; there are quite other causes at work here, though it must be admitted that education develops self-reliance in the people. But this is far from being a defect" (4:11–12, 37).

17. *PSS*, 8:327–28; Fyodor Dostoyevsky, *The Idiot*, trans. Henry and Olga Carlisle (New York: Signet, 1969), 414; and *PSS*, 14:210; Fyodor Dostoevsky, *The Brothers Karamazov*, trans. Constance Garnett, revised and ed. Ralph Matlaw (New York: Norton, 1976), 212.

18. Liza Knapp has argued convincingly that some of these convicts, in particular Orlov, are able to avoid the inertia that is characteristic of so many of Dostoevsky's other characters. "Abundant vital force courses through what Dostoevsky calls 'the house of the dead.' " Knapp, *The Annihilation of Inertia: Dostoevsky and Metaphysics* (Evanston, Ill.: Northwestern University Press, 1996), 24.)

19. Oeler, "Dead Wives in the *Dead House*," 525.

20. Andrei Sinyavsky makes a similar point, "Dostoevskii i katorga," 110.

21. Jackson has suggested that the primary link between *The House of the Dead* and *Notes from Underground* consists in the theme of suffering that is common to both. "In his later writings Dostoevsky tends to idealize suffering and to view it as having a salutary influence in the life of the individual and of the Russian people at large. Although such a point of view finds real expression in the personal drama of the narrator of *House of the Dead*, it finds little development in the drama of the common peasant convict. For the most part, Dostoevsky explores the suffering of the Russian people from a social and psychological point of view. He finds in the common convict's passive submission to suffering, for example, a kind of perverse and stubborn resistance to a cruel fate. As later, in *Notes from Underground*, he links suffering in general closely with man's primordial craving for freedom, with his need to express his deepest creative instincts and energies" (Jackson, *Art of Dostoevsky*, 10–11).

22. See Jackson, *Dialogues with Dostoevsky: The Overwhelming Questions* (Stanford, Calif.: Stanford University Press, 1993), 29–55; Miller, *Dostoevsky and* The Idiot, 184, 212–13; Jefferson Gatrall, "Between Iconoclasm and Silence: Representing the Divine in Holbein and Dostoevskii," *Comparative Literature* 53, 3 (2001): 214–32; Knapp, *The Annihilation of Inertia*, 90–91; Olga Meerson, *Dostoevsky's Taboos* (Dresden: Dresden University Press, 1998), 90–92.

23. Charles Robert Maturin, *Melmoth the Wanderer: A Tale* (Lincoln: University of Nebraska Press, 1961), 196–97.

24. Belknap, *Structure of* The Brothers Karamazov, 45–50.

25. *PSS*, 28(1):311–32; *Dostoevsky Letters*, 1:346.

26. This crucial episode from Rousseau and its tremendous impact on Dostoevsky has already been widely analyzed in the criticism. See, for example, Yurii Lotman, "Russo: russkaia kul'tura XVIII-nachala XIX veka," in *Zhan-Zhak Russo. Traktaty* (Leningrad, 1969); Miller, "Rousseau and Dostoevsky: The Morality of Confession Reconsidered," in *Western Philosophical Systems in Russian Literature*, ed. Anthony M. Mlikotin (Los Angeles: University of Southern California Press, 1979), 89–101; Martinsen, *Surprised by Shame: Dostoevsky's Liars and Narrative Exposure* (Columbus: Ohio State University Press, 2003), 38–43; Knapp, *The Annihilation of Inertia*, 16–20. These references are only partial but give the reader an overview of the assessment of Dostoevsky's response to Rousseau.

27. This essay is treated at some length in chapter one. The quotations here are from *PSS*, 18:77, 94; and *Dostoevsky's Occasional Writings* (Evanston, Ill.: Northwestern University Press, 1997; first printed 1963), 95, 124.

28. *PSS*, 28(1):210; *Dostoevsky Letters*, 1:235. This same letter to Maikov contains an amusing observation about Tolstoy: "I like L.T. very much, but in my opinion he won't write much (perhaps I'm mistaken, however)." And earlier, in 1855, he had made his very first mention of Tolstoy to Y. Yakushkin, "Please let me know who *Olga N.* and L.T. are (the latter published "Adolescence" in *The Contemporary*)" (*PSS*, 28(1):184; *Dostoevsky Letters*, 1:205–6).

29. *PSS*, 6:418; Fyodor Dostoevsky, *Crime and Punishment*, trans. Jessie Coulson, ed. George Gibian (New York: W.W. Norton, 1975), 459–60.

30. *PSS*, 6:415; *Crime and Punishment*, 456.

31. *PSS,* 6:421; *Crime and Punishment,* 463.

32. See my essay, "What Is Chekhovian about Chekhov?" in *Word, Music, History,* 2 vols., *Stanford Slavic Studies,* vol. 29, ed. Lazar Fleishman, Gabriella Safran, Michael Wachtel (Stanford, Calif.: Garth Perkins, 2005), 489–504.

33. This pivotal scene from *The Brothers Karamazov* receives a much fuller discussion in chapters seven and eight, as well as in the concluding chapter.

34. *PSS,* 6:422; *Crime and Punishment,* 464.

Chapter 3: Crime and Punishment *in the Classroom*

1. Konstantine Klioutchkine has brilliantly and meticulously analyzed the myriad ways in which *Crime and Punishment* arises from the St. Petersburg cultural environment of the 1860s — from its conversations, its journals, its newspapers. "In my view, Dostoevskii's literary achievement was in large measure a result of his opening his novel to the influence of the press. He assimilated the processes underway in the new discursive environment and investigated their effects on his contemporaries." See Klioutchkine, "The Rise of *Crime and Punishment* from the Air of the Media," *Slavic Review* 61, no. 1 (Spring 2002): 89. Klioutchkine is able to demonstrate concretely how the contemporary proliferation of accounts of murders in the St. Petersburg press "makes problematic the treatment of any one of them as *the* source for Dostoevskii's novel" (ibid., 98).

2. Recently, however, there has been a growing interest on the part of literary critics in writing about teaching. Important and fascinating work has been the result. See, for example, David Denby, *Great Books: My Adventures with Homer, Rousseau, Woolf, and Other Indestructible Writers of the Western World* (New York: Simon and Schuster, 1997). There is also the fine series published by the Modern Language Association, *Approaches to Teaching World Literature.* They have nearly one hundred such volumes published — these are edited books that all combine a variety of classroom approaches to particular works. See, for example, the collection of essays on teaching *Anna Karenina* (ed. Liza Knapp and Amy Mandelker). See also the essay by Gary Saul Morson, "Teaching as Impersonation," in *Literary Imagination* 4, no. 4 (Spring 2002): 145–51

3. I use the word *shocked* in the spirit of David Denby, who begins his book with a chapter on Homer's *Iliad.* "I was shocked. A dying word, 'shocked.' Few people have been able to use it well since Claude Rains so famously said, "I'm shocked, *shocked* to find that gambling is going on here," as he pocketed his winnings in *Casablanca.* But it's the only word for excitement and alarm of this intensity. The brute vitality of the air . . . ," *Great Books,* 29. Denby goes on to give his amusing, yet admiring account of the classroom professor, " 'Don't get sucked in by false ideas,' he said. 'You're not here for political reasons. You're here for very selfish reasons. You're here to build a self. You create a self, you don't inherit it' " (ibid., 31).

4. *Reading at Risk: A Survey of Literary Reading in America: Research Division Report #46,* to be abbreviated from here on as *RAR.* These quotations are drawn from the preface by Dana Gioia — a poet and the chairman of the National Endowment of the Arts (NEA) at the time of the preparation of this report. The report defines a reader as anyone who, during the past twelve months had read, during leisure time, any novel, short story, play, or poem. "No distinctions were drawn on the quality of literary works"

(2). There are problems with this definition of reader: it excludes the reading of non-imaginative literature; it excludes imaginative literature assigned as reading to students, and, conversely, it sets the bar for being designated a reader very low — the reading of a single, short poem during the course of a year is enough to make you a reader. And given the absence of any measuring of quality, that short poem could, in theory, be something on the order of an ad jingle. But any definition for a report such as this is the obvious product of compromise and utility. The report, despite its shorthand and its shortcomings, has yielded important results.

5. *RAR,* vii.

6. Ibid., 5.

7. Ibid., vii, xii.

8. Ibid., 7.

9. It may be worth asking whether certain approaches to literature or to the teaching of it *discourage* reading. On the positive side, Gary Saul Morson argues that the experience of reading long, realist novels can change students lives in some fundamental way, not because the teacher conveys some great idea or theory to students, but because "the student has so 'lived in' the work . . . that he or she has acquired a new set of eyes. . . . From monocular the student has gone to binocular vision, and now the world is a different place. . . . By the end of a class, the students need no persuasion to realize that in a realist novel, the truth of a moment is not just what happens, but is a combination of A's perspective, B's perspective, C's perspective, A's on B, B's on A's perspective on C; and the narrator's on all of these. And that the narrator's voice is not mere commentary but an orchestration of diverse perspectives and viewpoints" ("Teaching as Impersonation," 146–49).

10. Malcolm V. Jones, *The Novel of Discord* (New York: Harper & Row, 1976), 75. See also *"Crime and Punishment:* Driving other people crazy" (in Jones, *Dostoyevsky after Bakhtin: Readings in Dostoyevsky's Fantastic Realism* [Cambridge, U.K.: Cambridge University Press, 1990], 77–96) in which Jones finds a different, highly original organizing principle. "Almost any scene in the novel could be analyzed in terms of the strategies of driving other people crazy" (ibid., 91). Jones demonstrates how "the techniques of emotional confusion have paradoxically led to the possibility of gradual clarification" (ibid., 94).

11. All the following quotations from Mochulsky are taken from Konstantin Mochulsky, *Dostoevsky: His Life and Work,* trans. Michael A. Minihan (Princeton, N.J.: Princeton University Press, 1967), 300–313. Since these quotations all occur within a short thirteen-page span, and since there are so many of them, I have decided to cite them not individually but rather as a group. Steven Cassedy has extended Mochulsky's argument in an interesting and subtle way: "It is my contention that *Crime and Punishment* is formally two distinct but closely related things, namely a particular type of tragedy in the classical Greek mold and a Christian resurrection tale; that it successfully superimposes the two forms because they are, within clearly determined limits, identical; finally that the conflict between the two forms occurs at precisely the point where they cease to be superimposable." (See Cassedy, "The Formal Problem of the Epilogue in *Crime and Punishment:* The Logic of Tragic and Christian Structures," *Dostoevsky Studies* 3 [1982]: 171. Cassedy's essay calls to mind a similar reading of the book of Job — a book of the Bible that

Dostoevsky particularly loved. Some scholars have argued that theologians had tacked the book's pious "happy" ending onto what had possibly been an older Greek tragedy.)

12. Vyacheslav Ivanov, *Freedom and the Tragic Life*, trans. Norman Cameron, ed. S. Konovalov (New York: Noonday Press, 1952), throughout. Joseph Frank, *Dostoevsky: The Miraculous Years, 1865–1871* (Princeton, N.J.: Princeton University Press, 1995), 100.

13. The most interesting, original, and recent analysis of the precise nature and the ramifications of Raskolnikov's shame can be found in the work of Deborah Martinsen. See her article "Shame and Punishment," in *Dostoevsky Studies* (New Series) 5 (2001): 51–70. See also her incisive full-length monograph that explores the question of shame (and its links to the contemporary field of shame studies) throughout Dostoevsky's work, *Surprised by Shame: Dostoevsky's Liars and Narrative Exposure* (Columbus: Ohio University Press, 2003), 20–21 and throughout. The landmark monograph on *Crime and Punishment* is Gary Rosenshield's *Crime and Punishment: The Techniques of the Omniscient Author* (Lisse, Netherlands: Peter de Ridder Press, 1978).

14. *PSS*, 28(2):171, 173; and *Fyodor Dostoevsky: Complete Letters, 1860–1867*, ed. and trans. David A. Lowe (Ann Arbor, Mich.: Ardis, 1989), letters to A. Lyubimov (9 December 1866), 2: 214, and (13 December 1866), 2:216. In the second letter Dostoevsky writes, "That's the way it's turning out; that way it will be better and more effective in a literary sense." This volume is hereafter referred to in this chapter as *Dostoevsky Letters*.

15. Morson urges that teachers work to bring a different *voice* into the classroom. He argues polemically that too many of us, out of a desire to insure our own beliefs against challenge, allow authors and characters to "speak only to their times, not to ourselves." When that happens, according to Morson's reasoning, "instead of participants in a dialogue, we become eavesdroppers on old gossip." Moreover, the students are quick to sense this and will, he suggests, become bored and disengaged ("Teaching as Impersonation," 147–48).

16. Jay Parini, "The Well-Tempered Seminar," in *Chronicle of Higher Education* 50, no. 46 (23 July 2004): 16. This is not unlike Northrop Frye's statement that the text is like a picnic to which the author brings the words and the reader the meaning (in Frye, *Fearful Symmetry* [Princeton, N.J.: Princeton University Press, 1957], 427.

17. Martha C. Nussbaum, *Poetic Justice: The Literary Imagination and Public Life* (Boston: Beacon Press, 1995), v.

18. Ibid., xvi.

19. Ibid., 10.

20. Ibid., 120–21. The "blades of grass" reference here is to Walt Whitman (*Song of Myself)*, whose work is central to Nussbaum's overall analysis, as is that of Dickens (*Hard Times*), E. M. Forster (*Maurice)*, and Richard Wright *(Native Son)*, as well as several others.

21. It can be fascinating for students to recall and reflect upon their own first readings, and particularly childhood or early adolescent readings, of major texts like *Crime and Punishment*. George Orwell has written vividly, for example, about his own first reading of *David Copperfield*. "I must have been about nine years old when I first read *David Copperfield*. The mental atmosphere of the opening chapters was so immediately intelligible to me that I vaguely imagined they had been written *by a child*. And yet when one re-

reads the book as an adult and sees the Murdstones, for instance, dwindle from gigantic figures of doom into semi-comic monsters, these passages lose nothing. Dickens has been able to stand both inside and outside the child's mind, in such a way that the same scene can be wild burlesque or sinister reality, according to the age at which one reads it" (Orwell, "Charles Dickens," *A Collection of Essays by George Orwell* [New York: Harcourt Brace Jovanovich, 1946], 60).

22. V. S. Pritchett, *The Myth Makers: European and Latin American Writers* (New York: Random House, 1979), 72. Octavio Paz, *On Poets and Others*, trans. Michael Schmidt (Manchester, Eng.: Carcanet Press Limited, 1987), 94. I am grateful to Donald Fanger for turning my attention to these two works. Recently Richard Freeborn described Dostoevsky's still awesome power to "ambush a part of life and transform it forever." See his *Dostoevsky* (London: Haus Publishing, 2003), 137. Criticism abounds with powerful testaments to Dostoevsky's acute timeliness.

23. *PSS*, 6:419; and Feodor Dostoevsky, *Crime and Punishment*, trans. Jessie Coulson, ed. George Gibian (New York: W. W. Norton & Co., 1975), 461. Subsequent references to the novel in this chapter will appear in the main body of the text in parentheses with the Russian page numbers from *PSS* preceding those of the English translation. Dostoevsky returns to this theme of an infectious trichina in his story, "The Dream of a Ridiculous Man," which appeared in *Diary of a Writer* in 1877. See chapter six of the present study.

24. For an extended discussion of Dostoevsky and the practice of metaphysical homeopathy, see chapter eight.

25. Curiously, in his notebooks of the mid-1860s, before he began work on *Crime and Punishment* and while he was working on various articles, Dostoevsky twice made reference to the contrast between socialism and Christianity by associating, on one hand, loose twigs (*luchinochki*) with socialism, and on the other, brotherhood — or the collective idea of humanity — with Christianity. See *Neizdannyi Dostoevskii* 83 (Moscow: Literaturnoe nasledstvo, "nauka," 1971), 244–46; and *The Unpublished Dostoevsky: Diaries and Notebooks, 1860–1881*, I, introduction by Robert L. Belknap, ed. Carl R. Proffer (Ann Arbor, Mich.: Ardis, 1973). See the entries for August 19 and September 14, 1864, 94–95. Proffer (albeit a bit confusingly) glosses these references to twigs in a way that resonates with why the infected individuals in Raskolnikov's dream are doomed to failure: "When talking about Christianity versus socialism, Dostoevsky apparently uses this word as a shorthand reference to the biblical parable of the strength of many twigs together, while separate and disunited they break easily, seeing socialism as essentially composed of separate individuals — unlike a Christian community bound together by the indestructible idea of God" (*Unpublished Dostoevsky*, 142). The Russian editors also write, "Dostoevsky often speaks about 'luchinochki' " (see ibid., 246, 250) and indicate that he is referring to a parable. But neither source indicates what parable this is, and I have, even after my own researches and conversations with several colleagues in religious studies as well as a priest, unfortunately been unable to locate it by the time of this writing. I cite the reference anyway because of its intriguing nature.

26. E. M. Forster, *Aspects of the Novel* (New York: Harcourt Brace, 1927), 95–96.

27. Maynard Mack, *King Lear in Our Time* (Berkeley: University of California Press, 1965), 97, quoted by R. A. Foakes in his introduction to *The Arden Shakespeare: King Lear* (London: Arden Shakespeare, 2003), 1.

28. *Neizdannyi Dostoevskii* (83), 183; *Unpublished Dostoevsky,* 50; and Frank, *Miraculous Years,* 31.

29. Frank, *Miraculous Years,* 60, 85.

30. *PSS,* 18(2):127; *Dostoevsky Letters,* 2:63.

31. For a superb analysis and overview of the role of family in Dostoevsky's writing, see Susanne Fusso, "Dostoevsky and the Family," in *The Cambridge Companion to Dostoevsky,* ed. W. J. Leatherbarrow, (Cambridge, U.K.: Cambridge University Press, 2002), 175–90. Fusso writes movingly and wittily about Dostoevsky's sense that to create a real family is an "untiring labour of love" (Dostoevsky's own phrase from *Diary of a Writer*), 183–90. This essay is too full of original insights to be paraphrased effectively here.

32. *PSS,* 7:81; and *Dostoevsky: The Notebooks for Crime and Punishment,* ed. and trans. Edward Wasiolek (Chicago: University of Chicago Press, 1967), 79 (hereafter referred to as *NCP).* This continues to be an invaluable and thoughtful work, whose insights are on a par with the commentary within the masterly *PSS.* The Russian editors of the notebooks and Wasiolek have each ordered the segments of Dostoevsky's notebooks in a different way, so readers will notice a seeming lack of logic in the page cross-references for the two in my citations.

33. *PSS,* 7:48; and *NCP,* 145. Frank reminds us that at one point Razumihin "says that his name is only a shortened form of his real one, Vrazumihin. . . . The verb *vrazumit* means to teach or to make to understand, [and] . . . his own behavior in coping with adversity provides a lesson that Raskolnikov will ultimately have to learn" (*Miraculous Years,* 99).

34. *PSS,* 7:173; *NCP,* 209.

35. *PSS,* 7:155–56; *NCP,* 189–91.

36. Frank, *Miraculous Years,* 63. Dostoevsky's words may be found also in *PSS,* 4:87–88. Tolstoy's eccentric reading of *Crime and Punishment* in "Why Do Men Stupefy Themselves?" (1889, reprinted from the Maude translation [1937] in *Critical Essays on Dostoevsky,* ed. Robin Feuer Miller [New York: G. K. Hall, 1986]), suddenly seems uncannily astute and persuasive.

37. Leo Tolstoy, "Why Do Men Stupefy Themselves?," 101–2; emphasis added. My discussion of this essay in another context has relevance here: "Was Raskolnikov's decision to murder hanging in the balance in the way Tolstoy describes? Was the voice of Raskolnikov's conscience stifled by external forces and events? Or, as it may be argued, did Dostoevsky depict Raskolnikov as finding, buzzing in the air all around him, external confirmations of a transformation which had already taken place in his consciousness? Of course, Tolstoy and Dostoevsky, as two great artists, each portrayed the intermingling of these external and internal factors: Tolstoy's depictions of the interior monologues and dialogues of his characters are at least as compelling as Dostoevsky's, and Dostoevsky's ability to portray the countless factors, both insignificant and weighty, which hover behind and shape a particular event is, without doubt, comparable to Tolstoy's. But neither opted for the easy compromise, and in the end, the chains of causality depicted by Tolstoy clash head on with Dostoevsky's emphasis upon the ineradicable presence and the ultimate force of man's capacity for choice — his free will" (*Critical Essays on Dostoevsky,* 6).

38. There have been a number of important studies of the genesis of *Crime and Punish-*

ment that have also offered rich speculation and analysis of Dostoevsky's notebooks and especially his switch from a first-person to a third-person narration. See in particular Wasiolek in *NCP*, Gary Rosenshield in *Crime and Punishment: The Technique of the Omniscient Author*, L. M. Rozenblium, *Tvorcheskie Dnevniki* (Moscow, 1981), and Frank, *Miraculous Years*, 80–95.

39. *PSS*, 7:148–49; *NCP*, 52–53.

40. *PSS*, 28(2):136–38, 139–40; *Dostoevsky Letters*, 2:174–76, 177.

41. *PSS*, 28(2):141; *Dostoevsky Letters*, 2:179.

42. *PSS*, 28(2):150; *Dostoevsky Letters*, 2:188.

43. Frank, *Miraculous Years*, 93.

44. *PSS*, 7:141; *NCP*, 58.

45. Klioutchkine, "The Rise of *Crime and Punishment* from the Air of the Media," 103. He has cited *Vremia*, no. 4 (1861), pt. 2:13.

46. Frank, *Miraculous Years*, 84, 86.

47. Ibid., 87 and ff.

48. I have argued elsewhere that Dostoevsky used the first person more successfully in shorter forms than in long, although both *The Insulted and Injured* and *A Raw Youth* are due even more serious attention in this regard than they have yet received. See Robin Feuer Miller, *Dostoevsky and* The Idiot: *Author, Narrator, and Reader* (Cambridge, Mass.: Harvard University Press, 1981), 2–3.

49. Morson's analysis of this first part of the novel is keenly observed and executed with a style Dostoevsky might have enjoyed. "He does not plan but dreams of planning; he does not make meticulous preparations but argues abstractly that they could be made. Remote from the here and now, he never seems to know what time it is and, at the end of part I, is even late keeping his engagement to murder. . . . Indeed, even the murder itself is undertaken as if it were just another rehearsal. The fact is, Raskolnikov never decides to commit the murder, which is one reason he later has so much trouble in ascertaining *why* he decided to do so . . . Dostoevsky is at the height of his powers here. He shows us a murder, a dramatic and active event if there ever was one, consciously and freely committed by someone who never truly decides to do so and lives passively at several removes from reality" (Gary Saul Morson, *Narrative and Freedom: The Shadows of Time* (New Haven, Conn.: Yale University Press, 1994), 226–27). Morson's reading is close to Tolstoy's in its emphasis upon Raskolnikov's passivity at this crucial juncture. It seems to me that Frank's analogy with the peasant whom Dostoevsky writes about who gives way to a kind of drunken delirium is speaking toward an altered state of being, which, while perhaps trancelike, is not passive. These mutually exclusive readings are each persuasive. For another brilliant analysis of the first part of the novel, see Robert L. Belknap's "The *Siuzhet* of Part I of *Crime and Punishment*," in *Dostoevsky on the Threshold of Other Worlds*, ed. Sarah Young and Leslie Milne (Derbyshire, U.K.: Bramcote Press, 2006), 153–58. This article appeared just as this book was going to press.

50. John Jones, *Dostoevsky* (Oxford: Oxford University Press, 1983), 18–19.

51. Only occasionally does Dostoevsky overshoot his mark and land his narrative vessel in the swampy realm of saccharine sentimentality, as he does, one could argue, at certain moments in *White Nights*, "A Boy at Christ's Christmas Tree," "The Peasant Marey," and "The Dream of a Ridiculous Man."

52. Jones, *Dostoevsky,* 19–20.

53. Klioutchkine has identified several accounts in newspapers and journals, including "stenographical accounts" in *Golos* of similar crimes. There is, for example a man who, "in a burglary attempt, murdered two old women with an axe and left their bodies in puddles of blood." In Krestovkii's novel, *The Slums of St. Petersburg,* "a character sets out to murder a pawnbroker and his maid but reconsiders on his way up the stairs to the apartment. Instead of proceeding with the murder, he goes to the police and confesses his intention" (in "The Rise of *Crime and Punishment* from the Air of the Media," 98). Klioutchkine is at pains to point out that the very proliferation in the press of the reports of such crimes makes it impossible to identify any one of them as *the* source for the novel.

54. *PSS,* 7:88; *NCP,* 87. See also *PSS,* 7:88; *NCP,* 89.

55. *PSS,* 7:90–93; *NCP,* 90–93.

56. *Miraculous Years,* 85.

57. *PSS,* 7:79–81, *NCP,* 96–97.

58. *PSS,* 7:64; *NCP,* 165.

59. *PSS,* 7:182, 195; *NCP,* 218, 234. Russian readers would also associate here to Nikolai Karamzin's influential story "Poor Liza" (1792).

60. See the previous chapter, especially note 25.

Chapter 4: The Gospel According to Dostoevsky

1. For a fuller discussion of this letter in the context of Dostoevsky's other writings of the period, see chapter one.

2. *PSS,* 28(1):175; *Selected Letters of Fyodor Dostoyevsky,* ed. Joseph Frank and David Goldstein, trans. Andrew MacAndrew (New Brunswick, N.J.: Rutgers University Press, 1987), 68. It is important to take stock of the extraordinary degree to which Dostoevsky repeatedly uses the most precious and intimate ingredients from his own life in the service of his fiction. Thus in *The Possessed* Shatov attributes this same thought to Stavrogin: "But wasn't it you who told me that if someone proved to you mathematically that the truth is outside Christ, you would better agree to stay with Christ than with the truth?" (*PSS,* 10:198).

3. There is an extensive critical literature on Dostoevsky's readings of the Bible and of Russian Orthodox texts generally. I have chosen here to highlight the work of Jostein Børtnes because it combines deep religious and biblical knowledge with a keenly creative reading of literary texts. See his book *Visions of Glory* (Oslo: Slavica Norvegica, 1988), his many essays, and in particular, "The Function of Hagiography in Dostoevskij's Novels," *Critical Essays on Dostoevsky,* ed. Robin Feuer Miller (New York: G. K. Hall, 1986), 189. See also generally the critical work of Roger Anderson, Robert L. Belknap, Nikolai Berdyaev, David Bethea, Steven Cassedy, Leonid Grossman, Vyacheslav Ivanov, Malcolm V. Jones, Robert L. Jackson, Sven Linner, Olga Meerson, Harriet Murav, Victor Terras, Nina Perlina, Diane Oenning Thompson, Vladimir Solovyov, Valentina Vetlovskaia, and Vladimir Zakharov for some of the finest work on Dostoevsky and religious subjects. Many of these critics, as well as Mikhail Bakhtin, have also scrutinized Dostoevsky's extensive use of biblical quotation and have addressed the question of how fragments from the Bible, from hagiographic texts, and from theological writings commingle

in Dostoevsky's pages with quotations from newspapers, street anecdotes, parodies, and pamphlets.

4. Bortnes, "Function of Hagiography," 191. See also Priscilla Meyer, "*Crime and Punishment:* Dostoevsky's Modern Gospel," in *Dostoevsky Studies* (New Series) 2, no. 1 (1998): 66–79. Meyer recapitulates Gary Rosenshield's powerful argument (in *Crime and Punishment: Techniques of the Omniscient Author* [Lisse, Netherlands: Peter de Ridder, 1978]) that the last two pages of the epilogue to *Crime and Punishment* are "a completion of the scene in which Sonya reads the story of the raising of Lazarus to Raskolnikov" and are thus a "fulfilled prophecy" (69–70). She goes on to argue convincingly that one can read Dostoevsky's entire novel as a "modern gospel," in particular a kind of version of "the gospel according to John," in which Dostoevsky brings Raskolnikov through "a series of events that parody moments in the life of Jesus" (70–71). Meyer also states unequivocally that "John is emphasized over the first three gospels by Russian Orthodoxy" (71).

5. See Richard Lanham, *A Handlist of Rhetorical Terms* (Berkeley: University of California Press, 1969), 124; Karl Beckson and Arthur Ganz, *Literary Terms: A Dictionary* (New York: Farrar, Straus and Giroux, 1960), 173; and M. H. Abrams, *A Glossary of Literary Terms* (Fort Worth, Tex.: Harcourt Brace Jovanovich College Publishers, 1993), 6.

6. John J. Bonsignore, "In Parables: Teaching Through Parables," *Legal Studies Forum* 12, no. 2 (1988): 195–96.

7. Frank Kermode, *The Genesis of Secrecy: On the Interpretation of Narrative* (Cambridge, Mass.: Harvard University Press, 1979), 25.

8. Kermode has addressed at length this fascinating paradox of the parables. He has located the most intense focus on parable generally and, indeed, the beginning of the debate about the nature of parable, as stemming precisely from these verses in Mark and, in particular, from the translation of a single word, the Greek *hina*. This pivotal word, as Kermode tells us, is, in turn, a translation from the lost Aramaic text. In a nutshell: should the word be translated as "lest," or as "in order that," *or*, should it be translated as "because"? Matthew, Kermode tells us, "seems to have found Mark's *hina* intolerable. For though he does not omit the general theory of parable from his big parable chapter (13), he substitutes for *hina* the word *hoti*, 'because.'" See Kermode, *Genesis of Secrecy,* 29–32.

9. Ibid., 46–47.

10. G. P. Fedotov, *The Russian Religious Mind: Kievan Christianity, The Tenth to the Thirteenth Centuries* (New York: Harper & Row, 1960), 206, 218–19.

11. *PSS,* 18:53; *Dostoevsky's Occasional Writings,* trans. and ed. David Magarshack (Evanston, Ill.: Northwestern University Press, 1997; first printed 1963), 58–59. Further references throughout this chapter to Dostoevsky's works will appear in parentheses in the main body of the text with the Russian volume number and page reference from PSS preceding the English translation. The English translations cited here are (as they are throughout the rest of this book) from *The Idiot,* trans. Henry and Olga Carlisle (New York: New American Library, 1969); "The Peasant Marey," in Fyodor Dostoevsky, *A Writer's Diary,* 1 (1873–1876), trans. and annotated by Kenneth Lantz, introduction by Gary Saul Morson (Evanston, Ill.: Northwestern University Press, 1994); *The Brothers Karamazov,* trans. Constance Garnett, ed. and revisions in translation Ralph E. Matlaw

(New York: W. W. Norton, 1976). My discussion of *The Brothers Karamazov* throughout this chapter draws in part from my book *The Brothers Karamazov: Worlds of the Novel* (New Haven: Yale University Press, 2008), although my arguments here extend and revise those presented there.

12. For a fuller discussion of this letter and its echoes in his journalism see chapter one. The letter cited here is *PSS*, 29(2):101–2; *Dostoevsky's Letters*, trans. and ed. David Lowe (Ann Arbor, Mich.: Ardis, 1988), 4:304–5.

13. For excellent analyses of this work, see Robert Louis Jackson's "The Triple Vision: 'The Peasant Marey,'" *The Art of Dostoevsky: Deliriums and Nocturnes* (Princeton, N.J.: Princeton University Press, 1981), 20–33; and Joseph Frank, "The Peasant Marey," in *Dostoevsky: The Years of Ordeal, 1850–1859* (Princeton, N.J.: Princeton University Press, 1983), 2:116–28 and in *Dostoevsky: The Mantle of the Prophet, 1871–1881* (Princeton, N.J.: Princeton University Press, 2002), 5:342–45; and Gary Saul Morson, introduction to *Writer's Diary*, 1:24–28.

14. I return to this story in chapter eight and discuss it more fully as a classic conversion tale. My focus here is on the parabolic qualities of this work.

15. The paradigm of John 12:24, which is also the epigraph to *The Brothers Karamazov*, is also important to "The Peasant Marey." It has long been observed that the way in which grace travels through Dostoevsky's last novel is that a character witnesses an event or has an experience that inspires a sensation of miracle and mystery and the presence of something deeply harmonious and good. He then forgets it; then, at some critical moment in the future it is recalled, and the character himself experiences a conversion. After that he tries to impart his experience to others. It is interesting that this entire paradigm is operative in "The Peasant Marey" as well. The nine-year-old Dostoevsky has an experience that inspires and comforts him; he forgets about it, only to recall it in an hour of despair during his prison years. He then transmits this experience to others.

16. See the discussion in chapter one.

17. I discuss this moment more fully in *The Brothers Karamazov: Worlds of the Novel*, 39–41. For a rich account of Dostoevsky's experience at this tragic time, see Joseph Frank, *Dostoevsky: The Mantle of the Prophet*, 38?–89, and Marina Kostalevsky, *Dostoevsky and Soloviev: The Art of Integral Vision* (New Haven, Conn.: Yale University Press, 1997), 65–67. For a seminal reading of this passage, see Robert L. Belknap, *The Structure of the Brothers Karamazov* (Evanston, Ill.: Northwestern University Press, 1989; originally published 1967), 94–96.

18. *PSS*, 30(1):126–27; Frank and Goldstein, *Selected Letters*, 488–89. These are Dostoevsky's italics.

19. Sarah Smyth, "The 'Lukovka' Legend in *The Brothers Karamazov*," *Irish Slavonic Studies*, no. 7 (1986): 41–51. Smyth agrees with the hypothesis of Yurii Lotman that Dostoevsky was "deliberately misleading his editor" in saying that he was the first to record this legend, because Afanasev's book had been proscribed (42). See Lotman, *Realizm russkoi literatury 60-kh godov xix veka* (Leningrad, 1974), 307. Nevertheless, Dostoevsky's glee at transcribing this tale also harmonizes with his consistent search for originality and his tendency to boast when he had found new types, new anecdotes, new ideas to represent. It also meshes (as I stress here) with his own tendency to forget and then remember things at the needed time. See also Robert L. Belknap, *The Genesis of* The

Brothers Karamazov: *The Aesthetics, Ideology and Psychology of Making a Text* (Evanston, Ill.: Northwestern University Press [Studies of the Harriman Institute], 1990), 89–111. For two readings that focus on the ramifications of this passage for the novel as a whole see my *The Brothers Karamazov: Worlds of the Novel,* 81–86; and Gary Saul Morson, "The God of Onions: *The Brothers Karamazov* and the Mythic Prosaic," in *A New Word on* The Brothers Karamazov, ed. Robert Louis Jackson (Evanston, Ill.: Northwestern University Press, 2004), 107–25.

20. "One must . . . reject as misleading the common assertion that the east concentrates on the Risen Christ, and the west on Christ Crucified. If we are going to draw a contrast, it would be more exact to say that east and west think of the Crucifixion in slightly different ways . . . The Orthodox Church on Good Friday thinks not simply of Christ's human pain and suffering by itself, but rather of the contrast between His outward humiliation and His inward glory. Orthodox see not just the *suffering humanity* of Christ but a *suffering God* . . . The Crucifixion is not separated from the Resurrection, for both are but a single action . . . When Orthodox think of Christ Crucified, they think not only of His suffering and desolation; they think of Him as Christ the Victor, Christ the King, reigning in triumph from the Tree." See Timothy Ware, *The Orthodox Church* (Middlesex, Eng.: Penguin Books, 1964), 232–33.

21. Smyth, "The 'Lukovka' Legend in *The Brothers Karamazov*," 44.

22. In Part II, Book v, in "The Grand Inquisitor," chapter (five), Ivan is delineating to Alyosha "the preface" of his Grand Inquisitor poem.

> whew . . . I am a poor hand at making one. You see, my action takes place in the sixteenth century, and at that time, as you probably learned at school, it was customary in poetry to bring down heavenly powers to earth. Not to speak of Dante, in France, clerks, as well as the monks in the monasteries, used to give regular performances in which the Madonna, the saints, the angels, Christ, and God Himself were brought·on the stage. In those days it was done in all simplicity.

He then adds:

> But besides plays there were all sorts of legends and "verses" scattered about the world, in which the saints and angels and all the powers of Heaven took part when required. In our monasteries the monks busied themselves in translating, copying, and even composing such poems — and think when — under the Tatars. There is, for instance, one such poem (of course, from the Greek), "The Wanderings of Our Lady through Hell," with descriptions as bold as Dante's (14:225; 227–28).

Then follows his haunting summary of this twelfth-century apocryphal tale which is, in itself, so markedly and immediately redolent of Grushenka's parable of the onion that is to follow shortly in the novel. See the concluding chapter of the present study.

Chapter 5: Transformations, Exposures, and Intimations of Rousseau in The Possessed

1. Jean-Jacques Rousseau, *The Confessions,* trans. J. M. Cohen (Middlesex, Eng.: Penguin Books, 1954), 419–21. Rousseau completed *The Confessions* in 1765. In this

chapter subsequent references to this work and to others that are frequently cited will appear in parentheses in the main body of the text.

2. See, for example, Barbara H. Howard, "The Rhetoric of Confession: Dostoevskij's Notes from Underground and Rousseau's *Confessions*," *SEEJ* 5 (Winter 1981): 16–33 (reprinted in my edited volume, *Critical Essays on Dostoevsky* [Boston: G. K. Hall, 1986], 64–73). For further references to work on Dostoevsky and Rousseau, see note 25 in chapter two.

3. Leonid Grossman, "Stilistika Stavrogina," *Sobranie sochienii* (Moscow, 1928): 2:141–43. Translated as "The Stylistics of Stavrogin's Confession: A Study of the New Chapter of *The Possessed*," trans. Katherine Tiernan O'Connor, in *Critical Essays on Dostoevsky*, 148–58.

4. Brian Wolfson, "*C'est la faute à Rousseau:* Possession as Device in *Demons*," *Dostoevsky Studies* (New Series) 5 (2001): 97–117; 97. See also Malcolm V. Jones, "Dostoevsky, Rousseau, and Others," in *Dostoevsky Studies* 4 (1983): 81–93; and "The Marion Motif: The Whisper of the Precursor," in Jones, *Dostoevsky after Bakhtin: Readings in Dostoevsky's Fantastic Realism* (Cambridge, U.K.: Cambridge University Press, 1990), 149–63; Thomas Barran, "Dark Uses of Confession: Rousseau and Dostoevsky's Stavrogin," in *Mid-Hudson Language Studies* 1 (1978): 97–112; my "Dostoevsky and Rousseau: The Morality of Confession Reconsidered," in *Western Philosophical Systems in Russian Literature,* ed. Anthony M. Mlikotin (Los Angeles: University of Southern California Press, 1979), 89–101 (reprinted in *Dostoevsky: New Perspectives*, ed. Robert Louis Jackson [Englewood Cliffs, N.J.: Prentice Hall, 1984], 82–98); and "Imitations of Rousseau in *The Possessed*," in *Dostoevsky Studies* 5 (1984): 77–89; Deborah Martinsen, *Surprised by Shame: Dostoevsky's Liars and Narrative Exposure* (Columbus: Ohio State University Press, 2003), 38–43 and passim.

5. Wolfson goes on to develop the idea that although Stavrogin duplicates Rousseau's predilection for "'experiments' in thought," his all operate in a stark reversal of Rousseau's assumption that man is inherently good. Through Stavrogin, "Dostoevsky presents the chilling repercussions of the alternative." Wolfson comes to the surprising, but to this reader convincing, conclusion, "Not only is Stavrogin a kind of Rousseau, but Rousseau himself is, 'secretly,' a Stavrogin - as Dostoevsky's examples show" ("C'est la faute à Rousseau," 107).

6. Natalie Babel-Brown, *Hugo and Dostoevsky* (Ann Arbor, Mich.: Ardis, 1978), 120. Hugo's novel also asserts its presence in *Crime and Punishment* and *The Idiot*.

7. In addition to several of the articles and chapters cited above see, J. M. Coetzee, "Confession and Double Thoughts: Tolstoy, Rousseau, Dostoevsky," in *Comparative Literature* 37, no. 3 (1985): 193–232. Coetzee writes, "Confessions are everywhere in Dostoevsky. . . . In the later novels the level of gratuitousness mounts to the extent that one can no longer think of confession as a mere expository device: confession itself, with all its attendant psychological, moral, epistemological and finally metaphysical problems, moves to the center of the stage" (215). Coetzee cites Dostoevsky's skepticism about Rousseau's variety of secular confession and concludes that "it is possible to read *Notes from Underground, The Idiot,* and Stavrogin's confession as a sequence of texts in which Dostoevsky explores the impasses of secular confession, pointing finally to the sacrament of confession as the only road to self-truth" (230).

8. "Glava deviataia: u Tikhona," *PSS*, 11:12. See also Fyodor Dostoevsky, *The Devils*, trans. David Magarshack (Middlesex, U.K.: Penguin Books, 1953), 680–81. I have altered the English translation at certain points. Subsequent references throughout this chapter to the novel will appear in parentheses with the Russian volume and page number from *PSS* preceding the English translation.

9. Peter France, trans. and ed., in introduction to *Jean Jacques Rousseau: Reveries of the Solitary Walker* (Middlesex, U.K.: Penguin Books, 1979), 8.

10. Thomas W. Laqueur, *Solitary Sex: A Cultural History of Masturbation* (New York: Zone Books, 2003); Stephen Greenblatt, "Me, Myself, and I," *New York Review of Books* 51, no. 6 (April 8, 2004): 7 (available at *http://www.nybooks.com/articles/17015*).

11. Greenblatt, *"Me, Myself, and I,"* 9, emphasis added.

12. Greenblatt, "Me, Myself, and I," 10. In this context Greenblatt observes that pornographic images of women masturbating "frequently feature an open book, dropped on the ground at the moment that the overwhelming excitements of reading provoked the urge for immediate relief" (ibid.).

13. D. H. Lawrence, "On Dostoevsky and Rozanov" (a 1936 review of V. V. Rozanov's *Solitaria*), reprinted in *Russian Literature and Modern English Fiction,* ed. Donald Davie (Chicago: University of Chicago Press, 1965), 99–100.

14. Greenblatt, "Me, Myself, and I," 11.

15. See Wolfson, "C'est la faute à Rousseau," 100–101. His interesting discussion of Rousseau's account of being frequently woken in the night by his father during which time he acquired a singular familiarity with "every feeling" finds a haunting echo in Stepan Verhkhovensky's propensity for the waking of the little Nicolas Stavrogin when he was a boy. "They used to throw themselves into each other's embrace and weep." The overtones or undertones of these passages seem particularly dark in today's cultural milieu where it is not masturbation that is feared but child abuse. The ramifications for Stavrogin of Stepan's middle-of-the-night encounters and tearful embraces of the child are dreadful to contemplate.

16. See, for example, the editorial notes in *PSS*, 12:224–25; E. N. Dryzhakova, "Dostoevskii i Gercen, (u istokov romana 'Besy' ")," in *Materialy i isslodovaniia,* ed. G. M. Fridlender (Leningrad, 1974), 219–29. See also Joseph Frank, *Dostoevsky: The Miraculous Years, 1865–1871* (Princeton, N.J.: Princeton University Press, 1995), 4:401–9, 422–23, 454–60, 474–78, 492–97; Richard Peace, *Dostoyevsky: An Examination of the Major Novels* (Cambridge, U.K.: Cambridge University Press, 1971), 140–46.

17. On can, however, also discover in him traces of other characters of Dostoevsky such as General Ivolgin, though an Ivolgin rendered as more dignified and gentlemanly, and without such an overpowering, vaudeville-like dose of shame in his character. Such comparisons, however, when pursued, tend to yield as many interesting differences as similarities. See, for example, Martinsen, *Surprised by Shame,* 130–33.

18. Martinsen, *Surprised by Shame,* 105. Martinsen quotes Wilson, "Self-Deception and Psychological Realism," in *Philosophical Investigations* 3, no. 4 (1980): 58.

19. Grossman, "Stilistika Stavrogina," 143.

20. Thomas Barran, *Russia Reads Rousseau, 1762–1825* (Evanston, Ill.: Northwestern University Press, 2002), 220–23.

21. Dostoevsky wrote in his *Diary of a Writer* in January 1876 that while writing *A*

Raw Youth, "I almost began my *Fathers and Sons;* but I held back, and thank God I did, for I was not ready. In the meantime I wrote only *A Raw Youth,* this first attempt at my idea . . . I took a soul that was sinless yet already tainted by the awful possibility of vice, by a premature hatred for its own insignificance and 'accidental' nature; tainted also by that breadth of character with which a still chaste soul already consciously allows vice to enter its thoughts, cherishes it and admires it in shameful yet bold and tempestuous dreams — and with all this, left solely to its own devices and its own understanding, yet also, to be sure, to God. All such are miscarriages of society, the 'accidental' members of 'accidental' families" (*Writer's Diary,* 1:302). I am suggesting that these ideas provide at least as powerful a gloss on *The Possessed* as they do upon *A Raw Youth* or *The Brothers Karamazov.* See also *PSS,* 17:6–7, for Dostoevsky's notes written in 1874 for his projected *Fathers and Children.* Susanne Fusso also hypothesizes that the plans for a novel, *Fathers and Sons,* even though it was not actually jotted down until the mid-1870s, hover behind *The Possessed.* She writes, "Dostoevskii's creative efforts in the last years of his life were dominated by his desire to produce his own 'Fathers and Sons.' His last three novels, *The Devils, A Raw Youth,* and *The Brothers Karamazov,* can be seen as in part motivated by this quest to rewrite Turgenev (Fusso, "Dostoevskii and the Family," in *The Cambridge Companion to Dostoevskii,* ed. W. J. Leatherbarrow (Cambridge, U.K.: Cambridge University Press, 2002), 175. See also her fascinating "The Sexuality of the Male Virgin: Arkady in *A Raw Youth,*" in *A New Word on The Brothers Karamazov,* ed. Robert Louis Jackson (Evanston, Ill.: Northwestern University Press, 2004), 142–55.

Richard Peace finds that the conflict of generations motif in the novel is far broader than a simple tension between the men of the 1840s and the men of the 1860s. He writes, "for just as Stepan Trofimovich is responsible for Petr Verhovensky, so too Stavrogin is the intellectual 'father' of Kirillov and Shatov. It is typical of the dualism which everywhere informs the writing of this novel, that the reader should thus be presented, not with one theme of 'fathers and children,' but with two" (Peace, *Dostoevsky: An Examination of the Major Novels* [Cambridge, U.K.: Cambridge University Press, 1971], 155–56. I would expand Peace's canny observation further to suggest that there are multiple themes of fathers and children — including daughters as well — which, taken as a complete complex tapestry, form the texture and meaning of the novel as a whole.

22. Martinsen, *Surprised by Shame,* 116.

23. *PSS,* 5:179; *Notes from Underground,* in *Three Short Novels by Fyodor Dostoyevsky,* trans. Constance Garnett, intro. Ernest J. Simmons (New York: Dell, 1960), 140.

24. Dennis Patrick Slattery has argued that the importance of Rousseau's lifelong bladder complaint was central to his philosophical ideas and to shaping the structure of his *Confessions.* "He feels . . . the rhythms of revolt internally, when he informs us that a malformed bladder from birth begins to take on a life of its own and directs his feelings as well as his memories; like the disease that infects Ivan Ilych, Rousseau's agitated and stubborn bladder . . . shifts his entire way of seeing himself, the rapidly changing world around him, and his relation to others. *The Confessions* . . . is certainly an embodied narrative that seeks to define the figure of Rousseau, who in his physical and psychological ailments seeks some form of cleansing by writing his autobiography. Aristotle and others before him understood how confession and catharsis are so frequently two sides of

the same act of self-exposure." Slattery, "Autobiography, Body Cleansing, and the Invention of the Paris Sewer System," in *The Wounded Body: Remembering the Markings of the Flesh* (Binghamton, N.Y.: SUNY Press, 2000), 85. Slattery goes on to suggest the ways in which Rousseau's disease "implicates his culture, his own psychology, and his autobiographical project" (ibid., 87). He colorfully describes *The Confessions* (like the Paris sewer system that was then being developed) as a place of "intimate discharge" (ibid., 93). He cites Alfred Ziegler's observation that Rousseau's "bodily distresses center on his continual use of catheters 'draining his bladder to avoid uremia, self-contamination by his own excrement.' . . . I suggest that a similar danger lurked for him in the writing of *The Confessions* and analogously in his own life" (ibid., 107). Slattery's observations transfer well to Stepan Trofimovich: his words throughout the novel also constitute a kind of intimate discharge, his illnesses — both spiritual and physical — affect and shape his ideas. Unlike Rousseau, however, by the end of the novel Stepan Trofimovich may have managed to avoid that dreaded state of self-contamination. He expels the poison.

25. Rousseau, on the other hand, resolves to leave his possessions "in the open fields" (*Confessions*, 452).

26. Wolfson, "C'est la faute à Rousseau," 110–11.

27. From this point on in the novel, Stepan Trofimovich ceases to resemble Rousseau and takes on instead many of the qualities of Dostoevsky's beloved Don Quixote.

28. See, for example, Lionel Gossman, "The Innocent Art of Confession and Reverie," *Daedalus* 107 (Summer 1978): 60. Equivalent in Rousseau's moral and spiritual development to Augustine's youthful stealing of the pears is Rousseau's account of the ribbon episode with the servant-maid Marion. Although Rousseau's crime is the far greater one and the more complexly ridden with desire and moral perversion, both acts are impulsive, unpremeditated, and ultimately play a primary role in the avowed spiritual transformation of the narrator. For interesting analyses of this ribbon episode in Rousseau, see Coetzee, "Confession and Double Thoughts," 205–9, Paul De Man, *Allegories of Reading: Figural Language in Rousseau, Nietzsche, Rilke, and Proust* (New Haven, Conn.: Yale University Press, 1979), 280; and his "The Purloined Ribbon," in *Glyph* 1, no. 1 (1977): 28–50.

29. For a discussion of this passage from *House of the Dead*, see chapter two. There are also perhaps some comic overtones of King Lear and the heath.

30. See Martinsen's illuminating discussion of Sofya Matveevna's reading of these three passages from the Bible in *Surprised by Shame*, 126–28.

31. Gossman, "Innocent Art of Confession and Reverie," 66.

32. Rousseau, *Reveries of the Solitary Walker*, 64–65. This work was published in 1782, four years after Rousseau's death.

33. Maxim Gorky, *Reminiscences of Tolstoy, Chekhov and Andreev*, trans. Katherine Mansfield, S. S. Koteliansky and Leonard Woolf (London, 1968), 30. Coetzee sees in this tendency of Rousseau to believe his own lies (and hence, by extension here, Stepan Trofimovich) a manifestation of a different kind of truth — of authenticity. "Language itself therefore becomes for Rousseau the being of the authentic self, and appeal to an exterior 'truth' is closed off" ("Confession and Double Thoughts," 209). Thus we might also argue that when Stepan Trofimovich claims that he believes himself when he is lying, one cannot know whether or not he is speaking the truth at that moment (that knowledge

is "closed off" to us), but we can suppose that we are witnessing, through his language, Stepan Trofimovich's "authentic self."

34. It is interesting that the underground man, one of Dostoevsky's "self-deceivers" par excellence, here accuses his readers of being self-deceivers too.

35. Grossman, "Stilistika Stavrogina," 143; and *Dostoevsky: A Biography,* trans. Mary Mackler (Bloomington: Indiana University Press, 1975), 244. Strakhov's letter was not published until 1913.

Chapter 6: Unsealing the Generic Envelope and Deciphering "The Dream of a Ridiculous Man"

1. "The Dream of a Ridiculous Man" is Dostoevsky's fourth important monologic story (the others are *White Nights, Notes from Underground,* and "A Gentle Creature") whose narrator is an anonymous urban dreamer. Each of these dreamers has a single encounter with a young woman that becomes the shaping influence in his moral, spiritual, and ethical life, as well as the main focus of his possibly lifelong reverie. For illuminating readings of these stories as a kind of quartet, see Robert L. Belknap, " 'The Gentle Creature' as the Climax of a Work of Art that Almost Exists," in *Dostoevsky Studies* (New Series) 4 (2000): 35–42; and Deborah Martinsen, introduction to *Notes from Underground, The Double and Other Stories* (New York: Barnes and Noble Classics, 2003), xii–liv.

2. Henry James, preface to *What Maisie Knew* (Oxford, UK: Oxford University Press, 1982), 9.

3. Jonathan Swift, *Gulliver's Travels* (1726; New York: New American Library, 1960), 288, 296.

4. See chapter five, especially notes 2, 3, 4, 7, 22, 26, and 31.

5. The definition of confession I use here derives from Leonid Grossman. See his "Stylistics of Stavrogin's Confession," trans. Katherine Tiernan O'Connor, in *Critical Essays on Dostoevsky,* ed. Robin Feuer Miller (Boston: G. K. Hall, 1985), 156.

6. Jean Jacques Rousseau, *A Discourse on Inequality,* trans. and ed. Maurice Cranston (Harmondsworth, U,K.: Penguin Books, 1984), 101. Although we tend to juxtapose reason and passion, Rousseau attempts to show a link between them: "It is by the activity of the passions that our reason improves itself; we seek to know only because we desire to enjoy; and it is impossible to conceive a man who had neither desires nor fears giving himself the troubles of reasoning" (ibid., 89). His natural men were subject to passion only insofar as it was a simple "impulsion of nature" — the desire for food, for a mate, for rest, or the fear of pain or hunger.

7. F. M. Dostoevskii, *PSS,* 25:397–400. Subsequent page references to "The Dream" are included in parentheses throughout the chapter with the Russian page number from *PSS* followed by a citation from *Great Short Works of Dostoevsky,* ed. Ronald Hingley, trans. David Magarshack (New York: Harper & Row, 1968), 715–39. I have altered Magarshack's translations slightly when necessary. Citations to other volumes of the *PSS* also appear by Roman numeral and page number in the text. Dostoevsky's preface appeared in *Time,* no. 1 (1861): 230–31.

8. The editors also cite Dostoevsky's interest in Nikolai Strakhov's "The Inhabitants

of a Planet" (*Time,* 1861) and in the work of such astronomers as C. Flammarion (*PSS,* 25:400).

9. Edgar Allan Poe, "A Tale of the Ragged Mountains," in *Complete Tales and Poems* (New York: Vintage Books, 1975), 681, 683, 684–85. This experience is typical of what in popular psychology has come to be called a "near-death experience," in which one experiences, among other things, a detachment from the body and the sense of entering a tunnel and seeing a light at the end of it. Along with this comes a distortion of time and such phenomena as a life review, a sense of unity, or the reaching of a border at which one either advances or is sent back to life. These phenomena have been described by such psychiatrists as Kenneth Ring and Bruce Greyson, but they are, of course, most immediately familiar to readers of Russian literature through such works as "The Dream of a Ridiculous Man," or Tolstoy's *The Death of Ivan Ilych* (1886). The phenomenon of retaining one's consciousness and sensibility after death is also explored by Dostoevsky in his story "Bobok" (1873).

10. Czeslaw Milosz, "Dostoevsky and Swedenborg," in *The Emperor of the Earth: Modes of Eccentric Vision* (Berkeley: University of California Press, 1977), 122, 130. In *The Brothers Karamazov* the narrator describes how the starry sky is filled with countless stars, "each of which, in its place and in its system, is a seed plot [*rassadnik*] of the heavens" (*PSS,* 15:401). See also chapter eight and the conclusion of this book.

11. In the eighteenth-century French tradition, utopian works were most frequently called *rêves* (dreams), *codes, robinsonades,* or *voyages imaginaires.* The nineteenth-century French dictionary by Littre defined *utopie* as *chimère* (chimera). See Frank and Fritzie Manuel, *Utopian Thought in the Western World* (Cambridge, Mass.: Harvard University Press, 1979), 6. Thus the title of "The Dream of a Ridiculous Man" would carry these immediate utopian-dream associations to an educated reader of the nineteenth century.

12. J. Michael Holquist, *Dostoevsky and the Novel* (Princeton, N.J.: Princeton University Press, 1977), 156, 159, 162. Holquist quotes Sigmund Freud, *On Dreams,* trans. James Strachey (New York: Norton Library, 1952), 65.

13. Gary Saul Morson, *The Boundaries of Genre: Dostoevsky's Diary of a Writer and the Traditions of Literary Utopia* (Austin: University of Texas Press, 1981), 36, 181–82.

14. Manuel and Manuel, *Utopian Thought,* 2. They quote from Sir Philip Sidney, *The Complete Works,* vol. 3 (Cambridge, U.K.: Cambridge University Press, 1923), 15. Thus the title "The Dream of a Ridiculous Man" would carry these immediate utopian associations to an educated reader of the nineteenth century.

15. Manuel and Manuel, *Utopian Thought,* 6, 15.

16. The Manuels argue from the historical perspective that it is not important or necessary to distinguish between utopia and paradise. "Any strict compartmentalization of future utopia and nostalgia for an idealized bygone human condition is invalidated by their constant interplay in Western thought. In the fiction of the original Morean utopia, the idea already exists somewhere on a faraway island and has been seen by human eyes. . . . Similarly, the widespread Christian belief that the Garden of Eden, or earthly paradise, continued to exist in a particular place, even after the expulsion of Adam and Eve, fed the hope that a paradisical state was possible this side of heaven and provided a model for it" (ibid., 5). Granted, then, the utopian tree can produce many different kinds of fruit. But

may not our interest focus on one particular fruit—an apple, perhaps an apple with a tiny spider on its stem? That is, the very kind of compartmentalization that they argue against —the separation of future or present utopias from edenic nostalgia for a bygone human condition—can yield valuable insights. It seems to me that the impulse toward a future idea and the nostalgia for a bygone time cannot be construed as identical. It becomes as important to describe their differences as it is to acknowledge their similarities.

17. W. H. Auden, "Dingley Dell and the Fleet," in *The Dyers Hand and Other Essays* (New York: Random House, 1968), 409.

18. Auden, "Dingley Dell," 410. Richard Gerber has responded similarly to the different emotive atmospheres of paradise and utopia. He writes, "In the one case happiness is a state of grace, in the other it is the result of a conscious human effort." See his *Utopian Fantasy: A Study of English Utopian Fiction Since the End of the Nineteenth Century* (New York: McGraw-Hill, 1973), 5. Perhaps we may imagine the ridiculous man as experiencing the former and becoming imbued with a vision of the latter.

19. Such an oxymoron is best viewed consciously as such, keeping its separate interweaving strands intact. Thus, to use paradise and utopia as interchangeable terms leads to confusion. Consider, for example, the confusion generated by the following otherwise interesting statement, "Yet the myth of a hypothetical paradise persisted, a walled garden, as the etymology implied. . . . The entrance fee to utopia was conformity to behavioral rules." See Efraim Sicher, "By Underground to Crystal Palace: The Dystopian Eden," *Comparative Literature Studies* 22, no. 3 (Fall 1985): 378.

20. Edward Wasiolek, *Dostoevsky: The Major Fiction* (Cambridge, Mass.: MIT Press, 1964), 145, 147.

21. Robert Louis Jackson, *The Art of Dostoevsky: Deliriums and Nocturnes* (Princeton, N.J.: Princeton University Press, 1981), 273.

22. *PSS*, 25:118. Subsequent page references to the Russian text of "The Dream" are included in parentheses in the text, followed by page references to the English translation from *Great Short Works of Dostoevsky*, trans. David Magarshack, ed. Ronald Hingley (New York: Harper and Row, 1968), 715–39. I have altered Magarshack's translations slightly when necessary.

23. Jackson, *The Art of Dostoevsky*, 280.

24. Holquist, *Dostoevsky and the Novel*, 158.

25. Charles Dickens, "A Christmas Carol," in *The Christmas Books* (2 vols.), ed. Michael Slater (Harmondsworth, U.K.: Penguin Books, 1971), 1:134. Subsequent page references are included in parentheses in the text.

26. This gothic use of light will come under further consideration in the next chapter.

27. This passage may have been in Dostoevsky's mind again later when he was writing the scene in which Ivan Karamazov confronts his own otherworldly visitor, his devil. The devil taunts him about whether or not he is really appearing before him, "Listen, in dreams and especially in nightmares, from indigestion or anything, a man sometimes see such artistic visions, such complex and real actuality, such events, even a whole world of events, woven into such a plot, with such unexpected details from the most exalted matters to the last button on a cuff, as I swear Leo Tolstoy could not create." *PSS*, 15:74; *The Brothers Karamazov*, trans. Constance Garnett, ed. Ralph E. Matlaw (New York:

Norton, 1976), 606. See chapter eight for a fuller discussion of this passage and Ivan's confrontation with his devil.

28. Could Dostoevsky have had in mind the words of Shakespeare's Prospero in *The Tempest?* Near the close of the play, when Prospero is thinking to put aside his power and his magic in order to leave his enchanted island and return to the everyday world of men and women, he says, "We are such stuff / As dreams are made on, and our little life / Is rounded with a sleep." Shakespeare, *The Tempest* (4:(1):156–58).

29. Myshkin's parable about faith uttered to Rogozhin also strove to express the essence of religious feeling in a discourse that avoided logic and reason and depended instead upon patterns of correspondences that ultimately aspire to have a transformative effect upon both the narrator and his audience. See chapter four for a fuller discussion of this.

30. Deborah Martinsen has emphasized that in this passage the ridiculous man "is repeating a question raised by Nikolai Stavrogin. . . . By setting the action on another planet, both men distance themselves from their abuse of a young girl, turning their actual 'disgraceful and dishonorable action' into an abstract speculation" (Martinsen, introduction to *Notes from Underground*, xlvii).

31. Wasiolek, for example, has eloquently argued this position: "Both Stavrogin and Versilov are men without faith, and they should have given Dostoevsky's interpreters the key to the possibility that the ridiculous man's dream is a dream of a Golden Age without faith. We need to remind ourselves that the tiny spot of light (the ridiculous man's star) turns into a red spider for Stavrogin" (*Dostoevsky,* 145). See also Richard Peace, "Dostoevsky and the Golden Age," *Dostoevsky Studies* 3 (1982): 62–79.

32. George Gibian has noted that Dostoevsky's nature imagery, while intensely powerful, is curiously condensed: "In his later works Dostoevsky frequently concentrated the meaning of vegetation and 'the garden' into a leaf" (see Gibian, "Traditional Symbolism in *Crime and Punishment,*" in *Crime and Punishment,* trans. Jessie Coulson, ed. George Gibian [New York: Norton, 1975], 527).

33. See chapter three and its discussion of the epilogue to *Crime and Punishment.* As in "The Dream" this trichina is a wormlike parasite representative of Dostoevsky's bleak view of modernity in a world where men aspire to take the place of God and give themselves over to the beauty of lies and self-delusion.

34. Miguel de Cervantes, *The Adventures of Don Quixote,* trans. J. M. Cohen (Harmondsworth, U.K.: Penguin Books, 1961), 85–86.

35. Dostoevsky's use of leaves and Cervantes's of the acorn exhibit a strikingly similar use of synecdoche, a rhetorical device whereby a single part of nature stands for its idea as a whole: the entire garden of nature.

36. See chapter four, in particular the discussion of Grushenka's tale about the onion. There too a story with a message of despair becomes, in the act and process of telling, transformed into a parable of hope.

37. Quoted by Michael Slater in Dickens, *Christmas Books,* 1:33.

38. *PSS,* 22:12–13; *Writer's Diary,* trans. Kenneth Lanz (Evanston, Ind.: Northwestern University Press, 1994), 1:308.

39. This passage is also, of course, redolent of Dostoevsky's longstanding doctrine of *pochvenichestvo.*

40. See, for example, Michael Futrell, "Dostoevskii and Dickens," in *Dostoevskii and Britain*, ed. W. J. Leatherbarrow (Oxford, Eng.: Berg Publishers Limited, 1995), 97–98. See also Loralee MacPike, *Dostoevsky's Dickens: A Study of Literary Influence* (London: George Prior, 1981).

41. Jackson, *Art of Dostoevsky*, 261. Dostoevsky's description of the little boy's actual death, a grim moment transfigured for the dying child by a vision of beauty, also, it seems to me, calls to mind the death of Little Nell (*The Old Curiosity Shop*) and of Betty Higden (*Our Mutual Friend*).

42. Ibid., 266.

43. The numerous resemblances of this story to Hans Christian Andersen's "The Little Match Girl" are also striking and could be the subject of further study.

Chapter 7: Evocations and Revocations of Anxiety in the Metaphysical Novel

1. For the purposes of this discussion, I am making an analogy between genre and beauty in asserting that both of them exist partly in the perception of the beholder and partly in the inherent property of the thing (in this case, the text) itself. In doing this I am sidestepping a recent and fascinating indirect debate that has arisen between two contemporary thinkers about the nature of beauty and its relation to the imagination — the literary and cultural critic Elaine Scarry, and the mathematician and poet Barry Mazur. Both Scarry and Mazur are interested in the mental processes by which truth is constituted in its perception. Beauty is no less (and no more) real than the imaginary numbers of mathematics. See Elaine Scarry, *Dreaming by the Book* (New York: Farrar, Straus and Giroux, 2000), 40–74, and Barry Mazur, *Imagining Numbers* (New York: Farrar, Straus and Giroux, 2003), 3–4, 16–18. I am grateful to my colleague William Flesch for alerting me to this debate and for illuminating it for me.

2. Tzvetan Todorov, *The Fantastic: A Structural Approach to a Literary Genre*, trans. Richard Howard (Ithaca, N.Y.: Cornell University Press, 1973), 3. Subsequent page references to this work appear in the main body of the text in parentheses.

3. Sigmund Freud, *Studies in Parapsychology*, "The Uncanny" (1919; New York: Macmillan, 1963), 19–20. Subsequent page references to this work appear in parentheses in the main body of the text.

4. The next chapter explores the interaction between Ivan and his devil in more detail. And his devil is certainly most devilish in his details.

5. Peter Brooks, *The Melodramatic Imagination: Balzac, Henry James, Melodrama, and the Mode of Excess* (New Haven, Conn.: Yale University Press, 1976), ix.

6. Brooks, *Melodramatic Imagination*, 4, 25. The notion of taboo is crucial to the uncanny, the gothic, and the melodrama. Moreover, taboos are, by definition, productive of deep anxiety. David Punter has defined tabooed objects as "those to which we summon up not a simple emotional reaction but a dialectical one in which the mind oscillates between attraction and repulsion, worship and condemnation" (Punter, *The Literature of Terror: A History of Gothic Fictions from 1765 to the Present Day* [New York: Longman, 1978], 410.) In another context, he has offered a possible definition of the gothic mode as a "series of strategies for dealing with tabooed material" (see David Punter,

"Social Relations of Gothic Fiction," in David Aers, Jonathan Cook, and David Punter, *Romanticism and Ideology: Studies in English Writing, 1765–1830* (London: Routledge & Kegan Paul, 1981), 103. See also Olga Meerson, *Dostoevsky's Taboos,* Studies of the Harriman Institute (Dresden: Dresden University Press, 1998). It is impossible to summarize Meerson's complex and learned readings of Dostoevsky's fictional works with regard to the role of taboo within them, but I shall quote in full one paragraph from her concluding chapter that gives an indication of what she has argued throughout: "I found the term 'taboo' perfectly applicable to Dostoevsky's poetics because it crosses the boundaries between several realms, disciplines and approaches, thereby providing a unified vision of Dostoevsky's system of values without reducing any of these realms or approaches to each other. Thus for example the behavioral expression of an unclean conscience of a character or even a narrator may exactly correspond to the patterns observed by Freud, but the phenomenon of this conscience — which, I believe prompts the character in question to taboo — concerns not only psychoanalysis or even psychology, but also morality, theology, philosophy and, last but not least, narrative motivation. I submit that the overview of taboos in Dostoevsky allows one to unify all of these aspects of Dostoevsky's poetics in one vision. After all, tabooing is the only thing definitely common to *Dostoevsky's* conscious narrative technique and *his characters'* involuntary embarrassed silence, conscience-sanctioned or God-imposed reticence, and dread at the prospect of eternal torment in hell. Tabooing underlines characters' interaction with each other as well as the ways in which Dostoevsky provokes his readers to interact with his text. Tabooing signals to the reader the values and sore spots of characters, but while doing so, it also addresses the reader's own sore spots and values" (213).

7. Charles Robert Maturin, *Melmoth the Wanderer,* intro. William F. Axton (Lincoln: University of Nebraska Press, 1961), 271, 274. Subsequent references to the novel will appear in the main body of the text.

8. For an excellent and comprehensive analysis of the many rhetorical devices Dostoevsky used in *The Brothers Karamazov* as well as the specific locating of them, see the monumental study by Victor Terras, *A Karamazov Companion: Commentary on the Genesis, Language and Style of Dostoevsky's Novel* (Madison: University of Wisconsin Press, 1981), 89–90, 138–39 and passim. For the way in which oxymoron can modulate into catachresis, see Terras, 133, n. 89.

9. See the forthcoming essay by Caryl Emerson, "In Honor of Mikhail Gasparov's Quarter Century of Not Liking Bakhtin: Pro and Contra." Emerson offers a new analysis of how to understand Bakhtin's ideas about polyphony. In the context of its relationship to music she cites Michael Holquist, *Dialogism: Bakhtin and His World* (London and New York: Routledge, 1990), 18–20; and Alexander Makhov, "Muzika slova: iz istorii odnoi fikzii," forthcoming in *Voprosi literaturi* (2005–2006). In short, our understanding of what Bakhtin may actually have meant by the idea of polyphony is in transition.

10. For example, Northrop Frye's analysis of the menippean satire meshes well with Bakhtin's but also expands upon it in interesting ways. Like Bakhtin, Frye emphasized that the menippean satire dealt less with people as such than with characters as representations of mental attitudes and that the "short form of the Menippean satire is usually a dialogue or colloquy in which the dramatic interest is in a conflict of ideas rather than of characters." Frye put special emphasis on the combination of fantasy and morality that

existed within these satires, as well as the fact that the menippean satirist understood evil and folly as "diseases of the intellect," whereas, in his view, novelists tend to see evil and folly as social diseases. See Frye, *Anatomy of Criticism: Four Essays* (Princeton, N.J.: Princeton University Press, 1957), 309–12.

11. Coral Ann Howells, *Love, Mystery and Misery: Feelings in Gothic Fiction* (London: Athlone Press, 1978), 16; Devendra P. Varma, "Quest of the Numinous: The Gothic Flame," in *Literature of the Occult: A Collection of Critical Essays,* ed. Peter Messent (Englewood Cliffs, N.J.: Prentice-Hall, 1981), 43.

12. See Terras, *A Karamazov Companion,* 84–85. Terras in this context has cited PB. Bitsilli, "K voprosu o vnutrennie forme romana Dostoevskogo," in *O Dostoevskom: Stat'i, Brown University Slavic Reprint* 4 (Providence, 1966), 49–59.

13. Punter, *Literature of Terror,* 403.

14. Leonid Grossman was the first to point out the influence of the gothic tradition in Dostoevsky's work. See his "Kompozitsiia v romane Dostoevskogo," *Sobranie sochinenii* 2 (Moscow, 1928): 9–59. For another discussion of this influence on Dostoevsky, starting with Edmund Burke's theories about the sublime and the beautiful, up through Maturin's novel, see Miller, *Dostoevsky and* The Idiot: *Author, Narrator and Reader* (Cambridge, Mass.: Harvard University Press, 1981), 108–29, 267–77, or "Dostoevsky and the Tale of Terror," in *The Russian Novel from Pushkin to Pasternak,* ed. John G. Garrard (New Haven, Conn.: Yale University Press, 1983), 103–25.

15. G. R. Thompson, "A Dark Romanticism: In Quest of a Gothic Monomyth," in *Literature of the Occult,* 33. S. L. Varnado has written that the essential movement in the gothic novel is the quest for the numinous (a word created by the German theologian and philosopher Rudolf Otto to describe "man's underlying sense of supernatural fear, wonder and delight when he is confronted by the divine"). See Varnado, "The Idea of the Numinous in Gothic Literature," in *Literature of the Occult,* 52. Varnado has cited Otto's *The Idea of the Holy: The Nonrational Factor in the Idea of the Divine and Its Relation to the Rational* (1917). See also Varma's "Quest of the Numinous," 40–51.

16. Mario Praz, introduction to *Three Gothic Novels: The Castle of Otranto, Vathek, Frankenstein,* ed. Peter Fairclough (Harmondsworth, U.K.: Penguin Books, 1968), 20; and Miller, *Dostoevsky and* The Idiot, 112.

17. Punter, *Literature of Terror,* 135; Axton, introduction, to Charles Robert Maturin, *Melmoth the Wanderer,* xviii.

18. *PSS,* 14:18; Fyodor Dostoevsky, *The Brothers Karamazov,* trans. Constance Garnett, revised and ed. Ralph E. Matlaw (New York: Norton, 1976), 13. Subsequent references to the novel will appear in the text of this chapter, with the Russian citation from *PSS* preceding the English one. Terras specifically links this image of "the slanting rays of the setting sun" to the paintings of Claude Lorrain and cites Dostoevsky's use of the same imagery in *The Possessed* and *A Raw Youth,* in *A Karamazov Companion,* 133. See also the discussion in the previous chapter of Lorrain and of the same image of the sun as it appeared in "The Dream of a Ridiculous Man."

19. For more general discussions of Dostoevsky and his interest in the visual arts, see chapters one and two.

20. Robert Kiely has written that "Maturin's grouped portraits are not the mere whims of a warped aesthete but a romantic vision of man's fallen state as emblemized by his

incapacity to maintain stability and proportion in a life encircled by pain and death. If Maturin created new images of beauty in his dark art, they were images created in sorrow and longing for a beauty classically defined, an ideal lost, not rejected." See Kiely, *The Romantic Novel in England* (Cambridge, Mass.: Harvard University Press, 1972), 197. Kiely's words about Maturin could read as a description of many of Dostoevsky's most painterly verbal representations.

21. Grossman, *Sobranie sochinenii,* 2:73 and 3:32 (Moscow, 1928), and "Kompositsiia v romane Dostoevskogo," 2:21–32, 51–52; George Steiner, *Tolstoy or Dostoevsky: An Essay in the Old Criticism* (New York: Random House, 1959), 192–214 and passim. See also Vsevolod Setchkarev, "Ch.R. Maturin's Roman 'Melmoth the Wanderer' and Dostoevskij," *Sonderabdruck aus Zeitschrift fur slavische Philologie* 30(1)(MS1): 99–106.

22. "The structure of *Melmoth the Wanderer*," writes Kiely, "a series of narrations within narrations—often compared with a nest of Chinese boxes—defies conventional chronological sequence and replaces it with obsessive variations on the single theme of human misery" (Kiely, *Romantic Novel,* 71). Axton similarly describes the structure of the novel as "a system of interpolated tales nested one within another like the boxes of a child's toy" and finds this structure to be a "conscious artistic device which serves several important functions," (introduction to Maturin, *Melmoth the Wanderer,* xv).

23. Douglas Grant, introduction to *Melmoth the Wanderer* (London: Oxford University Press, 1968), xi. I have taken this quotation from Kiely, *Romantic Novel,* 190.

24. Punter, *Literature of Terror,* 135–40.

25. See *Eugene Onegin: A Novel in Verse by Aleksandr Pushkin,* trans. and with commentary by Vladimir Nabokov, 4 vols. (Princeton, N.J.: Princeton University Press, 1975), 1:33, 55, 285, 316; 2:35, 352–54, 356; 3:96, 97–98, 159. Setchkarev, "Ch.R. Maturin's Roman," 101. Also see his *Gogol: His Life and Works,* trans. Robert Kramer (New York: New York University Press, 1965), 127.

26. Quoted by Howells, *Love, Mystery, and Misery,* 137. For a further discussion of Maturin's preoccupation with the problem of human suffering, see ibid., 131.

27. *PSS,* 29(1):117; *Selected Letters of Fyodor Dostoevsky,* ed. Joseph Frank and David I. Goldstein, trans. Andrew MacAndrew (Rutgers, N.J.: Rutgers University Press, 1987), 331, (letter to A. N. Maikov from Dresden, March 25/April 6, 1870).

28. For extended discussions of the way the layers of narration work in *The Brothers Karamazov,* see Robert L. Belknap, *The Structure of The Brothers Karamazov* (The Hague: Mouton, 1967), 77–106 and passim; Terras, *A Karamazov Companion,* 50, 85; Miller, *The Brothers Karamazov: Worlds of the Novel* (New Haven: Yale University Press, 2008), passim; Diane Oenning Thompson, *The Brothers Karamazov and the Poetics of Memory* (Cambridge, U.K.: Cambridge University Press, 1991), 26–52; Joseph Frank, *Dostoevsky: The Mantle of the Prophet, 1871–1881* (Princeton, N.J.: Princeton University Press, 2002), 572–80, 623–45, and passim.

29. *PSS,* 29(1):63; Frank and Goldstein, *Selected Letters,* 464–65.

30. *PSS,* 29(1):68; Frank and Goldstein, *Selected Letters,* 470. Note too Dostoevsky's by now familiar habit of especially valuing and even allowing himself to point out the originality of his work.

31. *PSS,* 29(1):121–22; Frank and Goldstein, *Selected Letters,* 486.

Chapter 8: Perilous Journeys to Conversion

1. Dostoevsky, writing in his notebooks for *The Idiot,* described his writing as embodying a fantastic conception of reality. "It is true," he writes," that we have a different conception of reality, a thousand thoughts, prophecy — a fantastic reality" (*PSS,* 9:276). Evaluating what Dostoevsky may have meant by fantastic realism has preoccupied, to varying degrees, virtually all of Dostoevsky's critics. For an interesting discussion of this question, see Liza Knapp, *The Annihilation of Inertia: Dostoevsky and Metaphysics* (Evanston, Ill.: Northwestern University Press, 1996), 66–67. See also Malcolm Jones, in *Dostoyevsky after Bakhtin: Readings in Dostoyevsky's Fantastic Realism* (Cambridge, U.K.: Cambridge University Press, 1990). Jones presents a fine and full discussion of moments of fantastic realism as they occur throughout his work. See also Robert Louis Jackson, *The Art of Dostoevsky: Deliriums and Nocturnes* (Princeton, N.J.: Princeton University Press, 1981), 288–303, and his *Dostoevsky's Quest for Form* (New Haven, Conn.: Yale University Press, 1966), 71–91, and Joseph Frank, *Dostoevsky: The Mantle of the Prophet, 1871–1881* (Princeton, N.J.: Princeton University Press, 2002), 552–55. Frank argues convincingly that in the passage in which Ivan is visited by the devil, Dostoevsky is revisiting some of the problems that the fantastic had posed to him in his early work, *The Double.* "The 'enjoyment' he felt in depicting Ivan's devil may well have sprung from being able at last to rectify his literary failure as a debutant" (*Mantle of the Prophet,* 554). Frank also discusses Dostoevsky's fantastic realism in *Dostoevsky: The Miraculous Years, 1865–1861* (Princeton, N.J.: Princeton University Press, 1995), 301–2, 308–9, 314–15, 349–52.

2. William James, *The Varieties of Religious Experience: A Study in Human Nature,* intro. Reinhold Niebuhr (New York: Collier Books, 1970), 160. Subsequent references to this work will appear in parentheses in the text.

3. See chapters one and four as well as their notes.

4. Joseph Frank, *Dostoevsky: The Years of Ordeal, 1850–1859* (Princeton, N.J.: Princeton University Press, 1983), 116, 124. Frank has made an extraordinarily happy choice in the discovery of James's *Varieties* as a model for describing the earmarks of Dostoevsky's (or "Dostoevsky's") conversion experience as he portrayed it in "The Peasant Marey."

5. Thomas De Quincey, *Confessions of an English Opium Eater,* ed. and intro. Alethea Hayter (Middlesex, U.K.: Penguin Books, 1979), first published 1821 in *The London Magazine,* 104. Page references in the text are to this Penguin edition.

6. See earlier discussions of this idea throughout chapters one, four, and six.

7. In fact, James often sounds like the rebellious Ivan: "The normal process of life contains moments as bad as any of those which insane melancholy is filled with. . . . The lunatic's visions of horror are all drawn from the material of daily fact. Our civilization is founded on the shambles." Compare this insight of James's with Ivan's collecting of articles from the newspaper and his refusal, in "Rebellion," of a civilization founded upon the unjustified tears of a child. Like Ivan, James refers to the "geological cataclysm" and uses the metaphor of reptiles devouring each other: "To believe in the carnivorous reptiles of geologic times is hard for our imagination . . . , yet there is no tooth in any one of those museum-skulls that did not . . . hold fast to the body struggling in despair of some fated living victim" (*Varieties,* 140).

8. *PSS*, 22:47. Fyodor Dostoevsky, *A Writer's Diary*, 2 vols., (1873–76), trans. and annotated by Kenneth Lantz, intro. Gary Saul Morson (Evanston, Ill.: Northwestern University Press, 1994), 1:352; emphasis added. Subsequent page references to this work will appear in the text in parentheses.

9. For a fuller discussion of this work, see chapter four.

10. Robert Louis Jackson, "The Triple Vision: The Peasant Marey," in *The Art of Dostoevsky: Deliriums and Nocturnes* (Princeton, N.J.: Princeton University Press, 1981), 25.

11. See chapter one.

12. Jackson, "The Triple Vision," 28.

13. Alfred Adler, "Dostoevsky," lecture delivered in Town Hall of Zurich, 1918, in *The Practice and Theory of Individual Psychology*, trans. P. Radin (London, 1923; rev. ed., 1929), 287. Adler also makes an observation about Dostoevsky that could have come verbatim from the pen of Bakhtin, "There is no *image* so often occurring in his work as that of a '*boundary*' (ibid., 283). Adler's essay teems with insights and deserves further study. I am grateful to my late father, Lewis S. Feuer, for pointing out this obscure article to me, and I hope others will turn to it as well.

14. I. S. Zil'bershtein and L. M. Rozenblium, eds., *Neizdanny Dostoevskii. Zapisny knizhki i tetradi 1860–1861, Literaturnoe Nasledstvo*, 83 (Moscow, 1971): 416, 57, quoted by James Rice in his *Dostoevsky and the Healing Art: An Essay in Literary and Medical History* (Ann Arbor, Mich.: Ardis, 1985), 258.

15. It is well known that Dostoevsky consulted with a doctor, in fact several of them, about the details of hallucinations and of brain fever to prepare the description of Ivan's encounter with the devil. Hence the narrator-chronicler's almost clinical description, "And so he was sitting almost conscious himself of his delirium, and as I have said already, looking persistently at some object on the sofa against the opposite wall." (*PSS*, 15:69; 602) Yet one cannot help but think the consultation with a doctor was perhaps superfluous, given Dostoevsky's account how as a convict his reveries used to begin with "some speck." Golyadkin, as early as 1846 in *The Double*, stares fixedly into the black water just before his double appears; Stavrogin can spend a sleepless night, "his eyes fixed on a point in the corner by the chest of drawers," or he can describe how he lost count of the time while "looking at a tiny red spider on the leaf of a geranium." But time, for Stavrogin as it does for Ivan later, reenters with a jolt, "suddenly I whipped out my watch." Twenty minutes had passed; he waits another fifteen minutes, to give Matryosha more time to complete her dreadful act. It seems there is little a doctor could tell Dostoevsky about hallucinations and trances.

16. See sections "'The Dream:' A Utopian Dystopian Hybrid" and "Gardens and Paradises" in chapter six for an account and an analysis of some of these controversies.

17. Mikhail Bakhtin, *Problems of Dostoevsky's Poetics*, ed. and trans. Caryl Emerson, intro. Wayne C. Booth (Minneapolis: University of Minnesota Press, 1984), 147. Bakhtin links this work to Cyrano de Bergerac's *Histoire comique des etats et empires de la Lune* (1647–1650), to Grimmelshausen's menippea, *Der fliegende Wanderesmann nach dem Monde* and to Voltaire's menippea *Micromegas*. And, in chapter six, I have already suggested important connections to this story from works by Swift, Rousseau, Poe, and Dickens.

18. *PSS*, 25:104; "The Dream of a Ridiculous Man," in *Great Short Works of Dostoev-*

sky, trans. David Magarshack (New York: Harper & Row, 1968), 717. Subsequent page references will appear in the text in parentheses.

19. I have already explored Dostoevsky's ongoing obsession with Rousseau's *Confessions* and Rousseau's claim that the fundamental occasion for *his* confession was the harm he had, years earlier, caused a young girl. See chapters three, five, and six.

20. For a fuller discussion of these passages, see chapter six. The presence of the horrible trichina links the ridiculous man to equally critical moments for Raskolnikov and Stavrogin in which a dangerous trichina also appears.

21. James describes one Stephen H. Bradley who underwent a similar conversion experience one day earlier, on November 2, 1829, after which, like the ridiculous man, he rushed to tell others of his vision. "After breakfast I went round to converse with my neighbors on religion, which I could not have been hired to have done before this. . . . And I now defy all the Deists and Atheists in the world to shake my faith in Christ" (*Varieties,* 160–63).

22. *PSS,* 1:138–139; *The Double,* trans. George Bird, in *Great Short Works of Dostoevsky,* 38–39. It is a curious coincidence that *The Idiot,* the novel of Dostoevsky that is perhaps most preoccupied with the meaning of visionary experience, also opens on a wet, foggy morning late in November, as the two main characters, sitting opposite each other —doubles in their own right—approach St. Petersburg by train.

23. The November gloom had produced for Golyadkin a double who was physically familiar, but whose soul was alien and other.

24. Dostoevsky obscures the reference to the date by giving it much earlier, at the beginning of Book X, *The Boys.* Nevertheless, the same use of a precise location in time and place to encapsulate its opposite prevails.

25. Liza Knapp, "The Fourth Dimension of the Non-Euclidean Mind: Time in *The Brothers Karamazov,* or Why Ivan Karamazov's Devil Does Not Carry a Watch," in *Dostoevsky Studies* 8 (1987): 108. Knapp has tackled with great success and lucidity perhaps the most difficult moment in time anywhere in Dostoevsky's canon. See also her fascinating, sustained discussion about Helmholtz's, Flammarion's, and Strakhov's ideas about time and outer space and their import for Dostoevsky in *The Annihilation of Inertia,* 186–90. For another discussion of Ivan's encounter with his devil, see my *The Brothers Karamazov: Worlds of the Novel* (New Haven: Yale University Press, 2008), 108–12, 118–25. I cite my own text here rather than many instructive analyses of this scene by others simply because it relates tangentially to some of the ideas presented here.

26. Jacques Catteau, "Vremia i prostranstvo v romankh Dostoevskogo," in *Dostoevskii: Materialy i issledovania,* ed. G. M. Fridlender (Leningrad: Nauka, 1978), 3:52; quoted by Knapp, "Fourth Dimension," 100.

27. Bakhtin, *Problems of Dostoevsky's Poetics,* 149.

28. James discusses this very point in "Religion and Neurology," the opening chapter of *Varieties of Religious Experience.* This view tends to be echoed by those who want to allow serious discussion of visionary journeys and unearthly beings. Thus can the critic Jack Sullivan write that whether or not a ghost exists is unimportant, "what counts is the authenticity of the experience." Or, M. F. James, using an oddly Bakhtinian turn of phrase can observe, as early as 1927, "It is not amiss sometimes to leave *a loophole* [emphasis added] for a natural explanation, but I would say, let the loophole be so narrow as not to

be quite practible." As readers, we repeatedly return and are drawn to the fantastic journey, the ghostly, and the otherworldly. For the duration of our reading we may become jelly in the hands of the poet, novelist, and critic alike. Even as we seek to name, to categorize, or to dismiss such fantastic material, we may sheepishly crave "contact with other worlds." See Jack Sullivan, " 'Green Tea': The Archetypal Ghost Story," and M. R. James, introduction to *Ghosts and Marvels* (London, 1927), vi, quoted by Sullivan in *Literature of the Occult: A Collection of Critical Essays,* ed. Peter B. Messent (Englewood Cliffs, N.J.: Prentice Hall, 1981), 121, 124.

29. This word ("numinous") was coined by Rudolf Otto, in *The Idea of the Holy* in 1917. The term "numinous" describes a feeling that is closely connected to the intellect, and it is descriptive of a non-rational sense of supernatural fear, wonder, and delight. See S. L. Varnado, "The Idea of the Numinous in Gothic Literature," in *Literature of the Occult,* 22.

30. Varnado, "Idea of the Numinous," 62–63. He is quoting Rudolf Otto, *The Idea of the Holy,* trans. John W. Harvey (Oxford, U.K.: Oxford University Press, 1958), 68–69. The words of Coleridge's Ancient Mariner (which I have used as an epigraph in this chapter) crystallize for Varnado the feeling of the numinous: "Alone, alone, all, all alone."

31. In notes 1 and 12 of this chapter, as well as in the text itself, I cite some possible connections between the episode of Ivan's encounter with his devil and Dostoevsky's early work, *The Double,* about which he later wrote in his *Diary of a Writer.* I agree with Frank that Dostoevsky, in his last novel, endeavored to revisit certain ideas about the fantastic that were important to him already at the time of writing his first novel.

Thus it is fascinating to note that the only other time Dostoevsky seems to have used the word "homeopathic" in a work of fiction occurs in *The Double.* The narrator is describing "that festal day" on which Kara Olsufyevna, with whom the pitiful Golyadkin is wretchedly infatuated, celebrates her birthday with a ball. The narrator tells his readers that a "fitting description" of this ball is "beyond the powers of my feeble pen," but then, of course he attempts precisely such a description. He describes the "seemly medley of beauty . . . all the playfulness and laughter of the functionaries' daughters and wives . . . with their pink and lily-white shoulders and faces, their slender waists, their lively, twinkling, and—to use a grand word—*homeopathic* feet?" (*PSS,* 1.128–30; 26–29). The italicization is used by the translator but does not appear in the *PSS,* so I do not know if Dostoevsky himself had ever italicized the word in a manuscript edition. While the word homeopathic offers a way to begin discussing the phenomenon of the appearance of one's double, it does not tell us anything about feet. It does give us a clue to the narrative voice of the novel, however, and suggests that the narrator himself is either uneducated, unreliable, or—as an extension of Mr. Golyadkin himself, mad.

32. *PSS,* 8:36; *The Idiot,* trans. Henry and Olga Carlisle (New York: New American Library, 1969), 424.

33. Czeslaw Milosz has pointed out that Dostoevsky's use of seed imagery, particularly the notion of God having taken seeds from different gardens in different worlds, may show the influence of Emanuel Swedenborg, whose works Dostoevsky had read in A. N. Aksakov's translations. See Milosz, "Dostoevsky and Swedenborg," in *Emperor of the Earth: Modes of Eccentric Vision* (Berkeley: University of California Press, 1977), 120–44. Also see the editors' commentary in *PSS,* 15:401. Indeed, Milosz shows that Dostoev-

sky's ideas about ghosts, his fascination with that state between dreaming and wakeful-
ness, and particularly his interest in visionary travels to other worlds could all have been
reinforced by his reading of Swedenborg. It is here that an interesting triangulation of
Dostoevsky, Swedenborg, and, not William, but Henry James Sr., an avid Swedenborgian
explicator, might be explored. See Linda Simon, "William James: The European Connection," in *William James in Russian Culture*, ed. Joan Delaney Grossman and Ruth Rischin (New York: Lexington Books, 2003), 16.

34. Stephen Cummings and Dana Ullman, *Everybody's Guide to Homeopathic Medicines*, foreword by James S. Gordon (Los Angeles: Jeremy P. Tarcher, 1984), 8. In the late
1700s the founder of homeopathy, the German physician Samuel Hahnemann, coined
the phrase *similia similibus currentur.*

35. Cummings and Ullman, *Guide to Homeopathic Medicines*, 17.

36. Rice, *Dostoevsky and the Healing Art*, 50.

37. Ibid., 50. Rice's interest in this event stems from his desire to establish the possibility that this throat ailment, which resisted treatment, might have been an early sign of
Dostoevsky's epilepsy — for Dostoevsky's disease was characterized, among other symptoms, by severe throat constrictions.

38. *PSS*, 15:324–32; *The Notebooks for The Brothers Karamazov*, trans. and ed.
Edward Wasiolek (Chicago: University of Chicago Press, 1971), 219–25.

39. The reference, of course, is to the episode in the novel where Grushenka tells
Alyosha the parable about the wicked woman and the onion. For a discussion of this
important little story, see chapter four.

40. Victor Terras, *A Karamazov Companion: Commentary on the Genesis, Language
and Style of Dostoevsky's Narrative* (Madison: University of Wisconsin Press, 1981),
392. Terras also points out that many echoes of this idea of palingenesis occur in the
Notebooks for *A Raw Youth*. This interest of Dostoevsky's would be a fascinating subject
for future investigation.

41. The devil's experimentation in homeopathic medicine has an interesting parallel in
the alternative medical procedures that William James continued to seek in curing his
own aliments. As Linda Simon, William James's recent biographer, recounts, James, in his
own efforts to cure himself of depression and numerous physical ailments, not only
sought out the services of a "mind-cure 'doctress'" but tried hallucinatory drugs, galva-
nism, various kinds of folk healing and alternative medicine. To treat his bad heart, Simon
reminds us, James had himself injected with a compound prepared from the organs of a
goat, lymph from the thoracic ducts, together with extracts from the lymphatic glands
and brains. See Simon, *Genuine Reality: A Life of William James* (New York: Harcourt
Brace, 1998), 211. James, in his derision of establishment medicine and his attraction to
what might be called crackpots and those who ventured into hallucinating states via
drugs, shares the irreverence of Dostoevsky's devil for conventional medicine and its
fancy practitioners. (I am grateful to Ruth Rischin and Joan Delaney Grossman for
suggesting this analogy to me and for pointing out the relevant reference in Simon's
book.)

42. See chapter four for a reading of this folktale of the onion and how it functions as a
parable in *The Brothers Karamazov*.

43. James goes on to link the figure of the saint to the nineteenth-century utopian

socialist. "In this respect the Utopian dreams of social justice in which many contemporary socialists and anarchists indulge are . . . analogous to the saint's belief in an existent kingdom of heaven. They help to break the edge of the general reign of hardness and are slow leavens of a better order" (*Varieties*, 285). What would Dostoevsky have thought of this linkage? Certainly he too was fascinated by that dangerous borderline generated between the saint and the utopian dreamer.

Concluding Fragments

1. For more extensive close readings of this final passage see, for example, Victor Terras, *A Karamazov Companion: Commentary on the Genesis, Language and Style of Dostoevsky's Novel* (Madison: University of Wisconsin Press, 1981), 441–44; Diane Oenning Thompson, *The Brothers Karamazov and the Poetics of Memory* (Cambridge, U.K.: Cambridge University Press, 1991), 270–72; Robin Feuer Miller, *The Brothers Karamazov: Worlds of the Novel* (New Haven: Yale University Press, 2008), 130–33; Joseph Frank, *Dostoevsky: The Mantle of the Prophet, 1871–1881* (Princeton, N.J.: Princeton University Press, 2002), 701–3; Robert L. Jackson, "Alyosha's Speech at the Stone: The Whole Picture," in *A New Word on The Brothers Karamazov,* ed. Robert L. Jackson, with an introductory essay by Miller and a concluding one by William Mills Todd III (Evanston, Ill.: Northwestern University Press, 2004), 234–54.

2. *PSS*, 1:45; *Notes from Underground, Poor People, The Friend of the Family: Three Short Novels,* trans. Constance Garnett, intro. Ernest J. Simmons (New York: Dell, 1960), 186.

3. W. H. Auden, "As I walked out one evening," in *The Collected Poetry of W. H. Auden* (New York: Random House, 1967), 198.

4. Joseph Frank writes, "If we are to judge by his references to it later, no creation of Hugo meant more to Dostoevsky than the grisly little novel, *Le dernier jour d'un condamné.* This book — filled, as Herzen suggestively put it, with 'the strange, terrible lights and shadows of a Turner' — is the imaginary diary of a condemned criminal awaiting execution for some unspecified crime . . . and there is something truly prophetic in Dostoevsky's evident fascination with this work. For he was one day to suffer exactly the same agonies as Hugo's character, and, in reliving all his torments, to reveal how indelibly Hugo's book had bitten into his mind. On returning to prison after the mock execution in 1849, when he had believed himself to be only a moment away from death before a firing squad, his first reaction was to write a letter to his brother Mikhail. And this moving document contains the French phrase, not otherwise explained — *on voit le soleil!* These are almost the very words used by Hugo's condemned man to express his desire for life at any price, even at the price of exile and hard labor that Dostoevsky had just learned he was to be forced to pay himself. It is not surprising that, having ingested this text so thoroughly, Dostoevsky should later have drawn on it for his novels." Joseph Frank, *Dostoevsky: The Seeds of Revolt, 1821–1849* (Princeton, N.J.: Princeton University Press, 1976), 109. See also chapter one of the present study for a reading of this particular letter that endows it with major importance for Dostoevsky's life and art.

5. Charles Dickens, *David Copperfield* (Oxford: Oxford University Press, 1981), 53.

6. *PSS*, 14:10; *The Brothers Karamazov,* trans. Constance Garnett, revised and ed.

Ralph E. Matlaw (New York: Norton, 1976), 4; emphasis added. Subsequent page references to the novel will appear in the text in parentheses.

7. In October 1870 Dostoevsky had written to his niece, Sonya Ivanova, "The thing is that I always choose themes beyond my power. The poet in me pulls the artist back and forth, and this is bad." See *PSS*, 29(1):143. For a more complete discussion of Dostoevsky's emphasis on the competing qualities of the poet and the artist within him, see "The Narrative Imperative," in Robin Feuer Miller, *Dostoevsky and* The Idiot: *Author, Narrator, and Reader* (Cambridge, Mass.: Harvard University Press, 1981), 23–32.

8. W. H. Auden, "Dingley Dell and the Fleet," in *The Dyers Hand and Other Essays* (New York: Vintage Books, 1968), 407–8.

9. See chapter four for a fuller discussion of Ivan's allusions to this apocryphal story.

10. See Jackson, "Alyosha's Speech at the Stone," 239–40, 242, 249.

11. Thomas Wolfe's *A Stone, a Leaf, a Door* is a little book that is a text, now largely unread, for adolescents. Its terrible poetry is nonetheless a powerful evocation of youth. I borrowed and adapted its title here as a header in part to remind us that *The Brothers Karamazov* is a novel populated with adolescents and young adults — Alyosha, Ivan, Dmitry, Smerdyakov, Lise, Katerina Ivanovna, Ilyusha, Kolya, Smurov, Rakitin, Grushenka, and others. We know Dostoevsky wanted to write about children, but he ended by writing about young people. As we become immersed in the stories and the potential stories of these characters, we can forget that they are adolescents or young adults. Moreover, Wolfe did not even write these poems for which he is so well remembered; they were "discovered," selected and culled from his prose by the obscure editor Sergeant J. S. Barnes, in a manner not unlike the way in which Alyosha collated his account of Zosima's thoughts and exhortations. Thomas Wolfe, *A Stone, a Leaf, a Door: Poems,* selected and arranged in verse by John S. Barnes, foreword by Louis Untermeyer (New York: Charles Scribner's Sons, 1945).

12. See Robert L. Belknap, *The Structure of the Brothers Karamazov* (1967; reprinted Evanston, Ill.: Northwestern University Press, 1989), 39–45, 90–97; and Miller, *Brothers Karamazov,* 84–86, 88.

13. Interestingly, the fine Pevear and Volokhonsky translation of the novel, in its effort to be accurate, actually misleads the reader here. They substitute an actual quotation from *Hamlet,* in which Polonius uses the phrase "implorator of unholy suits" (*The Brothers Karamazov,* trans. Richard Pevear and Larissa Volokhonsky [New York: Vintage, 1991], 239) but this correction obscures Ivan's important misquotation. The translators tell us that they "have substituted an appropriate line from the passage Dostoevsky quotes in Russian translation" (ibid., 785). Unfortunately, in this case as in many others in the novel, the meaning lies in the character's misquotation and faulty translation.

14. He had written, as we saw earlier in chapter four, to his editor, "I particularly beg you to proofread the legend of the *little onion* carefully. This is a gem, taken down by me from a peasant woman, and of course published for *the first time* [Dostoevsky's italics]." In *Letters* Frank and Goldstein tell us that in fact this story had already appeared in two versions of A. N. Afanasev's collection of Russian legends published in 1859 (*Letters,* 489). See also Sarah Smyth, "The 'Lukovka' Legend in *The Brothers Karamazov,*" *Irish Slavonic Studies* 7 (1986): 41–53. This correspondence is discussed more fully in chapter four.

15. Lodge's emphasis upon the novel as narrative that converts human problems and contradictions into process resembles that of the early Stanley Fish in *Surprised by Sin: The Reader in* Paradise Lost (London and New York: Macmillan, 1967). And, as is well known, it is Fish who provided important inspiration for one of Lodge's most compelling, loveable, humorous characters — Morris Zapp, who appears in several of Lodge's novels. David Lodge, *The Practice of Writing* (New York: Penguin Books, 1996), 181–82. This important essay was originally published in 1990 in a collection entitled *Ways of Communicating*. Gary Saul Morson has also written at length and interestingly about what he calls the processual or processual intentions. See, for example, his *Narrative and Freedom: The Shadows of Time* (New Haven, Conn.: Yale University Press, 1994), 142–45.

16. Lodge, *Practice of Writing*, 192. It is interesting that Tolstoy also compared conversation to a game of ball in his early work, "A History of Yesterday," which remained unfinished and was not published in his lifetime.

17. Leo Tolstoy, *War and Peace*, ed. George Gibian, trans. Louise and Aylmer Maude (New York: Norton, 1966), 421.

18. James Gleick, *Chaos: Making a New Science* (New York: Penguin Books, 1988), 8.

19. E. O. Wilson, *Consilience: The Unity of Knowledge* (New York: Random House [Vintage Books], 1998), 8–9.

Index

Adler, Alfred, 156
The Adventures of Don Quixote (Cervantes), 124, 213n. 27, 217n. 34, 217n. 35
Afanasev, A. N., 81, 228n. 14
air, 44–46, 50–54, 58–61, 65, 67, 204n. 37
Alexander II, 8
Allen, Woody, 178
analytical style, 29, 39–40
anatomy, 133
Andersen, Hans Christian, 218n. 43
Anderson, Roger, 206n. 3
anxiety, 53–54, 130, 131, 134–37, 218n. 6. See also melancholy; suffering
"Apropos of the Exhibition," 10–13, 17, 78–79
art: for art's sake, 8–13, 30–34, 38–40; criticism, 9–13, 29–30, 177; in The House of the Dead, 29–41; in journalism, 8–21, 29–30, 38–39; peasants and, 8–13, 14–16, 18–21, 38–39. See also painting

"As I walked out one evening" (Auden), 174–75
Aspects of the Novel (Forster), 54
Auden, W. H., 114–15, 174–75, 179
author, 22–23, 25–26, 28–29, 57–58, 61. See also narrative
Axton, William, 135, 221n. 22

Bakhtin, Mikhail, 133, 158, 165, 191n. 9
Balzac, Honoré de, 131
Barnes, Sergeant J. S., 228n. 11
Barran, Thomas, 92
Barsht, Konstantin, 193n. 23
beauty, 9, 129, 135–36
Belinsky, Vissarion, 29, 92, 104
Belknap, Robert, 36, 193n. 19, 197n. 6, 203n. 25, 205n. 49, 206n. 3, 208n. 17, 214n. 1, 221n. 28
Berdyaev, Nicholas, 196n. 48, 206n. 3
Bethea, David, 206n. 3
Blood, Benjamin Paul, 160–61
The Boatmen of the Volga (Repin), 10–11

Evdokimoff, Paul, 116
evidence, 180–82
evil: in *The Brothers Karamazov*, 132,
 166–67, 177–78; conversion and, 153;
 freedom and, 32–36; genre and, 132;
 in *The House of the Dead*, 32–36; in
 The Idiot, 74, 78; motivation for, 105–
 6; narrative and, 177–78; parables
 and, 74, 78; Shakespeare and, 105–6.
 See also punishment; suffering
"The Exhibition in the Academy of Arts:
 1860–1861," 9–10

faith: of Bradley, Stephen H., 224n. 21; in
 The Brothers Karamazov, 79–85,
 138–40, 142–47, 166–68, 176–77; in
 correspondence, 5, 69–70, 180; in
 "The Dream of a Ridiculous Man,"
 118, 217n. 31; in *The Idiot*, 20, 73–
 75, 79, 80–81, 84–85, 217n. 29; notebook entries on, 191n. 9; in "The Peasant Marey," 20, 75–78, 79, 81, 84–85,
 150–51, 156; of Tolstoy, 149–50. *See
 also* conversion
family: in *The Brothers Karamazov*, 79–
 80; in *Crime and Punishment*, 55; in
 The Diary of a Writer, 190n. 5, 211n.
 21; in *The Idiot*, 74; in *The Possessed*,
 92–93, 95–97. *See also* children
Fanger, Donald, 189n. 3
the fantastic: in *The Brothers Karamazov*, 129–30, 130–31, 136–37, 149;
 conversion and, 149, 224n. 28; in *The
 Double*, 161; in "The Dream of a
 Ridiculous Man," 109–11
Fathers and Children, 93
Fathers and Sons (Turgenev), 93
Faust, 167
Fedotov, G. M., 72
Feuer, Lewis S., 223n. 13
Fish, Stanley, 229n. 15
Fonvizina, Natalya, 5, 69–70, 180
forgetfulness: in *The Brothers Karamzov*,
 80, 81, 82, 172, 180–82, 208n. 15;
 conversion and, 152–53, in *Crime and*

Punishment, 64–66; of Dostoevsky
 generally, 152, 177, 208n. 19; in
 nature, 42; in prison, 38. *See also*
 memory; originality
Forster, E. M., 54
Frank, Joseph: on conversion, 4; on
 Crime and Punishment, 48, 55, 56,
 58–59, 60–61, 204n. 33, 205n. 49; on
 the fantastic, 222n. 1; on father, 190n.
 5; on *Le dernier jour d'un condamné*,
 227n. 4; on originality, 228n. 14; on
 "The Peasant Marey," 150–51; on
 peasants, 3, 192n. 16
Freeborn, Richard, 203n. 22
freedom, 31–36, 38–39, 40, 42, 146–
 47
Freud, Sigmund, 112, 129, 130, 131,
 137, 156
Frye, Northrop, 133, 202n. 16, 219n. 10
Fusso, Susanne, 204n. 31, 212n. 21

Ge, Nikolai, 12–13
genre: anxiety and, 130, 131, 134–37;
 beauty and, 129, 135–36; of *The
 Brothers Karamazov*, 128–47; of confession, 87–93, 101–2; of "The Dream
 of a Ridiculous Man," 105–27; evil
 and, 132; of the fantastic, 109–11,
 129–30, 130–31, 136–37; gothic, 23,
 119, 129–30, 134–36, 138, 218n. 6;
 of *The House of the Dead*, 22–24;
 light and, 135–36; of melodrama,
 129–30, 131–34, 136–37; of the
 metaphysical, 129–30, 136–47; music
 and, 132–33; painting and, 9–13; of
 parables, 70–73; realism and, 130–31;
 of the uncanny, 129–31, 136–37; utopian, 111–16, 122–27
"A Gentle Creature," 109–10, 214n. 1
Gerber, Richard, 216n. 18
Gibian, George, 217n. 32
Gioia, Dana, 200n. 4
God, 82–84, 138–40, 142–47
Golden Age, 121, 122–27
"The Golden Age in the Pocket," 124–25

parables: in *The Brothers Karamazov*,
14, 79–85, 182–84; on Christianity v.
socialism, 203n. 25; on conversion,
81–85; in *Crime and Punishment*, 70;
Dostoevsky's use of generally, 69–70,
72–73; dramatic action and, 74–75,
80–81; evil and, 74, 78; function of,
70–73; in *The House of the Dead*, 13–
14; in *The Idiot*, 20, 73–75, 78–79,
80–81, 84–85; on love, 74, 76–77, 78,
82; narrative and, 74–75, 78–79; in
"The Peasant Marey," 75–79, 80–81,
84–85; peasants and, 13–14, 19–21,
73–74, 75–78, 79–81; in *The Possessed*, 99–101; truth in, 70–73, 74.
See also onion; seeds
paradise, 113–16, 142. *See also* utopia
paradox, 132
Parini, Jay, 50
passion, 214n. 6
Paz, Octavio, 53
Peace, Richard, 212n. 21
"The Peasant Marey": children in, 76–
77, 156, 157, 158; conversion in, 75–
79, 150–51, 153–57, 158, 172;
dreams in, 155–56; faith in, 20, 75–
78, 79, 81, 84–85, 150–51, 156; grace
in, 78; journey in, 150–51, 153–57,
172; love in, 76–77, 78; memory in,
36–37, 76–78, 153–57; narrative in,
78–79; parables in, 75–79, 80–81,
84–85; peasants in, 19, 20, 75–78;
time in, 115, 155, 156–57
peasants: art and, 8–13, 14–16, 18–21,
38–39; in *The Brothers Karamazov*,
79–81, 145–46, 163, 176–77, 193n.
19; conversion and, 4–8, 27–28, 150–
51, 153–57, 163; education of, 8–9,
13–14, 38–39, 124–25, 198n. 16;
grace and, 13–14; guilt and, 14–16,
24–27; in *The House of the Dead*, 13–
14, 14–16, 24–29, 31; in *The Idiot*,
19, 20, 73–74; in journalism, 8–21,
27, 73–74, 75–78; murder and, 3–4,
56; in novels, generally, 13–21; para-

bles and, 13–14, 19–21, 73–74, 75–
78, 79–81; in "The Peasant Marey,"
19, 20, 75–78; problem of, generally,
1–3; suffering of, 18, 145–46; transformation and, 13–14
"Pedantry and Literacy," 13, 38–39
Perlina, Nina, 206n. 3
Perov, Vasily, 12
Petrashevsky Circle, 3, 137
Pickwick Papers (Dickens), 114–15
plagiarism, 166, 182–86. *See also*
originality
Pobedonostsev, Konstantin, 145
Poe, Edgar Allan, 109–11, 138, 158
poetry, 179–82
polyphony, 132–33
Poor People, 29, 62, 174
The Possessed: children in, 93, 95–96,
122–23; confession and, 87–93, 98–
99, 100–101, 102, 103–4; conversion
in, 98–101; disease in, 101; dreams in,
122–23; dress in, 97; family in, 92–93,
95–97; ideas in, 93–95, 98–99, 102–
4; illness in, 97–98; memory in, 99–
100; the new in, 100; parables and,
99–101; sources for, 88–92; sun in,
122–23; time in, 94, 223n. 15; transformation in, 88–92; truth in, 100–
102, 206n. 2; unwritten work in, 93–
94; women in, 86–87, 95–99
prayer, 36–37
Pritchett, V. S., 53
process, 31–32, 185–86
Proffer, Carl R., 203n. 25
Proust, Marcel, 90–91
punishment, 32–33, 34–36, 38, 139. *See
also* evil
Punter, David, 134, 135, 138, 218n. 6

Radcliffe, Ann, 135–36
Raphael, 9
A Raw Youth, 61, 123, 211n. 21, 226n.
40
reading: air and, 50–54; by children, 52,
137, 175–76, 202n. 21; *Crime and*